RENEWALS 458-4574

## DATE DUE

OCI 10.

G.

PRINTED IN U.S.A.

D1165468

# DEMOCRATIC THEORY AND SOCIALISM

WITHDRAWN
UTSA LIBRARIES

# Democratic Theory and Socialism

Frank Cunningham

*Professor of Philosophy*
*University of Toronto*

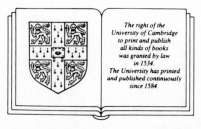

## CAMBRIDGE UNIVERSITY PRESS

*Cambridge*

*London    New York    New Rochelle*

*Melbourne    Sydney*

Published by the Press Syndicate of the University of Cambridge
The Pitt Building, Trumpington Street, Cambridge, CB2 1RP
32 East 57th Street, New York, NY 10022, USA
10 Stamford Road, Oakleigh, Melbourne 3166, Australia

© Cambridge University Press 1987

First published 1987

Printed in Canada

*Library of Congress Cataloging-in-Publication Data*

Cunningham, Frank.

Democratic theory and socialism.

Bibliography: p.
Includes index.
1. Socialism.  2. Democracy.  I.Title.
HX72.C86  1987    320.5′31    87-18280

*British Library Cataloguing in Publication Data*

Cunningham, Frank

Democratic theory and socialism.

1. Socialism  2.  Democracy
I.  Title
335    HX550.D4

ISBN 0 521 34039 X  hardcovers
ISBN 0 521 33578 7  paperback

LIBRARY
The University of Texas
At San Antonio

# Contents

v

# Preface

This book is written with the aim of helping to make progress in the theory and practice of socialism and democracy. Nearly two decades of attempted theorizing and practising to this end has persuaded me, in agreement with many other socialists, that this is the political order of the day. It has also persuaded me that the task of uniting socialism and democracy is not just one of having good will, but requires empirical research and political-theoretical work as well.

The book's organization and the motivation for addressing the topics it does are explained in Chapter One. Though no attempt is made systematically to survey the large contemporary body of literature on democracy and socialism, pertinent works of several authors, both socialist and nonsocialist, are drawn on and summarized when this helps to situate debate. Detailed argumentation and textual analysis are confined to end notes.

Thanks are due to the following people, who, with Jonathan Sinclair-Wilson and the editorial staff of Cambridge University Press' New York office, helped me with the book: Derek Allen, G.A. Cohen, Phyllis Clarke, R.B. de Sousa, Daniel Drache, David Galbraith, André Gombay, Terry Heinrichs, Marlene Kadar, Ernesto Laclau, Andrew Levine, C.B. Macpherson, Dale Martin, Chantal Mouffe, Calvin Normore, Maryka Omatsu, Andrew Ranachan, Alejandro Rojas, David Schweickart, and Bob Ware. Of these all but Maryka are fortunate they did not live with me during the book's production. Special thanks are due her.

Toronto *January, 1987*

## Postscript

On July 21, 1987, as production of this book was in its final stages C.B. Macpherson died, having continued his research on democracy to that very day. He will be missed by all of us who found his work so stimulating

*July 1987*

vii

# Introduction

# 1 What Is To Be Asked?

SOCIALIST THEORISTS of the last century had in common with their strongest opponents that both thought socialism and democracy were kindred phenomena. Socialism was projected by advocates as the fulfilment of the broken promises of the French Revolution and as the democratic wing of the movements of 1848; while opponents warned against socialism precisely because of its association with democracy, which they viewed as mob rule and social chaos.[1] Battle lines in the late 20th century are not so neatly drawn, as socialists must now argue against a conception that counterposes democracy and socialism. The reason for this is clear: to all appearances present-day socialist societies have more in common with authoritarian regimes than with the advanced democracy envisaged by early socialists.

Some defenders of existing socialism grant the point but urge that severe checks on democracy are required to secure socialism against counterrevolution. Others maintain that such societies *have* achieved a high level of democracy and contrary opinions are ill-informed or ideologically warped.[2] The first view supposes that securing working-class power ('socialism' on one definition) is an overriding goal. The second argument supposes that 'democracy' is not a univocal concept, but that there are kinds of democracy each unique to some social system. Socialists sceptical of these defences may be divided into two broad categories. In one category are those who *share* the suppositions while differing over whether present-day socialist societies embody working-class power or have actually realized 'socialist democracy.' By contrast, the present work places itself within a category of socialist theory that challenges the suppositions themselves. It shares with a growing body of democratic-socialist literature the opinion that so-

3

cialism must be regarded primarily as a means for making advances in democracy and that fragmenting the concept of democracy into kinds works against achieving this goal.

Of course, it is one thing to make assertions in support of democratic socialism and another to produce useful theories on the subject. Perhaps the latter requires a 'unified democratic-socialist theory' to which existing work may contribute. However, the task this book sets itself is more modest. It suggests answers to a selection of questions that must be addressed by any practically relevant theory of socialism and democracy. Chapter Two outlines the political, methodological and philosophical dimensions of the work's orientation. The present chapter motivates the questions to be addressed. The main body of the book is divided into three parts, each concerned with theoretical questions but in ways that make increasingly explicit its relation to the demands of political practice.

### i. Democracy, Equality, and Socialism

The work's underlying political question is: How, if at all, can one have both socialism and democracy? A satisfactory answer to this question supposes that certain other questions can be answered. This task will be addressed in Chapters Three through Six. The questions and their short answers are:

1. Why socialism? – To make possible and to preserve major advances in democracy.
2. Why not capitalism? – Because it too severely restricts democracy.
3. Why democracy? – To expand the scope of human freedom.

The project at hand, then, fits within a larger argument that replacing capitalism with socialism is necessary for advancing democracy.

Chapter Five takes up questions of definition concerning 'capitalism' and 'socialism.' Use of these terms by the democratic socialist must take account of nonaccidental associations of capitalism with freedom and of socialism with equality without begging the question about the relation of each to democracy. 'Democracy' is treated at length in Chapter Three, where it is regarded as having to do with self-determination in both institu-

4

tional political environments and in civil society, but where self-determination or 'popular sovereignty' is characterized in such a way as to retain room for majority rule and the formal protection of minority rights. Key terms must be defined so that: a) claims about socialism being necessary for democracy or capitalism inhibiting democracy do not become true by definition, and b) the definitions bear useful resemblance to the things pro- and antisocialists can agree match their conceptions. The second requirement is in tension with the first, since many conceive of their favoured systems as necessarily democratic. Thus, a pro-capitalist might view evidence that capitalism inhibits democracy as proof that the society is not really capitalistic, but has been tainted with protosocialist welfarism or the like. Or a socialist might explain undemocratic features of existing socialist societies by denying that they could be truly socialist.

Alternatively, self-serving definitions of 'democracy' are adopted. Typically this involves thinking of democracy so that freedom, and in particular the freedom to be a capitalist, is paramount, or of socialism to make the provision of relative material equality definitive of 'democracy.' More concretely, the procapitalist regards a multiparty, parliamentary system as an indispensable condition for democracy,[3] while the socialist distinguishes between 'bourgeois' and 'proletarian' democracy or 'representative' and 'direct' democracy, where these are thought of as radically different.[4] A main task of this work is to resist this division of democracy into 'democracies.'

Chapter Three argues that democracy is always a matter of degree and that the question to ask about an economic structure, a political institution, or a political culture is not simply whether it is democratic but how democratic it is. There are two grounds for thinking it undesirable to divide democracy into kinds. First, in fragmenting the concept of democracy, political theory denies itself an important standard by which different political and economic arrangements can be evaluated, namely, 'progress in democracy.' One might argue that this is not a good standard to employ. Alternatives might be 'satisfaction of basic human needs,' or 'promotion of rule by the most capable.' Or some claim that an alternate standard is more appropriate to the present time, such as 'advancing the interests of the working class,' even though it is thought the two standards are ultimately compatible. Thus

Lenin argued against Kautsky that if, contrary to Lenin's advice, one insists that democracy is a univocal concept, then socialism must be seen 'a million times more democratic' than capitalism.[5] But in either case there is some question begging about ruling out a progress-in-democracy standard by definition.

The second ground for resisting the division of democracy into kinds is based on political morality. Even someone who does not place a high value on democracy must think the actions of authoritarian regimes (mass arrests, torture, and police state intimidation) are to be avoided. Most such regimes have made no pretence of behaving democratically, but those appropriately called 'Stalinistic'[6] have acted in the name of democracy. This is surely a most pernicious practice, adding ideological cover to authoritarianism and allowing honest accomplices to rationalize their support. If a practice such as abnegating civil liberties seems undemocratic, it is held that this results from thinking in terms of the *wrong kind* of democracy. In this form of political discourse 'democracy' soon comes to refer to whatever the regime does, in the same way that 'preservation of freedom' is used today by apologists of United States foreign policies to describe economic and military practices that obviously inhibit freedom.

Chapter Four, which defends democracy, is much more than preaching to the converted. Would that this were the case. Democratic gains, great though they have been in the last two centuries, are obviously fragile. One manifestation of this is the scepticism with which democracy is regarded by many whose humanistic values are not at all in question. In this category are socialist activists worried about false consciousness, those who see a threat to minority rights in democracy, and theorists of social choice who question the very coherence of democratic concepts. In attempting to meet these concerns, Chapter Four lays the ground for the outline argument in Chapter Six that socialism is a necessary (though evidently not a sufficient) condition to make and protect 'major advances' in democracy.

## ii. The Retrieval of Liberal Democracy

If 'democracy' is taken univocally, and if socialism is said to represent a potential advance in democracy, then some additional questions are raised. The theory and practice of democracy in most if not all contemporary capitalist societies have been liberal democratic. So the question arises about the relation between democracy in a socialist environment and this phenomenon so far unique to capitalism. The range of positions is that democracy in socialism is of an entirely different sort, that liberal democracy should be retained intact in socialism, or that socialists should seek a supersession of liberal democracy.[7] This last view is most famously advanced by C.B. Macpherson, whose main contribution to democratic theory has been to defend socialist 'retrieval' of liberal democracy.[8]

When a course I offered on Marxism and democracy addressed Macpherson's views, I had expected strong opposition from pro-capitalist class members. But such opposition never got expressed, since all the time was taken with stormy debate among the course's socialist students. Opinion was divided between those who saw Macpherson's views as a vital link between socialist economic and political theory and those who regarded his views as beyond the worst revisionism. Though muted by customary scholarly civility and qualifications, the same division exists in the academic journals.[9] The importance of this debate cannot be underestimated. It will make a difference both to how one envisages democracy in socialism and how one thinks democratic socialism can be achieved if this democracy is regarded as continuous with liberal democracy. Chapters Seven and Eight attempt to make progress in the retrieval of liberal democracy by defending some suppositions of this project and by clarifying concepts typically left vague by retrievalists, including 'retrieval' and 'liberal democracy' themselves.

The approach differs from most socialist analyses, which address the shortcomings of liberal-democratic political practices as evidence of flaws in liberal-democratic values and institutions. In this work the order of argumentation is reversed. First a provisional list of liberal-democratic values and institutions is given and then some implications of adopting these for socialist practice will be drawn. Or rather, implications of acting on 'superseded' liberal democracy will be treated, thus necessitating a characterization of 'supersession' that allows one to prescribe going beyond traditional liberal democracy while retaining continuity with it. Existing retrievalist literature offers little help in this endeavour. Nor does it directly address some time-honoured socialist attacks on political theories that take general values as their starting points. The chapters of Part II address these and related challenges, while defending the supersession of a selection of liberal-democratic prescriptions: upholding the rule of law, protecting 'negative' freedom, and promoting pluralism.

Many socialist critics point to the underdeveloped world, where liberal-democratic traditions and institutions are lacking and where political repression is especially harsh, as evidence that the retrievalist project is only relevant to limited segments of the world. By confining itself primarily to conditions of the developed capitalist world, the arguments of Part II (as of the rest of the book) will not contest such a claim. Nor, however, will its soundness be granted. In my experience most of those who raise this objection do so to cast doubt on the feasibility of retrieval in the 'first world' as well as in the 'third.' The implied message is that whenever and wherever socialists seriously challenge capitalism, flight of capital, subversion, and military threat combine to create conditions like those in the third world, making democratic-socialist politics impossible. This is a direct challenge to the first-world retrievalist. Moreover, claims about the limitations of retrieval suppose that analogues of socialist retrieval of liberal democracy are not possible in the developing world, but this is contested by some third-world socialists themselves.[10]

### iii. The Politics of Democratic Socialism

The charge that retrieval is impractical is at its strongest as a challenge to produce realistic strategies for attaining superseded liberal-democratic goals.[11] Macpherson's views offer little help here since he confines himself to addressing the values of liberal democracy, rather than its institutions and practices. As will be seen, there are limitations to how far a general theory of socialism and democracy can go toward prescribing political institutional forms. Nonetheless, some defence can be given to the claim that democratic *means* are both realistic and required to attain democratic socialism.

This topic has been placed on the socialist agenda by Antonio Gramsci, whose Italian Communist Party has doggedly pursued such a project since the end of World War Two. Gramsci's work and attempts to put it into practice have inspired debate among socialists over whether or how there can be a democratic road to democratic socialism. Thus, practical discussions of the book supplement Macpherson's retrievalist approach with the fruit of work sparked by Gramsci. The concluding chapter (Eleven) joins efforts of democratic socialists trying to find organizational alternatives to traditional revolutionary vanguardism and to traditional social-democratic or labour politics: a 'third way.' Similarly, the chapters of Part III take up two main topics of socialist theory – class reductionism and false consciousness – which, though usually addressed abstractly, are better approached by situating them within the broadly Gramscian project.

*Class and People.* What has socialism to do with working-class struggle? Since Marx's time a widespread socialist response has been, 'everything.' If 'socialism' is defined as 'the dictatorship of the proletariat,' then, of course, this is true. We shall see, however, that there are good reasons to reject this definition and to see working-class political power as an important component of means for attaining socialism. But this is the end of a story, the beginning and middle of which have become increasingly problematic.

The story begins with systematic pain and suffering, dashed hopes, frustration in the pursuit of what should be easily attainable goals, ennui, and in general 'oppression.' The planet, shrunken though it has become, does not seem all that harsh a place that people cannot share its fruits without going at each other's throats, and the demonstrated ability of people to cooperate and to enjoy each other's company suggests that this could be the normal human condition. We know that instead the human community is split along a variety of lines – class, occupation, sex, sexual orientation, race, nation, age, religion – such that some people are systematically, structurally subject to oppression.

If the first part of the story is to ask from where these oppressions come, the middle part is to ask how they might be eliminated. Marx's theories are the most powerful to date in addressing these questions. The dominant sustaining causes of various systematic oppressions for him are in the domination by first one then another economic class over those who produce the world's wealth. Divisions among this vast majority are advantageous to oppressing classes, which accordingly create or exacerbate them. With capitalism, however, an oppressed class comes to have the incentive and the ability to overthrow the ruling class, but unlike any previous class, does not have an interest in itself becoming an oppressor. Its interests are to eliminate class oppression and with it other systematic oppressions altogether. Accordingly, it is the essential rallying point for all antioppressive movements. Main left-wing challenges to the Marxist tradition come from two sources.

On the one hand, many activists have reacted against the persistent claims of socialists in and around their movements that things like the domination of women or national oppression really are of a class nature.[12] On the other hand, criticisms have come from socialists trying to understand political phenomena recalcitrant to traditional Marxist analysis. People from countries with strong but troubled socialist movements (for instance, France, Japan, and Chile) have developed one set of critiques, and socialist students of political culture have produced another.[13] Ernesto Laclau, examining Peronism in his native Argentina, used the phrase, 'class reductionism,' to describe a socialist disposition to subordinate all struggles to class struggles, and this term has now gained prominence.[14] Antisocialists have denied claims about working-class oppression ever since there has been that oppression. What differentiates the work of democratic-socialist theorists is their quest for an approach that will neither deny the importance of class oppression and struggle nor submerge other oppressions and struggles in it. Chapter Nine joins this effort.

*Paternalism and Populism.* Suppose it is agreed that more democracy is better than less, that socialism is necessary for making major advances in democracy, and that there are realistic measures to avoid the undemocratic potentials of socialism. The question democratic socialists must then ask is why their own societies have not achieved this. Why do not the people make democratic socialism come to pass? This question is very difficult to answer without referring to beliefs and values the socialist thinks false and wishes were not harboured, but this poses a problem described by one theorist, Ted Benton, as 'the paradox of emancipation: '[if democratically-motivated radicals] are to remain true to their political values they may implement no changes without the consent of those who are affected by them, and if they seek to implement no such changes, then they acquiesce in the persistence of a social system radically at odds with their political values.[15]' Two well-known radical orientations are best seen as attempts to resolve this 'paradox,' but it is not hard to see difficulties with each of them.

One critic of Marx grants the ultimately democratic aspirations of Marxism, but says that in its theory of interests Marxism 'dispensed with consent theory,'[16] thus attributing to it a position that might be called 'democratic paternalism.' The democratic paternalist sees false beliefs and values in the present as the major impediment to democracy in the future and recommends that those who do not suffer these faults act on behalf of those who do, even if this requires that a minority force a majority to be free. This approach depends on the notion of 'false consciousness' and hence requires some criterion for identifying true interests. Additionally, a case can be made that once antidemocratic measures are taken in the short run, it becomes extremely difficult if not impossible to return to democracy in the long run, even if the short-term measures are designed to further democracy.

An alternate approach of some socialists is the 'populist' one that denies the category of false consciousness altogether.[17] This faces the problem that if the values of the democratic socialist are shared by the large bulk of a population, then an explanation is needed for political behaviour apparently at odds with them; but if the values and beliefs are not shared, then very fancy conceptual footwork will be required to avoid regarding widely held opinions as false. In Chapter Ten an antipaternalist way of retaining the notion of false consciousness will be hypothesized. As in the treatment of reductionism, the approach will hinge on situating the problem of false consciousness within a political setting (that of 'systematic oppressions') instead of addressing it as an abstract question of epistemology.

SUMMARY

These, then, are the main questions to be asked in this work:

### Part I

1. What is democracy and what reasons are there to suppose that socialism is necessary to make progress in it? (Chapters Three through Six)

11

## Part II

2. How, if at all, should socialist theory and practice retrieve liberal democracy? (Chapters Seven and Eight)

## Part III

3. How are the main types of people's efforts to overcome
systematic oppressions related to class struggle? (Chapter Nine)

4. How, if at all, can democratic-socialist theory recognize
false consciousness? (Chapter Ten)

A concluding section makes suggestions regarding the question:

5. What might be done? (Chapter Eleven)

There is no pretence that these are the only questions to be
addressed about socialism and democracy. Nor does the work try
more than to outline and begin defending some hypothesized
answers. Its major parts have sufficiently different focuses to be
read alone (I have found that among theorists of democracy and
socialism, political philosophers usually concern themselves with
the topics of Part I, political scientists with II, and those wishing
to bring theory to bear on movement politics with III), but the
chapters are meant to supplement one another. Chapter Two
concludes this introductory segment of the book by defending its
methodology and reviewing some of the literature against the
background which its arguments are developed.

# 2 Marxism and Methodology

THE POLITICAL POINT of view motivating the present endeavour is broadly prodemocratic and prosocialist. Beyond this, however, the book simply aims to answer the questions posed above, drawing on work from whatever political perspectives are found useful, and it will try as far as possible to avoid basic philosophical questions. This approach supposes a certain orientation toward theory and practice.

### i. Theory and Practice

The arguments of subsequent chapters will be relentlessly theoretical. Although some references will be made to actual socialist practices, the bulk of the work is devoted to posing theoretical questions and hypothesizing answers. Of course, to be realized, democratic socialism requires concrete thinking about institutions and modes of practice informed by close historical analysis. Some suggestions about the sort of research required will be made in this work, and those readers equipped with appropriate skills and experience are invited to test or, better, improve the book's various hypotheses.

Some socialist activists might object that the work's theoretical orientation could dampen practical political resolve by immersing one in theoretical speculation. An objection like this cannot be met to the satisfaction either of the dogmatic socialist, who thinks that all important questions of socialist theory have been answered, or of anti-intellectual socialists, who regard all theories as rationalizations. At the same time, the objection is too easily dismissed by the hyperabstract theorist who ignores actual circumstances within which political-philosophical questions are posed, seeking

13

instead to perfect models far removed from the messy world of real politics. There remains a range of orientations that reject these extreme positions while differing in how they blend theoretical and practical considerations. This work will attempt to weave a path between two such orientations – one with an activist emphasis and one with a rationalist emphasis – without rejecting all aspects of either.

*Leap Before You Look.* Lenin's criticism in 1923 of those socialists who had considered the Russian Revolution premature because it did not fit a plan derived from Marxist texts has much to be said for it. In the course of this critique Lenin approvingly quoted Napoleon as saying: 'On s'engage et puis... on voit'[1] – freely, 'first take action, then see where you are.' Whatever the merits of Lenin's point against his specific opponents, it must now be recognized that Napoleon's advice is not without its limitations. Indeed, less than a month earlier Lenin himself had expressed concern about what he saw, namely Stalin as the likely next head of state.[2]

I make this observation neither to second-guess the Russian Revolution, nor to speculate about whether such efforts to secure a socialism that lived up to the democratic aspirations of Marx, Engels, or Lenin could have succeeded in the conditions faced by those who have tried.[3] Rather, the point is made to urge that successful activism by democratic socialists requires more sober reflection than somebody taking Lenin literally might condone. It is clear from the history of socialist movements that what one sees after the engagement is usually not what one had hoped for. Stalin is one example, and Pinochet is another. In 'the Allende experiment,' a conscious effort to integrate democracy with both the goals of socialism and the means for attaining it was ended with the 1973 right-wing military coup in Chile. Chapter Eleven will return to current debate over what 'might have been done' where protagonists are divided between those who say that if the coup could have been averted, this would have required a *less* democratic approach than that of Allende's Popular Alliance and those who maintain the Alliance should have been *more* democratic.

*Political Rationalism.* Defenders of a 'leap before you look' approach might argue that nobody has ever acted otherwise, since the alternative is an unrealistic rationalism. Extreme antirationalists see the formulations of goals, and even of means, as nothing but rationalizations for actions people are going to take, regardless of reasons, but one need not go this far to see the merit of a practice-oriented mistrust of the rationalist, who demands complete formulation of goals and of strategies as a precondition for any political undertaking. Regarding means, the 'data' needed to estimate effectiveness are frequently unavailable until after some course of action is actually taken. Similarly, while people no doubt do 'raise projects in their imagination,' as Marx put it, goals as complex as the transformation of a political and economic structure are such that one's conceptions of the nature of goals change as means are taken. This reacts on estimations of means themselves, which in turn affect views of ends, and so on. The attitude of the modified antirationalist is not to despair of rationality, nor to give up formulating goals, but to proceed with understanding of the dialectics involved.

This critique of rationalism in politics suggests a compromise in which forging ahead and advance planning interact.[4] Arguably this interaction is exhibited in all political projects and in the everyday life of each human being as well, and success partly requires striking the right balance. The guiding aim of this work defines 'success' as achieving a socialism that makes major advances over capitalism in expanding democracy. Further, it maintains that the 'right' balance requires work, both on socialist and on democratic theory. It will neither suffice to confine oneself to ridding the world of capitalism on the supposition that democracy will follow, nor to rely on what theory of democracy there is in classic socialist texts.

### ii. Marx and the Post-Marxists

It is to be expected that the spectre of Marx haunts contemporary theorizing about democracy and socialism. Unlike other socialists, Marx's views have been adopted as official theory in socialist countries, thus making them central to arguments about their levels of democracy. Also there has now come of age a generation of Western theorists who were introduced to socialist ideas largely

15

through Marx's earlier writings, where his intention to link socialism with democratic values was most explicit. A manifestation of the pervasiveness of this influence is that many theses pertinent to democracy and socialism are in works that explicate Marxism. In addition to synoptic evaluations such as Richard Miller's, Jon Elster's, and Allen Wood's,[5] there are the attempts of those like G.A. Cohen and John McMurtry to reconstruct Marxist historical theory[6] and the several debates, exemplified in Allen Buchanan's book and elsewhere,[7] over whether Marx had or could have had a theory of justice or morality.

In following chapters little effort is made to evaluate these texts as interpretations of Marx. This abstention is also maintained in the case of the many works couched in the form of criticisms of Marxism. Jean Cohen's useful *Class and Civil Society* is one example and Leszek Kolakowski's impressive history, *Main Currents of Marxism*, is another.[8] Works such as these will be drawn on for their positive contributions; however, it is worth expressing a reservation about Kolakowski's contention that there is a nearly direct line from Marx's views to Stalin's practices. Those acquainted with my own earlier writings on Marxism will note that I am now more inclined to call some of its theses into question than I once was,[9] nor do I think that Marx produced enough in the way of political theory to answer the questions addressed in this book. Nonetheless, any view that Marx was an antidemocrat seems to me entirely unwarranted.

Only the most arbitrary sorting and strained readings can make Marx out to be a power-political instrumentalist rather than a humanist who valued socialism as an indispensable means to the realization of values related to democracy.[10] Moreover, sweeping attacks on Marx from democratic socialists detract from what will surely someday be acknowledged as his major contribution to the history of democracy: his relentless insistence that human self-determination will be meagre at best in a world where society is divided into economically exploiting and exploited classes and his efforts to explicate the mechanics of exploitation that make this so. Uncharitable interpreters of Marx's writings, like some supportive interpretations, also often divert energy for advancing democratic-socialist theory into exercises to show that Marx must really have held what they think one should be against or for.

The present work has profited more from the endeavours of

those who get on with the job without worrying about which classic socialist theorists agreed or disagreed with the fruit of their theoretical labour. In this category are books and articles addressing specific topics. A few representative examples are: the work of Mihailo Marković, Agnes Heller, and David Schweickart on workers' self-management; of Carol Gould on socialist rights and freedoms; of Kai Nielsen and Philip Green on equality; of Zillah Eisenstein and Heidi Hartmann on the relation of feminism to socialism; of William Connolly on false consciousness; and of Benjamin Barber and Carole Pateman on participation.[11]

Insofar as the present work is influenced by the theories of Gramsci and of Macpherson, two clusters of literature have been especially important. One cluster concerns pluralism especially as treated by Ernesto Laclau and Chantal Mouffe, in their *Hegemony and Socialist Strategy*.[12] They agree with Gramsci that a successful transition to socialism and a democratic-socialist outcome require winning overwhelming support for socialism which can only be accomplished by engaging with people in a variety of popular democratic struggles. However, Mouffe and Laclau challenge Gramsci's notion that such struggles must make working-class opposition to capitalism their centre.

Insisting on the centrality of working-class struggle, according to them, militates against achieving the pluralism crucial to a socialist transition and to democratic socialism itself. It presupposes a suspect theory of human nature in which people are thought of as having 'fixed' essences. Mouffe and Laclau draw on explorations by André Gorz, Claude Lefort and François Furet of the antipluralistic threats to democracy posed by traditional socialist approaches to political power, and on theories like those of Alain Tourrain about the variety of social movements and groups making for social change.[13]

While Laclau and Mouffe make use of these European traditions of democratic theory, Samuel Bowles and Herbert Gintis arrive at similar conclusions drawing upon a growing body of democratic-socialist literature in the United States. In their *Democracy and Capitalism* they argue that 'no capitalist society today may reasonably be called democratic in the straightforward sense of securing personal liberty and rendering the exercise of power socially accountable,' and they employ a model of social power as 'heterogeneous' to sketch an alternative society where the pro-

17

cesses that shape people are under democratic control, rather than results of 'the interplay of property rights.'[14] This effort helps to deepen Macpherson's interrogation of liberal democracy, as do those of Joshua Cohen and Joel Rogers, in their popularly written *On Democracy*.[15]

Summarizing work of the socialist political scientist, Adam Przeworski, Cohen and Rogers address the question of how capitalism can continue to command popular consent within liberal-democratic structures. They respond by tracing ways these structures and capitalist economic institutions mutually reinforce one another to limit the demands people can prudently pursue to those compatible with capitalism. This conclusion is in some ways akin to that of Jürgen Habermas and other Critical Social Theorists. In his influential *Legitimation Crisis*,[16] however, Habermas is also concerned to explore ways political-economic arrangements contain self-destructive internal strains, and he wishes to relate a descriptive theory of such 'crises' to a normative theory which grounds pluralist democracy by appealing to requirements for free, undistorted communication. It is worth noting that despite some important political and philosophical differences, the society Habermas envisages – one allowing for free and equal 'democratic will-formation' – is in certain respects similar to the 'radical and plural democracy' Laclau and Mouffe project.[17]

Other authors who have investigated the 'fit' between liberal democracy and capitalism and the tensions between them include Claus Offe and Andrew Levine. Offe's collection of essays, *Contradictions of the Welfare State*,[18] pursues suggestions made in *Legitimation Crisis* regarding states when they find themselves impelled to bypass liberal-democratic political institutions in favour of corporatism. Among other things, this opens the way for new social movements to exercise political power, as through the Green Party in the Federal Republic of Germany. Levine, working outside of a Habermasian tradition, has written a most rigorous critique of Macpherson's project (*Liberal Democracy*) that explains limitations of liberal democracy by reference to a postulated fit between it and capitalism. But Levine has also exhibited the structural failure of capitalist society to permit full realization of liberal-democratic values in his more recent *Arguing for Socialism*.[19]

Readers acquainted with these authors know that they exemplify a wide variety of philosophical orientations. Mouffe and Laclau draw on discourse theory, while Offe and Connolly are Critical Theorists. The training of Nielsen and Levine is in Anglo-American analytic philosophy, while Habermas and Lefort employ approaches typical of the European Continent. This book assumes that democratic-socialist theory is insufficiently developed to require lining up for or against any one 'school.' Accordingly, material may be appropriated regardless of what perspective has generated it. Those disquieted by this approach may misperceive it as an effort to produce a grand synthesis, but its intent is much less ambitious, namely to make progress in the solution of selected problems. Another source of concern may be that different schools are based on conflicting philosophical foundations among which one must choose. The chapter concludes by questioning this claim.

### iii. Nonfoundationalism

Adopting a phrase of Robert Merton's, this book will pursue 'philosophy of the middle range.'[20] Instead of basing its conclusions on fundamental principles of epistemology, ethics, or philosophical anthropology, it engages in more methodological activities that can be brought into rapport with empirical social science and practical political activity, on the one hand, and fundamental philosophical inquiries, on the other, but which can be carried on in relative independence of these disciplines. Examples of such methodological activities are: posing questions and defining terms; formulating hypotheses; distinguishing elements of a complex conceptual field; and suggesting where key choices must or need not be made. For some theorists philosophy of the middle range is not philosophy at all, but should be considered methodology or social theory. They may reclassify the arguments of this book and evaluate them according to whatever standards are thought appropriate to 'extraphilosophical' endeavours.

The foundationist may rejoin that extraphilosophical theories are flawed unless they have deep philosophical support. However, the claim that there are necessary connections between philosophical perspectives and social/political theories is suspect. It is noteworthy that similar political prescriptions not infrequently are paired with conflicting foundations. The case of Mouffe/Laclau and Habermas is one example. Another is to be found in the rich body of work by contemporary feminists on the family. Analysis of the family, and of the oppression of women generally, is approached from a wide variety of viewpoints (traditional Marxist, psychoanalytic, multicausal, structuralist), yet there seems consensus on the importance, as a central prescription for the liberation of women (as of men), that child care be democratized.[21]

Yet another example may be found by comparing the works of the Eastern European theorists, Branko Horvat, Svetozar Stojanović, and Mihaly Vajda.[22] Despite major philosophical differences among them (ranging from Horvat's neopositivism to Stojanović's antideterministic 'teleology'), their analyses of existing socialism (as nonsocialist statism) and their prescriptions (for workers' self-management supplemented by society-wide political democracy) are virtually identical. Of course, there are also political differences among these theorists. Still, given that the prescriptions in question are so central to their practical concerns, and given that the foundations are in some instances radically at odds, one wants to question which is the guiding force in their work: their prescriptive inclinations and the 'middle range' theory immediately supporting them or their foundational orientations.

The nonfoundational approach of this work extends to maintaining agnosticism about antifoundationalism. That is, while middle-range theorizing is compatible with the viewpoint that there is something misguided about seeking deep philosophical foundations, it does not commit one to such a viewpoint. Those who think it important to pursue philosophical foundations might adopt the plausible suggestion of John Rawls that progress in normative political philosophy requires putting founding theories in 'reflective equilibrium' with moral intuitions.[23] If nonfoundational views require the conclusions of foundational inquiry for support, the reverse also holds: because deepening, correcting, and extending theories of a foundational nature require adjusting them in the light of methodological, social-theoretical, and empirical work.[24] Thus those who wish may regard the present effort as extrafoundational work both to be evaluated by theories of a more fundamental philosophical nature and to be employed in evaluation of such theories.

In the same vein, and edging a bit closer to profoundationalism, an advantage to pursuing political philosophy nonfoundationally is that this helps keep foundational options open. Tying political analyses to fundamental philosophical positions forces choices that may be unnecessary. I am thinking in particular of positions for and against social-scientific realism and causal determinism. A widespread view among democratic theorists is that these two perspectives are inherently antidemocratic.[25] However, unless realism must be naïve, uncritical realism, or determinism must be fatalistic (both debated views),[26] it is not obvious why this must be the case.

One could speculate that Stalinism is partly responsible for the contrary opinion. Its putative philosophical underpinnings were militantly objectivistic and deterministic. Anyone who questioned either was labelled an antisocialist revisionist.[27] Also, realist and determinist language is used in the Stalinist tradition to claim special insight into the nature of history, from which 'correct lines' are read as from a cookbook, and impersonal 'world forces' are blamed for misdeeds of autocratic leaders. One of the many lamentable legacies of Stalinism has been to cast aspersion on scientific approaches to social theory. This has resulted in a reverse tendency of some democratic socialists to label any position that includes room for causal determinism or social-scientific realism as antidemocratic.[28]

One way to avoid pairing political and fundamental philosophical views, suggested by Mouffe and Laclau, is to pursue democratic political theory in a variety of philosophical idioms, without making judgments from within one of them about the viability of the others.[29] This approach might prove difficult to sustain, since some foundational idioms do not allow such tolerance. How, for example, can the radical antirealist and the realist advance compatible conclusions if each relates them directly to basic philosophical positions? An alternate approach is time-buying agnosticism.

When, for example, the causal determinist, the structural determinist, and the antideterminist employ phrases of the form, 'X leads to Y,' each might consider this a philosophically problematic phrase, if not for himself or herself, then for the adherent of other positions. For instance, the antideterminist will doubt that the causal determinist can avoid supposing fatalism, and the causal determinist will think that, if pushed, the antideterminist is forced

21

to interpret such phrases in ways only verbally different from determinism. Or anti- and prostructuralists could disagree over the stability of concepts like 'structural generation.' Similarly, realists and antirealists might agree to disagree about how to interpret political assertions which are advanced as 'true' or as 'false.' But each would regard these as problems for future work in which results of the current exercise in nonfoundational theory may or may not figure in striving for reflective equilibrium.[30]

Perhaps advancing nonfoundationalism is to be viewed as itself a fundamental philosophical matter, in which case what is requested of the reader is that full defence of it may be set aside for the purpose of the work at hand, to which we now turn.

# I Justifying Democracy and Socialism

# 3 Democracy: More or Less

IN *DEMOCRACY, IDEOLOGY AND OBJECTIVITY*, Arne Naess and others list the 311 definitions of 'democracy' they found in surveying literature from Plato's time to the 1950s.[1] Reading these definitions and considering subsequent ones, it is clear that, like all politically important definitions, they conflate reports of usage and prescriptions. One reason for this is that most definitions regard democracy in a 'substantive' way, that is, as a quality which social or political phenomena either entirely have or lack. Political theorists who both value democracy and think of it substantively will want definitions congruous with the social and political arrangements they favour. As a result the definitions will be value laden.[2]

A contrasting approach is that democracy is always a matter of degree. Instead of asking whether something is or is not democratic, one should ask *how democratic* it is. On this view political theorists ought to seek definitions of the phrase 'more democratic.' Accordingly, this chapter sketches an informal definition of 'A is more democratic than B,' draws out some consequences of the definition, and contrasts it with approaches that fragment the concept of democracy into kinds.

### i. 'A Is More Democratic Than B'

'A' and 'B' stand for social units, that is, collections of people in which the actions of at least one person—directly or indirectly, deliberately or unintentionally—affect at least one other person. A household, the inhabitants of a city, a university, a state, a neighbourhood, the workers in a plant, or the secretaries and clerks in an office are all social units. Indeed, the entire world is

25

a social unit, as are such collectives as the passengers on a bus between two stops. Though the term 'more democratic' is not value laden, a value judgment is implicated in employing a degrees-of-democracy approach.

A sufficiently general definition should make it possible to compare *different* types of social units (some work place and some university, for example), to compare different units of the *same* type (two different universities), or to compare the same social unit at *different times* (a university before and after a change in its governing structure or a country before and after a socialist revolution). Comparing the degrees of democracy of the same unit at different times is the least problematic: one is clearly comparing comparables. This might be thought a good reason to regard democracy substantively, since then any two units can be as easily compared as any other two by ascertaining what democracy-constituting qualities each has or lacks. The present work does not consider this an important advantage.

What makes pursuit of democratic theory worthwhile is its potential for helping to increase democracy in *one's own* social units. The substantive approach lends itself to the fruitless activity of hurling brickbats at others. While it is sometimes desirable to make cross-unit comparisons, these should be guided by concern to increase democracy in one's own backyard. Thus a Canadian might fruitfully compare state enterprises, cooperatives, workers' self-managed firms, tripartite corporatism, and paternalistic capitalism in, respectively, the Soviet Union, Bulgaria, Yugoslavia, Sweden, and Japan with an eye to prescribing changes in the organization of work in Canada. Or one might ask what political parties can learn about internal democracy from the women's or students' movements.

Somebody comparing degrees of democracy requires standards of comparison, and thus a definition of 'more democratic' is indispensable. This involves some thorny problems, but as a first approximation the following characterization illustrates what is involved in regarding democracy as a comparative concept. To say that the social unit 'A' is more democratic than 'B' is to say that:

1.  proportionately more people in A have control over their common social environment than do people in B; and/or

26

2. people in A have control over proportionately more aspects of their social environment than do people in B; and/or
3. the aspects of their social environment over which people in A have control are more important from the point of view of democracy than those over which people in B have control.

While they may differ about its desirability, members of a university community would surely agree that, other things being equal, a situation in which faculty, students, and support staff contribute to university decisions is more democratic than one in which only administrators have this ability. A state with effective popular input to both domestic and foreign policies must be recognized (or would be if any existed) as more democratic than one where this input is restricted to domestic matters. Even though clerks and secretaries in two offices may participate in making the same number of decisions, the office in which those decisions extend to the governing structure of the business would be thought (barring the bizarre circumstances some philosophers are good at dreaming up) to be more democratic than one where instead of this ability there is only the power to determine the location of coffee machines.

### ii. Specifications and Defences

The proffered definition, rough though it is, should suffice to indicate how democracy might be considered a matter of degree. Fully to explicate the definition would be a considerable task involving contested issues of decision theory and philosophical psychology. In this respect the notion of degrees of democracy is like any key concept of political theory, including the more traditional, substantive ones. Without suggesting that they are more than first steps toward sharpening and defending the idea of 'more democratic,' this section makes some observations for these purposes.

CONTROL

As the term is used here, a person has 'control' over something when what that person wishes to happen to it does happen in virtue, at least in part, of actions he or she has taken with this end in view. Many democratic theorists think that when talking of control in connection with democracy, one must specify the channels through which control may be exercised (for instance, elected parliaments, referenda, political party structures, and so on) or the degree of directness of people's involvement (for example, to insist that people actively participate in all facets of governance rather than allowing elected officials to make some decisions). Standard 'substantive' approaches make some such specifications definitive of 'democracy.' By contrast, the 'degrees-of-democracy approach' prescribes sorting channels of control and degrees of involvement by estimating what is likely to make progress in democracy in local circumstances, without identifying any such channels or sorts of involvement as essentially democratic.

The reason for not identifying institutional or other means by which control might be achieved as essential for it to be democratic is that these means are highly context bound and indefinite in number. No attempt to specify in advance of actual efforts to expand popular control those means which are truly democratic could account for all the contingencies, and the attempt could discourage innovation. A similar point may be made about degrees of involvement. At one extreme, people may be said partly to control an outcome when their 'activity' is no more than to refrain from inhibiting someone else from doing it. At another extreme, people may be directly involved in all stages of whatever process is needed to secure the outcome.[3]

One more possible misgiving about this characterization of control is that the *content* of the preferences of those said to have control is not specified. Some democratic theorists fear that a decision issuing from some preferences might be out of accord with what one conceives of as democratic because it does not have a 'socially acceptable' outcome[4] or because the preferences are not 'enlightened.'[5] In the first case people realize a state of affairs that one wishes to call undemocratic (office workers vote for coffee machines as a trade-off cleverly designed by the employer to bar them from future voice in office government). In the second situation they are mistaken about what will satisfy them (they vote for guns and later wish they had voted for butter).

The view adopted here is that individuals exercise control insofar as they succeed in making things conform to their preferences at the time they wish them thus to conform, whatever their preferences then are. The phrase 'democratic control' will be used to refer to exercise of control in one time and place that facilitates securing more control for yet more people in other times and places or at the very least does not inhibit these things. In general, this is how the characterization of values or institutions as being simply democratic or undemocratic is interpreted in this work. For example, the statement that electoral politics in a modern society constitutes a 'democratic institution' means that normally a modern society with provisions to elect representatives is more democratic than one without them. That this is in keeping with the ways most people talk of democracy is indicated by the fact that many who agree with this judgment also recognize that the possibility of electing government officials every few years does not guarantee very much in the way of popular democratic control.

*Participation.* Someone would have 'sole control' over an environment if all aspects of that environment susceptible to human control were brought about by that person's actions and were in accord with his or her preferences. Such a person would be a complete dictator, but it is unlikely that any social unit could be a complete dictatorship. In all except the shortest-lived social units, one person's control will be constrained by attempts of others to exercise control. 'Dictatorial' mechanisms are ones designed by would-be dictators to monopolize in their own hands means of control over a social environment they share with others.

Democrats are more ambitious. They seek means of control over a shared environment which many people employ, each in an attempt to make the environment conform to his or her wishes.[6] The activity of employing such means may be called 'participation,' of which there are many varieties. Voting in elections or referenda might be a form of participation, but so might talking through an issue until consensus is reached, joining a strike or demonstration, or empowering someone to make decisions. Depending on the circumstances, some of these activities will be more likely than others to enable (or at least not impede) an increasingly large number of people to exert control over increasing aspects of their shared environment. Hence, as in the case of 'control,' we can describe participation as being more or less democratic.

Participation in which each participant has equal access to rel-

29

evant means of control will usually be more democratic than participation in which there is unequal access, and majority-rule voting is almost certain to be a more democratic form of participation than empowering one person to make decisions for everyone else. Chapter Four shows why 'anonymous majority' rule, which involves these things, is conducive to democratic control; however, a degrees-of-democracy approach cannot condone the laying down of exceptionless rules about such matters. There may be circumstances where unequal access in the form of weighted voting, for instance, constitutes more democratic participation than otherwise. Similarly, as Carl Cohen and other theorists point out, it is a mistake simply to identify democracy with majority rule, as elected minority governments would then be no more democratic than an autocracy and insisting on consensus on democratic grounds would be ruled out.[7]

More generally, it is a mistake to define 'democracy' by exclusive reference to participation, as in Cohen's own definition: 'Democracy is that system of community government in which, by and large, the members of a community participate, or may participate, directly or indirectly, in the making of decisions which affect them all.'[8] To square this definition with the degrees-of-democracy approach employed here, it must be specified (contrary to Cohen) that not all members of a social unit need be able to participate in decisions for there to be *some* degree of democracy, though a unit in which participation is available to everyone will most likely be more democratic than one where it is not. It must also be specified (in accord with Cohen) that 'community government' include informal as well as formal means for making social decisions and that participation requires engaging in activity that has a realistic chance of success in making something conform to participants' preferences. When voting is a sham, it makes no sense to talk of it as a form of participation in means of control, much less as 'democratic participation.'

Thus qualified, it can be agreed that for there to be any measure of democracy at all, means of control over a social environment which (at least some) people may 'participate' in employing must be available. Some democratic theorists raise another problem here. They note that means for making social decisions may inhibit the satisfaction of first preferences. The outcome of a majority vote, for example, may be to implement a policy that is the first preference of nobody, because all those who voted for it compromised their first choices to avoid being in a minority position. This matter is studied as an abstract problem of social decision theory (in addressing paradoxes of constrained choice) and by political theorists such as Robert Dahl and Anthony Downs who note the way that political parties are obliged to compromise their most favoured policies to win votes.[9] Chapter Four will take up the question of whether these considerations invalidate the notion of 'democratic decision.'

*Perfect Democracy.* In characterizing 'control' and 'participation,' it does not seem damaging to recognize that a mechanism for participating in a social choice (majority rule, weighted voting, negotiated agreement, and so on) can sometimes interfere with reaching a result in accord with the first preferences of some or all participants. In a 'perfect democracy' means of control would always enable everyone to participate in bringing about a social environment at least 'acceptable' to each. An acceptable outcome may not conform to everyone's or even anyone's *first* preference, but, as the term is used here, people must be able to live with the outcome, that is, they must prefer it to any alternative outcome that would jeopardize retaining future participation at least of the level they already enjoy. An outcome is 'unacceptable' when changing it to accord with a person's first preferences is more important to that person than maintaining the cooperative institutions and cultural attitudes under which increasing numbers of people will be able to enjoy control over their lives.

In a social unit comprised of people who are both very selfish and very shortsighted, few outcomes would be acceptable. In this society, progress in democracy would be most difficult to achieve. In a social unit whose members are either so timid or have so few aspirations that a society affording them very little control is nonetheless acceptable, perfect democracy would be too easily achieved. In the first society, prescriptions for making progress in democracy would be impractical; in the second, extrademocratic norms would be the important ones by which to prescribe social policy. In neither society would there be much use for the labour of democratic theorists. I shall assume, however, that the pictures of human nature in these imagined societies are unrealistic, despite the popularity in some circles of theories advancing them as normal.

In a society acceptable to all but where not everyone's first preferences are satisfied, a number of different combinations of preference satisfactions will be possible (half the population have their first preferences satisfied and half their third; everyone's second preference is satisfied; and so on). A well-known problem of ethical theory is to find principles for adjudicating among different combinations of this sort, for instance to decide whether it is better to maximize average satisfaction or to minimize the distance between the most and the least satisfied. Anyone concerned with political theory and practice will want to address this problem, but the task specifically pertinent to democracy is restricted to ascertaining what distribution of satisfactions would best promote progress toward enduring and world-wide perfect democracy. (Chapter Six argues for equality in this connection.)

### PROGRESS IN DEMOCRACY

Maybe the concept of perfect democracy employed here has, in Aristotle's phrase, 'as much clearness as the subject matter admits of,' but there are alternative conceptions, and it is unlikely that this one could not be improved upon.[10] Democratic theorists persuaded by the 'degrees' approach are invited, indeed urged, to strengthen some such concept, since it plays important prescriptive and descriptive roles. Thus, the notion of perfect democracy will be used to address what any reader will have seen as a problematic feature of the definition of 'more democratic.' Suppose that one social unit is more democratic than another regarding the number of aspects over which people have control, but less democratic regarding the number of people who have it. Or suppose there is disagreement over what counts as 'important.' How can one determine which social unit is more democratic? The notion of perfect democracy makes this a surmountable definitional problem, though it undoubtedly shifts the burden to difficult tasks of social research.

In a postulated perfect democracy everybody always participates in employing means of control sufficient to make their shared society at least acceptable to each of them. It is unlikely that any such society could ever exist, but this does not prevent ranking alternatives by estimating progress toward perfect democracy. For example, it is probably more important for office workers to have control over the governing structure of the office than over placement of coffee machines, since the former opens up many more possibilities for increasing control over other aspects of their lives at the office and perhaps outside of it as well. It should be emphasized that positing this criterion does not eliminate the problem of making democratic comparisons,[11] but it situates it. Making actual determinations will be the hard, rough edged, often tentative work typical of any political research and practice that aspires to more than sophisticated name calling.

Similar considerations apply to the problem of social units that overlap so that increasing democracy in one unit decreases it in another. Robert Dahl confronts this 'dilemma' of democracy when he asks whether there is an ideal size of democratic government, for instance, the world or the nation state.[12] Given the interdependencies of the world's communities the problem Dahl raises needs to be addressed. Any nation and the world are overlapping social units, and an increase in control of people in one of them will in some cases decrease control in the other. Using the criterion of progress in democracy in ascertaining what balance would maximize progress toward world-wide perfect democracy would be difficult, but not impossible.

Nor, it might be noted, would it be biased in favour of the macro entity, since arguably either relative microdemocracy, being easier to sustain, is more secure than macrodemocracy, or a high level of democracy in the micro unit is necessary to make supplemental democracy in the macro one possible. This view is held by the nonaligned nations in the United Nations, who argue that national self-determination is compatible with a strengthened role for the U.N. Examples of other trade-offs involving overlapping social units come quickly to mind, and a test of this work's approach is to see whether it situates debates about them more usefully than a substantive approach to democracy.[13]

'DICTATORIAL' DEMOCRACY

A consequence of combining a degrees-of-democracy approach with one that places no limits on the scope of democracy is that democracy permeates humanity. The point is approached by John

Dewey: 'Regarded as an idea, democracy is not an alternative to other principles of associated life. It is the idea of community life itself.'[14] Expressed as a matter of degree (as Dewey also does), there is no society of humans, no social unit, that contains no degree of democracy whatsoever.

This raises another problem. When we think of ancient despotic empires, modern authoritarian dictatorships, the Boss Tweed city government, or the typical patriarchal family, among too many other examples, it runs against our intuitions to view them as containing any democracy, and we are tempted to seek a threshold below which something is simply void of democracy. The alternate solution is to recognize the presence of some measure of democracy even in autocracy. Perhaps this was in the young Marx's mind when he described democracy as 'the truth of monarchy.'[15] It is also a theme implicit in Gramscian analyses, which regard the state as 'hegemony protected by the armour of coercion.'[16] For Gramsci, no society is dominated by a ruling clique maintained in power only because it is feared by the entire population. Rather, even in the most despotic societies there is a measure of active support by a minority, and there is passive acceptance by larger sectors who believe there are compensating advantages to themselves and no realistic alternative.

In acknowledging patently antidemocratic situations to be partially democratic, we are addressing the 'paradox of dictatorial democracy.' However, this paradox depends for its force on viewing democracy substantively and not as a complex process. On the contrasting degrees-of-democracy view it is unlikely that any social unit will be absolutely democratic, though each will approximate an ideal perfect democracy to some degree. By the same token, each will also approximate absolute *undemocracy* to some degree. Examples of absolute undemocracies are an ant hill or Hades, and while there may be autocrats who have fantasies about presiding these ways over human societies — countries, schools, families, and so on — and may even do their best to achieve this, full success in such ignoble ventures is probably also impossible.

Recognizing that any social unit simultaneously approximates full democracy and full undemocracy helps explain how people can legitimately accept as democratic things like parliamentary electoral systems lacking accountability between elections or single party political systems. To a certain extent they are democratic. It also suggests that those who passively accept autocracy are not necessarily to be branded as irredeemable antidemocrats. And it reminds the prodemocrat that it is always possible to continue expanding democracy. Recognition that democracy is in one way 'the human condition' is no cause for complacency when one also recognizes that so is a measure of undemocracy, and, worthy as democracy is, there is not very much of it in today's world.

### iii. Kinds of Democracy (Ideal)

We can now examine the widespread view that there are 'kinds' of democracy. Reasons for being wary of this view were given in Chapter One: it removes an important standard of comparison and encourages making favoured systems democratic by definition. To this might be added that taking this approach is tantamount to rejecting socialist retrieval of liberal democracy; if there are good reasons to favour retrieval these will also be reasons against fragmenting democracy into kinds.[17]

Some socialists have been vocal critics of the 'fragmentist' perspective on democracy. Nicos Poulantzas, for example, considers Lenin's counterposing of representative and direct democracy a major step toward Stalinism,[18] and Alain Touraine maintains that those 'who oppose real democracy to formal democracy, proletarian liberties to bourgeois liberties, only show that they are either foreign or hostile to democracy.'[19] Still, fragmentist positions are held by many theorists whose commitment to democracy is hard to question. In fact Touraine, himself, in a different work, might well hold the record in listing *eight* kinds of democracy.[20] It is unlikely that such apparent contradictions are mere oversights. Rather, it is difficult not to classify 'democracies' when one surveys the vast array of measures, institutions, mechanisms, and attitudes all said to be democratic.[21]

An advantage of a degrees-of-democracy approach is in taking account of this diversity without purchasing the disadvantages of fragmentism. When viewing democracy as a matter of degree, things said to constitute kinds of democracy will be recognized as important features of the social and political world to be evaluated by seeing how far they advance or impede progress in democracy. Before contrasting this orientation with standard left-wing fragmentist attempts, the view that 'democracy' must be sorted into radically different ways of conceptualizing collective decision-making will be examined. This will also serve further to sharpen the notion of perfect democracy.

### NEGOTIATION VS. CONSENSUS

Some political theorists distinguish between democracy as a forum for negotiation among self-interested individuals and as a way of generating cooperation and consensus. This distinction parallels that between the concepts of a social contract held by Hobbes and Rousseau, and many contemporary theorists relate their views to one or the other of these conceptions. Alan Ryan puts the point in terms of conflicting conceptions of human nature: 'If two conceptual schemes depict man as on the one hand a private being, a consumer who comes into the market for goods, whose behaviour is to be understood in contractual and bargaining terms, and on the other hand as an agent, a being whose need is to make the world conform to plans he shares or as a member of a community, then it is no wonder that we are still in difficulties about simple questions, such as whether we live in a democracy.'[22] Similar to this distinction are Macpherson's between the 'possessive individualistic' and the cooperative dimensions of liberal democracy[23] and Barber's between democracy as a 'multilateral bargaining association' and as a force to create 'democratic community.'[24]

A related distinction is that between democracy thought of as an arena for conflict management and as a means for maintaining social order. Brian Barry sorts democratic theorists into these two categories, which he calls the 'economic' and the 'sociological' approaches,[25] and the distinction was central to debates among the Pluralist theorists.[26] If the peace-keeping sort of democracy is one which promotes consensus, and if consensus requires community spirit, then this distinction comes close to the others, and some theorists seem to identify it with one of them.[27] But as Barry discusses the distinction, it rather describes points on a scale such that democracy 'sociologically' conceived has some features of negotiation and some of community building. From a degrees-of-democracy perspective the notion that there is a scale will be more attractive than the notion of kinds. It allows the antifragmentist to consider 'kinds' of democracy mechanisms for collective self-determination, some facilitating negotiation, some the building of community spirit.

## MIXED-MODE PERFECT DEMOCRACY

It might be argued against this approach that it tries to combine Hobbesian and Rousseauean political prescriptions, thus illegitimately mixing radically different concepts of human nature. This charge must be taken seriously by the degrees-of-democracy advocate.[28] One could meet it by entering the time-honoured debate over whether people are basically selfish, altruistic, both, or neither. For our purposes, people are assumed to be not so selfish as to make democratic progress impossible. However, instead of defending this assumption, the approach taken here expands its grounds for justifying political prescriptions. It will be recalled that these prescriptions require estimating what would constitute progress toward a world of perfect democracy. To the question about what kind of world this would be, there are two classic answers which I shall label 'the harmonious negotiation forum' and 'the global community.'

In the negotiation forum conflict exists, but it is always possible to resolve disputes to the satisfaction of each party. What happens will not be in accord with everyone's first preferences, but the outcome will always be at least 'acceptable' to everyone. People will agree to disagree on some matters, but will strive nonetheless to maintain peaceful means for cooperating in the pursuit of whatever goals they share (even if this is just to keep distance from each other). In the global community there is no conflict to be resolved. Consensus will have been reached, where each will have been won over to a common point of view and the outcome of social decisions will be in accord with everyone's first preferences. Unlike Hobbes himself, the optimistic Hobbesian thinks human ingenuity and foresight can find approximations to harmonious negotiation mechanisms; the Rousseauean communitarian believes that a human disposition to make the interests of others one's own can be developed.

One might ask of each world whether it is desirable as a goal. Objections come readily to mind: the negotiation forum inhibits efforts to reach consensus; the global community rules out anyone being a rebel. What is more, the coherence of each as a pure model is questionable. As Jürgen Habermas has argued, negotiation, like speech, supposes some measure of consensus.[29] In particular, every individual in the forum would have to place more value on trying to reach a negotiated agreement than on any other goal, and it is hard to imagine a forum that would allow harmonious resolution of dispute over whether *this* measure of consensus should persist. It is also hard to imagine a society of complete and persisting consensus where everyone had an overriding preference that others' first preferences not be thwarted. The resulting situation would be that of the four friends in the satirical review 'Beyond the Fringe,' who spend time at a restaurant asking of each other what each wishes for lunch, and then simply order 'four of the same.'[30]

Maybe one of these models can be fixed to meet such objections, but there is an alternative: to describe an ideal perfectly democratic society that conjoins *both* consensus and negotiation. In this society:

> there are ways of acceptably negotiating disagreement, *or else* there is universal consensus, *provided that* negotiation does not sociologically or institutionally block the possibility of reaching consensus in the future and consensus is not reached in a way that sociologically or institutionally inhibits future negotiation should there come to be a failure to reach or maintain consensus.

Objections to the global community and the negotiation forum as unmixed models are muted when adopting the mixed one. No doubt some advocates of the global community will resist the criterion on the grounds that allowing mechanisms for negotiations might discourage effort to reach consensus, and an advocate of the negotiation forum might think that always allowing for future consensus inhibits negotiation by encouraging hasty compromise.

Considerations of real-life approximations suggest that these elements of the model may be complementary rather than at odds. The negotiator (for example, in collective bargaining) who always leaves open the possibility of reaching consensus can be shown to be better *as a negotiator* than one who does not, because areas of potential agreement are found that might otherwise be overlooked and because discovering some areas of consensus puts him or her in a stronger position to press for concessions in other areas. Similarly, members of a consensus-based community, such as a living commune, who allow the possibility of negotiation avoid all-or-nothing situations where the community might break up when it need not. The existence of means for negotiation thus *facilitates* efforts to reach consensus by allowing open expression of differences without fear on anyone's part of putting the community in jeopardy.

Somebody using this criterion to decide which of two or more comparable social/political arrangements is the most democratic would estimate which struck the best balance among: reaching consensus, effective negotiation, keeping open possibilities for consensus, and protecting future negotiation. Determining what constitutes the 'best balance' requires both quantitative estimates (for instance, about the number of trade-offs that would have to be made among the variables) and historical considerations about preferences for some ordering of variables by members of the social unit involved or their ability to implement a prescription.

The idea of a mixed-mode perfect democracy is formal to the extent that it does not specify the content of preferences, and it does not specify exactly what form structures for negotiation must take. A limitation on its formality is that in the perfect democracy there would at least have to be consensus on the desirability of maintaining ways harmoniously to resolve conflict. This specification is arguably less ad hoc in the mixed-mode, which allows both consensus and conflict, than in a nonmixed one, but it nonetheless constitutes a limit on the model's formality. Also mixed-mode perfect democracy likely shares with all attempts to describe an ideal society a failure in completeness.[31] Though I have not tried to do it, I am sure that situations can be imagined where appeal to perfect democracy would fail to produce a unique prescription.

How serious these problems are depends on how many real-life situations match the imagined ones and how important it is for people to have a complete decision procedure.[32] An hypothesis of this chapter is that some such mixed-model criterion will be more realistically employable than an unmixed one. This hypothesis can be tested, and perhaps in its testing readers skilled at ideal model construction and sympathetic to the degrees-of-democracy approach can think of ways to improve on mixed-mode democracy. Now, however, it is time to examine some fragmentist approaches which concern themselves with the nonideal world.

## iv. Kinds of Democracy (Real)

While any democratic theorist must no doubt presuppose a stance on ideal democracy, most defenders of the fragmentist approach explicitly discuss actual political practices. The two main candidates are those pairing kinds of democracy with economic classes and those making a radical distinction between representative and direct democracy. Though often collapsed, these distinctions are treated separately in this section.

### CLASS-RELATIVIZED DEMOCRACY

The most common socialist view distinguishes between capitalist or bourgeois democracy, on the one hand, and socialist or proletarian democracy, on the other. In their book, *Democracy*, Cohen and Rogers maintain: 'Capitalist democracy is neither just capitalism, nor just democracy, nor just some combination of the two that does not change its component parts. Indeed even to think of such separate "parts" is to miss the vital integrity of the system.'[33] Later in the same work they write: 'A democratic society is an ongoing order characterized in the first instance by a certain principle of justification, or principle of democratic legitimacy (PDL). The PDL requires that individuals be free and equal in determining the conditions of their association.'[34] Then they list conditions for the PDL, concluding that 'for its realization, democracy requires the abolition of capitalism.'[35]

Taken literally the passage defining the PDL entails that capitalist democracy is not democracy at all, something denied in the first quoted passage. If one interprets 'realization' to mean 'full realization,' democracy becomes a matter of degree, but this interpretation opens the door to distinguishing the relatively democratic and the relatively undemocratic 'parts' of capitalism. The alternative is to say that capitalist democracy is one kind of democracy and democracy in accord with the PDL another. Reasons given by socialist theorists for thus fragmenting democracy do not justify this drastic move.

40

Cohen and Rogers themselves give two sorts of reasons. One is that capitalism is able successfully to constrain the 'resources' necessary for noncapitalists to make use of formal freedoms and equalities.[36] The argument is well-known and well-taken. Rich and poor alike, as Anatole France put it, are prohibited from sleeping under bridges. The millionaire and the welfare recipient may both run for public office. People can get the information required for effective political involvement from any newspaper or TV station in their city. And so on. The second reason Cohen and Rogers give is that capitalism constrains 'demand,' by creating needs in people (for short-term, mainly material satisfaction) that it can satisfy and by making it arduous to pursue satisfaction of other needs.[37]

Neither of these observations is incompatible with an antifragmentist position. Arguing more radically than Cohen and Rogers, someone might claim regarding the first observation that a capitalist society allowing formal rights is *worse* than one that denies them. At least the gloves are off. People know where they stand and are not deluded into thinking they have any control over their lives. A less radical interpretation sees formal rights as having the potential for challenging capitalist constraints on substantive freedoms and equality. Both interpretations are consistent with a degrees-of-democracy approach. The radical view sees the existence of formal rights as an impediment to progress in democracy rather than as somehow constituting one kind of it. The tempered interpretation sees institutional protection of rights as a potential democratic advance.

The argument about demand constraint also can be taken more or less strongly. In its strongest version capitalism is a functionally closed system creating people all of whose preferences will be realized within the system. A contrasting interpretation, that of Marx and probably of Cohen and Rogers, holds that capitalism creates *contradictory* preferences, some of which do not support it. Marx and Engels argued that capitalism frees people from constraining traditions and both necessitates and engenders collectivist and eventually revolutionary values by socializing work and impelling workers to form defensive organizations like trade unions.[38] There is clearly no problem reconciling this view with a degrees-of-democracy approach. Capitalism is seen to be more or less democracy inhibiting, depending on whether and how it digs

41

its own grave. A nonfragmentist approach is also compatible with capitalism's being perfectly self-sustaining, but this is a more problematic case.

## CLOSED SYSTEMS

A social system would be completely 'closed' if it produced all and only those preferences that it also satisfies. It is unlikely that any system could ever be thus closed. For one thing the resulting social unit could not overlap with any other units in such a way as to thwart preferences in them. Moreover, the closed system would either have to be void of preferences for calling its own closedness into question or somehow allow them while remaining closed. In the first case there would be nobody to raise the objections considered here, and in the second case there would be nobody to complain about such 'repressive tolerance,' as this could not be viewed as repressive.

Sometimes the thoroughly 'bureaucratized' society is thought a closed system and, as Max Weber argued, there do seem to be mechanisms in modern societies that condition people to be willing participants in the bureaucratic hierarchies that permeate their lives.[39] Addressing this problem, John Keane maintains that bureaucratic control undermines itself by requiring active political participation on the part of depoliticized citizens.[40] Keane's point suggests yet another reason to doubt that a social system could ever be completely closed. It is unlikely that any system permitting people to act in accord with their wills could also contain will-manipulating mechanisms that *never* thwarted at least some of the aspirations people may come to have.

The fragmentist might, at this point, weaken the requirements for closedness and appeal to a 'quasiclosed' system which produces and satisfies all the preferences of a large majority. Here there would be dissenters, but they could never carry the day against a robotized majority. One reason to doubt the views of many North American socialists that they live in a quasiclosed system is that this does not explain the existence of these socialists themselves. Unless all of them are direct descendants of survivors (somehow ghettoized through the generations) of the Haymarket Police Riot or the Winnipeg General Strike, some must have come from

42

largely uncritical, antisocialist backgrounds which they successfully challenged.

Assuming this socialist is not to be viewed a freak of nature, a
luckily superior being, it must surely be allowed that the populace
from which he or she comes is not, after all, divided in the mass/
elite way a quasiclosed system would require. Moreover, there is
an alternative way to regard North American political culture,
namely in terms of there being significant contradictory preferences and system-challenging values in the populace which are
not developed in part because many of the most vocal on the left
fail to recognize them and even dampen active popular discontent
by advancing unrealistic or undesirable images of socialism, by
proposing impractical means for social change, and by putting
people off with elitist and sectarian political practices.

Suppose, however, that a quasiclosed system could exist. Why
should it be marked off as a separate 'kind' of democracy, instead
of being recognized as *more* democratic than a society in which
the will of the majority is always thwarted but *less* democratic than
one where minorities have the ability to try to change the values
of the majority and can sometimes succeed? A good reason to
reject the 'kinds' option is that it breeds a 'democracy be damned'
attitude which will be pernicious if one has hastily jumped to the
wrong conclusion that his or her system is closed. Also, this attitude
could only justify paternalistically substituting a 'democracy' people do not like for one they do.

### THE CONTENT OF PREFERENCES

Perhaps what concerns the fragmentist is not the self-perpetuating
nature of a system incorporating a measure of democracy but the
*content* of the preferences people in it have. This is the point of
view discussed above of democrats who want to specify the nature
of preferences people must have. Thus Jane Mansbridge distinguishes between 'unitary' and 'adversary' democracy, where the
former is principally marked by the fact that in it people act from
enlightened interests.[41] One of Macpherson's characterizations of
democracy by reference to people's ability (equally) to realize their
human potentials is of this variety,[42] as is Marković's distinction
between two senses of 'power' (to dominate and to create).[43]

It also figures in many definitions of favoured 'kinds' of democracy, where not just procedures but goals of a procedure are specified, for example Benjamin Barber's definition of 'strong democracy' as: 'politics in the participatory mode where conflict is resolved in the absence of an independent ground through a participatory process of ongoing, proximate self-legislation and the creation of a political community capable of transforming dependent, private individuals into free citizens and partial and private interests into public goods.'[44] According to this definition a society responsive to the wishes of 'capitalist persons' who prefer to seek private goods would certainly not count as being democratic in the good sense, even if they composed the entire citizenry.

Of course a democrat should not sanction control of a society in accord with preferences leading to antidemocratic consequences even if the preferences are shared by a majority. However, the notion that one can sanction thwarting a population's will in the name of democracy also should rest uneasily with the democrat. There is a problem here, and one that will be addressed more than once in this work, but it is less acute for somebody using a degrees-of-democracy approach than for one using a kinds-of-democracy approach.

For the former, a trade-off may exist where it would further progress in democracy to thwart the present will of a majority. In fact, this is often done when minority rights of certain kinds are legally protected. In this circumstance it is not concluded that the thwarting is entirely democratic or entirely undemocratic; rather it is seen as on balance the most democracy-promoting or the least democracy-inhibiting thing to be done in less than ideal conditions. It is logically possible that nearly an entire population has antidemocratic values so strong that the criterion of progress in democracy would always prescribe thwarting this population. In Chapter Ten it will be argued that such systematic will-thwarting is not in fact justified except under the most contrived of imaginary situations, but even if such an occasion should arise, it should not be viewed as a matter of exercising a good 'kind' of democracy against a bad 'kind.'

## REPRESENTATIVE VS. DIRECT DEMOCRACY

When Marxist views on democracy are discussed, Lenin's critique of Kautsky is usually cited. It is true that Lenin denounces Kautsky for writing of 'pure (i.e., nonclass? or above-class?) democracy,' instead of always putting the question, 'democracy for *which class?*,' and Lenin himself consistently modifies the word 'democracy' with either 'bourgeois' or 'proletarian.'[45] But on closer reading Lenin's position is less class fragmentist than his language suggests. His arguments can be divided into two parts. Usually Lenin is not arguing that democracy is divided into kinds on class lines, but that institutions of the state called 'democratic' are instruments of a ruling class. When the bourgeoisie rules, it makes institutions called 'democratic' serve its class interests; when the proletariat rules, analogous institutions serve its interests.[46] The other part of Lenin's argument is that representative-democratic forums and the formal equalities and freedoms associated with them are well suited for use by the bourgeoisie.[47]

Lenin was not the first or the last to claim that representative government and the voting procedures and formal rights that accompany it are favoured by capitalists.[48] But it does not follow from the fact that members of some economic class prefer a political form that the form is exclusively biased toward their class interests. Capitalism inaugurated many facets of modern technology, but only the most radical Luddites conclude that therefore this technology is irretrievably procapitalist. Indeed, the question of whether the proletariat can or should itself make use of parliamentary bodies was a hotly debated topic in Lenin's time. Thus Rosa Luxemburg:

> In place of the representative bodies created by general, popular elections, Lenin and Trotsky have laid down the soviets as the only true representation of the labouring masses. But with the repression of political life in the land as a whole, life in the soviets must also become more and more crippled. Without general elections, without unrestricted freedom of press and assembly, without a free struggle of opinion, life dies out in every public institution, becomes a mere semblance of life, in which only the bureaucracy remains as the active element.[49]

Lenin's fragmentation of democracy is only indirectly a form of class fragmentation. It is closer to one that counterposes representative to 'direct' or 'participatory democracy' (that is, shared control of a social environment unmediated by governmental representatives). Sometimes, as in Carole Pateman's book on participation, it is argued that representative and direct democracy each has its place, even if the latter is superior.[50] This accords with the antifragmentist perspective, though there will be room for debate over the circumstances in which one or the other mechanism is superior. A stronger view sees no role for representative democracy except a destructive one.[51]

Though loath to lay down very many general rules about what mechanisms are to be preferred, the degrees-of-democracy theorist can also agree with many of the strong criticisms of representative democracy. Are we not all too familiar with the bind of having as sole candidates people that almost nobody wants or likes, backed by small minorities with vested and selfish interests, often condescending elitists (even when they are in fact parliamentary cretins) given to habitual promise breaking and underhanded back room politics? It is not surprising that political apathy and cynicism are widespread in modern parliamentary democracies. Pateman and others are surely also right to react against those mainstream political theorists who cannot think of an alternative to delegating decision-making to someone else and who consider notions of direct public input, local self-government, or striving for consensus as somehow foreign to democracy as they conceive it.

Recognizing these things, the antifragmentist will nonetheless probably reject strong criticisms of representative structures that would abolish them altogether. Defenders of exclusively direct democracy sometimes construe the issue as if it were a matter of combatting elitism and narrow pragmatism. Thus Isaac Balbus counters those who claim people are incompetent directly to govern themselves by calling attention to the educative features of participation. He has one standard response to the claim that direct democracy is not possible in large, cosmopolitan communities, namely that people do not need to live in such communities and would be happier if they did not.[52] A commonly encountered alternative participationist response is that modern technology makes instant referenda possible on almost any question.

These arguments do not get to the heart of the matter. The difficulty with exclusive participationism is not that people are incompetent to govern themselves or that they are stuck in large communities, but that they do not always *want* to be involved in day-to-day or month-to-month government and wish to delegate some decision-making to others, and that many *prefer* living in large communities. (Insofar as the use of instant referenda goes, it should also be noted that someone has to pose the questions asked in referenda, and hence there are limits to how far this can go completely to replace representation.) The exclusive participationist might conclude that people's preferences have been warped and made undemocratic by representative-democratic structures. Fragmentists are obliged to justify such uncharitable judgments about their peers. This view also presupposes that representative and participatory mechanisms are in opposition rather than being complementary.

One reason the mutual support of representation and direct participation is possible is that each admits of degree. One might expect, for example, that the involvement of neighbourhood councils in the formation of municipal housing policies is more democratic than citizen review of policy once formulated; yet both are extrarepresentative forms of participation.[53] Similarly, representative structures are more democratic when they provide for recall and accountability between elections. Representatives may be entrusted to make decisions by a constituency that feels itself inadequate to make them directly, but this delegation will be more or less democratic depending upon whether the constituency has control over the *range* of such decisions and upon whether one obligation of a representative is to provide for sufficient education to make delegation increasingly unnecessary.[54]

These considerations suggest that combinations of different degrees of direct and representative practices should be regarded as complementary rather than exclusive, global alternatives. A public that had gained firsthand political knowledge through local participation, for instance, would be in a better position to understand the activities of a representative and to call him or her to task, than somebody who only knew politics from T.V. Conversely, by delegating some tasks to representatives, people's time will be freed to participate directly where and when it is appropriate do so.

### v. Conditions for Democracy

In the remainder of this chapter, two approaches to democracy that share some fragmentist and some nonfragmentist characteristics will be examined: one distinguishing between democracy and

47

its conditions and one limiting the scope of democracy. On the first approach, democracy is thought of substantively, while its conditions admit of degree. This approach attracts those who want to know not how democratic something is, but what democracy, considered by itself, is. Its main problem is to motivate a list of preconditions. Unless criteria are carefully spelled out and justified suspicion is warranted that the list is the result of thinking backwards from something one wants to be necessarily democratic. The following examples of lists of putative conditions for democracy illustrate the problem.

Joshua Cohen and Joel Rogers:
1. The capacity to form reasoned judgments.
2. Equal freedom and reasoned deliberation.
3. Manifest processes for decision-making.
4. Possession of autonomy and respect for others' autonomy.
5. Formal guarantee of individual freedoms.
6. Organized expression of political debate.
7. Absence of material deprivation.
8. Public control of investment.
9. Work place democracy.
10. Removal of all materially based disabilities.
11. Mutual respect by states of each others' autonomy.[55]

Michael Margolis' list of conditions for 'viable democracy.'
1. Adequate access to information.
2. The smallest unit of government possible makes policy decisions.
3. Criticism of government encouraged.
4. Members of the public are on corporation boards.
5. Institutionalization of social and environmental cost/benefit accounting.[56]

Radoslav Selucky's list of (necessary but not sufficient) requirements:
1. Separation of economic and political power.
2. Dispersion of economic power.
3. Decentralized economic decision-making.
4. Horizontal political and social relations.
5. Voluntary cooperation mediated by the market.
6. A pluralism of economic subjects.
7. Free and educated consumer choice.
8. Social mobility.

48

9. Free competition.
10. Ability to pursue self-interest.[57]

J. Roland Pennock's list:

1. Historical identification of a people with the interests of their shared community.
2. Open mindedness.
3. Power not concentrated in a few hands.
4. Absence of great economic inequality.
5. Respect for persons.
6. Belief in individual rights.
7. Mutual trust, tolerance, willingness to compromise.
8. Literacy and education.
9. Commitment to democratic procedures and values.
10. Public spirit.
11. Nationalism.
12. Certain kinds and balances between consensus and cleavage.
13. Certain institutions of political culture, such as political parties.[58]

A reading of almost any other work on democratic theory will produce additional lists. Sometimes they are set down as (empirically) necessary and sufficient conditions for democracy, as in the case of Cohen and Rogers, sometimes as necessary conditions as in Selucky's case, and sometimes, as Pennock holds, just as lists of items none of which is necessary, though all of which are 'favourable to the formation and survival of democratic regimes.'[59] Even in this case there is a tendency to talk of the conditions as necessary or sufficient,[60] and this is to be expected. What is the point of setting down a list of *general* conditions 'favourable' to democracy if its items are not to be thought jointly necessary and sufficient?

This marks an additional problem with the substantive-cum-conditions approach to 'democracy.' In the degrees-of-democracy orientation, the question of what conditions will facilitate, impede, guarantee, probabilize, and so on, progress in democracy is open. One needs to look at the sort of social units involved and their specific internal and surrounding social environments to make such judgments. For instance, there have been major debates in the peace movement over whether it extends public power over weapons policies to have citizens on corporate boards of firms manufacturing weapons; but on Margolis' view the debate is settled in advance. A similar point can be made about whether workers' self-management and a noncapitalist market are required for democracy, as they *necessarily* are for Selucky in the explication of his condition 3. Or again, in discussing the multinational state, Pennock lays it down that 'state-wide nationalism overrides that of the constituent nations'[61]—a comment that is certain to grate on anyone acquainted with the complex and condition-bound debates of those in bi- and multinational states.

This is not to say that less global conditions cannot or should not be explored. There is surely some space between universal theorizing and the absence of generalization altogether in these matters. Indeed, in arguing (as in Chapter Six) that socialism is a precondition for making major advances in democracy, many of the observations of Cohen and Rogers construed in relation to contemporary, industrialized capitalism are endorsed. However, as their list stands it is possible to deduce the undemocracy of capitalism from a general theory about the conditions of democracy.[62] In this way an approach that insists on laying down general conditions becomes the sort of view criticized in Chapter One that makes claims about democracy true by definition. Theorists who disagree with the political conclusions of the author of one list will find it easier to adopt another list than to examine the social and political realities of the case.

### vi. Scope

To say that democracy is pervasive is to say that there are no situations of social interaction about which the question 'how democratic is it?' cannot be appropriately asked. A competing view agrees that democracy is a matter of degree, but delimits its domain. Three examples will illustrate what this means: limitation of democracy to activities and forms of the state; limitation to the realm of the 'political'; and limitation to social units with a certain level of social and intellectual sophistication.

*States.* The most common view of the field of democracy limits it to the state. Citizens of a state may or may not be able systematically to influence it. If a certain proportion of citizens, typically a majority, have influence, the state is called (more or less) democratic. This was the view of mainstream political theorists from Aristotle's time and has been the dominant view of liberal-democratic theory.[63] It is also the view of one stream of Marxist theory (while specifying that states include not just governmental institutions but also instruments of coercion). Thus Lenin: 'Democracy is a form of the state, one of its varieties.'[64]

For some Marxist socialists, any presocialist state is an instrument of an oppressive, minority class whose activities are the overriding determinant of people's social interactions,[65] while for other socialist theorists (notably anarchists) the state itself is the overriding influence.[66] Debates both among socialists and between them and nonsocialists are surely important ones, but they should not be confused with debates over the proper domain of democracy. Any social unit is part of the domain of democracy, and the democrat's job is to ask what means in given conditions (embedded in states or otherwise) facilitate collective self-determination within a social unit and what structures (again of the state or otherwise) inhibit it.

*Politics.* Limitations of the scope of democracy often take the form of defining the realm of the 'political.' An extreme example is a definition of Barber's: 'One can understand the realm of politics as being circumscribed by conditions that impose a necessity for public action, and thus for reasonable public choice, in the presence of conflict and in the absence of private or independent grounds for judgment.'[67] This is surely too restrictive. It is just in circumstances where conflicting parties are convinced the truth is on their side that it is *most* important that democratic procedures be followed. Hard-line fundamentalists of either the religious or the secular variety can agree with Barber and claim that democracy is not appropriate to a vast range of issues about which they are sure the truth is known.[68]

A less extreme characterization of the political refers to purposes. An example is Michael Walzer's definition of a 'political community' as 'a group of people committed to dividing, exchanging, and sharing social goods, first of all among themselves.'[69] Here democracy is thought appropriate to those circumstances when people might reasonably choose it to accomplish certain ends. This approach will limit the scope of democracy when the ends are specified or when people must actually, deliberately choose democracy. On the face of it, however, it does not seem democracy should be limited in either way. Unless one drew up a list of every possible end people could have and specified this list (disjunctively) as the end in question, it is hard to imagine any one end that would exhaust the scope of democracy. Walzer's specification, for instance, is in terms of a division of goods, but people might reasonably choose democratic processes to achieve other goals, for instance, not just to divide goods but to select a constitution, only some aspects of which would be goods-dividing; or people might decide not on the distribution of goods, but on their contents (for example, that a public TV network will be predominantly educational).

The question about whether democracy is the sort of thing that must be deliberately chosen leads to problems about contract theory. The contract theorists are no doubt right that democratic procedures or any others appropriately called 'political' are ones people *might* deliberately choose and hence 'contract for,' depending on how loosely this activity is regarded.[70] But, some of Locke's comments to the contrary,[71] it would be most odd to say that somebody subject to political processes which he or she did not deliberately choose was thereby outside the realm of the political.

*Reason and Community.* Identifications of the realm of the political and hence of democracy is sometimes attempted by selecting a subset of putative 'conditions' for democracy. Carl Cohen's way of marking off those conditions determining the scope of democracy is to seek ones that are 'commonly or universally met with in human society,' thus showing that democracy may be an omnipresent option.[72] Like many democratic theorists he identifies two such conditions: reason and community.[73] These terms can be defined broadly enough to be compatible with the conception of the scope of democracy employed in this work. Any social unit is a community if this requires human interaction, and 'control' requires reason if this is thought of as no more than the ability to formulate preferences and to make them known to others. Theorists who wish to limit the scope of democracy by reference to these things, however, always have more in mind. The problem is in deciding how much more.

*Democracy: More or Less*

Michael Davis wants an interpretation sufficiently sophisticated to sustain deliberate constitution-making.[74] John Harris, in arguing that children above a certain age should have democratic rights, characterizes 'persons' as 'reasonably competent language-users, who have wants for themselves and their future which they can plan plausibly, not necessarily most successfully, to achieve and who are reasonably responsible for their actions.'[75] As in the case of ends advanced as definitive of democratic scope, the burden is on one using some concept of reason or of community to show that it does not rule out situations where democratic debate and evaluation is appropriate.

For example, Davis's conception might well entail a dubious stand on whether questions of democracy appropriately pertain to traditionally organized tribal societies,[76] and Harris's view is at variance not only with those who do not think democracy is applicable to children at all (his main targets of criticism), but also with those who wish to extend democratic rights to the retarded and to very young children. However, why not extend the scope to any socially interacting ensemble including young children, the severely mentally handicapped, or indeed many animals as long as they are able to form preferences and to make them known? One might argue that in some of these cases less democracy is better than more, but this is not a foregone conclusion; one might argue instead that at least some of what happens in a social unit should be partly determined by the wishes of these people and/or animals. Be this as it may, if debate is appropriate, then the scope of democracy should not be set in a way that would rule it out.

The concept of democracy as pervasive is not by any means new to democratic-socialist theory. Here are two close approximations:

> [U]nder *politics* in the wide sense of the word I understand all those human activities of decision-making and realization whereby important, public, social processes are regulated and directed.
>
> —Marković[77]

> Democracy is now seen, by those who want it and by those who have it...and want more of it, as a kind of society—a whole

53

complex of relations between individuals—rather than simply a system of government.

—Macpherson[78]

Sharing this view of the unlimited scope of democracy, Chapter Four now addresses itself to the question of why people *should* want more of it.

# 4 Justifying Democracy

THAT DEMOCRACY NEEDS to to be justified indicates
the low degree of it in today's world. In some socialist circles,
sad to say, use of the word except for the consumption of others
generates scepticism about one's socialist determination. This
chapter addresses significant worries about democracy that socialists share with nonsocialists; later chapters address specifically
socialist sources of concern.

## i. Why More Democracy?

The principal reason to favour more democracy over less is that
as social units become increasingly democratic, more people become increasingly free. If 'freedom' refers to the availability of
options to do what one might prefer, the thesis can, of course, be
challenged by rejecting this concept of freedom. This topic will
be pursued in Chapters Seven and Eight, along with an examination of the objection that one ought only to favour maximizing
the freedom of those in a certain group, such as the working class.

Some fundamental questions of ethical theory are also set aside.
One concerns the entirely self-interested person who only wishes
personally to be free. Perhaps there are arguments proving that
democratic progress makes any one person's freedom secure, and
that people who have the concern of others at heart are generally
better off than those who do not. But such arguments will not be
pursued here.[1] Nor will the ethical debate be joined about whether
a prescription for freedom, or democracy, or any other goal may
ever justifiably be overridden.

Instead it is stipulated that such prescriptions at least carry a
strong presumption in their favour. I recall a debate with a socialist

friend who takes a far less critical attitude than I do toward the Soviet occupation of Afghanistan or the use of martial law against Poland's Solidarity movement. 'So,' he said, 'you favour that democracy be promoted in any circumstance, at any time, no matter what the surrounding conditions or the consequences?' When I allowed that one might conceive of exceptional situations, this elicited the response that we agreed after all. In fact, we did not agree, but I realized that the dictatorship of the proletariat, so to speak, needs only a crack in the door to fill the whole house.

To forestall this sort of thing, it is here maintained that there must be overwhelmingly conclusive reasons for limiting democracy. Defining 'overwhelmingly conclusive' would be difficult, though not impossible. It certainly rules out making an exception on the basis of just any reason. There are likely always some reasons that weigh in the direction of shelving democracy, and most defences of antidemocratic actions can be seen as seizing on excuses rather than seriously taking up the burden of proof. Also, defence of an overwhelmingly strong case would not give one *carte blanche* to limit democracy in any way, since there would still be a burden to show that a prescribed democracy-limiting measure is the least undemocratic one available.

As to the argument favouring more democracy, it must at least be shown: a) that increasing freedom is a worthwhile goal and democracy is to be valued as a means to it; and b) that increasing democracy does in fact increase freedom. Claim a) will be resisted by those who think of democracy not as a means for maximizing individual freedom, but as a means for establishing a morally good society and who fear that people might not choose one. It will also be resisted by theorists who think democracy should be valued as an end in itself and not as a means to something else. Claim b) is challenged by those who doubt that a highly democratic society is attainable by making incremental advances. These challenges are examined before turning in ii and iii to classic critiques of democracy.

### BAD FREEDOMS

In his book, *The Justification of Democracy*, William Nelson criticizes attempts to defend democratic procedures by appeal to freedom: 'When we evaluate legislation or policy from a moral point of view, we must reject some laws or policies even when they reflect the tastes or desires of individuals.... Indeed, it could be argued that we must sometimes reject these laws just because they are responses to desires – the *wrong* desires.'[2] Nelson's alternative is to value democracy as a force for creating a society of people with good characters.[3]

The distance between Nelson's defence of democracy and one appealing to freedom may not be very great; since a society of people with morally good characters would presumably be one where everyone was free to do as he or she wanted (though having good characters, they would only want to do morally acceptable things). A substantive difference between an approach focussing on the good society and one focussing on individual freedom concerns their different views about the extent to which democratic tolerance for possibly morally objectionable preferences can be sustained short of full democracy. It is hard to deny that in an imperfect world considerations of democracy and of morality will · sometimes pull in opposite directions. The problem this poses may be conceived globally to question whether (imperfect) democracy is in general a suitable means for progressing toward perfect democracy. The problem can also be addressed on a case-by-case basis of conflict between the requirements of morality and of democracy. Thus regarded, the following considerations may allay Nelson's concerns:

1. It is consistent to favour maximizing freedom while also limiting it. This will be the case when it is necessary to limit the freedom of some to protect the freedom of others. Judgments about whose freedoms to curtail might be made on other than freedom-maximizing grounds, but they need not be. An alternative is to use the criterion of 'progress toward complete freedom,' (therefore toward perfect democracy).

2. One might favour the freedom of people to do whatever they wish, while hoping that they will not wish to do certain things. Should people wish to do them anyway (and a 'progress toward complete freedom' criterion does not rule this out), then there is a conflict between a norm in favour of freedom and the norm on which such acts are negatively evaluated. Availability of a criterion for adjudication in such cases would allow a choice, but if none is available,

one would be stymied. Neither situation is ideal, but then neither is entirely unencountered in a world where complex moral decisions must be made, and life goes on.

3. Perhaps in some social unit the situation just described is not an exception but the rule. In this society freedom may not be something to value, and Nelson's approach would be appropriate. But also appropriate would be that in such a social unit democracy is not to be valued. I suspect that were the human community sufficiently depraved (for instance, globally possessed of Nazi values), increasing democracy would cease to be a worthwhile collective activity. Though it might be questioned what would be worthwhile in such a world.

### DEMOCRACY AS AN END IN ITSELF

These observations will be resisted by those who think that the sincere democrat must see democracy itself as an end. Thus, Seymour Martin Lipset: 'Democracy is not only or even primarily a means through which different groups can attain their ends or seek the good of society; it is the good society itself in operation.'[4] This view makes favouring democracy difficult unless one already accepts the value it is supposed to embody. A developed example may be found in Philip Green's arguments for replacing the 'pseudodemocracy, liberal capitalism' with a genuine democracy conceived as political equality. In *Retrieving Democracy* he argues that 'social equality' (a form of material equality plus nonoppressive divisions of labour and equal access to the means of production) is necessary for 'political equality,' a state of affairs equivalent to 'real democracy' in which 'everybody should count for one and nobody for more than one.'[5]

Green describes a demand for political equality as 'an ultimate desire of public opinion,' by which he must mean that it *should* be ultimate, since it is unrealistic to think this a presently universal motivation.[6] This work questions whether the democrat must or should endorse such a prescription. We shall return to this topic in iv and again in Chapter Eight. Suffice it here to observe that in a highly democratic society, people recognize that protection of political equality is required, not as an ultimate end, but as a means for pursuing their various goals. Moreover, it is debatable whether a society in which democracy itself, as interpreted by Green or by anyone else, is desirable, since insisting that democracy is an end in itself limits people's courses of action to ones consistent with whatever the goal 'democracy' is said to be.

Brian Barry is too unkind when he charges those who view democracy as an end in itself with 'giving aid and comfort to the politics of the beautiful people – the radical chic of the Boston–Washington corridor and the London–Oxbridge triangle.'[7] Perhaps some democrats are accurately described by Barry, but others who value democracy for its own sake are more seriously motivated. An example is Roy Medvedev, who associates democracy definitionally with certain moral rights to avoid the sort of 'class instrumentalism' exhibited in the following judgment: 'Democracy under capitalism is to be welcomed, even fought for, not as an end in itself, but in order to demonstrate the material basis, the real roots of political power.'[8] Avoiding such class instrumentalism is an appropriate motive to think of democracy in noninstrumental terms, but this is neither necessary nor sufficient. It is not necessary because there are other ends which democracy serves and because good '*democratic*-instrumental' reasons can be given to resist class instrumentalism.[9] It is not sufficient because class instrumentalists can simply reject as 'bourgeois' any defence of democracy making reference to values they think stand in the way of advancing working-class interests.

The view that democracy is an end in itself is often combined with approaches that regard it as a matter of moral rights. Some fear that otherwise democracy will be sacrificed in the interests of expediency. Perhaps the association of rights-based ethical theories with anticonsequentialism is so strong that anyone friendly to democracy and hostile to utilitarianism feels it imperative to put democracy on a par with rights. But this mixes up two questions: how moral principles are to be justified (by reference only to consequences of acting on them or by something else) and how things other than moral principles are to be justified.[10] Another challenge concerns political equality. Green's view discussed above reflects the opinion of many that democracy essentially involves not just participation but *equal* participation, and it might be thought that unless democracy encompasses the right to political

59

equality as an end, this important value will be sacrificed in the name of democracy itself. This concern will be addressed in due course.

## DEMOCRACY IN AN IMPERFECT WORLD

A perfectly democratic society would probably be as freedom maximizing as any society could ever be. Granting, however, that perfect democracy is not attainable, it is central to the argument of this chapter that much closer approximations to it than exist anywhere today are realistic and desirable goals, and that these goals can be reached only by relentlessly working to increase democracy wherever and whenever possible. Both claims are contested. Critics who think of democracy as a form of mob rule, a tyranny of the majority, or a font of incompetence and inefficiency might agree that perfect democracy would not suffer from these things. But they may still claim that when the trade-offs typical of any imperfect democracy are made, less democracy will be preferable to more. These challenges will be the subject of subsequent sections of this chapter. However, there is a certain purchase on credibility to scepticism about imperfect democracy's ability for improvement sometimes expressed on the political left.

In a world short of perfect democracy, democratic advance will often involve deliberately limiting the control some people have over some aspects of their social environments. Even sanctions against stuffing ballot boxes is a limitation. It is therefore hypothetically possible that progress in democracy is best made by paternalistic denial of control to most people over most aspects of their social environments up to the golden day when they are kicked out of their protected nest into a garden of full democracy. This extreme position could be modified by allowing limited non-paternalistic measures provided they could be justified on a case-by-case basis. That is, the burden would now be placed on the antipaternalist.

The alternate position is that progress toward full democracy requires maximizing individual freedoms except where limitations are: demonstrably necessary for progress in democracy; of short duration and minimum expanse; and imposed in such a way as to be reversible if they turn out to be a mistake. (For instance, laws protecting a minority, though clearly necessary for demo-

60

cratic progress, should be carefully laid down and capable of repeal.) More freedom for effective input to collective decisions, on this view, promotes democratic progress because restrictions on such freedom create a downward democratic spiral, while removal of restrictions creates an upward one. (Readers are invited to consult their own experiences and whatever lessons we can learn from history to test these claims.)

The counterclaim that stepping backwards in democracy is required for making progress in the long run has the additional deficiency that the costs of being wrong are so great as to justify strong scepticism, despite the appeal of simplicity. Indeed, this very appeal should be cause for doubt. Any social unit will be an historically inherited blend of democratic and undemocratic habits and attitudes. It is understandable that somebody might think major progress can be made in one fell swoop, wiping the slate clean and starting again near the top. However, rather than making for progress, this ahistorical approach is apt to create a reaction against attempts to construct new democracy-promoting structures and to prompt retrenchment into antidemocratic traditions on the part of a populace which must view such Draconian efforts as contrary to their interests.

In this work, then, perfect democracy is taken as something to be valued by somebody who, for whatever reasons, values the maximization of human freedom, and imperfect democracy is to be valued so long as one always tries to improve upon a secured level of it. Explication of the case that more democracy lays the basis for yet more will show that this is a realistic prescription, and it will afford an opportunity (in section iii of the chapter) to meet some traditional political arguments against democracy. Core concepts in this endeavour – the 'democratic fix' and the 'anonymous majority' – are introduced in section ii by examining some abstract challenges to democracy.

## ii. The Feasibility of Democracy

Though most political philosophers from Plato's time to the 18th Century were critics of democracy, they still recognized it as an option. It is only in our century that the very coherence of democracy has been called into question. The question is not about whether perfect democracy can ever be attained. In addition to obvious impediments (the complexity of overlapping and always changing social units, the fact that people's visions often exceed their grasp, and the many sources of potential conflict in human affairs), it is possible that some people may not *want* to live in a perfectly democratic society. Considering this possibility creates a paradox. A society including such people could not be perfectly democratic; but excluding the possibility of such wants puts restrictions on the content of preferences. The conclusion to be drawn is not that therefore the idea of perfect democracy is incoherent, but that the possibility of a preference that could not exercise control in a perfect democracy is an additional reason to suppose that this level of democracy will never actually be reached.

### 'PARADOXES OF DEMOCRACY'

The question raised by Kenneth Arrow, among others, is whether *any* democratic mechanism is feasible. Arrow lays down some conditions that must be satisfied by any procedure for making a social choice which is both rational and democratic, and he shows that no procedure (or 'rule of social choice') simultaneously meets all of them. For example, the possibility of cyclical majorities means that majority vote would fail to meet a condition that a social choice rule will always select a single option (the 'collective rationality' condition).[11] Prodemocratic theorists approach this problem in three ways: by modifying Arrow's conditions;[12] by indicating methods for circumventing the problems on a case-by-case basis when they arise in political practice (for instance by logrolling or arbitration in the case of cyclical majorities);[13] or simply by noting that usually workable rules are justified even if one can imagine circumstances when they would not work.[14] The latter, practice-oriented, reactions are on the right track, but they must be focussed in a certain way.

In criticizing the democratic component of liberal democracy, Andrew Levine notes that it will not do to show that in practice Arrow-type paradoxes seldom arise or can usually be gotten around, since it is alleged that democratic social choice rules suffer 'incoherence' and are thus 'profoundly defective' and 'fatally flawed.'[15] The point can be sharpened by asking what a procedure for making social choices must be to avoid such a flaw. One of Arrow's own descriptions is typical in holding that a 'social decision process' or 'constitutional rule' should be capable of 'selecting a preferred action out of every possible environment.'[16] Arrow's emphasis is on the word 'every' in such characterizations, and for those with a proclivity for orderliness it makes sense to say that a rule which fails in this respect is to that extent defective. The question is whether this defect is 'fatal,' but here intuitions differ. For the practically oriented democratic theorist to consider this defect fatal is to put unduly stringent demands on collective decisions. Indeed, such stringency would probably also invalidate decision rules commonly employed by *individuals*. Yet it seems strained to claim that someone who follows usually decisive procedures, making ad hoc adjustments when they fail, is thereby necessarily acting irrationally.

An alternate way to make out a profound defectiveness case is to focus not on the word 'every' in Arrow's phrase but on the word 'preferred.' Leaving aside the question of how individual preferences are ascertained, describing a person as having made a rational decision based in part on his or her preferences is not problematic from the point of view of the political theorist. But ascribing preferences and decisions to *collections* of people is problematic. Were the social choice theorist's only task to evaluate procedures whereby social groups with their preferences attempt to make rational choices, Arrow's problem could be met on a case-by-case basis by anyone for whom ad hocery is not anathema on general principle. However, the social choice theorist faces a more grave problem at the very first step, namely to *identify* group preferences themselves.

In this version of the view about what would make a social decision process fatally flawed, phrases like, 'the collective preference of group X' are supposed to be *defined* by reference to some decision procedure that the members of X might follow, such as voting, drawing lots, or following a leader. When a putative decision-making rule of this kind is shown flawed (for instance, because it conflicts with other indispensable rules), then irrationality would be, as it were, within the very attempt of a group to formulate a preference, and hence the political theorist would not be able to identify group preferences at all, much less ascertain the rationality of actions taken to further them.

The approach of this chapter sides with the practically-oriented defenders of democracy on the question of whether completeness is a necessary condition for rationality (of groups or of individuals), and it suggests a way to avoid the problem of identifying group preferences. The degrees-of-democracy theorist is not concerned to discover what, if anything, would constitute group rationality in the formulation of preferences. Rather, this theorist wants to know how progress toward perfect democracy may be made. 'Perfect democracy' is not defined by reference to collective preferences, but to individual preferences and to the availability of some means of control which people may jointly employ, where the list of such means is open ended.

In a perfect democracy means must be available whereby negotiation can take place when consensus is not reached (or sought), but it is unnecessary to identify some means as ideal, much less as definitive of 'negotiation.' Activities like voting or seeking a consensus before acting are devices that may make progress toward perfect democracy or that might function as a means of negotiation in a perfectly democratic society, but they are not meant to be definitive of 'democratic social choice.' Thus conceptualized, many considerations advanced to solve Arrow-type problems can be valued as suggesting techniques to be employed when circumstances merit it, even if none of them constitutes an acceptable definition of 'democratic decision.'[17]

## COMPROMISERS AND FREE RIDERS

This approach can be applied to two more problems addressed by social choice theory: that of the free rider and of the autocompromiser. Democracy-promoting mechanisms and institutions are 'public goods' for those enjoying their benefits. But while it is of benefit to everyone that democratic institutions exist, no one will consider it necessary to put out any effort, even if this is only to vote, to secure it. One should expect, therefore, that nobody will make the effort with the result that nobody benefits from democracy. Reflection on this dilemma has generated quite a body of literature trying to explain why people do in fact exert such effort.[18]

Autocompromising was touched on in the last chapter in discussing 'control.' Political theorists who study it note the way platforms of competing political parties often fail to match the first preferences of their mainstream adherents. Policy makers of each party fear that unless the party takes a stand close to the political centre, it will lose to a party that itself employs this strategy. The result, again, is a situation in which whoever wins the election, it will be on a platform that is nobody's first choice. Rather than each party running on a platform reflecting its members' primary values, uncertainty prompts advance compromise.[19] The problem is an instance of that studied by decision theorists as one version of 'the prisoners dilemma,' where choices must be made by conflicting parties in justified mutual mistrust and with severely limited options.[20]

If these sorts of 'dilemmas' are associated with the project of defining 'democratic social choice,' then similar considerations are pertinent. As part of the ongoing effort to maintain and expand democracy, however, they raise somewhat different difficulties. There is obviously something wrong with the first problem as a deduction about how people must behave, because many people do in fact exert the effort to participate in democratic procedures. While some of them may be irrational (lunatics with a deranged compulsion to fill out ballots), most do not seem either crazy or stupid, and to conclude that they *must* be because they are not free riders is objectionably antiempirical. Hence, considered at the most abstract level, this is a problem for theories of rationality, not for democratic politics.

But viewed practically, the free-rider problem must be addressed by someone who wishes to make progress in democracy.[21] Low voter turnout and other forms of nonparticipation are well-known phenomena, no doubt partly to be explained by the possibility of being a free rider. The practical question for the democrat to ask is how free riding can be limited to the degree that it does not make democracy-enhancing practices impossible. One mechanism often suggested is to attach a cost to nonparticipation, for instance, fines for not voting or penalties for not attending meetings. This sort of approach is too pessimistic, since there is an alternative.

THE DEMOCRATIC FIX

In the 1960s some technophiles liked to talk of the 'technological fix,' the view that problems created by technology are best rectified by the employment of more technology.[22] We know the disastrous consequences of this view; one need not be a technophobic to realize that machines, whatever their virtues, are incapable of taking an interest in human well-being. But there are some reasons to suppose that an analogous theory of a 'democratic fix' is sound. The free-rider problem is created by the achievement of a certain level of democratic society, one that can provide everyone with benefits even if not everyone helps to maintain that level.

By the democratic fix, solutions to this problem are found by *increasing* democracy. People who do not vote in elections are not just lazy. They are also reacting to the fact that few have effective input to the selection of candidates and that there is sparse correlation between what candidates promise and what they do. People who have an opportunity to participate in the governing of their affairs in a more direct way, for instance, in voluntary neighbourhood or issue-related organizations, but refrain, are influenced by the fact that these activities take up much time with relatively meagre results that are often later reversed. On the argument of the democratic fix, increased popular control of the conditions that impede participation is required to rectify this situation.[23]

It is noteworthy that the most extreme example of autocompromising, the prisoner's dilemma, is an abstract model in which constraints are so severe that the democratic fix cannot be applied. The parties in question have no opportunity either to try reaching consensus or to negotiate with one another. Being players in an abstract model, the prisoners do not live in a real world where there would be more room for movement (for instance, carried on by the prisoners' lawyers), nor is there a world outside the prison and the courts subject to democratizing measures which (the democrat argues) can in the long term increasingly minimize crime and hence the need for prisons and their constraints. This is not to deny that the practical problem of autocompromising is a real one, as the problem of political party platforms illustrates, but in this real-life example there are ways of minimizing constraints.

The most frequently encountered response is to take *antidemocratic* measures. Faced with pressures to move away from stating preferred political policies, parties compromise in platforms, but do whatever they want when elected. The contrasting democratic prescription is to increase democracy. Political theorists have noted that autocompromising ought to lead to a two party-system. It is accordingly instructive to see what sorts of counteracting pressures have prevented this, as they have in most of the world where there are parliamentary systems with competing political parties.

One hypothesis is that convergence is less likely when parties have an active, popular base of support with effective input to their decision-making structures. Examples are some labour, socialist, and communist parties with trade union support, and the Green Party in the Federal Republic of Germany, which has active support from ecological, peace, and feminist movements. To the extent that this hypothesis is sound it illustrates the democratic fix. Dependence on support by people actively pursuing goals outside of a party structure provides an incentive for it to advance policies in accord with these goals. Internal political party democracy also helps to keep leaders honest. Perhaps one can imagine circumstances within which the democratic fix is unlikely to work, and there are problems other than those of the free rider and autocompromising. But once these problems are considered practical ones, instead of challenges to the coherence of notions like 'democratic choice,' the impossibility of the democratic fix cannot be established in advance of concrete inquiry.

### iii. Constitutions, Majorities, Minorities

Dennis Mueller's book, *Public Choice*,[24] explores the question of how democracy can get started and by whom. Mueller distinguishes between methods for making decisions over the allocation of goods within a political structure and methods whereby 'constitutional' decisions about the principles of such a structure are made. His main concern is with constitutional decisions, where he sees problems with both unanimity and majority vote.

Requiring unanimity can prevent a constitution from ever being agreed to or allow a small minority to blackmail the majority with its veto power. Majority decision can leave a minority feeling itself shut out or unbound by a constitution. Mueller suggests that social choice theorists are therefore attracted to social contract theory, where the most basic normative decisions are thought somehow to have been made in advance of ongoing political society. But a serious problem for contractarians concerns the locus of 'primary citizenship' or the question of who makes the contract: 'If primary citizenship is vested in the inclusive polity, citizens in unfavourably endowed local communities are able to tax those living in other local communities. How then is the writing of the social contract envisaged, as a pact among all members of the inclusive polity, which sets aside certain rights for the local polities? Or do the citizens first form a pact for the local polity, and then delegate authority over some issues to the larger one?'[25] Mueller's challenge offers an opportunity to sharpen a degrees-of-democracy approach.

### GETTING STARTED

The question of an 'Ur-Constitution' does not concern a degrees-of-democracy approach (though the question of deciding how inclusive an actual constitution should be and whether people should have a right to opt out is of concern). On the degrees approach, democracy never has to be gotten off the ground because it is never on it. There is always some measure of democracy, and the problem is how to increase it. People always have found themselves in social units, some partially shaped by formal constitutions, most not, but all of them more or less democratic. When it is important to construct or to alter a constitution (that is, collectively and deliberately to set out principles in accord with which further actions affecting a shared social environment will be taken), this is done against the background of these overlapping social units and of the degrees of democracy each possesses. Democracy enhancement is of the lifting by one's boot straps variety of processes rather than of the fundamental construction variety.[26]

Nevertheless, Mueller's considerations throw into relief some problems about the relation among the three indices of 'more democracy' outlined in the last chapter (number of people having control, number of aspects over which control is exerted, and the importance of aspects over which control may be had). In one respect the 'proportion of people' measure has no claim to being more important than the others, and a democrat may recognize that in some imaginable circumstances progress would be made by disallowing wide public input to a range of decisions, whether unanimity, majority vote, or something in between, for a considerably long period of time. This logical possibility keeps the imposition of emergency legislation or the imposition of revolutionary dictatorship on an unwilling majority from being antidemocratic *by definition*.

However, we know, do we not, that these things are in fact antidemocratic, that is, that they contribute to regress in democracy? Not only is control limited in the short term, but well-known social, political, organizational, and psychological processes are set in motion that inhibit democracy and are hard to reverse. I have no doubts that were one ever written, a world history of democracy[27] would justify thinking of it as a spiral, to employ the image of Bowles and Gintis,[28] such that motion in either an upward or a downward direction creates an impetus to keep moving in that direction. Thus viewed, the 'proportion of people' measure takes on special significance. To do something against the will of the majority is to set in motion dynamics that will lead to less and less democracy, even if it could lead to more democracy were one able to think these dynamics out of existence.

Most constitutions limit a majority's ability to force an election at any time on any issue, and the leaders of many postrevolutionary or nationally liberated states often refrain from holding elections immediately after attaining statehood. Such measures can be sorted according to whether there is popular support, measured in a variety of ways, for them.[29] In these cases intuition gives unanimity and/or majority agreement special place among ways to ascertain popular support. It is thought that were there unanimity, this would be an ideal situation, and if a majority agrees, then taking into account only the 'proportion of popular control' measure, the result would be at least more democratic than one agreed to by less than a majority.

UNANIMITY AND CONSENSUS

The problem addressed by Mueller that unanimity might become de facto rule by minority veto can be ameliorated by seeking criteria to identify situations where on balance more democracy is promoted than retarded when a minority has this power. But there are bound to be limitations on how well such criteria could function in an ever-changing world. There is also the question of how a choice of the criteria themselves is to be made: by unanimous consent or otherwise. However, these problems will, again, be less acute for the degrees-of-democracy advocate than for others.

Unanimity itself admits of degree, one limit of which is veto by a minority of one, the other, consensus. Theorists of participatory democracy have done a good job of describing the difference between decision-making by consensus and by what might be called 'voting on fixed interests.' Benjamin Barber describes the strongest form of consensus as: 'an agreement that arises out of common talk, common decision, and common work but that is premised on citizens' active and perennial participation in the transformation of conflict through the creation of common consciousness and political judgment.'[30] This form of consensus is not just acquiescence to a stubborn majority; it requires coming to agreement. Nor is it a case of people happening to agree already. Barber calls this weak form of consensus 'substantive' as opposed to 'creative' consensus. This is an apt term, signalling as it does that consensus is a process during which people's preferences change as a result of engaging in discussion and debate with others engaged in shared projects. (In Japanese the phrase *sodan kai* refers to a group that strives to reach consensus by talking together.) Habermas describes the same phenomenon in his description of democracy as the 'participation of citizens in discursive processes of will-formation.'[31]

When there are good reasons both to seek more than majority rule and also to avoid a minority veto, the degrees-of-democracy approach will prescribe striving for consensus in this strong sense. One standard objection is that people can be expected to enter social decision-making forums and to exit from them with the same, probably selfish, preferences. This mean-spirited view of human nature has been more than adequately treated by democratic theorists and will be touched on in later chapters. A much different objection is that anything other than consensus, and in particular majority vote, fails to be democratic at all. This is Barber's own view: 'Majoritarianism is a tribute to the failure of democracy: to our inability to create a politics of mutualism that can overcome private interests. It is thus finally the democracy of desperation, an attempt to salvage decision-making from the anarchy of adversary politics.'[32] This criticism of majority rule supplements that of Mueller, but both can be met.

## THE ANONYMOUS MAJORITY

Writing from a degrees-of-democracy perspective, Felix Oppenheim persuasively argues that in order to maintain an acceptable level of democracy, the 'majority principle' itself requires constraints on what any one majority may do.[33] The point applies especially to the protection of minority rights. If majority rule is to be ongoing and secure it must avoid a situation where a minority ceases to feel bound by majority will or where restrictions on minority rights trigger a downward spiral that finally undermines the power of the majority itself. Oppenheim also notes that minority-protecting rights serve the interests of majority rule by protecting the minority's ability to change the minds of the majority. This justifies a large number of traditional civil liberties and some equality rights. Members of a minority subject to discrimination, threatened by arrest without recourse, lacking information and political skills, or hamstrung by poverty will hardly be in a position to try educating members of the majority to their opinions; yet it is surely not in the interests of ongoing democracy that a majority should do things to keep itself ill-informed.[34]

Implicated in these considerations is that the notions 'minority' and 'majority' are more complex than usage sometimes suggests. Each is a group concept, but groups *per se* do not, strictly speaking, vote or otherwise make decisions. Hence, to talk of a minority changing the mind of a majority is misleading; rather it is the actual contours of the majority that change. The point is made by Carl Cohen who discusses the 'fluctuating majority,'[35] and by public choice theorists who insist that, in a democratic decision, who votes for what on one issue should not determine the outcome of a subsequent vote. Kenneth May called this open-ended majority 'anonymous.'[36]

It is too strict to make anonymity necessary for any democracy at all. Even fixed majority rule will be more democratic, other things being equal, than minority rule. But it will be less secure, less likely to be ongoing majority rule and less likely to provide fertile ground for developing other methods, like seeking consensus. Thus, the democrat will strive to protect the anonymity of the majority. The implications of this for pluralism and class reductionism will be discussed in due course. The point here is

71

that the democrat need not be stuck with an alternative between a simply interpreted unanimity procedure and an equally simply interpreted majority rule. Each, like democracy itself, is a complex matter of degree.

## iv. The Practicality of Democracy

So far the strategy of this defence of democracy has been to displace abstract problems to the terrain of real political practice. Now, however, we must confront some practical reservations which many have expressed about democracy: that it constitutes a tyranny of the majority; that it promotes rule of the incompetent; and that it is inefficient.

### THE TYRANNY OF THE MAJORITY

Elaine Spitz, a strong defender of majority rule, argues that the force of this criticism can be dampened if majority rule is seen as a 'social practice,' embodying certain values and modes of comportment, but she grants there is something to the objection.[37] In terms of a degrees-of-democracy approach, a situation where a majority oppresses a minority may well be more democratic than one in which a minority has the ability to oppress the majority, but at the same time minority rule might also be justified under certain conditions. Neither alternative can sit well with the democrat. However, once the notion of democracy as ongoing is introduced, the intuition can be captured that there is something out of keeping about both a majority tyrannizing a minority and minority rule. Promoting minority rule will require dismantling political mechanisms difficult to rebuild, thus leading to far more antidemocratic consequences. Similarly, many democratic theorists concur with the view explicated above that unconstrained majority rule is autodestructive.[38]

Here it is appropriate to return to the question of political equality raised in section i, since this principle also finds a source of justification in the anonymous majority. The point is almost made by Green: 'Since the rule of political equality is everybody to count for one, nobody for more than one, political equality cannot exist when there are permanent or long-term minorities in the polity.... A minority must be nothing more than a random collection of people who lost the last vote; if that proviso does not generally hold true, then we have not political equality but majority tyranny.'[39] This argument may be inverted to maintain that equality of participation is a requirement for prevention of majority tyranny. Democracy might be best served if those most strongly affected by the outcome of a decision have greater input to the decision than those little affected (hence the rule 'one-person-one-vote' ought not to be advanced as inflexibly universal). But democratic progress is not promoted if certain people always have disproportionately advantageous input.

Clearly, the more such situations there are, the greater the possibility of a tyranny of a minority with its attendant consequences of creating cynicism and political apathy in the majority. At the same time systematic disproportionate advantage also threatens majority anonymity. Though it is misleading to say with Green that a minority or a majority on any one issue should be 'a random collection' (there must, after all, have been reasons for them to have voted the same way), full anonymity would be impeded if there were a tendency for some always to be members of a majority. Those with disproportionate input will be just such people, since others will see an advantage to getting them on their side, not because of the content of the majority's opinions, but just because they are thus privileged.[40]

### THE EMPTY SPACE OF DEMOCRACY

Anonymous majority rule is what Green calls 'the true ideal' of majority rule: 'not that everyone has equal influence, but that no one has any influence.'[41] The description is appropriate, but it suggests a problem addressed by some theorists about the stability of democracy. Claude Lefort and François Furet argue that democracy requires sovereignty to be 'empty': 'The legitimation of [democratic] power is based on the people; but to the image of popular sovereignty is attached that of an empty place, impossible to occupy, such that those who exercise public authority cannot claim to appropriate it. Democracy joins these two apparently contradictory principles: one that power comes from the people, the other that it is the power of nobody.'[42]

Neither Lefort nor Furet link their idea of the empty space of democracy with the anonymous majority, and perhaps they can be criticized for supposing a theory of fixed interests. However, their concept of popular sovereignty sits more comfortably with the notion of the anonymous majority than with a doctrine of fixed interests. If the majority becomes so fixed that decisions are always made by the same configuration of people, they become the occupants of the space of sovereignty. Lefort's concern is rather that the space of democracy can be 'occupied' by a minority acting in the name of the people.

Furet thinks this happened after the French Revolution when the Jacobins assumed this role, and Lefort sees the Bolsheviks as having done the same thing after the Russian Revolution. These are intriguing hypotheses, and one can find illustrations closer to home in parliamentary governments when representatives who are barely responsive to a population authoritatively pronounce on some issue in the name of 'the people.' Thus, the problem is not that the majority becomes tyrannical but that to prevent its so becoming, the door is opened to unresponsive minority rule. One need not conclude that therefore all is lost, but attention is drawn to the fact that, like almost anything else worth pursuing, progress in democracy involves a certain risk. An important way to prevent the space of democracy from being misused is to ensure that a populace is aware of the importance of keeping it open. This applies both to a majority, who should have a conception of the importance of protecting minority rights at the same time that it opposes a specific minority, and to a minority, who should value abiding by the will of the majority, even while disagreeing with it.[43]

### RULE OF THE INCOMPETENT

Democrats are no doubt right that those who question the people's moral or intellectual abilities to govern their own affairs are usually elitists and snobs. But one must still confront the substance of this charge. The main counter argument must be empirical. It must be denied that people are incapable of self-government. Evidence for this is not easily found outside of participation with people who are not professional politicians in efforts at self-determination. My own experience (in left-wing politics, the peace and civil rights movements, and in my own work place and professional associations) has informed me, to be sure, of the problems

74

to be overcome when people try collectively to direct some portions of their lives in a political, cultural, and economic environment often hostile to this task. I think it also cured me of any
populist romanticism I may have had and shows that some people
seem to have a special aptitude for this kind of activity.

But it has also revealed that people concerned with issues close
to them and given half a chance do not bifurcate into the few
who are smart and capable and the many who can never hope to
be more than good followers. People can and do rise to the occasion. This is one thing that makes voluntary organizations, for
example, women's or peace movements, tenants and environmental protection organizations, or trade unions, as effective as
they sometimes are against powerful adversaries, who typically
underestimate people's ability to get their acts together. Further,
where there are problems of apathy or insecurity among 'rank
and file' members of an association, my experience has been that
this is rather an effect than a cause of elitist domination of leadership by a few.

*Participation.*   Observations such as mine are no doubt of a highly
subjective nature and not likely to convince a hostile critic of democracy. (Although it should be noted that the view often supporting such scepticism that knowledge about things social and
political requires detachment and nonparticipation can be challenged.)[44] But additional, burden-shifting arguments are available
to the democrat. One of these appeals to the possibility of education. Moses Finley concludes his book on democracy in ancient
Greece: 'The conviction of Socrates is not the whole story of freedom in Athens. . . . I have tried to argue that [exclusive concern
to erect protections against the public] is a way of preserving
liberty by castrating it, that there is more hope in a return to the
classical concept of governance as a continued effort in mass education. There will still be mistakes, tragedies, trials for impiety,
but there may also be a return from widespread alienation to a
genuine sense of community.'[45] Like most other democratic theorists Finley has in mind not just formal education but the education that comes through democratic participation itself.

Proving that participation educates people for self-government demands much argumentation, but some features of a
participationist argument might be noted, all supposing ver-

sions of the 'democratic fix.' Required for effective, ongoing and increasing participation in collective self-determination by members of a social unit is: 1) that they have the *desire* to participate, that is, that they are not apathetic; 2) that they have appropriate *values*, for example, simultaneous respect for majority rule and minority rights; and 3) that they have the *skills* required for self-governance, including the ability to use good judgment in negotiation, debate, coordination of self-governing efforts in overlapping social environments, and in general practical knowledge about human nature and political processes.[46]

The democrat believes that activity that increases shared control over a social environment (democratic participation), once engaged in, is found effective at solving long-run problems and yields short-term rewards, as bringing people together in common action helps to break down alienation, isolation, and a sense of impotence. Thus, unless somehow counteracted, a desire for increased democratic participation should grow as its benefits are learned. The process needs to be started, but as noted, it always does exist in some measure. Extending it requires people's becoming involved in such things as community associations, home and school organizations, unions or caucuses in unions, national or cultural organizations, or issue-related movements. Involvement can be more or less democratic, and education in democracy requires also that the involvement be deliberately and critically democratic. A main task of democratic theory and social research is to explain why and how such things take place or fail to take place where and when they do.

The participationist notes that the more local and modest the democratic enterprise the less difficult it is for people to engage in it and the more direct the incentive to do so. Hence there is the possibility of entering a process. Potential for increasingly acquiring the values and skills required for more democracy is found within the process. One learns how to negotiate by doing it. Success in changing a majority's mind educates one to the role of protecting minority rights even when in the majority. The values of respect and tolerance are initially learned by people seeking the same goals but differing on means, and it can then be extended to respect and tolerance for people sharing some goals but disagreeing on others. Democracy-inhibiting prejudices (racial, sexist, or national chauvinist) thrive on mutual isolation, but begin to be called into question in the interaction that participation in joint projects facilitates. To challenge the participationist it will not do simply to adduce examples where participation has not had the desired effects, but further to show that there were no' counter-acting tendencies (for example, opposition so strong that shared goals were thwarted and morale broken), and that impediments to the development of relevant skills and attitudes could not have been removed by more democracy (for instance, in the internal organization of a collective itself).

*Philosopher Kings.* Another defence against the 'people are in-competent' challenge is to ask who *is* competent to control human affairs if not all the humans whose affairs they are. The question-begging response, 'those who happen to have the incentive and skills necessary to rule,' does not suffice. In the first place, there is the question of what they are to do as rulers. Controlling human affairs means doing things that will affect some society, and un-democratically responsive rulers will have to decide how to use their supposed skills and knowledge. The main alternatives seem to be: to promote satisfaction of a ruler's own preferences no matter what effects this has on others; to promote satisfaction of needs shared by every member of the community (to stay alive, for example); or to try maximizing preference satisfaction across the society.

Each alternative is problematic. The first is overt tyranny. The second two alternatives are forms of paternalism and raise the question of how the ruler knows what universal needs or individ-ual preferences are. If the ruler relies on people's expressions of them, this approaches the democracy that was to be avoided. If the ruler has some other access to knowledge of these things, then one wants to know how this knowledge is obtained and who has it. This suggests another weakness in the elitist's argument. Walzer addresses it in discussing Plato's claim that philosophers should decide what is best for people. He comes down against the phi-losophers: 'The interventions of philosophers should be limited to the gifts they bring. Else they are like Greeks bringing gifts, of whom the people should beware, for what they have in mind is the capture of the city.'[47] The point is surely apt. Who is to judge whether decisions of supposed leaders are in people's real interests? If the people themselves are the judges, this elitist position again turns into that of the democrat. If the rulers are to judge, there is no way to check against bad and self-serving decisions, thus leading to tyranny.

Supposing that either of these arguments against the elitist can be sustained, there remain two alternatives: democracy and 'traditionalist conservatism.' The latter view is that those people should rule who find themselves in the traditional roles of rulers, whether they are competent or not.[48] Among the problems with this profoundly pessimistic viewpoint is that even if one agreed with its premises, it is *too late* to act on in countries which have achieved a degree of democracy that includes an ethos hostile to such blind obedience. Unless the traditionalists are to take the status quo as the 'tradition' to follow (in which case this would often involve more democracy than they want), they will have to be 'reactionaries,' advocating return to some past tradition. It is hard to see how a criterion telling one which tradition should be reverted to and consistent with traditionalism could be found.

### EFFICIENCY

While pro- and antidemocrats take opposing views about whether democracy is more or less efficient,[49] it is not always made clear what democracy is supposed to be more or less efficient *at*. Presumably there are tasks requiring coordinated activity to be performed. More or less democracy may enter at one or both of two stages: deciding to confront a task and agreeing on means to undertake it. Relatively undemocratic situations regarding both ends and means are ones forced on people by circumstances like a natural disaster, pursued in accord with blind tradition, or dictated by a few to suit their purposes (as when a government, responding to the arms industry, determines that 'defence' will be promoted by massive arms spending). Most who claim democracy to be inefficient avoid the topic of the selection of goals, as well they might.

To argue that goal selection should be undemocratic requires maintaining that all such selection is forced or blindly traditional or else that the few who know what goals people ought to have make these decisions. Surely the first alternatives are objectionably fatalistic, and the last is a version, again, of Platonic elitism. Perhaps it is in recognition of these weaknesses that most critics of democracy concern themselves with its putative inefficiency as a means for realizing goals. The arguments are familiar. Democracy is said not to allow sufficient coordination or to be too slow and clumsy in emergencies. Or it is urged that while people may be the best judges of their ends, special expertise is required in the choice of means.

Evaluation of the critic's claims requires comparison of success in solving problems of joint concern carried out more or less democratically. The democrat argues that despite regular denunciations of democracy as inefficient (almost always levelled by people whose own power would be curtailed by more democracy) such comparisons tell another tale. Of course, the comparisons must be thorough ones. In a thin slice of space and time Hitler made trains run on schedule, but not many were running when he surveyed a country in rubble from his bunker a few years later. This is not the place to carry out such evaluation, but some general considerations on the democratic side can be noted. Lipset appropriately points out that when special expertise is required, a democratically 'legitimated' society is better able to produce and call upon qualified experts, because people are more likely to be recognized and promoted on the basis of real achievement than on superficial characteristics such as skin colour.[50] And Habermas criticizes as an unjustified, technocratic assumption that planning and citizen participation must be in contradiction.[51]

There are also the advantages often and justly referred to by democratic theorists of democratic debate and the need for accountability to advance knowledge and develop expertise. Moreover, democracy allows utilizing the practical 'expertise' of people locally affected by decisions.[52] The relatively rare city planners who consult residents of neighbourhoods, school superintendents who consult students and teachers, hospital administrators who consult nurses and patients, or factory managers who consult workers almost always make better decisions than the many who do not.

'Emergency' situations said to require the shelving of democracy in the interests of expediency are often suspect.[53] Sometimes the emergency which requires autocracy turns out to be no more than democratic threat to autocrats themselves. Genuine emergencies, for instance, ones caused by natural disasters, economic collapse, or military invasion, are almost always better met democratically than autocratically. They demand sacrifices which people who have had input to a decision will be more committed to making than if someone else has declared that they must endure them, and there is less danger that temporary checks become permanent ones. Also, means and ends have a way of turning into each other. Democratically secured commitment to seek a common goal can atrophy when there is little participation in choosing means, and relative lack of democracy in the choice of means can change a social environment in such a way as to create new problems.

These are not meant to be more than outlines of defences for full democracy. Once they are developed the importance of seeking always to advance democracy is established, so the democrat maintains. On this premise, then, one wants to know about social units as large as entire countries what political/economic structures will best promote democracy. Chapter Six will make a case for socialism in this respect. First some key and controversial problems of definition need to be addressed.

# 5 Capitalism, Socialism, and Equality

HISTORICALLY, SUPPORT FOR capitalism was associated with rebellion against the freedom-inhibiting aspects of feudalism, while a main appeal of socialism has been its opposition to the gross inequalities of capitalism. This has promoted the practice of making claims about the relation of capitalism and socialism to democracy true by definition. Nonetheless, question-begging practices can be avoided while taking account of these associations. A capitalist society will here be considered one legally and politically structured to facilitate the freedom of a few (capitalists) individually to dispose of the bulk of the society's wealth; while a socialist society is one structurally favouring material equality.

These are the most important essential features of capitalism and socialism from the point of view of one primarily concerned to make advances in democracy. Definitions sufficiently full for any purpose a student of social/economic systems may have would require much more work and confront many contested issues. Among the contested features of the approach in this chapter is its agreement with Marx that capitalism and socialism should be identified by structural features of which people living in them may be unaware and its departure from a standard Marxist definition of 'socialism' as 'the dictatorship of the proletariat.'

### i. 'Capitalism'

Adam Przeworski and G.A. Cohen provide convenient concepts for making the partial definition above a bit more precise. Central to Przeworski's treatment is that capitalism and socialism are both modern, industrial, commodity-producing economic systems where goods are mass produced for an impersonal market, and where 'part of the total societal product is withheld from the immediate producers' for future use. What marks off capitalism is that this withheld surplus accrues 'in the form of profit...to owners of the means of production,' while 'wage earners *qua* immediate producers have no institutional claim to its allocation.'[1] Cohen wishes to defend Marx from the charge that his definition of 'capitalism' by reference to private ownership of productive means makes explanations employing the base/superstructure distinction incoherent. 'Ownership,' Cohen argues, refers not just to legal facts, but to actual economic power.[2] The base/superstructure theory need not concern us (until Chapter Nine), as what is useful is the notion of economic power over deployment of a surplus protected by legal and other institutions of the state.

Like socialism, a capitalist system (or 'structure,' or set of 'practices,' 'relations,' 'institutions,' or other terms deliberately used vaguely here) is one where commodity production requires and yields a surplus of wealth. 'Capitalists' are those individuals (including corporate individuals) who privately 'own' means of production, which is to say that they have the state-facilitated ability to make use of or sell such means. Petty capitalists do this directly; capitalists in the full sense of the term employ workers. When sale or rent of commodities (including services, money, raw materials, and energy, in addition to manufactured goods) realizes a profit, its deployment is at the discretion of that capitalist whose profit it is. A society will thus be noncapitalist either if nobody privately owns means of production and employs workers or if the allocative discretion of those who do is severely constrained, not by the market but by social and political structures deliberately put in place to further goals other than to protect continuing capitalist discretion.[3]

Cohen's conception is slightly narrower when he gives as one of two extensionally equivalent definitions of 'capitalism,' that it is 'the society whose production serves the accumulation of capital,'[4] Reference to capital accumulation reflects the common practice of making it a matter of definition that capitalists use their power to expand capital or to maximize future profit. Though this is no doubt the case, it need not be included in our definition. In this respect the approach here is more in keeping with that of Samuel Bowles and Herbert Gintis, who describe capitalist private ownership simply as 'conferring' power to make decisions limiting the powers of others over such matters as investment.[5] One advantage of such a broad conception is that it allows for the fact that in capitalism workers are 'exploited,' without wedding one to use of this term, thus avoiding the need to defend a stand on how to define it (by reference to the controversial labour theory of value or in another way).[6]

Exactly how far the approach is from that of Marx need not be addressed here.[7] The less specific concept is adopted to reflect the opinion held by procapitalists that their favoured system is not plan-bound, and to make clear the empirical nature of Marx's demonstrations that regardless of the motives of individual capitalists, their economic circumstances compel them to sacrifice other goals they may have to the maximization of profit. (Some procapitalists are loath to accept this conclusion, since it greatly mitigates claims about how capitalism is supposed to promote freedom. Others accept the conclusion and try to argue that even if capitalists are constrained to maximize profit before anything else, the system is still to be preferred in virtue of putative 'trickle down' effects.)

Like most social-theoretical definitions, this one is of an ideal type. In real circumstances the allocative power of capitalists is not absolute. Being state facilitated, there are laws with means for enforcement protecting the ability in question, and with them are such things as institutions of the civil service, regulatory and planning agencies, educational and research facilities, government commissions, and so on, likewise structured to maintain an economy with the ability. There may *also* be state practices that put constraints on what capitalists can use their capital for and taxes that remove some capital from their hands altogether. This is clearly the case in all real capitalist societies, which are nonetheless capitalist if constraints function to limit capitalist ability in the short term to protect or expand it in the long term, or if they function to limit some capitalists in the interest of other capitalists. The work of Claus Offe illustrates the pervasiveness and complexity of such constraints, including contradictory constraints that do not work to the advantage of capitalist ability at all.[8]

*Welfare Capitalism.*  A society may remain capitalist when there are laws and the rest that do not even indirectly protect the capitalist ability to dispose of wealth provided that these are 'outweighed' by structures that do protect it. Fully to define 'outweigh' would be an important exercise, not undertaken here. Evidence that a capitalist-limiting state measure, function, or institution is outweighed by capitalist-promoting ones is that the former is more fragile in terms of its effectiveness or its preservation than the latter. Or one might say that the origin and persistence of state-supported things that limit capitalists require special explanation to be understood (for instance, by reference to a large-scale national disaster or the efforts of a uniquely effective pressure group), whereas institutions or laws that support capitalist freedom are easily understood as what is to be expected given usual patterns of behaviour and the felicitous 'fit' between them and what is required for capitalists to exercise this freedom.[9] 'Welfare capitalism' might thus be described as a society with nonnegligible and persistent constraints on capitalists, most of which are capitalist serving in the long run (for example, by providing purchasing power or by dampening social unrest), even if there are a few truly countercapitalist constraints.

*Social Democracy.* There may also be state ownership of means of production and employment of labourers coexisting with private ownership. In this circumstance it is possible to talk of a capitalist society when the state comports itself compatibly with the continued (relative) freedom of capitalists to allocate wealth. Sometimes state ownership interferes with this freedom by running paying industries or by forcing up wages. A society with both large-scale capitalist ownership and state ownership that inhibits deployment of wealth by capitalists could still be counted a capitalist one if, as in the case of welfare capitalism, state-supported capitalist power on balance outweighs impediments to this power deriving from state ownership. A 'social-democratic' society may then be conceived of as one where there is a near balance between capitalist-serving legal and political structures, including state ownership, that do not interfere with capitalist freedom, on the one hand, and capitalist-inhibiting state ownership, on the other, but where the 'weight' favours capitalism in that the society's anticapitalist dimensions are more precariously maintained than its procapitalist ones.[10] Right-wing social democrats see this as a desirable form of capitalism. Optimistic left-wing social democrats regard

84

it as a stepping stone to full-blown socialism; while pessimists consider it the closest to socialism one can hope to aspire.


## ii. 'Socialism'

'Socialism' is usually defined negatively, but it is not always clear what is negated. One approach is to negate the feature of capitalism that some own major means of production and employ labour. The resulting conception of socialism is not inaccurate from the point of view adopted here as long as Cohen's broad concept of 'ownership' is kept in mind. However, this concept leaves open the possibility that leading party and state officials or plant managers exercise the powers enjoyed by capitalists. There may be no formally legal possibility of privately owning means of production, but the state might still be structured so that the analogues of capitalists – those who make decisions about the allocation of wealth and the deployment of labour – are relatively unconstrained in their decision-making.

At this point the theorist of socialism must make a choice. Marković suggests that 'society as a whole' make decisions about the allocation of wealth in socialism. That is, a socialist society must be relatively democratic at least in economic matters. Alternately, Levine distinguishes between 'democratic' and 'state bureaucratic' models of socialism.[11] In the latter model, which we shall also call 'thin socialism,' officials of the state and not the populace make crucial economic decisions, but such socialism is different from capitalism in being more egalitarian.

Just as legal and state institutional features of capitalism are biased in favour of the ability of capitalists individually to make decisions about the disposition of wealth, so one can say that analogous structures of socialist societies are biased in favour of the outcome of decisions *not* being thus open; rather they are directed toward promoting material equality. Even in thin socialism, when state officials relatively unresponsive to popular pressures are the economic decision makers, laws and attendant agencies and state practices constrain them to employ societal wealth (by direct distribution to individuals and communities, by reinvestment in wealth producing enterprises, by expenditures in public services, and so on) equally to benefit everyone in the society, as they understand what this would be.[12] The system is what Robert Nozick calls an 'end state' or 'goal-directed' one.[13]

Specific constraints under which socialist decision makers labour will vary from society to society and with time. Some private ownership of means of production and the limited employment of labourers may be allowed, but not in the extended way compatible with capitalist allocative powers. For example, private ownership of workers' self-managed firms is compatible with socialism provided there are checks against generating inequalities in the society in which they function. Limited employment of labour conjoined with full employment policies, job mobility, and wage floors might also be an option in some socialisms. Though income variations can be allowed, the gross disparities common to capitalist societies will not be tolerated.

*Statism and State Capitalism.*   Why do not decision makers in thin socialism allocate resources unequally to themselves so that they can override structures protecting equality? Hypothesized answers include that:

1. the decision makers are principled thin socialists who do not want to dismantle egalitarian structures;
2. even if some or all did want to do this, they realistically fear they could not get away with it given that they were brought to power by a revolution, as their populace is often told, against gross inequality;
3. the organization of a socialist economy would make it counterproductive for a selfishly motivated official (who already has a secure position in life) to make the major efforts required to replace it with a capitalist one;
4. generally inadequate as they may be, there are still political mechanisms sufficiently democratic to allow people to prevent such a drastic counterrevolution.

Decisions still might be effectively made that escape constraints favouring equality. If such decisions 'outweigh' those in accord with the constraints, then one would want to call the society in question something other than socialist. It might be called *statist*, if the effect is to shift the dominant constraining goal from equal social well-being to strengthening the power of state institutions and the security of personnel within them. If the effect is to remove constraining goals, giving decision makers the relative free hands capitalists have in allocating wealth, the society might be called *state capitalist*. Statism would still be economically goal-directed, but with a different goal than material equality; while state capitalism would no longer be goal-directed.

*Degrees of Socialism.* The conception of 'socialism' advanced here is deliberately narrowly economic. Thin socialism, structured to facilitate material equality, is essentially different from capitalism and may be legitimately grouped with a socialism that also embodies political equality and fosters democratic participation in all areas of life and work. All democratic socialists want to see thin socialism democratized. Other democratic socialists do not want thin socialism to count as socialism at all (even if it is neither statist nor state capitalistic) in virtue of its relative undemocracy. However, in addition to the advantage a narrowly economic definition has in avoiding a question-begging defence of socialism's democratic potentials, there are historical considerations.

A charitable interpretation of the intentions and activities of main decision makers in existing socialisms is that they think of socialism as a society in which much more democratization over all matters should exist than at present, and they believe that meeting basic human needs, educating the people, and protecting socialism from its enemies is also important. The problem as they see it is that these two goals work against one another, since a populace as yet ignorant of its main interests might make decisions which would leave it vulnerable to capitalist economic or military assault. The solution is to pursue the second set of goals until, by the very success of so doing, the people are ready for more democracy. To be sure, this interpretation is sometimes strained,[14] and it must be supplemented to take account of the way paternalism has of subverting originally honestly held prodemocratic attitudes. As argued in the last chapter, I think that paternalistic socialism is dangerously flawed. Still, the paternalist's position is coherent, and one, moreover, that I am inclined to attribute to most if not all people in positions of authority in those societies which now call themselves socialist.[15]

### iii. 'Equality'

Fully to explicate the concept of equality would constitute a very large task, requiring such things as sorting and ranking the 140

87

'ways of being equal' that Louise Marcil-Lacoste has discovered.[16] Instead, this section will review two generic concepts of equality – of opportunity and of benefits and burdens – noting a stronger and a weaker variety of the former and defending a relativized version of the latter. In each case, we shall address 'substantive' and not merely 'formal' equality.

Equality may be conceived of as the possession of legal rights or the possession of extralegal things like wealth, power, or opportunity.[17] Sometimes these are conflated in the notion of a 'moral right,' thought of as some power, opportunity, or share of wealth to which people ought to have a legal right. One can also distinguish between having *equal legal rights* to something and having a *legal right to the equal possession* of it. In the first case there is 'formal' equality in respect of that thing. People may have an equal legal right to seek medical care if a doctor or hospital may not refuse to treat anyone who can pay, but there is no obligation to treat those who cannot pay. A legal right to equal provision of medical aid, by contrast, requires that provision of comparable medical aid for everyone needing it must be seen to.

## OPPORTUNITIES AND BENEFITS/BURDENS

When it is said that socialism legally favours equality this means that it institutionally protects and promotes equal possession on the part of its members to something. There are two main candidates for what that something is: substantive (as well as formal) opportunities on the one hand and benefits and burdens, on the other.[18] Other candidates some socialists may be tempted to adopt – such as Michael Walzer's concept of 'complex equality,' Philip Green's 'constrained inequality,' or Brian Barry's 'integration' and 'nondiscrimination' – are parasitic on one or both of these notions.[19]

In a society fully egalitarian in respect of substantive equality of opportunity nothing would inhibit anyone from seeking to enjoy the benefits to be had in that society except his or her own lack of talent, skills, perseverance, and perhaps other characteristics said to be 'personal,' plus whatever legal or moral constraints are required to regulate conflicts with potentially inegalitarian results. The sincere advocate of this equality would demand special justification for anything that deviated from it. While many such advocates hope that equality of opportunity will eventually lead to equality of benefits and burdens, most see these things as conflicting norms for determining social policy. According to them inequalities in a society's distribution of benefits and burdens may be sanctioned so long as receipt of someone's share does not depend on anything except his or her efforts and/or contributions to society. Thus, one should not be disadvantaged for being of a certain race or sex but should able to be rewarded for using special talents.

By contrast, a benefits and burdens norm prescribes that nobody should suffer more of the burdens of life or enjoy more of its benefits than anyone else. Like equality of opportunity, this is a pure position usually advanced in an ameliorated form. Thus it is allowed that providing welfare floors should supplement an equality of opportunity standard, and equality of benefit and burden advocates typically advance this as a base line or presumptive goal, deviations from which are permitted in the light of special circumstances, provided the necessity of deviation can be justified and progress toward full equality is not undermined.

The opinion of socialists like Levine that substantive equality of opportunity is the one appropriate to socialism is subject to the same sort of criticism Levine, himself, levels at formal equality of opportunity advocates. He distinguishes three versions of equality of opportunity: a 'right-wing' one which is no more than absence of legal or customary impediments; a 'centrist' view favouring special provision of educational and other facilities to disadvantaged groups; and a 'left-wing' position promoting affirmative action and similar undertakings to attack the broad social sources of unequal opportunity. Then, like other critics of merely formal equality, he argues that the centrist view 'veers toward the left-wing position,' and that the right-wing version is 'vacuous' and renders the notion of equality of opportunity 'otiose,' since there can be no effective equality of opportunity unless institutional causes of inequalities are rectified.[20] But if the centrist position on equality of opportunity is unstable, then so is the left-wing one; since, as other democratic socialists argue, inequality in benefits and burdens is a main social source of continuing inequality of opportunity.[21]

89

# Justifying Democracy and Socialism

## POLITICAL AND MATERIAL EQUALITY

A rough distinction might be made between material and political benefits. Material benefits are those goods and services required for sustenance and desired for recreation, physical comfort, security for one's old age, and the like. Effective participation in governmental and analogous decision-making activities is a political benefit. There is a great temptation for the democratic socialist to make equality in the enjoyment of political benefits definitive of 'socialism.' Similarly, 'socialism' is often defined by reference to what are sometimes called 'cultural,' 'spiritual,' or 'social' benefits, such as the sense of leading a personally meaningful life or enjoying good companionship (while recognizing that the line between these and material benefits is not always sharp).

For reasons to be developed in the next chapter, these temptations will be resisted. This does not mean that socialism should not promote political and spiritual equality. Structural bias in favour of promoting equal material benefits and burdens as a baseline goal is, rather, a minimum feature of socialism, and one that clearly differentiates it from capitalism. Political and cultural inequalities are widespread features of all existing societies. Equality of opportunity is by now valued in at least some capitalist as well as socialist societies. That is, each has legal sanctions against (different sorts of) discrimination, and promotes (again various forms of) affirmative action programmes. A main difference between capitalism and socialism on this score is that the sanctions and programmes in the one case must be adjusted to the discretionary ability of a few over wealth gained from privately owned means of production and in the other case to structures favouring equality of material benefits and burdens.

## WELFARE RELATIVITY

Subjectively interpreted, somebody is said to have 'benefited' from the presence or absence of something if having or lacking it is in accord with his or her preferences (and analogously with burdens), but preferences are notoriously relative. Some people have champagne taste, others beer taste, and as Marx notes, some have greater demands on them than others. Thus, to equalize benefits and burdens, more social wealth must be expended on one person

90

than on another simply in virtue of the relative expense of their tastes or of their circumstances. Obviously, treating everyone in just the same way (the same transportation facilities in both city and country, the same work conditions for disabled and able bodied, and so on) fails to take into account their differing circumstances. This leads some to reserve the term 'equity' for equal treatment adjusted to circumstance.[22]

The subjective relativity of tastes raises problematic difficulties. These can be ameliorated by specifying that what is to be equalized are actual satisfactions as opposed to possibly false beliefs about what would satisfy, and by controlling against the deliberate cultivation of expensive tastes just to get more of the pie of social wealth (a contrived worry of some political theorists). But as long as we have a subjective definition of 'benefits and burdens' the problem of relativity remains. Substituting an objective standard brings with it the need for criteria and allows the odd (and for the democrat dangerous) situation that people could be said to be equally benefited without knowing it.[23]

An alternate solution is to recognize the relativity of benefits and burdens and prescribe approximating full equality of them insofar as this is possible. The egalitarian will, as Kai Nielsen puts it, strive for 'a condition where everyone alike, to the fullest extent possible, has his or her needs and wants satisfied.'[24] The more people there are with sadistic or perversely meddlesome preferences, or with champagne taste, the more often conflict will prevent full equality, but it would be a harsh society with a strange population indeed where there were no 'lowest common denominator' of compossibly satisfiable preferences. Such preferences are sometimes called 'needs,' but it is unnecessary to engage in the problematic search for a criterion of 'need'[25] to see satisfaction of preferences to have food, shelter, clothing, and so on as both possible for everybody in today's world and as a minimum approximation to full equality.

### iv. Equality As A Socialist Value

Many socialists who resist identifying socialism with equality invoke Marx's views on this subject and in particular his criticism of the Lassallean wing of the German Social-Democratic Party in his *Critique of the Gotha Programme*,[26] where those who advocated equality as a central socialist goal are criticized. The argument may be put that if the Lassalleans mean legal or formal rights of equality, they forget that these rights serve nobody but the bourgeoisie despite, and partly because of, their supraclass appearance. If material equality is meant, then one fails to recognize that such equality is entirely relative to needs, which differ from person to person. Marx's own position was that the guiding distributive principle of socialism is that each should be rewarded according to his work, while in a stateless, communist society each is to be rewarded according to need.[27]

The stipulation that socialist equality be substantive as opposed to merely formal and the recognition of the relativity of benefits and burdens meets the objections formulated this way. However, as most commentators have noted, Marx's misgivings about the *Gotha Programme* relate more profoundly to his stance (insofar as he had worked one out) on rights and on morality generally,[28] a topic to be taken up later.

### EQUALITY AS A BYPRODUCT

The egalitarian definition of 'socialism' does not maintain parity with our definition of 'capitalism.' One might criticize this by urging that if the efforts of those who privately own means of production to seek maximization of profit is taken as an effect of capitalism, not part of its meaning, then approximation to equality of benefits and burdens should likewise be seen as an effect of a socialist system.[29] But why not say that it is of the essence of socialism to possess such mechanisms? If socialism, unlike capitalism, is a goal-directed system it is appropriate to specify goals in a definition. Many such goals are no doubt best left unspecified, but approximation to equality should not be unspecified. It is not sufficient just to say that in socialism deployment of social wealth will be constrained. One wants to know what sorts of constraints, at the bare minimum, the socialist has in mind, and if, as Levine notes, socialists are agreed on the desirability of material equality, there is no reason not to recognize this in a definition. Surely socialists *are* agreed on this point. But even a purely negatively motivated socialist, who only favours blocking a return to capitalism, should realize that this requires active promotion of material equality.

92

Socialist equality is one of the principal things procapitalists object to, because they support the 'right' of capitalists to dispose of great wealth as they wish and because they claim socialism would fail to reward talent. Socialists challenge the legitimacy of the right partly on the grounds that it can only be enjoyed by a limited number of people.[30] Good grounds for rejecting the argument about natural talents are: that there are reasons to doubt the extent of wide ranges of differences in talent and initiative; that where there are such differences these are rather results than causes of material inequality; and even if they are not conditioned by inequality, 'the arbitrary effects of the natural lottery,' to use Rawls's phrase, should be compensated for.[31]

### REFORMISM

Another sort of socialist might object not to the presence of reference to equality in a definition, but to the absence of reference to noncapitalism, fearing that this might leave the door open to capitalist reformism. Such an objection misses the mark, since political mechanisms effective in promoting equality are surely incompatible with the free hand capitalists must have in deploying wealth and hiring labour. This might prompt one to opine that it makes no difference whether socialism is seen primarily as a matter of the negation of capitalism, an effect of which is to promote equality, or as an equality-promoting system that must negate capitalism to secure a society structured to protect this value.

One problem with such a viewpoint is that there is more flexibility in the ways that capitalism may be negated than there is in ways material equality can be interpreted. Accordingly, the equality goal should be more fixed than specification of any mechanism to advance it, and room for wide adjustment to circumstance should be permitted regarding ways to foster equality. China now permits limited private ownership of productive means. Yugoslavia promotes workers' self-management. Most Eastern European countries permit limited private employment of labour. Algeria and Nicaragua permit the continued existence of some relatively large privately owned manufacturing and financial concerns. These situations can be evaluated by reference to their estimated consequences: whether they block achieving (or regaining) a socialist society; whether they promote socialism; whether they can be accommodated in a socialist system, though they are a drag on it; and perhaps other criteria. Unless one is primarily concerned to have ammunition to hurl charges of nonsocialism about, it seems more useful to make judgments on a case-by-case basis and not by appeal to an overly specific definition.

Those who agree with Etienne Balibar that 'socialism is nothing other than the dictatorship of the proletariat,'[32] will be wondering by now where the notion of working-class power may be found in the egalitarian characterization of socialism. They might agree that socialism is primarily goal-directed, and they might even agree that equality is not a bad thing to strive for, but strongly object to any approach where equality or anything else could eclipse what they see as the overriding aim of socialism. Socialists may be divided into two categories on this question. For one group, socialism is that state form by which the working class exercises power. For the other group socialism is a state structurally embodying certain valued principles.[33]

On the egalitarian view, socialism is incompatible with political domination of a society by capitalists since this impedes equality. Some who are both anticapitalist and antiproletarian think a society incorporating egalitarian goals with any working-class input is also to be avoided, but such theorists are rare.[34] It is more common for egalitarian socialists to resist the idea that people acting exclusively to benefit the members of any one class should dominate a socialist state. Those in the 'working-class power' category consider this opinion the worst sort of revisionism. Whether the egalitarian socialist approach of this chapter is an instance of 'revisionism' or not depends on how one uses this word. The democratic-socialist orientation of this book is obviously out of keeping with a variety of socialist thought in which the dictatorship of the proletariat is viewed as the overriding end of socialist activism. It is also out of keeping with a weaker variety in which working-class power, egalitarianism, and democracy are seen as compatible and coextensive goals.

### HISTORICISTIC POWER POLITICS

The approaches are clearly incompatible if the view that socialism is nothing but the dictatorship of the proletariat is embodied in a certain theory of history. The orientation supporting this view

94

is not uniquely socialist, but an amalgam of power politics and historicism. Briefly, history is thought of as the clash of conflicting parties (nationalities, races, sexes, forces of good and evil, God and the Devil, economic classes, or perhaps other things), and political, cultural, and other institutions and practices are all viewed as expressions of these conflicts; whereas the values and beliefs people have about what they are doing and why, including accurate ideas about being in locked combat with representatives of an opposing force, are effects and not causes of historical forces.

A socialist theory of the state can be derived from this orientation whereby state forms are seen as nothing but efforts to advance economic classes by people who are motivated by class forces. These people will be most effective if they can accurately sort things like political institutions and popular ideas into those that serve the working class and those that thwart it. But to do this they must understand the historical dynamics at work and not be deceived into thinking they are promoting supraclass values. The 'Cunning of Reason' might make it come to pass that people who think they are promoting egalitarianism are in fact advancing the cause of the working class, but at least the most active militants must know that it is the quest for working-class state power that is the goal.

Few socialist theorists endorse so bold a form of the dictatorship of the proletariat. Most espouse modified views which at least apparently come closer to the orientation of the egalitarian socialist. On one such view, the dictatorship of the proletariat is seen as a transition to an egalitarian society, and on another its realization is held to be coextensive with the achievement of equality, though not identical with it. We shall examine these viewpoints in turn.

*Socialism and Communism.* 'Socialism' is sometimes used to describe an intermediary form between capitalism and communism and sometimes to describe 'communism' itself. On the well-known view of Marx defended by Balibar, communism is a classless and stateless society, and it is also an egalitarian society, where wealth is allocated to people in accord with their needs. To achieve communism, capitalist remnants need to be dismantled, and only the working class, using a state apparatus designed to serve its interests, is both capable and motivated for this task. What Marx calls

95

'communism' is here classified as highly democratic socialism (with the possible large exception that communism is supposed to be stateless and therefore presumably without legal institutions[35]). It might then be argued that once the transitional nature of the dictatorship of the proletariat is noted, the major debate is not over goals but over how to attain them.

One problem of this approach is to specify how the dictatorship of the proletariat is to be regarded by those trying to achieve it at the time they are doing this. Should it be thought of in a power-political way as an end in itself or not? If so, then this is in danger of creating a strong barrier – of the kind Stalin and company so graphically illustrated – to a shifting of perspective after the revolution and adopting different goals. Closer to the egalitarian position is the view that sees the proletariat as having a stake in equality, since it suffers the effects of inequality, and sees rule of the proletariat to promote this and other values as democratic, since it comprises the majority of the population.[36] But this approach is also problematic.

*Workers and Majorities.*   With the possible exception of a few countries or regions of countries, it was likely untrue in Marx's time that the proletariat constituted a majority, even if it were conceived of more broadly than in its proper designation as 'workers at the point of production.' By our times, however, drastic shrinkage in the proportion of self-employed farmers, producers, professionals, retailers, and others, along with increased entry of women into the labour force, has probably made the working class broadly considered the majority class in many if not all countries. It may even have made the proletariat a majority, if technology has sufficiently stretched what counts as 'points of production.' There are still many self-employed people and many whose class location is not clear (the 'middle classes'), and this fact has led some, like Selucky, to object to identifying a postcapitalist society with worker's power.[37] But if democratic socialism is a society where major economic decisions are democratically made, and if 'working-class power' means that these decisions are made by members of a class comprising a majority of the population, then would not its dictatorship be highly democratic? The society might not be fully egalitarian, but it would be much more egalitarian than capitalist society.

This deceptively simple argument overlooks the fact that nobody is just a worker. Each worker is also a person of a certain sex and sexual orientation, race, age, nationality, ethnicity, who has a certain state of health, who lives in a certain region and community, who is engaged in extraemployment activities such as those related to child rearing and recreating, and who has scales of values not all of which put advancing his or her interests as a worker at the top. If, as was argued in the last chapter, majority rule is to comprise anonymity then it must always be possible for configurations of people cutting across class lines to form a majority or for a majority to be made up of people who, even if they are workers, do not make advancement of specifically working-class goals their first priority. Accordingly, there will be a difference between a group's being a numerical majority of a society and that same group's always being its democratic majority. In Chapter Eight, we shall return to this topic. Suffice it to say here that the egalitarian socialist can accommodate this plurality of dimensions to the human character. It is not clear that someone defining 'socialism' as 'the dictatorship of the proletariat' can.

## 'SOCIALISM' AND DEMOCRACY

It remains to show that the proffered definitions do not beg the question that socialism is necessary for advances in democracy. The outline of this argument can now be presented easily. Reference to democracy does not enter the definitions of 'socialism' and 'capitalism,' though references to substantive freedom to dispose of wealth and material equality of benefits and burdens do. Freedoms and equalities, whether substantive or formal, are not definitionally democratic, as the latter term is used here, but are putative conditions for making progress in democracy in sufficiently large and complex enough social units to sustain state structures. But to prove any one sort of freedom or kind and degree of equality a precondition of or guarantor for democracy requires argumentation beyond attention to the meaning of words.

Libertarians, for instance, often argue that a democratic society cannot be socialist because it *must* include the economic freedom to be a capitalist. However, as Cohen and Nielsen have ably argued against Nozick on this score, the existence of this freedom does not at all guarantee the maximization of freedom generally.[38]

Similarly, to show that constraints favouring relative material equality advance democracy, the socialist is obliged to confront arguments that socialist planning and bureaucracy are themselves sources of relative undemocracy. These are the sorts of considerations that will occupy us in the next chapter.

# 6 Justifying Socialism

OF THE MANY WAYS to demonstrate that socialism is a requirement for democracy, the argument from definition is the most economical. Here are two examples:

- Should it be a matter of democratic social decision how national (or international) resources are to be allocated and how the economic life of society is to be organized? Should it be a matter of democratic social decision how the smaller institutions of everyday life – the shop floor, the school, the neighbourhood, advocational groups – are to be organized and to carry out their activities? The affirmative answer to the first question might be called 'planning democracy,' and that to the second 'participatory democracy.' The two together constitute 'socialism' in the sense I will use that term.—Lawrence Crocker[1]

- [T]he concepts of democracy and socialism...entail each other. For the principle of democracy states that each individual has an equal right to participate in the co-determination of all social activities in which he or she is engaged....[This] requires also co-determination or common control over the conditions of this activity....But the common control over the conditions by those engaged in the activity is precisely what I designated as social property which is one of the fundamental aspects of socialism.—Carol Gould[2]

Crocker leaves the term 'democratic' unanalysed, and unpacking terms like 'common control' in Gould's definition requires making several important theoretical decisions. Still, these arguments have the merit of placing socialism and democracy into the same genus. Each is a 'goal-directed' phenomenon, the telos of which is to maximize shared control over human environments. This means that an attack on the claim that socialism is necessary for democracy cannot be an attack on valuing something for having this telos (as a conservative traditionalist might have it), nor can it be an attack on valuing any sort of 'goal-directed' society (as some libertarians do), since socialism and democracy stand or fall together in these respects.

At the same time, an argument from definition confronts the problems summarized in the first chapter. It is subject to the counterargument that nothing is democratic and that the nearest approximation is capitalism. Also from a rhetorical point of view the definitional approach invites contradiction without appeal to facts. For example, Carl Cohen argues against socialism by criticizing the notion of 'economic democracy.' He reconstructs the socialist argument to be that socialism, tersely described as 'public ownership and the like,' constitutes 'economic democracy,' and that therefore any nonsocialist system will necessarily be deficient in democracy.[3] But, according to Cohen, 'economic democracy' is properly regarded not as partially definitive of 'democracy' but as an empirical condition for it.

In this attack on the definitional argument, Cohen is able to fudge on whether socialism is in fact such a condition. Thus, criticizing both procapitalists and prosocialists for theoretical confusion, he concludes that: 'intense concern with economic matters has brought Marxists to see, correctly, that economic conditions essential for democracy are not being met in large parts of the globe under Western influence. The Marxists may be mistaken about what the needed conditions are, but their philosophical position has made them sensitive to the absence of material requirements....'[4] Aside from a two-paragraph argument purporting that only elimination of gross inequality is necessary for democracy, Cohen does not pursue the substantive question of whether elimination of capitalism is or is not a 'needed condition,' yet this is clearly the crucial question.

Definitional arguments can be viewed as encapsulated empirical arguments, which may be how Crocker and Gould intend them. Crocker's argument can be formulated that socialism extends the range of matters over which people have collective control, and Gould can be seen as arguing that socialism provides the conditions (empirically) necessary for realizing democratic values in practice. Taken together, these claims represent an argument from 'expanded scope,' where scope is both extensively and intensively regarded (the reformulated views respectively of Crocker and of Gould). This argument is outlined in section ii of the chapter. Perhaps a fully developed version of the argument from scope would convince some. However, more is needed for one who sees democracy as a matter of degree such that no society, capitalist or socialist, ever completely lacks some measure of it. Since this work is written from a degrees-of-democracy orientation, the bulk of the chapter (section iii) defends a case from within it. A socialist must also meet the countercharge that even if socialism has democratic potentials, it has stronger antidemocratic ones; section iv suggests how to meet this charge. Section i appeals directly to equality.

### i. The Value of Equality

Reasons to favour a society institutionally structured to favour material equality might initially be divided into those that appeal to the advantages of increasing democracy and see equality as necessary for this and those that appeal to some other standard. The fact that this chapter addresses mainly the first sort of argument should not suggest that other sorts cannot be given. In particular there is a moral argument appealing directly to equality, the premises of which are:

1. Material inequalities are, other things being equal, morally unjustified;
2. Capitalism creates and sustains these inequalities, and gross ones at that.
3. There are no essential features of a socialist, egalitarian society that outweigh its moral advantage over capitalism in respect of equality, and inessential negative features can be overcome or compensated for.

In this section, summary democratic-socialist arguments will be made about each of these premises, starting with the last.

*Capitalist 'Efficiency'.* The most common challenge to 3) is that socialism is essentially undemocratic. This charge will be taken up in section iv of the chapter. An alternate challenge is that socialism is in one way *too* democratic. Thus Arthur Okun argues: 'Any realistic version of American socialism that I can visualize would not encroach dangerously on the rights that are precious to me. But precisely because it would operate within the constraints of preserving these rights, the collectivized system would . . . achieve only a small improvement in equality at the expense of a significant worsening of efficiency. I regard it as vital that private enterprise continue to be the main mechanisms for organizing economic activity in those areas where experimentation and innovation are important, and in those where flexibility matters more than accountability.'[5]

Okun grants that the moral advantage of socialism is not shared by capitalism, the ethical case for which, he says, 'is totally unpersuasive.'[6] Though different from most procapitalists in this honest admission, Okun's argument in broad outline is the familiar one: a) that capitalism is and socialism is not capable of efficient flexibility and innovation, and b) that this is desirable since in the end everyone benefits from a more economically efficient system. Later in this chapter some questions about socialist planning will be taken up in a way that bears on claim a). Despite frequent repetition, claims about the putative superiority of capitalism over socialism in respect of flexibility, innovation, incentive, and the like are by no means established.[7]

David Schweickart observes that the term 'efficiency' is often deceptively used as if it were not normative.[8] His point is well-taken regarding both claim a) and claim b). One might ask whether there should be democratic input to decisions about the 'benefits' that are supposed to trickle down from capitalist efficiency. Military production, for example, is a main locus for capitalist investment, and much ingenuity has indeed been invested in the design, production, and marketing of military wares. Spin-offs are jobs – though relatively few, as military production is capital intensive – and some high tech nonmilitary goods.[9] Should people be able to determine whether this production, with its byproducts, is to be pursued or not? If so, then more democratic limitations on capitalists will be required than Okun can likely sanction. If not, then people will be constrained to make do with whatever capitalist production happens to spawn. Someone convinced this is the best to be hoped for will have to decide whether such a meagre 'benefit' is worth maintaining a system of gross inequality.

*Capitalist Inequality.*   Regarding premise 2), that large inequalities are pervasive throughout capitalism, few democratic theorists try to deny this,[10] and it would be futile to try. A society structured to facilitate a few disposing of its wealth as they wish will not surprisingly yield the inequalities of all capitalist countries. Capitalists' wealth may either be kept by them for personal use or fed back into future wealth-producing enterprises. To facilitate material equality the first category of wealth would have to be shared and the second would have to be invested in a planned way to maximize things like employment, high wages, and social services. No capitalist can willingly reinvest capital in such ways, since any who did would risk losing out to competitors who did not.

For the same reason no capitalist can afford to spread around very much of whatever is held back for personal use, since this might sometime be needed as capital. These are two ways that having major allocative decisions in capitalist hands inhibits equality. Less direct ways also function. For example, egalitarian measures set precedents dangerous to a capitalist, and whet workers' appetites. Also the life conditions of a capitalist concerned to maximize profit, often in cutthroat competition and regarding workers and consumers instrumentally spawns and reinforces a personal morality in which sharing wealth does not rank very highly. As Green puts it, 'the ethos of capitalism is systematized inequality.'[11]

*For Equality.*   The 'other things being equal' qualification in the first premise (that inequality is morally unjustified) is to indicate a presumption in favour of equality while allowing exceptions. This is one way socialists can appropriate the part of John Rawls's famous second principle of justice, which favours equality but allows inequalities, provided that they benefit the least advantaged.[12] Socialists are divided on whether Rawls's views generally are to be adopted or condemned.[13] On a critical reading, his principle could be interpreted as a rationalization for supply-side economic arrangements which are supposed to benefit everyone by trickle-down effects or for welfare capitalism with ceilings on social benefits, but the principle need not be interpreted to necessitate one of these things.

While rejecting the rationalization charge, a Rawlsian might be prepared to accept one of these interpretations as a conceivable but not as a required application. If the principle really does express a presumption for equality as well as a recognition that exceptions can sometimes be made, this places a burden on the procapitalist to demonstrate and not just assert that welfare ceilings or putative tricklings down of capitalist wealth promote equality better than would a socialist alternative. This is an especially heavy burden if the notion of something's being 'to the benefit of the least advantaged' requires that it help create a situation where nobody *is* less advantaged than others. The claim that there is no realistic alternative but to implement inegalitarian measures (for instance, to reward industriousness), even when they do not contribute to the eventual lack of need for such measures, is looked on with suspicion by the egalitarian.

Nielsen considers equality a rock bottom value such that: 'a person who has a good understanding of what morality is, has a good knowledge of the facts, is not ideologically mystified, takes an impartial point of view, and has an attitude of impartial caring, would, if not conceptually confused, come to accept the abstract egalitarian thesis. I see no way of arguing someone into such an egalitarianism who does not have that attitude of impartial caring, who does not in this general way have a love of humankind. A hard-hearted Hobbesist is not reachable here.'[14] The point is well-taken, though it might be qualified to note that some of slightly softer heart can be reached by an argument of the 'there but for fortune go you or I,' variety.

It is a mere accident of circumstances, largely out of my own control, that I have four good limbs while someone else is handicapped, that I have had access to good education, others not, and so on. There are, to be sure, people who deny this on the belief that they are somehow personally responsible for their advantages as are others for their disadvantages. (I thank fortune that I did not grow up to be such a megalomaniac.) But there are also those who recognize the role of blind chance and yet feel no obligation to correct its 'injustices.' Such people will probably not be swayed by an argument for socialism based on the value of equality. Anyone else ought to be swayed and should accordingly favour a social system promoting equality.

### ii. Expanded Scope of Public Control

Levine summarizes the argument that socialism expands the scope of human control:

104

> For democrats... matters affecting the public ought to be decided by the public.... [T]he sorts of decisions capitalists make – about the use of the productive resources they own and about the allocation of the product derived from the employment of these resources – plainly affect the public.... However, under capitalism, questions of this sort are privatized, to the extent that they have to do with the utilization capitalists make of the assets they own. Thus, many public questions never come before the public, and therefore can never become, even in principle, objects of democratic collective choice. In this way, capitalism restricts the scope of democratic choice.[15]

The socialism to which Levine refers is beyond thin or 'state bureaucratic' socialism, since it includes public control of economic decisions. We shall return to the effect of this fact on the argument. Still, it is not exactly an appeal to definition, since it depends on the truth of some empirical premises. In particular, the argument assumes that public control is incompatible with capitalist ownership of major economic assets, and it assumes that the gain of public control over economic matters is important for expanding democracy. Each premise is contested by defenders of capitalism.

### THE CAPITALIST MARKET

Libertarians argue that a capitalist free market, unconstrained by egalitarian and most other measures of the state, is the best mechanism to promote freedom.[16] Cohen, Nielsen, Macpherson, Bowles and Gintis, among others, have already adequately criticized this position, and their work will not be reproduced here.[17] Also, put one way, the position does not touch the argument from expanded scope.

It might be granted for the sake of argument that a capitalist market would maximize freedom at least in economic matters. But at issue is whether economic policy should be made democratically or not. A public with effective control over this policy might decide to retain or to recover a capitalist market. This is the claim of some procapitalist government officials who pretend to express the will of the people in dismantling state-owned enterprises and implementing 'deregulation' or 'free trade.' Levine's complaint is that at present there is not even public control over whether there should be a capitalist market. Indeed, while some, such as von Hayek, advance their position as a democratic one, Nozick and other more consistent libertarians recognize that given the choice, a majority might opt to institute an egalitarian state. Accordingly they oppose democratic mechanisms that could allow this.[18]

A stronger libertarian argument would note that a free market constitutes a form of control over economic matters which is public in a 'monadic' sense: each and every actor pursuing his or her interests in the market, without concern that there be any collective decision over net outcomes, nonetheless has some effect on what these outcomes will be. However, the libertarian might continue, once a different kind of public control is exercised – collective action through the state – the free market can only with great difficulty be regained. There is some truth to such a view, but it would not be decisive against Levine's point. In the first place, if collective public control would make future monadic public control more difficult to gain or regain, the reverse is also the case. So one must ask which mode of economic control is the least autoentrenching. Socialists argue that the economic inequalities of a capitalist market make it the hardest to challenge.

Moreover, the libertarian faces the well-known paradox of monopolies. If people are to be as free as libertarianism requires, they should be able to contract to form monopolies (as self-interest often dictates). To prevent this by state measures surely gives the state greater power than the libertarian would wish. Another problem is that no free markets exist anywhere in the world. Hence, one must use mechanisms other than a free market to bring one into existence. Barring collective, democratic mechanisms, it is hard to see what these might be. The governments of Thatcher and Reagan advocated using state power to enforce market capitalism, while limiting the state itself, but instead they have *expanded* the state, mainly into the military. Post-1973 Chile, with a state economic policy specially designed for it by Milton Friedman (shortly after the democratically elected President Allende was machine gunned to death in his office by soldiers of the government that replaced him[19]), is a more grotesque example. The resulting 'free' market, in addition to bringing economic chaos, has coexisted with one of the most coercive police states in our times.

## INCREASED PARTICIPATION

The assumption that public gain of economic decision-making powers is sufficiently important to justify reorganization of a society's political economy is best defended by reference to the material preconditions for democratic participation. Michael Parenti offers a typical summary when he argues that in capitalism 'important structural and material factors so predetermine the range of electoral issues and choices as to raise a serious question about the representative quality of the political system. Mass politics requires mass resources; being enormously expensive affairs, elections are best utilized by those interests endowed with the resources necessary to take advantage of them. Politics has always been largely a "rich man's game." '[20]

Capitalism creates a situation where very few people have sufficient wealth to make effective use of democratic mechanisms and turn them to their advantage. To be sure, the procapitalist can assert that any alternative will be worse. But there is an onus to explain how it could be anything but antidemocratic that wealth buys effective access to forums for public debate, means to nominate candidates and to put issues on an agenda for a vote, or else it lets people get around democratic constraints when this suits their purposes or, in the case of owners of capital, to get their way by the blackmail of what Bowles and Gintis call threatened 'capital strikes,' where needed capital is simply moved away.[21] To see how heavy an onus the defender of capitalism has here, one need only look at the conditions for democracy recognized by most nonsocialist democratic theorists, such as the lists of Margolis and Pennock reproduced in Chapter Three (pp. 48–49), and ask how feasible it is to meet these conditions in the capitalist world.

The arguments of Levine and Parenti are complementary, but there is also a trade between Parenti's realistic criticisms of capitalism and Levine's portrayal of a yet nonexistent socialism. Critics can grant that capitalism is a rich man's game, but ask what reason there is to expect that socialism will be any better. Will it not instead, they might say, be a 'bureaucrat's game' or a game of nobody at all, but one in which human beings are pawns of an impersonal state plan. The argument from scope as exemplified by Levine avoids this challenge at the expense of building democratic control of the economy into its definition of 'socialism,' thus inviting the critic to question whether such a society is realistic. These charges must and will be met after sketching a third type of argument available to the democratic socialist, namely that major democratic progress is incompatible with capitalism.

### iii. Democratic Progress

Only the most abstract left-winger would claim that no progress at all can be made in democracy without socialist revolution. Usually, workers who win a strike, citizens who manage to elect a principled representative to a city council, women or blacks who

successfully lobby for antidiscrimination legislation, or tenants who organize an association in their building gain more control over their lives than they had before, and it is sometimes possible to enforce laws limiting the ability of money to distort democratic mechanisms. A 'hyperrevolutionary' might claim that such measures retard democracy by legitimating an undemocratic system, but even if this extreme antireform position were right, it would not prove that no additional control and hence marginally more democracy had been secured.

The problem is the classic bind for the hyperrevolutionary whose approach usually requires people to do everything or to do nothing. To be democratically regressive, small gains must not only legitimize an antidemocratic system, but it would also have to be the case that the system could be toppled were the gains not made. Such choices are rarely confronted, as people are seldom in a position to deliberate whether they should go for crumbs when it is possible to go for the whole cake. If people do not revolt it is because they think it undesirable or impossible or because it does not occur to them at all. Hence the hyperrevolutionary must either conclude that nothing can be done or that the handful who perceive the truth should prevent small gains and force the big one alone. Since this latter course is itself extremely unrealistic, it, too, amounts to inaction.

#### 'MAJOR DEMOCRATIC ADVANCES'

Anyone who thinks socialism is necessary to make progress in democracy, but who rejects the hyperrevolutionary's view, must distinguish between different orders of democratic progress.

Thus one might designate advances in democracy as major if they are 'global.' By definition, any democratic advance will increase the control some people in a social unit have over some aspects of their social environment, and in defending the 'democratic fix' it was argued that these advances lay the groundwork for future advances. However, most advances in democracy will be local in not creating an impetus for similar advance in other social units, and future advances they make possible will be piecemeal and largely unpredictable.

By contrast, a global democratic advance in a social unit initiates relatively rapid, broadly supported, and consciously pursued programmes aimed at making yet more progress in democracy in it, while sparking movements for similar democratic advances in other social units. A global advance in democracy is the sort of thing the antidemocrat Tennyson complained about regarding the 1789, 1830, and 1848 revolutions in France. He described a voice:

> Proclaiming social truth shall spread,
> And justice, ev'n tho' thrice again
> The red fool-fury of the Seine
> Should pile her barricades with dead.[22]

Tennyson's negative attitude toward democracy attuned him to the revolutionary potential of democratic advances to multiply. Some democrats also describe major advances as 'revolutions' in democracy, but this terminology will not be employed here. This way we avoid conceptualizing the history of democracy within the framework (to be criticized in Chapter Eleven) of 'reform and revolution.'

This chapter's application of the notion of a major democratic advance to capitalism is akin to Marković's treatment of 'crises,' which he sees occurring when a socio-economic formation 'exhausts its possibilities of development' and 'its necessary characteristics become inner limitations, the barriers for further development.'[23] His central claim is that expansion of democracy at the present time has come up against the inner limitations of capitalism and now requires decentralization, pluralism, and nonstatist socialism.[24] One advantage of this orientation is its avoidance of talk about a 'capitalist crisis' per se. Instead Marković addresses capitalist crises in respect of democracy to argue that advance in democracy requires major changes in present socio-

109

economic systems (capitalism and statism). The perspective of this chapter is compatible with this conclusion modifying it to hold that there is a crisis in capitalism with respect to democracy when capitalism does not allow full development of major democratic gains already made and blocks future major gains.

### THE CHALLENGE TO TRADITION

What advances in democracy have been or might be 'major'? Preferring to err on the side of parsimony, I think there have been very few, one of which was the challenge to traditional relations of authority and power in the 18th and 19th centuries. These are what Ernesto Laclau and Chantal Mouffe, drawing on work of Claude Lefort, François Furet, Hannah Arendt, and others, call 'democratic revolutions.' Their view is that relations of subordination could not be perceived as things to be overcome until there was a challenge to their supposed inevitability as 'natural' and/or as divinely sanctioned:

> [By 'democratic revolution,'] we shall designate the end of a society of a hierarchic and inegalitarian type, ruled by a theological-political logic in which the social order had its foundation in divine will. The social body was conceived of as a whole in which individuals appeared fixed in differential positions. For as long as such a holistic mode of institution of the social predominated, politics could not be more than the repetition of hierarchical relations which reproduced the same type of subordinated subjects.[25]

Mouffe and Laclau single out the French Revolution, while other democratic theorists, such as Shingo Shibata, focus on the American Revolution. Shibata argues that the American Declaration of Independence marked a watershed in the history of democracy and should be the model for contemporary democratic-socialist political values,[26] just as Mouffe and Laclau hold that 'socialist demands should . . . be seen as a moment internal to the democratic revolution.'[27] These authors might agree that the democratic revolutions were not unique causes of the challenge to tradition but dramatic points in protracted processes, and perhaps they would agree with reservations about use of the word 'revolution.' Also, one who sees democracy as a matter of degree

110

will want to qualify Furet's assertion that these major advances marked 't' birth of democracy.'[28]

The point of the authors is not that the changes of which the French and American Revolutions were parts ended all forms of subordination. What gave them special place is that they marked a democratic advance over traditionally accepted political inequality. The complex relations of these things, considered as major political advances to the economic revolutions, in virtue of which the former are called by most socialists 'bourgeois revolutions,' will be taken up in Chapter Seven. The fact that the political revolutions were nonaccidentally associated with change to an economy oriented around a capitalist-dominated market is central to explaining their limitations. But that they constituted advances in democracy is undeniable. More people gained control over important aspects of their social environments than they had before, and many more again came to see expansion of their own control as possible and legitimate. Things previously accepted because they were traditional became, for the first time on anything but an isolated scale, matters of deliberate choice.[29]

*Traditionalism and 'Critical Appropriation.'* This advance opened up possibilities and demands for further challenges to tradition because it is very hard to reverse. Calling tradition into question is like admitting to oneself that the emperor has no clothes. Once the recognition is made that tradition need not bind, it is hard to pretend otherwise. The main failing of a 'back to rule by tradition' prescription is that if one *chooses* to follow some tradition, the tradition does not rule. What has been chosen for can later be chosen against. And to choose to follow tradition blindly is not to choose at all. Only by desperate, self-induced psychosis could one hope to adopt a tradition in such a way as to forget that this had been deliberately done.

The point is not that the democrat must reject traditions. Carlyle presented 19th-century democrats with a false choice when he complained that democracy, 'abrogates the old arrangement of things and leaves...*zero* and vacuity.'[30] Carlyle's charge was not justified regarding the intentions of the most radical democrats of his time (the strongest defenders of the French Revolution), whose target was not tradition per se. Rather they wanted to replace the moribund traditions of the decadent monarchies with

111

what they saw as newly emerging traditions embodying the values of liberty, equality, and fraternity. Carlyle's criticism of the strongest foes of existing traditions is thus incomplete without an argument to show that such a project is not feasible. Moreover, it is unnecessary to reject all aspects of one's traditions in order to reject some aspects of them. Consider the theory and practice of liberation theologians in the developing world and of their democratic counterparts in the religious communities of developed countries. Though vocal critics of important tenets of their religious traditions, they do not thereby reject all tenets.[31]

No doubt theological debates over the liberation theologians' project are possible,[32] but there is nothing incoherent about its form. If a tradition is comprised of culturally inherited habits of everyday life, there is no reason to suppose that calling one's tradition into question necessitates rejecting all its aspects. Rather, there are good reasons for people to respect traditions, both those of others (to learn from them and to maintain pluralistic tolerance) and of one's own (to protect and nurture the communities that are shaped by and shape traditions). Moreover, the democratic interrogation of tradition strengthens it by promoting understanding of the traditions of others and the healthy pruning of aspects of one's own traditions (sexist, racist, elitist, national chauvinist, and so on), which are objectionable in themselves and detract from enriching dimensions of our cultures. Democratic advance is thus not opposed to tradition but is a requirement for, in Habermas's phrase, its 'critical appropriation.'[33]

*Political Authority and Tradition.* The advances to which Lefort and others refer were mainly in the political realm, and limitations on their global potential were evident from the beginning. Main examples are the traditionally supported domination of women by men, the colonized and later imperialized developing world by the industrialized world and, as in the American South, even the continuation of slavery. Nonetheless the challenge to feudal political tradition also opened up potential gains in these domains. It set in motion challenges to antidemocratic authority that claimed tradition for support in all areas of life, beginning almost immediately after the political revolutions and growing to bear fruit within the next century and a half – historically speaking, a short time period. All these movements reject the legitimacy of traditional constraints, which they challenge on explicitly democratic grounds.

In Chapter Four it was noted that as one approaches the deliberate construction of constitutions, problems of getting started come to the fore which admit of solution if the 'democratic fix' can be employed to make majority rule anonymous and to move unanimity in the direction of creative consensus. Whenever traditional authority is challenged, one is faced with such constitutional questions (both at a formal, state level and informally among members of various communities). We might ask how successfully such exercises in democratic reconstitution have been. How effectively has the democratic fix been employed to promote a culture and practice favouring such things as consensus building, majority rule, and minority rights? The answer is all too clear. For some socialists, capitalism is the entire cause of a relative failure to take full advantage of this global democratic advance. In Chapter Nine reasons to doubt this class reductionist view will be discussed. But the prosocialist need not take such an extreme position. What needs to be shown is that a capitalist society prevents full development of the democratic potentials of the challenge to tradition by putting in the way of the democratic fix impediments that socialism can remove. The case is best made by regarding discrimination.

### FREEDOM AND DISCRIMINATION

In traditionalist societies control over major aspects of life was overtly limited to a few people from specified demographic ranges, those born into positions of traditional authority. In capitalist societies control over major economic matters is still overtly limited to a few, which in turn gives them indirect and sometimes covert control over a broad range of political and social matters as well. That capitalists have such disproportionate control has often been well-demonstrated by socialists, whose arguments need not be repeated here.[34]

Despite the disgust of each generation of 'old' capitalist money at letting the new rich into the club, the demographic range from which those with disproportionate control may come is more open in capitalist than in older societies. But it is still limited while capital can be inherited, and in any case no economy can support more than relatively few capitalists. Arguing against a distinction Rawls wants to make between 'freedom' and 'the worth of freedom,' Norman Daniels defends the point that freedom from formal, and one might add traditional, constraints constitutes very little actual freedom if people do not have the material means to take advantage of them.[35] G.A. Cohen addresses the claim that in capitalism anybody is free to be a capitalist by arguing that this is only true in the sense that categories of people who may become capitalists are not specified.[36]

More insidious is the way capitalism blocks attempts to overcome discrimination. Racial, sexist, and other such discriminations impede the democratic fix, tolerance of minority rights, and a culture of seeking consensus and harmonious negotiation. Not only do they serve as yet another block to people's ability to take advantage of formal freedoms, but they create their own downward spirals. Some discrimination leads to more until it becomes entrenched and 'systemic,' that is, a feature of social, economic, and political life that does not depend exclusively on the ill will of individuals who are bigots or sexists to be perpetuated.[37] The point has often been made that capitalists profit economically from systemic discrimination. This helps to keep wages down and makes some desperate enough to do especially distasteful jobs at low pay. In the case of women, housewives perform work essential to continuing capitalist enterprises (caring for members of a family who work outside the house), and discrimination prevents this work being recognized or paid for.[38]

Although the claim that capitalism is therefore the sole and originating cause of all discriminations can be called into question, there is little doubt that it is a sustaining one. Capitalism perpetuates discrimination in direct relation to the economic costs and large-scale social planning required to eradicate it. Insofar as systemic discrimination can be combatted, this requires: a) legislation prohibiting such things as hiring, promoting, firing, or training in discriminatory ways; b) education; and c) 'affirmative action,' 'including things like retraining programmes and preferential hiring. Measure a) is no doubt found inconvenient by capitalists, but it is affordable within the system. Education and affirmative action are also possible, but on a severely limited scale.

The socialist's argument is that sexist and racist discrimination, for example, nurtured for centuries and ingrained in the social

114

and psychological fabrics of life, require massive and sustained effort to be overcome. Effective antidiscriminatory education means more than just reviewing school text books. It must include education through the news and entertainment media, both privately and publicly owned, 'practical' education through efforts to combat racist and sexist attitudes in unions, communities, churches, and other institutions, and the educators themselves must be educated. Preferential hiring programmes are ineffective if they produce only a few ghettos of equal opportunity employment, and they can be counterproductive by reinforcing resentment against preferred groups unless they are coupled with programmes for reducing unemployment generally.[39]

Capitalism is a system structured to protect the ability of the few who own means of production to produce as they like and to do what they want with profits gained. Large-scale social planning and social expenditures, the costs of which cannot be defrayed without taxing profits, severely constrain this ability. With reluctance capitalism can adapt to such limitations, but if a system is to remain capitalist there must be a limit on what can be accommodated. The main argument that capitalism perpetuates discrimination thus hinges on the claim that the limitations required to end systemic discrimination are ones capitalism cannot sustain.

## THE DEMOCRATIC PRODUCTION OF WANTS

Democracy involves people having control over their social environments, and having control entails its conforming to what one might want. Among the elements of one's social environment are wants themselves, both of others and of oneself. Hence it is appropriate to ask whether it expands people's control over their lives when they can control their own future wants, that is, when they are self-determining. The answer certainly must be in the affirmative.[40]

People sometimes set out to shape their own wants, and on a limited scale can succeed. Somebody who takes evening courses in a liberal arts programme may do so expecting that his or her values will change as a result. People who refrain from watching television sometimes do this to avoid rotting their minds. On a more collective level, consciousness-raising and self-help are deliberate efforts by people to shape their own preferences. Still,

115

such collective and deliberate control over what kinds of people the members of the collective will be is not widespread. It is generally assumed that people are what they are, with whatever preferences they happen to have, and that although manipulation of wants by advertisers or politicians is something to avoid, designing social institutions both locally and globally to facilitate people's collective control over their own wants is not presently a live political project. Realization of this project under the control of those affected by it would constitute a major advance in democracy. This democratic advance will have been achieved when there exists both a widespread culture favourable to people valuing control of their own values and social and political structures allowing this on more than a limited scale.

It is important to be clear about what is involved in this projected democratic advance. It takes as a point of departure that people do not often have very much control over what they are, that they are largely 'created' by the cultural, economic, technological, and environmental circumstances into which they are born.[41] To advocate bringing the creation of wants under deliberate control is not to advocate doing this no matter how or no matter by whom, but to advocate methods involving everyone who will be affected. The position is incompatible with paternalistic utopian schemes where mind control techniques are used by authorities to mold people into what they think desirable. Rather, processes that are already facts of life must be democratized, partly to prevent being brought or kept under the control of a few, whether paternalistically or worse.

An understanding of how the democratization of wants might function is not easily come by, requiring as it does comprehension of social, psychological, and political processes as yet little experienced as objects of collective self-determination. Habermas approaches this subject in characterizing the goal of democracy as 'discursive processes of will-formation,'[42] and I have the impression that some of the more tentative recent work of radical social theorists is best understood as efforts to explicate this theme. Bowles's and Gintis's theory of the 'unification of learning and choosing,' which (after Dewey and Mead) prescribes the democratization of the way people collectively determine themselves,[43] is another example.

One might also read Benjamin Barber in this light. When he

refers to democracy as a form of 'political knowledge,' or to politics as being 'its own epistemology,' he means to link these theses with a notion that political communities are autocreated as opposed to being things predetermined by already existing interests or by tradition: 'The past exists to be consulted as abridgments of tradition, but it is the future that political judgment must produce from a present community.'[44] Or the view of Laclau and Mouffe that subjects are always articulated in such a way that their identities can never be fixed[45] is related by them to the prospect of a 'radical and plural democracy,' in which nonfixity is itself valued.[46] And prescriptions of Gilles Deleuze and Félix Guattari that 'schizoanalysis' be employed in the service of postcapitalist 'production of desire' might be read in a similar vein.[47] That some of these views are obscurely expressed will be no surprise to one who considers them related to a not-yet-achieved second major advance in democracy.

### HUMANISM, PLURALISM AND CRITICAL THOUGHT

Whatever differences there are in ongoing democratic-socialist speculative theory, perhaps there is presently agreement on the importance of encouraging humanistic concern for the well-being of others, pluralistic respect for differences among people's aspirations, and critical thought. To favour these values being deliberately inculcated is to favour educational and cultural policies that promote their becoming 'second nature' and discouraging policies that breed antihumanist, antipluralist, and anticritical values. To favour this being done democratically is to favour winning people to their implementation, while protecting the ability of a minority to try changing the majority's mind on the content of the values and, in fact, on whether they should be deliberately inculcated.

There are many tensions in such a project. Promoting critical thought is promoting the habit of calling accepted values into question, and this allows calling into question democratic and humanistic values themselves. Another tension is that winning democratic support for democratic values requires a populace that already has some such values. Democratic inculcation of values with these tensions is surely not the creation of a monolithic society

117

of autohypnotists or some other Orwellian nightmare. Indeed, the paternalistic humanist might complain that democratic humanist projects are undesirable or impossible due to these very properties.

Against the paternalist it can be argued: a) that progress in democracy is a bootstrap process whereby small gains make possible greater ones; b) that paternalistic efforts to instill humanistic and critical values usually backfire (a phenomenon we may have witnessed in existing socialism where autocratic attempts to teach humanistic values seem to breed cynicism); and c) that favouring tolerance, pluralism, and critical thought does not require regarding the views of racists and sexists as legitimate, and sometimes it may even be justified to limit their expression if this can be shown necessary to preserve democratic tolerance itself.[48] The more widespread and strongly held the values of humanism, pluralism, and critical thought, the less difficult the decisions about such matters and the less frequently they arise – yet another reason to promote these values.

The notion that humanism, pluralism, and critical thought are to be valued is not new. The notion that they should be deliberately and democratically inculcated on a society-wide basis is more radical, seldom advanced by procapitalists, and then by those whose commitment to capitalism is questionable, such as Rousseau and Mill. Mainstream democratic theory holds that it is not the business of society to develop people's values, but to design mechanisms for accommodating to them whatever they might be, or even to design them for the 'worst case scenarios' when selfish, intolerant, and uncritical values are dominant. It is appropriate for the procapitalist to take this view, since it is hard to see how the democratic production of wants could be effected on a society-wide scale without socialism.

All of the considerations about taking advantage of the challenge to tradition pertain to this point as well. The kind of 'pluralism' most compatible with the perpetuation of capitalism is not consistent with either humanism or critical thought. It is the pluralism of tending one's own garden without concern for the plight of others and without questioning what garden one has or whether there is not a more cooperative and honourable way to spend one's life. Thus, as in the case of discrimination, there is a negative incentive for anyone wedded to this system to encourage humanistic and critical values. In addition, the measures required for effective education are, again, too expensive and require more planning than capitalism allows. This is clearly so regarding critical thought. To do more than pay lip service to the value of thinking critically, people must be provided with access to the highest quality formal and informal education and information facilities from a very early age. How will this be provided in a system where even the richest countries still have functional illiteracy rates of twenty-five percent and higher?[49]

It is worth considering the sort of 'people construction' that takes place in a capitalist society, usually without intention and as a rule undemocratically. Centrally engendered values are those typical of egoism and consumerism, the combination of which is well-labelled, 'possessive individualism,' by Macpherson. Like Marx, he argues that capitalism requires and creates people with this sort of personality.[50] Macpherson's case is not that capitalists deliberately indoctrinate people with false values, but that life in a system where everything is treated as a potential commodity leads one to think of people themselves as commodities. Also, as Joshua Cohen and Joel Rogers argue, the organization of work and production in capitalism constrains people to think in terms of short-term material gain, which is conducive, again, to possessive individualistic attitudes.[51]

## BOUNDARIES OF SOCIAL CHOICE

The phenomena referred to so far primarily concern the 'expansiveness' of capitalism, its tendency to commodify everything and to make people conform to a profit-oriented society. In this way capitalism is a flexible system. But in another way it is quite inflexible. Deliberate and democratic 'people creation' is not only or even primarily a matter of applied social psychology. Rather, just as earlier advances in democracy involved calling into question traditional authority, this democratic advance requires challenging and changing entrenched and previously largely accepted 'boundaries of social choice.' By this is meant principles embedded in social structures and practices prescribing what categories of people have what control over what dimensions of a social environment. Some examples will clarify the notion.

119

*The Public and the Private.* From his earliest writings, Marx challenged the view that the state was independent of civil society. Against Hegel in particular, he argued that there was a fit between what ethical, religious, and especially economic norms and activities existed in civil society and the political institutions of the state, and he noted the historicity of both realms.[52] This theme has been pursued by all Marxists and by anarchist and feminist theorists as well. The 'private' domain is characterized in their work as that where there is a presumption that neither the law nor considerations of public morality has a place. It has also been noted that the boundary between this domain and a 'public' one shifts, usually in response to special interests and seldom, if ever, as a result of collective decision.

For instance, echoing the views of many other feminists, Zillah Eisenstein shows how confinement of women's work to the household is facilitated by classifying this a private matter. She criticizes liberal feminists because they accept the boundary between the public and the private in this respect, arguing for parallel equality for women in each domain. Eisenstein holds that instead it should be made a matter of public and political concern who does what kind of work both in and out of the home and, she might have added, what should count as 'housework' itself.[53] Nicos Poulantzas maintained that the contours of the private realm, far from being independent of the public, are pervasively and undemocratically shaped by the state,[54] and Göran Therborn argues that the 'location and sharpness of the line of demarcation between private and public has varied considerably with the conjuncture of the class struggle.'[55] The point is not that there should be no private realm at all (a view of some radicals to be criticized in Chapter Eight), but that the boundary between public and private is not fixed and is therefore potentially a matter for democratic choice.[56]

*Divisions of Labour.* Another prescription of radical theorists is that divisions, of labour ought to be democratized. Referring mainly to work-related divisions, such as manual and mental labour, Marxist literature criticizes pairing kinds of work with social worth for reinforcing class suppression and ignoring the interconnectedness of different tasks humans must perform. Marxists have also challenged the notion that an individual must be locked into one kind of labour (rather than being simultaneously a car-

120

penter, philosopher, and fisherman as Marx famously put it).[57]
The point can be generalized, as, for example, in Iris Marion
Young's critique of the division of labour, to apply to any socially
structured principle in virtue of which people are confined to
limited and variously valued life activities.[58]

*Property and Use.*   Criticizing Nozick, Tony Honeré describes a
norm among certain tribes of the Hottentots whereby 'a person
who dug a water hole or opened a spring made this his property
and all who wished to use it had to have his permission, but he
was under an obligation to see that no stranger or stranger's stock
was denied access to it.'[59] Honeré offers this example as evidence
that a 'participatory' as opposed to an 'exclusive' system of property is both imaginable and possible. The boundary addressed in
his argument demarcates what people have exclusive use of from
what they must share. Honeré notes that people can always be
compelled to share the fruits of what they own by a state. But in
a society where property is regarded as giving one a right to
exclusive use, this will have to be justified by special considerations
and will likely be limited; whereas in a society governed by a
'participatory' concept of justice in ownership, the state will simply
be ensuring that a recognized obligation is carried out. To open
a choice between these two sorts of society is to challenge a boundary entrenched in the laws and concepts of justice of one of them
(and not even unequivocally in it).[60]

*The Divisible and the Indivisible.*   Comparing the economic theories
of Marx and Aristotle, Cornelius Castoriadis refers to things that
Aristotle considered 'divisible' into equal or unequal shares and
things that are not. An example of the former is wealth, and of
the latter language.[61] Castoriadis is too concerned to criticize Marx
in his essay to note that Marx also challenged the fixity of distinctions of this sort. In the *Grundrisse* he pointed out that with
the advent of money people could possess more wealth than they
could use and that therefore upper limits on the magnitude of
inequality in the distribution of wealth were removed.[62] This point
can be generalized to any boundaries between what can and cannot be unequally distributed. Thus, contrary to Aristotle's example, the facility to use language can sometimes be an unequally
distributed one, as George Bernard Shaw so nicely dramatized in

the case of culturally supported class distinctions in Britain. When language facility is taken to include literacy, inequalities in its distribution become yet more obvious.

*Sex and Gender.* In a course in political philosophy, we were examining some abstract criticisms by J.R. Lucas of the coherence of the notion of 'equality' as a principle of distributive justice,[63] when one student produced another article by Lucas giving practical content to his position. In an attack on full equality of opportunity for women he grants that some opportunities should also be denied men: 'However much I, a male, want to be a mother, a wife or a girlfriend, I am disqualified from those roles on account of my sex, and I cannot reasonably complain. . . . I have to acknowledge that it is reasonable for society to [disqualify me] and for the state to legislate accordingly. The state is justified in not countenancing homosexual "marriages," because of our general understanding of what marriage really is and the importance we attach to family life. For exactly the same reasons, women are debarred from being regarded in a fatherly or husbandly light.'[64]

The boundaries assumed here group certain life activities and psychological profiles with biological gender. The inevitability of these groupings are justly challenged by many theorists, especially by those supporting women's, gay, and lesbian liberation. Their critique often takes the form of challenging the naturalness of any one form of what Gayle Rubin calls a 'sex/gender system': a 'set of arrangements by which a society transforms biological gender into products of human activity, and in which these transformed sexual needs are satisfied.'[65] Roles like 'father' or 'wife' are socially constructed products that need not be identified with one or the other of the biological sexes. This confuses biological gender with humanly created social-sexual roles. The identification and the supposed naturalness of the roles themselves are subject to challenge.[66]

*The Individual and History.* The Hungarian philosopher, Eva Ancel, argues that a communist movement makes individual people responsible for history, because:

> [It] is only with the development of the Communist movement that the social process is brought under the control of conscious

122

planning by freely united individuals, since both of these indispensable conditions – *conscious* planning and *freedom* of union – emerge for the first time as part of this development. Thus in that sense too, revolutionary praxis is a genetic antecedent, for it means that history 'reconnects' the broken circuit between aims and social results, removing the spontaneous, 'natural' character of development. The sometimes halting but nevertheless irreversible process of the true recovery of responsibility begins therefore with the Communist movement, and mainly for those taking part in it.[67]

The 'boundary' challenged is that between the domain of deliberate individual activities, susceptible to being effective or ineffective, responsible or irresponsible, and the domain of world history, which seemingly goes on in accord with laws of its own.

Many democratic theorists charge Marx with believing in a metaphysically conceived historical force of which individuals are pawns. A more charitable reading is that Marx saw class-divided society as the main impediment to a situation where major social decisions affecting large numbers of people including future generations could be made deliberately and democratically. Marx thus challenged a boundary between the personal world of limited control by individuals over a small part of their social environments and an impersonal world of historical forces. This is the sort of boundary also challenged by Georg Lukács, who saw the perpetuation of the division of labour as central to 'reification,' a state in which people are identified and identify themselves with only a few of their potentialities. Though he mainly has economic reification in mind, Lukács' point that 'history is the history of unceasing overthrow of the objective forms that shape the life of man,'[68] may be taken as a general illustration of what is involved in democratizing the boundaries of social choice.

Can the critique and alteration of boundaries of social choice be effectively accomplished in a capitalist system? The democratic socialist claims that, like the things needed to realize the full potentials of the rejection of traditional authority, they cannot. Successful challenges to entrenched principles of property and of distribution are at loggerheads with capitalism. Marxists have advanced many considerations in support of the claim that constraining and discriminatory divisions of labour are endemic to

123

capitalism,[69] and feminists have advanced comparable arguments in the case of the public and the private and sex and gender.[70] In my view the burden of proof rests on the procapitalist.

### v. Socialism and Democracy

But what about socialism? So far the view has not been addressed that even if capitalism cannot advance democracy, neither can socialism. The chapter concludes by addressing two sides of this question: the potential for socialism to advance democracy and the possibility of overcoming antidemocratic features of socialism that might counteract this potential. The first part of the case can now be briefly summarized.

Relative material equality gives more people the time, security, and resources to make use of formal freedoms effectively to participate in political processes should they wish. It also provides a basis from which those who do not accept traditionally sanctioned roles can effectively challenge them, as in the case of the woman who rejects subservience to her husband and is in a better position to alter this role when she is not economically tied to him. Relative economic equality removes one of the worst effects of systemic discrimination, and it provides support for members of discriminated groups when they organize against noneconomic aspects of discrimination. An economy aimed at promoting material equality will be more conducive to cooperation and hence consensus building and the mutual tolerance required to respect minority rights.

All of these advantages also accrue to the democratization of want-production. Economic dependence is a powerfully conservative force. In addition to denying people time to equip themselves with skills for critical thought, it produces a despairing acceptance of one's lot in life and all too often a cynical attitude toward the human condition and mean-spirited antihumanism. Socialist equality removes these impediments, as it removes a weapon from those with vested interest in maintaining traditional boundaries. It also eases the justified fear that deliberate collective want-production could turn into an oppressive, herd mentality-type attempt to force individuals to mold themselves to fit existing social norms. Freedom from poverty and economically supported subservience to others should assist people to experiment with a variety of life-styles and to resist pressures to conform.

These arguments for socialism are all well-known, but they only persuade those who hate capitalism so much that they are prepared to take their chances on any alternative. The reason is that this portrayal of socialism seems unrealistic and contradicted by much present-day socialist experience. This consideration leads some democrats who think that capitalism is an insurmountable obstacle to the levels of democracy they envision, nonetheless to refrain from saying this outright.[71] An alternate response is that negative potentials of socialism can be overcome. The task has several dimensions.

André Gorz maintains that democracy is incompatible with working-class rule and with a planned society. His arguments on the first point do not pertain to characteristics unique to the working class (about which his analysis is less dismissive than the title of his book, *Farewell to the Working Class*, suggests) but to the nature of centralized state power. He holds that to unseat capitalism by occupying the positions of state power now held by its supporters is to replace one oppressive force with another.[72] Regarding planning, his view is that: 'To the extent that socialist political theory prescribes a social integration that no longer results from the uncertain play of initiatives and multiple conflicts but from a conscious and deliberate planning and programming of social activities, it implicitly gives primacy to society over the individual and their common subordination to the state.'[73] Even the most careful attempts to formulate plans democratically will fail because the required decisions are so complex. The result is that the plan 'will inevitably be the work of a state technocracy.'[74]

Gorz thus aims to show that in socialism there are potentially antidemocratic structures (of the state) and a reason to maintain them (to plan). This argument is supplemented by the considerations of Furet and Lefort, referred to earlier, regarding the possibility of dictatorship in the name of popular sovereignty opened by democracy itself. Laclau and Mouffe summarize this position: 'If in the nineteenth century the limits of every attempt at radical democracy were found in the survival of old forms of subordination across broad areas of social relations, at the present those limits are given by a new possibility which arises in the very terrain of democracy: the logic of totalitarianism.'[75] This logic is that of occupying the 'empty space' of democracy discussed in Chapter Four (section iii).

These arguments describe what should be recognized as a genuine set of problems for the democratic socialist. The question to ask is not whether the problems exist, but whether there are realistic measures to temper and compensate for them. If not, if the antidemocratic aspects of bureaucracy will overcome democratic efforts as an 'iron law,' in the phrase of Robert Michels,[76] then the democratic-socialist project will require major rethinking. However, a survey of work by socialists who address this problem suggests that although there may be no one measure to guarantee democractic progress in socialism, a combination of measures might do the job.

### BUREAUCRACY

Democratic theorists posit two checks against bureaucracies becoming authoritarian: institutional impediments and citizen participation in government. Each measure is feasible, and to the extent that they have been employed, each has exhibited bureaucracy-checking potential. By 'institutional' measures are meant the 'constitutional' structures, as William Connolly calls them, to assure such things as an independent judiciary, a free press, and the right to strike.[77] By 'citizen participation' is meant, on the one hand, the protection and encouragement of citizens to have direct input to governmental matters through referenda, recall, review and initiation of proposed legislation, and similar governmentally administrated means of control over shared social environments and, on the other hand, the taking over of hitherto state-administered functions directly by associations of citizens. These measures are well-described by participationist theorists.[78]

In projecting means to check bureaucracy one must thread a course between drawing up detailed blueprints and assuming that ad hoc solutions will be found when needed. It is no surprise that political theorists are inclined toward the former, and practicing political actors toward the latter. But it is surely possible to compensate for these predilections. (It helps for the theorist to engage in political practice, and the political actor to become theoretically educated.) Detailed blueprints are insufficiently tuned to changing circumstances, and simply assuming solutions will be found leaves too much to chance.

Another tendency to avoid is dogmatism about some measures. One example is the stance many democratic-socialist theorists take toward political parties. There is little doubt that formal channels for citizen participation in existing socialisms are largely nullified by the fact that participation is mediated through political parties, the dominant one of which is virtually identical with the state.[79] Similarly, political parties in capitalist societies function in ways that make it very difficult to challenge the capitalist system through formal democratic mechanisms.[80] Reflection on these facts has led some theorists, such as Branko Horvat, to view absence of political parties as necessary for democratic socialism,[81] thus running counter to a dominant socialist view that what is needed are parties of the right kind.

Now whether there should be any political parties at all would seem to depend on a number of contingencies, not the least of which concern the political culture and traditions of a society in which a transition to democratic socialism is sought. It would seem a mistake to prescribe for or against the existence of political parties no matter what the situation. At the same time, some projections can be made about ways to accomplish what political parties traditionally do in their absence or about ways in which the antidemocratic potential of political parties can be protected against in their presence. The experience of politics in societies with strong party systems suggests, for example, that their negative effects can be curtailed by democratic access and internal functioning, by assuring that there are alternate, extraparty mechanisms of which people may avail themselves, by enforcing a separation of party and state on the one hand and party and citizen's organizations, such as unions, on the other, and so on.

Another dogmatism that may affect thought about ways to inhibit antidemocratic bureaucracy is linked with the effort to divide democracy into kinds. On the face of it, a combination of institutional and participatory measures should be more effective in checking bureaucracy than either alone. But institutional checks now exist in liberal-democratic capitalist societies, thus prompting socialist critics of liberal democracy to be suspicious of them. By contrast, pondering how Marx's projected stateless society would handle problems of distribution without creating an undemocratic bureaucracy, Allen Buchanan concludes that it could not do this unless a way of protecting some standard liberal-democratic rights were found.[82] However, this runs against the view sometimes attributed to Marx that communism will be a society 'beyond rights.'[83]

If the rights in question are always legal, Buchanan's prescription also runs counter to the view that socialism should lead to a stateless society. But perhaps one need not choose between two exclusive viewpoints here. Perhaps there is room to question what a right or a state must be so as to project modes of collective self-determination that can draw on a variety of traditions. This is one way to interpret a view of Gorz in his treatment of postcapitalist and poststatist 'politics,' where he argues for replacing elimination of the state with ongoing critical reinterpretation of its role and nature:

> Politics is the locus of the tension and the always conflictual mediation between the enlarging of the sphere of autonomy, which requires the growth of movements throughout civil society, and the necessities managed by the state, which result from the functioning of society insofar as it is a material system. Politics is the specific place where society is aware of its production as a complex process of striving to master effects and control constraints.... This is why politics cannot perform its function if it is confused either with the state or with the growing aspirations of civil society.[84]

Similarly, in his *The Real World of Democracy*, Macpherson warns against identifying democracy with the specific forms that promote it in various parts of the world.[85] The same point can be made about ways of combatting bureaucracy. Flexibility of approach to this problem is a main condition for successfully meeting it.

### PLANNING AND WORKERS' SELF-MANAGEMENT

Measures to check bureaucracy pertain also to the formulation of plans. Institutional safeguards and citizen participation should ensure democratic input to planning. But this does not address misgivings such as those of Gorz regarding the content of plans.

128

Three related problems will be addressed, each put as a putative dilemma:

1.  Socialist planning has as a primary goal to promote the equality of benefits and burdens, but no plan can predict people's changing preferences; therefore some things must be singled out as 'objective' benefits and burdens to be equalized even if these are not thought important by those affected by the plan.
2.  One advantage claimed for plans is that they are long term and society-wide; however, this means that they must preclude many people from acting on many preferences, including ones it cannot be predicted they will have at the time a plan is installed.
3.  Planning is supposed to facilitate people's taking control of their own lives, but an effect of a plan is to mould people to have characters consistent with its goal, thus inhibiting their freedom to determine what sorts of people they will be.

It has been largely in response to the first problem that some democratic socialists prescribe workers' self-management where a noncapitalist market replaces much governmental decision-making mechanisms. This has generated hot debates with those socialists who see markets as just what socialism should overcome since they inhibit planning and perpetuate a competitive society. Some headway can be gained in evaluating this debate by distinguishing two broad versions of workers' self-management. On one version, a workers' self-managed economy is nothing but a free market constrained by prohibitions against forming monopolies or hiring labour. Such a system is not 'socialist' as the term is here understood, since there is nothing about it to guarantee or to probabilize approximation to equality of material benefits and burdens. Its main virtue would be a potential for maximizing certain freedoms, but if the arguments about socialism and freedom given above are sound, it would have to be further constrained in a socialist direction.

Most advocates of workers' self-management are socialists who favour democracy and equality. Thus, Schweickart advances a workers' self-management model as superior to capitalism in being able to realize both equality and democratic autonomy, and Agnes Heller and Ferenc Feher defend workers' self-management on

129

explicitly egalitarian grounds.[86] Socialist workers' self-management schemes are best seen as attempts simultaneously to democratize the work place and to solve the problem labelled 1) above about avoiding the legislation of wants. If benefits and burdens are to be equally distributed in a society, then by what means will it be determined how much of what is how great or little a burden or benefit to whom? The least problematic way of doing this, the workers' self-management advocate maintains, is to allow people as far as possible to 'vote,' so to speak, by means of their economic activity on an everyday basis in a relatively free market.[87]

Thus regarded, the distance between democratic socialists who favour workers' self-management and those critical of it is not too great. The point can be sharpened by considering this objection by Barry Clark and Herbert Gintis:

> In the Good Society, justice is produced in the main by institutions themselves, and individuals act justly by affirming these institutions. Freedom of speech is guaranteed in the first instance by the Bill of Rights, not the continual refusal of just individuals to exercise their right of censorship. Slavery is constitutionally prohibited; its absence is not predicated on the refusal of ethical individuals to enter into immoral relations.... The problem with capitalism, market socialism, and other distributional-redistribution economics, then, lies in their requiring individuals continually to make and remake choices which are either immoral or loftily virtuous.[88]

The argument would have some force against an advocate of a nonsocialist market, but all market socialist advocates recognize the need for institutional coordination and regulation. Deciding what and how much to withhold from social consumption for future development and how to distribute public goods requires extramarket structures. Thus, in advocating workers' self-management, Marković lists among six requirements for democratic socialism that there be 'a high level of coordination and conscious rational direction of social activities' to avoid 'the mutually exclusive actions of different unrelated individuals,' and of everyone 'doing his own thing.'[89] And Heller and Feher see the need for placing upper and lower income limits on all members of a society such that: 'The lower limit must enable the satisfaction of all needs within the given cultural context so as to allow individuals to participate in the appropriation process.... The upper limit ... would

130

prevent any one person from gaining power over others, especially over entire groups of people.'[90] These are very strict limitations on what can result from market interactions.

This suggests that institutional and market structures can be combined to offset problems endemic to planning.[91] Institutional checks on the market prevent antiegalitarian results; whereas market interactions among members of self-managed firms is a way that preferences get directly expressed. That is, these things can be combined if they are combinable. In the opinion of some people, concepts like 'an institutionally constrained yet relatively free market' or 'a planned society incorporating a market' are blatantly contradictory. Insofar as there are tensions between planning and markets, or market freedom and institutional constraints, such an opinion is not without foundation, but this brings us to a question of political-theoretic and practical methodology.

These tensions can be viewed on the level of abstract political concepts as simple contradictions. But viewed practically, they can be seen as problematic elements in ongoing processes. As Crocker puts it regarding representative and participatory practices in a projected socialism: 'The best set of mechanisms for realizing a socialist democracy should be determined by experimentation and debate in the process of creating a good society. One of the most difficult of the issues that will have to be settled in this fashion is the exact mix between the centralization of planning democracy and the decentralization of participatory democracy.'[92] Crocker's conclusion is not that therefore democratic socialism is impossible, but that successful democratic-socialist politics requires hard work and careful thought. What of importance does not?

### PLANNING AND FREEDOM

Whether one thinks planning is incompatible with freedom in either of the ways described as problems 2) and 3) will also partly depend on whether the abstract or the practical perspective is taken. That there are problems is again undeniable. Planning is a necessary part of the egalitarian project, which is in turn required to maximize freedom. But once a plan has been put in place it is bound to frustrate some aspirations such that, had its course been anticipated, the plan would either have been designed differently or not implemented at all (problem 2). Or else, plans

131

can ensure that there are not such aspirations by conditioning people affected by them to conform to the needs of the plan, which then takes on a despotic life of its own (problem 3). Abstractly viewed these problems might lead to despair or to 'playing it safe' by foregoing the advantages that planning promises. Regarded concretely, planning, like any other problem-solving activity, creates problems of its own to be offset, minimized or gotten around. There is no mystery about this orientation, and it has philosophical expression in more than one tradition, notably Pragmatism, Marxist Dialectics, and Process Philosophy.

Is human ingenuity up to the job regarding planning? It is the nature of a concrete orientation to demur at making absolute guarantees about such things, but there are considerations favouring a positive response. Plans that, where possible, allow for independent adjustments to changing circumstances by protecting local community and work place autonomy and for some market-type mechanisms will create room for at least these measures of relative 'plan independent' freedom. Moreover, one can plan for potential undesirable consequences with contingency plans and provision of mechanisms for recognizing and reversing mistakes. The 'democratic fix' also figures here. When people affected by a plan have effective input to its formulation and review, the plan may be more flexibly pursued than when few people have this control. More experience can be drawn on in anticipating and recognizing problems, and people involved in formulating a plan will both be motivated to try to make it work and knowledgeable enough to spot weak points.

To the observation that a society planned to further some goal creates people to fit it,[93] two sorts of reactions are appropriate. First sometimes this is *desirable*. The point can be argued on either of two grounds. One appeals to the moral preferability of a world without certain values. If life in an increasingly democratic and egalitarian society led to the eventual absence of racist or sexist attitudes, would this not be a good thing? It will not do to respond negatively on the civil libertarian ground that, however noxious, it is dangerously antidemocratic to deny people the right to their own opinions, since the supposition here is not that these opinions are forcibly suppressed, but that society has arrived at a point when nobody has them.

One counterargument, of course, would be that the attitudes

132

are justified due to the inferiority of some race or sex. It is important for the egalitarian to keep showing that people who think these things are wrong; however, what is now at issue is the claim that it is morally desirable that some opinions are not held by anyone. A radical relativist could continue this line of argumentation by maintaining that nobody can know what is morally right or wrong, and therefore any society that tends to inhibit or promote certain attitudes ought to be avoided. There are deep and murky philosophical waters here, but I am not sure the democratic theorist needs to enter them. If the relativist is right that morally relevant opinions cannot be justified, then there is no more ground for prescribing *against* the deliberate eradication of some opinion than there is for prescribing for it. The word 'ought' in the above characterization of the relativist's position is without force. We shall see that there are more secure ways to ground valuing tolerance of differences than to embrace ethical relativism.

Another ground for favouring the causative nature of an egalitarian plan pertains not to specific values, but to the creation of personality types. The point is broadly Rousseauean in seeing merit to a society that creates people who come to have an interest in the common good. Mansbridge makes this point when she advocates measures to transform 'adversarial' democracy into 'unitary' democracy, where each embodies its own form of equality:

> The ideal of equality in an adversary democracy is quantitative ...and mandates that in a decision each individual's interests have equal weight. When interests conflict, a secret ballot minimizes the cost to individuals of pursuing their interests. In a unitary democracy, the similar interests of the citizenry allow them to make their decisions by consensus. Because they need not worry about weighing each individual's interests equally in the decision, the kind of equality that concerns them is qualitative – the feeling of equal respect that prevails among friends. The unitary process of making decisions consists not in the weighing of votes but in the give and take of discussion in a face-to-face setting.[94]

There are pros and cons to this sort of argument. Insofar as democratic planning fosters personality traits favourable to resolving differences in the nonadversarial way Mansbridge describes, we have a 'limitation' that can surely be defended as desirable. Among other things, this is required to facilitate conversion of weak forms of un-animity to consensus. But if democracy creates people with 'similar interests' beyond one in harmonious settlement of dispute, the position may be subject to sound criticism. Antisocialists often charge that socialism will create a boring homogenous society without conflict, not because people seek to avoid it if possible, but because there are no differing interests to conflict. This image (as Chapter Eight will argue) is both an undesirable and unrealistic one for the socialist to project. It was precisely to recognize this that 'perfect democracy' was characterized to retain room for negotiation as well as the reaching of consensus.

Thus the point is well taken that to the extent a plan fosters over-powering conformity there is another problematic dimension of planning. But, again, there is also reason to think that this potentiality can be allowed for. Plans affect people's values directly as in formal education and indirectly by producing positive and negative inducements to conform. Conformist tendencies can be counteracted in the first case by promoting the value and skills of critical thought. They can be countered in the second case by measures whereby people may challenge a plan at any stage of its development or use. With this as an open possibility, there are options to conformity which do not carry the disincentive of being considered antisocial. More radically, plans may include as part of their goals the promotion of pluralism itself. Individual initiative and offbeat experimentation can be encouraged in schools and work places. Forming voluntary organizations to pursue special interests can be facilitated. Employing these sorts of measures, like the others, would involve many trade-offs between factors protecting the integrity of a plan and those inviting challenges to it, and finding the right balance involves fine judgment. But there is no reason to suppose humans incapable of this judgment, and practice makes perfect.

### vi. Imposed Socialism

The above arguments (or sketches thereof) are designed to show that there are no impediments beyond human will and ingenuity to prevent socialism from developing the global potentials of major democratic advances. But nothing has been said about whether or how it is desirable to try to attain such a state of affairs. Critics of socialism sometimes put the challenge this way: If people in

present-day liberal-democratic capitalist countries wanted socialism, they would vote it in, and the fact that this has not happened
shows that they do not want it. Therefore, such a state must be
imposed, which is what has happened, with the result of 'thin
socialism' at best. An imposed socialism, however, will perpetuate
antidemocratic structures and practices that will make its democratization impossible.

Many socialists are tempted to respond that once relative economic equality and a modicum of public input to economic decisions are attained, an upward spiral leading to full democracy
will ensue. This is not a promising response. It can just as well be
argued that when input is limited, people come to accept relative
undemocracy. It can also be maintained that the argument rests
on a crude economic deterministic theory which is not borne out
by comparisons of the various world's societies. To prove the hypothesis one would have to find correlations between levels of
economic equality and progress in democracy sufficient to demonstrate that the former was the cause of the latter.

A better, though weaker, response is to argue that *if* a highly
democratic socialism can be attained then people's control would
be widened into new and important domains; therefore, anything
that constitutes progress toward this goal is to be favoured by the
democrat. It is just this possibility of progress that the antisocialist
calls into question. If it were true that democratic advances could
not be made once 'state bureaucratic socialism' is in place, then
there would be no hope for existing socialisms. Democratic-
socialist theorists from such societies who address this question
dispute the claim and advance a variety of measures that give
them cause for hope.

Roy Medvedev surveys trends conducive to democracy both
within the Soviet Communist Party and outside it.[95] Mihaly Vajda,
despite his pessimism regarding the prospects for democracy in
'statist' societies, thinks that at least in Hungary democracy
requires a 'public sphere,' free of party and state domination
and that present conditions for this are 'very favourable.'[96] Horvat
and Svetozar Stojanović discuss the prospects for democratic advance in more detail and suggest a variety of measures, chief
among which is the introduction or expansion of workers' self-
management. Like other theorists from existing socialist countries,
they also see a toehold in the prodemocratic constitutions of these

societies and note 'constitutionalist' or 'legalist' movements to force governments to abide by their own laws.[97] Challenging this side of the antisocialist claim is the overriding task of any democratic socialist living in an existing socialist society, but it is unnecessary for the democratic socialist in a capitalist one.

Granting the obvious fact that an imposed socialism is at least a major obstacle to taking advantage of socialism's democratic potentials, one should aim to challenge the view that socialism could only be imposed on a population. Two dimensions of this task – roughly the theoretical and the practical – might be distinguished. The theoretical task is to produce good reasons to favour socialism. The more practically oriented task is to address the question of how and why recognition of these reasons can become a motivation for political activity by the bulk of a population. Parts II and III of this book will address some key dimensions of the practical task. Along with earlier chapters, this one has been taking up the first task. In addition to the truncated argument from equality, the claim so far has been: that making progress in democracy is feasible (the concept makes sense and there are mechanisms to accomplish it); that such progress is desirable; that socialism contains potentials not found in capitalism to make major advances in democracy; and that antidemocratic potentials can be overcome.

Some hard-line socialists might be tempted to argue (to one another if not to the world) *in favour* of imposed socialism. They would find themselves agreeing with one of Nozick's premises. He finds it intolerable that in a socialist society 'capitalist acts between consenting adults' would not be permitted.[98] Nozick is certainly right that typical capitalist acts would be prohibited in socialism. However, in a sufficiently democratic socialism, capitalist activity could be restored if enough people were convinced to dismantle its socialist structure. I am inclined to agree with G.A. Cohen that in such a society it is highly unlikely people could in fact be thus convinced,[99] but if they were, the autodestruction of thick socialism would have to be allowed.

Many socialists view this attitude as completely unacceptable, and condemning it has produced some of the most colourful prose in the history of socialist movements. The stand one takes on this question divides socialists into two importantly different categories. In addition to trade-off situations within planning activities there are also risks for entire plans. An extreme example concerns the relation between bureaucratic or thin socialism and more democratic socialism. In one respect planning to promote material equality is more secure in the thin socialist society, because it cannot be voted out. But then many of the checks on the negative sides of planning are lacking. This makes the plans in another way *insecure*, since they support authoritarian bureaucracy and the possibility that a few will subvert planning mechanisms to their own purposes. Which insecurity should the socialist choose?

The answer depends on whether a person is primarily a socialist or primarily a democrat. In the one case, democracy is favoured just because and to the extent that it furthers gaining and securing socialism. From this perspective the risks of democratic socialism, even if they are slim, may indeed not be worth taking. In the other case, socialism is favoured mainly because it protects and advances democracy. On this latter view the 'insecurity' of a highly democratic socialism is the clear choice.

# II The Retrieval of Liberal Democracy

# 7 Liberal Democracy

WHEN ALAN HUNT writes that, 'the project of socialism has as its goal the completion or realization of the democratic project initiated by the bourgeois revolutions of the eighteenth and nineteenth centuries,'[1] he likely has in mind the liberal-democratic tradition. Not all democratic socialists agree. Thus Andrew Levine concludes his book on *Liberal Democracy*: 'Neither adding a theory of justice to liberal-democratic theory nor expunging "possessive individualist" elements from [it] will suffice to produce a genuine and satisfactory "supersession" of liberal democracy. We should not hesitate, then, despite what is meritorious in the dominant tradition, to abandon the attempt at continuity.'[2] Levine's arguments depend on Arrow-type critiques of democratic decision procedures and on what he sees as an irreconcilable conflict between democracy and the liberal-democratic value of freedom.[3] Other socialists appeal to theories fragmenting democracy into kinds, in opposition to what Macpherson calls the socialist 'retrieval' of liberal democracy.[4]

To evaluate the debate over retrieval one must identify what is supposed to be retrieved or irretrievable and specify criteria for deciding the issue. An example of the problematic nature of the first task is indicated by asking who counts as a liberal democrat. For Levine, Mill and Locke are liberal democrats; Hobbes, a nondemocratic liberal; Rousseau and Kant, nonliberal democrats; and Hegel, neither a liberal nor a democrat. Rawls and Macpherson are what Levine idiosyncratically calls 'social democrats,' that is, democrats who wish to add justice to the liberal value of freedom.[5] By contrast, it is central to the argument of Amy Gutman's book, *Liberal Equality*, that Kant and Rawls count as liberals.[6] Zillah Eisenstein includes Rousseau as a liberal democrat in her book, *The*

141

*Radical Future of Liberal Feminism*;[7] and one author, Renato Cristi, argues that Hegel, though a conservative, was also a liberal.[8] Leo Strauss classifies Hobbes as a liberal,[9] and in an approach from the left, Frank Coleman argues that Hobbes was a liberal *democrat*.[10]

In fact each of these classifications can be justified depending on what dimensions of liberal democracy are focused on and what is included in each dimension. If one attends to a liberal-democratic theory of society and human nature (what Carol Gould calls a 'social ontology')[11] and concludes that its principal explanatory category is the self-interested individual, Hobbes is a prototypical liberal democrat. But if one focuses on the political values espoused by liberal democrats, Hobbes' antidemocratic views disqualify him. If the dimension of liberal democracy in question is the normative basis of its prescriptions and moral autonomy is included, Kant counts as a liberal democrat. And so on. We shall return to this problem of classification.

### i. Retrieval

Two questions are involved in evaluating the retrievalist's project: whether a position claiming to have effected socialist retrieval has succeeded and whether it is worthwhile to try. On the first point, one might say that the position succeeds if the projected political theory and practice in a socialist environment is sufficiently similar to liberal-democratic theory and practice to be recognized as of the same species. For what might be called the puritanical retrievalist, defining 'sufficiently similar' is easy; it means 'exactly the same.' For this retrievalist, socialism is just the realization of liberal-democratic values and institutions in a socialist society.

There are few puritanical retrievalists. More often, retrievalists wish to 'supersede' liberal democracy. Macpherson, himself, views liberal democracy as an amalgam of values and theories of human nature, some of which – (possessive) utility maximization and psychological egoism and social atomism (individualism) – can be stripped away. The result – a socialism that promotes the equal development of uniquely human potentials – is a supersessionist retrieval of liberal democracy.[12] The claim that this supersession is a retrieval depends on the accuracy of Macpherson's interpretation of liberal democracy and on a supposed method of supersession by subtraction. One who denies that these views are found in liberal-democratic theory[13] or thinks that subtraction from a theory loses similarity with it will be sceptical.

## OPPORTUNISM AND LIBERAL DEMOCRATS

There is a bad reason to endorse the retrievalist's project and a bad one to oppose it. Many socialists use the term 'opportunist' just to mean, 'You are less a true socialist than I,' but the concept need not be restricted to *ad hominem* attacks. A political opportunist is one for whom no consideration is more important than to be accepted by some intended audience. This does not mean that a nonopportunist should be unconcerned about the acceptability of a favoured position. Rather, it means that one should not disguise the position or hold no position except to be accepted. One kind of *socialist* opportunist takes as an audience militant members of a revolutionary organization or the leaders of some socialist country from whom support is sought and produces appropriate rhetoric to curry favour.

Other socialist opportunists adopt liberal-democratic rhetoric for the purpose of being accepted, for example, in one's work circles or by an electorate that, it is believed, cannot be persuaded to support a socialist candidate for what he or she actually believes. This latter opportunism is a bad reason to support retrieval. Among other objectionable features, it inhibits retrieval by perpetuating an antidemocratic politics of dishonesty. The resulting environment is more conducive to cynical power politics than to the healthy pluralism essential to socialist retrieval of liberal democracy.

One bad reason to *reject* retrieval is out of sectarian left opportunism; another is distaste for liberal democrats. One socialist defined 'a liberal' to me as 'somebody who is a democrat toward activities of the right and a totalitarian toward those of the left.' Anybody who has been politically active on the left will recognize the phenomenon. So too will the phenomenon be recognized of the liberal democrat whose activity is restricted to hand wringing and tear shedding. Such a person might refrain from doing business with a bank that invests in South Africa, but helping to mount a concerted divestment campaign is considered too radical. One might react by claiming an essential connection between such activity or inactivity and liberal democracy. However, the more obvious conclusion to draw is that the totalitarian or inactive liberal democrat is a hypocrite to be criticized on his or her own espoused values rather than taken as proof against these values.

### WHY RETRIEVAL?

There are two reasons to want the retrievalist project to succeed. One of these has to do with a transition to socialism. In Chapter Eleven it will be argued that in today's world only an approach to socialist organization that builds overwhelming, committed support from many sectors of a population has any chance of securing socialism and maintaining it without Stalinistic measures and that continuity with democratic dimensions of existing political cultures and practices is required to gain this support. The other reason is that liberal democracy does in fact contain these dimensions.

The argument turns on the relative independence of political history from economic-class history. One who thinks that political ideas, institutions, and practices are nothing but servants of dominant economic classes and who notes the ability of capitalists to make use of liberal democracy will likely see it as both undesirable and impossible to attempt retrieval. Alternately, liberal democracy may be viewed as an advance in democracy requiring socialism to become global. Given the features of capitalism that retard democratic progress discussed in the last chapter, the present integration of it with liberal democracy will be seen as an excellent reason *for* socialist retrieval.

## ii. Dimensions of Liberal Democracy

Anyone trying to characterize liberal democracy faces a hermeneutic problem. To arrive at a definition inductively by studying works of liberal-democratic authors, criteria are needed to identify these authors. To generate a description, Plato like, from the 'idea' of liberal democracy opens one to the charge of question begging in selection of an idea. An alternate approach is stipulative. Characteristics are hypothesized as central to liberal democracy, and arguments about socialist retrieval are made on this basis. Somebody who thinks the hypothesized characteristics completely fail to capture liberal democracy will find the arguments beside the point. Someone who thinks the hypotheses only partially accurate may make appropriate adjustments in evaluating a position depending on what errors of omission or commission are thought to have been made.

Putative characteristics of liberal democracy listed below are derived from consideration of what is advanced in the name of this political perspective or criticized by this name both in political-theoretic scholarship and in daily politics, but no effort is made to prove that this is a sound induction. Central to the task is considering separately four often conflated dimensions of liberal democracy: 1) the political values liberal democrats typically advocate; 2) ethical bases of these values; 3) liberal-democratic viewpoints on the nature of human beings and society; and 4) the political institutions and practices prescribed by liberal democrats to promote the values they advocate. In this section, each of these dimensions will be stipulatively characterized. Section iii will then defend the normative aspect of a liberal-democratic approach to political theory and practice, and the chapter will conclude with criticisms of unsuperseded liberal democracy.

### VALUES

Liberal democracy is taken to embody three generic values – freedom, equality, and democracy – plus a stance on their relative weight. It is probably impossible to find consensus among all liberal democrats on the precise meaning of any one of these terms, but certain convergences can still be identified. Students of liberal democracy do not always include equality, but this omission seems to me illegitimate. Chantal Mouffe makes the point that the 'new right' has been trying to redefine 'liberalism' in the public mind along antiegalitarian, libertarian lines,[14] and it does seem a dubious concession to exclude equality from a list of liberal-democratic values. It is, after all, the egalitarian dimension of liberal democracy that evokes the ire of conservatives who see this as ruining the economy and promoting injustice against the rich.

As to what kind of equality liberal democracy favours, there is no doubt a spectrum running from formal equality of opportunity through full equality of benefits and burdens. The mainstream liberal democrat is here interpreted to favour limited substantive equality of opportunity, where this requires antidiscriminatory

145

laws and modest affirmative action, economic welfare floors, and some universally accessible social services such as education and medical care. Deviations from substantive equality of opportunity in either direction call for special justification.

Isaiah Berlin's essay 'Two Concepts of Liberty' is often taken as a definitive liberal-democratic treatment of freedom. In opposition to a 'positive' concept, he regards liberty as the absence of 'coercion,' where this is defined as 'the deliberate interference of other human beings within the area in which I could otherwise act.'[15] Many liberal democrats no doubt share this definition. Others agree with left critics that inclusion of deliberate interference is too restrictive. Perhaps there are some who call their views liberal democratic but disagree with Berlin's attack on positive liberty (where the content of what one is free to do should be specified), but this strains liberal democracy.

Ronald Dworkin must express the mainstream view in holding that liberal theory 'supposes that political decisions must be . . . independent of any particular conception of the good life, or what gives value to life. Since the citizens of a society differ in their conceptions, the government does not treat them as equals if it prefers one conception to another.'[16] Liberal democrats are not barred from disvaluing certain things people want, and in fact are committed to sanctioning coercion when it is required to maximize freedom. But central to their view is that people cannot be 'forced to be free' by compelling them to do or forbear doing certain things against their wishes while calling this an exercise of their freedom.

Democracy as a liberal-democratic value means that those affected by some decision directly or indirectly take part in making it. Liberal democrats also favour certain sorts of governmental forms, but this has to do with their estimation of the institutions that will best advance valued goals rather than the goals themselves. Contrary to this interpretation, Levine holds that a liberal-democratic preference for representative government derives from its antidemocratic dimensions and reflects a weighting of their values such that liberty takes precedence over democracy.[17] My own impression is that liberal democrats deliberately refrain from weighting their values at all.[18] Life in political society for the liberal democrat is bound to be fraught with conflict such that trade-offs must be made among freedom, democracy, and equality. The art of politics is the art of making these trade-offs judiciously. If there is any guiding principle it is that no trade-off be made in a way that prejudices the kind of trade-offs that can be made in the future. Equality-promoting welfare measures, freedom-protecting laws, and popular input to government must be balanced, each of them hedged against becoming dominant over the others.

### ETHICAL BASES

One source of dispute over who counts as a liberal democrat is that those in the running exhibit a wide range of positions in the field of ethics. Approximation to consensus in norms is not matched at the philosophical level where those norms are to be justified. John Stuart Mill and John Rawls are liberal-democratic theorists if anyone is, yet Mill was a utilitarian and Rawls is a contractarian, each a strong critic of the alternate view. Another frequently encountered basis for liberal-democratic values is rights theory, where certain rights are taken as primitive (as Dworkin argues), and yet other liberal democrats, such as David Easton, are ethical relativists.

I doubt it is possible to select one of these approaches, or some combination of them, as either a mainstream favourite or one to which liberal democrats are committed whatever their expressed preferences. Selection depends on one's focus. If the negative freedom aspect of liberal democracy's normative dimension is the focus, classic utilitarianism might get the edge. Relativism might more comfortably fit with an emphasis on a liberal-democratic approach to trade-offs, and contractarianism with an approach focussed on an individualistic theory of human nature. We shall see that socialist antiretrievalist arguments do not usually depend on which ethical basis liberal democrats embrace, and that the same is true for the retrievalist.

### HUMAN NATURE AND SOCIETY

Steven Lukes identifies eleven species of 'individualism,' some of which are again divisible into subspecies.[19] His list can be initially sorted into normative and nonnormative categories. In the first belong moral prescriptions, like 'individuals should be allowed as

147

much as possible a private space to do as they wish,' and ethical doctrines such as that 'people deserve equal respect in virtue of being potentially autonomous individuals.' In the second category are social and psychological theses, for instance, that people are self-interested by nature, that deliberate human actions are not externally caused, or that there exist no super individual social or historical forces.

This chapter posits a convergence of liberal-democratic norms lacking in the case of ethical theories. It is similarly difficult to find common ground among liberal-democratic theorists about such matters as psychological egoism, causal determinism or even methodological individualism. Thus, despite the way he sometimes describes a social contract, it is clear that Rawls does not espouse psychological egoism.[20] Mill was a causal determinist, and Emile Durkheim favoured liberal-democratic political values while defending a holistic approach to social science. However, there is a third category of individualistic doctrines sharing normative and nonnormative features where some typical liberal-democratic views may be found.

This category might be called 'prescriptive political-theoretical methodology.' It includes recommendations about how human beings and societies ought to be conceptualized for the purpose of advancing political theory and practice. Any such prescription should be compatible with a favoured approach to social science generally and be capable of supporting normative prescriptions. But unless the political theorist is guilty of question begging, the prescriptive/explanatory views of this category should not be logically tied to any one viewpoint in the other categories. Three theses of this sort seem crucial to liberal-democratic theory: that individuals can make free choices; that people are the best judges of their own interests; and that the individual 'precedes' society.

The first view is inconsistent with fatalistic determinism, but whether it is consistent with the 'compatibilist' or 'reconciliationist' position that sees no conflict in principle between freedom and determinism is a matter of ongoing philosophical debate.[21] Crucial to the liberal-democratic position is that society comprise individuals capable of making deliberate choices. Freedom is then conceived of in terms of whether there are impediments to succeeding in what one has chosen to try to do. The thesis that people are the best judges of their own interests is further treated in Chapter

148

Ten. This thesis is compatible with recognizing that one can be mistaken about his or her own interests, but it prescribes taking seriously people's estimates of their interests both as an initial understanding of their actions and to evaluate political institutions and practices.

One kind of individualism described by Lukes pictures individuals 'with given interests, wants, purposes, needs, etc.; while society and the state are pictured as sets of actual or possible social arrangements which respond more or less adequately to those individuals' requirements. Social and political rules and institutions are, on this view, regarded collectively as an artifice, a modifiable instrument, a means of fulfilling independently given individual objectives. . . . '[22] This is one way that individuals can be said to 'precede' society. The liberal-democratic claim is that for the purpose of making political prescriptions, individual interests may be taken as fixed and social arrangements as modifiable. Thus, society must be changed to meet individuals' needs and not the other way around.

## INSTITUTIONS AND PRACTICES

In putting these values and political-theoretical theses together an expected set of political prescriptions is generated. On the liberal-democratic view certain values, capable of being in conflict, must be kept in balance, and individual goals are whenever possible accommodated rather than questioned. These things require certain formal structures and the promotion of a certain political culture. In particular the consistent liberal democrat might be expected to prescribe just what is typically prescribed: representative-democratic political structures; a 'rule of law' to protect individual rights; the protection of a private realm within which people are free from state interference with their pursuits; and a culture with supporting institutions to promote pluralism and tolerance.

If people's interests as they see them are taken as given and their freedom to act on those interests facilitated, then it would be most improbable to find that the interests meshed so as never to inhibit equality, democracy, or freedom itself. Hence political structures are needed to minimize conflicts among these things and to facilitate adjudication. Representative democracy provides one way of, if not guaranteeing that the best trade-offs will be made, at least promoting a method by which people have some say in governing their affairs. Public leaders are elected both to represent specific interests of a constituency and to take a peace-keeping stand above these interests. Since a tightrope like this is hard to walk and since representatives have their own interests and cannot be counted on to be altruistic, laws binding everyone and protecting rights of equality and individual freedom must also govern human interactions. In turn, such governmental and legal structures themselves pose obstacles to freedom, and hence it is important to maintain a private realm in which people are free from regulations of the state.

Being neither libertarians, who think a political free market will avoid self-destructive conflict, nor social engineers who advocate indoctrinating people to have only compatible interests, liberal democrats promote a political morality that highly values plural-ism and tolerance. This institutional prescription joins the shared values to produce a typical and central liberal-democratic nor-mative orientation toward the political world. It is this orientation that draws the strongest fire from some socialists.


### iii. Political Normativism

It has been urged that there is no core liberal-democratic ethical position, and to the extent that this claim is right, there would seem to be nothing in the way of ethical theory to inhibit retrieval. Indeed, one can see the various ethical positions of liberal dem-ocrats mirrored in the works of socialist theorists. Thus, David Schweickhart and Jeffrey Reiman give contractarian arguments for socialism,[23] Derek Allen argues that key normative political views of Marx are compatible with utilitarianism,[24] and Carol Gould derives a prescription for democratic socialism from an ethical principle of 'equal rights of access to the conditions of self-development.'[25] All the (ethical) bases are covered by socialists.

However, some socialist challenges to liberal-democratic ethics do not attack one or another of its varieties, but the enterprise itself and with it an approach to liberal-democratic normative prescriptions probably shared by retrievalists. Here are three sam-ple attacks:

- Macpherson's critique of liberal democracy is and always has been essentially an exercise in moral persuasion.... This project implies a number of crucial assumptions: above all, the project implies a particular audience and assigns to that audience a predominant role in the transformation of society.... A careful consideration of Macpherson's work as a whole and the tasks he has set himself may suggest that [a] lapse into 'classical Fabianism'...lies at the very heart of his intellectual and political project.— Ellen Wood[26]

- As the ideological companion (indeed spiritual justification) of Capital as it enters the world 'dripping from head to foot, from every pore, with blood and dirt,' these 'human rights' and 'liberal values' which some are so anxious to 'recover' brought slavery, misery, exploitation, and war in their train. This makes it difficult to see how they can simply be incorporated into Marxist theory as they stand: how theories of democracy tied organically to systems of exploitation and (some form of) slavery, can be said to provide that necessary 'political' ingredient which Marxism apparently lacks.—John Hoffman[27]

- One of the biggest stumbling blocks to according revolutionary rights comes from an absolutist conception of ethics.... [S]ome gradualists ultimately rest their case...on the view that a *class* is not the basis for rights but *humanity* is. Workers must then join with all other humans to change society from within the present system.—Milton Fisk[28]

These critics agree that trying to retrieve liberal democracy for socialism requires arguing for certain values. Wood thinks that this alone is objectionable, because it supports the view she associates with Fabianism that intellectuals can effect a socialist transformation by force of moral argument. Hoffman refers to the content of liberal-democratic values, and Fisk objects to the way socialist 'gradualists' and liberal democrats advance values as class independent. These criticisms must be met by the retrievalist.

If retrievalist values are not identical to liberal-democratic values, they are probably still too close for someone advancing Hoffman's argument, since otherwise the result would be too distant from liberal-democratic values to count as a retrieval. Similarly, the values could not be class or otherwise group relativized without, again, distancing the approach too much from that of the liberal democrat. Although liberal democracy need not be hostile to group rights (for example, in promoting equality), it certainly advances individual rights as generally applicable, regardless of class or other group membership. Reasons are required not to abandon the retrievalist project before it starts in the face of these arguments.

## NORMATIVE POLITICAL THEORY

Wood's criticism of Macpherson wrongly supposes: a) that in addressing arguments to intellectuals one is thereby biased in favour of seeing intellectuals as the most likely agents of social change; b) that those who advance arguments are only advancing them for consumption by intellectuals; and c) that addressing intellectuals with the idea that they might play a role in social change entails thinking they will play the only role. Regarding c), intellectuals may have *a* role to play in social change and hence are worth addressing, but this does not mean they have the only or the primary role. Moreover, arguments like Macpherson's are not made under the illusion that argumentation alone will bring about socialism. A more reasonable hope is that people will take actions compatible with these values. Regarding b), even if the retrievalist advances arguments in academic forums, using idioms familiar to intellectuals, this does not mean they are the primary intended target. Intellectual viewpoints find their way into popular consciousness through the media, through education, through the direct involvement of some intellectuals with social movements, and other avenues.

Regarding assumption a), the mere fact of arguing in an intellectual forum (such as the journal in which Wood's arguments appear) cannot by itself be proof of Fabianism. The argument must be strengthened to show that there is something misguided about socialists engaging in rational argumentation about morality. Wood does not develop this point, but three possibilities come to mind: that it is the task of the revolutionary to help find the best means to serve ends given within working-class movements themselves, not to question these ends; that any social ends worth pursuing embody values that everyone already agrees with; or

152

that moral argumentation is inconsistent with socialist partisanship. These are debatable views.

*Power Politics and Historicism.* Despite the ingenious efforts of some to present an entirely extranormative defence of socialism while avoiding moral nihilism,[29] there is room to doubt that this can be accomplished. Either one will suppose a moral viewpoint after all or else fall back on a pure power-political view of society or a drastic historical fatalism. A rational argument about political morality will be accepted or rejected on the power-political view to the extent that its conclusions are believed to further or retard the already adopted ends of some group. On the fatalistic view, the argument again will be accepted or rejected not in recognition of the merits of its content, but because it is believed somehow fated to be accepted. Any weaker view would leave space for meaningful rational argumentation about morality, and the retrievalist position would at least get off the ground. It could not be dismissed as necessarily a waste of ink or breath.

There are good reasons to be sceptical of strong power-political or historical-fatalistic positions. In addition to it being hard consistently to give arguments for them (why should anyone give or entertain such arguments?), the cost of being wrong is so high that the burden of proof should lie strongly on their advocates. These positions invite one to forego morality in the conduct of political affairs. The fact that much political behaviour exhibits immorality, however, does not prove that this must always be the case; while the terrible effects of such politics give us good reasons to want not to be complicit in them. On the power-political orientation ends are given (for instance, furthering the political position of the working class as interpreted by its often self-appointed representatives), and the only considerations entertained about means are whether they further these ends. As a result neither means nor ends are subject to moral constraint. The worst excesses of Stalinism were defended on power-political grounds.[30]

*Socialism As the Obvious Choice.* A different reason to think there is something suspect about socialist argumentation regarding morality is suggested by Michael Teitelman. In an article nicely titled 'On the Theory of the Practice of the Theory of Justice,' he contends:

153

> The debate over competing socially abstract ethical conceptions is jejune.... Contrary to Rawls' picture of the situation, the choice between capitalism and socialism is not an open one.... The [theory of justice] poses the problem as a debate over competing ethical conceptions. But if any plausible entry of principles or values – fairness, utility, freedom, self-realization, respect for human dignity, or even plain old decency – must endorse, when applied to our present circumstances, a socialist conclusion, then the problem of deciding between these can be bypassed. The question of basic [social] structure gets settled before the philosophical project gets started.[31]

Argumentation about political morality is unnecessary for Teitelman, since it is clear to anyone who knows the facts about the modern world that only socialism can realize any value people are likely to endorse.

There are two main problems with this approach. First, it is not clear what values socialists ought to favour. If the power-political orientation is rejected, then the socialist will not espouse whatever values are expedient to espouse in the interests of securing socialism but will want reasons to adopt one or another possible value. That there is room for choice is evidenced by the debates among socialists over many matters. To my knowledge there is nothing approaching consensus among socialists over whether or how freedom of speech or association should be limited either in capitalism or in socialism. There is no consensus on where priority should be placed when choices must be made as among conflicting demands of working-class, nationalist, feminist, or other causes. There is no consensus on when material inequalities are justified. And so on.

Secondly, it is also not clear whether and to what extent socialism will in fact promote the values on which everyone is supposed to agree. Of course, suitable definitions of 'socialism' can make the choice of it over capitalism clear for anybody except one with the values of a Nazi. But considering some of the less noble parts of the history of existing socialisms, the issues become clouded, and many can be excused for thinking that they confront a 'frying pan/frying pan' situation. A main aim of the retrievalist is not only to secure socialism but to secure a socialism with some assurance that it will be humane and democratic. For this task the interrogation of political values is essential.

*Morality and Radical Politics.* Richard Miller attributes to Marx the view that a moral case for socialism is inconsistent with radical political activity. According to Miller, basing important political prescriptions on moral viewpoints supposes that there are general norms 'valid for all societies' such that any rational person would accept sound arguments premised on them, and such that all individuals should be shown equal concern or respect.[32] Marx's belief in the historical variability of values disbarred him, Miller claims, from believing in transhistorical moral norms,[33] while his 'implicit noncognitivism' did not allow for belief in universal rationality.[34] The problem Miller sees with taking the 'humanitarian outlook' of equal respect is that for the radical to advance working-class interests, many people who are 'personally decent,' such as some capitalists or police, will necessarily be harmed in strikes, demonstrations, or social revolutions. Hence, '[t]o give sharp confrontations a crucial role for all would be either hypocritical or self-defeating.'[35] Clearly, the retrievalist cannot accept this conclusion.

Liberal democrats themselves are not of one mind regarding such philosophical questions as whether morality can admit of changing norms through history or whether there is universal human rationality. A successful argument that belief in these things is required consistently to make political prescriptions conjoined with arguments against universality and rationality would indeed show the futility of making such prescriptions. To my mind the jury is by no means in regarding these matters, and to forego political morality on the chance that the philosophical amoralists are right would be risky. However, the argument regarding equal respect challenges the retrieval of liberal normativism more directly.

The retrievalist will agree that people ought to be treated with equal respect in arguing for socialism partly on the grounds that capitalist inequality is morally unjustified. Miller's argument can thus be put that because attaining socialism requires less than equal respect for some people (decent capitalists), the socialist cannot nonhypocritically suppose an appeal to equal respect.[36] In summary:

1. Socialism cannot be secured without doing things that considered by themselves are counter to the principles of a general human morality.
2. Therefore, one ought not to pursue or to advocate pursuing socialism for such reasons.

The retrievalist's counterposition hinges on the inverse argument:

1'. Pursuing socialism and advocating its pursuit for exclusively extramoral reasons has morally bad consequences (namely, a power-political, instrumentalism that breeds the ruthlessness and callousness of Stalinism).

2'. Therefore, one ought not to pursue or to advocate pursuing socialism for exclusively extramoral reasons.

Assuming the accuracy of both premise 1 and premise 1', which way is one to go? In his critique of utilitarian Marxism,[37] Miller assumes that only a radical who was also a utilitarian could consistently opt for 2'. Perhaps this is true, in which case the debate over utilitarianism would take on special importance. However, it is not obvious that accepting 2' commits a radical to utilitarianism. The retrievalist could, fully in the tradition of the liberal-democratic viewpoint that all politics involve trade-off decisions, simply recognize that morally imperfect choices must sometimes be made and try to minimize their severity. Only the most austere moralist would see conflict as a reason to despair altogether of trying to make moral choices.

Miller's own response is to modify conclusion 2, by arguing that for Marx socialists typically adhere to a 'catalogue of general [moral] goods,' such as promoting freedom and not inflicting pain. When trade-offs must be made, these goods are ordered by appeal to the requirements for attaining socialism, which is regarded as having 'intrinsic worth' for workers. Socialism is in the interests of workers, and they make a 'basic social choice' to try securing it. But despite some subtle argumentation on Miller's part regarding the ethical status of this viewpoint, it would seem to fall either into instrumentalism (if the catalogue of goods is ranked by reference to the end of gaining socialism, while this end is not itself regarded normatively) or it becomes a form of the normativism Miller thinks radicals must avoid (if socialism is viewed as of morally intrinsic worth). Another option, is to say that socialism *is* to be morally valued, but only for those whose interests it serves. This is the group relativist approach of Fisk, to which we shall shortly return.

### CAPITALIST ORIGINS OF LIBERAL DEMOCRACY

It would be easy to dismiss Hoffman's argument as an example of the genetic fallacy. The point has already been made that even supposing that liberal democracy came into being entirely as an effect of capitalist needs, it would not follow from this fact alone that it is morally bankrupt or nothing but a servant of capitalism. Still, it seems undeniable that capitalism and liberal democracy are historically associated, and this should give the retrievalist pause for thought.

On a strong economic deterministic view, capitalism was the originating cause of liberal-democratic theories and institutions, and on a weaker view it was a partial cause. On either view, and on a yet weaker one in which liberal democracy and capitalism were effects of a common cause, a case can be made that capitalists found ways to make use of liberal-democratic attitudes and practices to serve their ends. It will not suffice for the would-be retrievalist to grant one of these possibilities but to maintain this has nothing to do with whether liberal democracy is unavoidably capitalist serving today. An historically originating connection between two things is not conclusive evidence of continuing connection, but it is *some* evidence. Also, it is claimed that one requirement for liberal democracy to serve capitalism is that people be deluded about its class nature, so the retrievalist must contemplate the possibility that he or she is thus deluded.

These observations must be tempered to note that appeal to the genetic fallacy is not without any force at all. The antiretrievalist also has a burden to show that a one-time historical association between capitalism and liberal democracy in which the latter serves the former cannot change in character. There is an inverse relation between the force of antiretrievalist arguments denying such a change and the plausibility of hypotheses about the original association. If capitalism is thought of as an impersonal and all-encompassing organism that destroys or incorporates anything it encounters, it will be hard to sustain the retrievalist case. It will also be hard to sustain on an alternative view in which capitalism is personalized and liberal democracy is seen as a deliberate and concerted conspiracy on the part of powerful capitalists. Few socialist theorists endorse either of these simplistic views. Like Marx and Engels (so it seems to me), most socialists view social systems as having *aspects* of organic 'totality,' but also as containing contradictory features that work counter to the stability of a system and as offering opportunities for individuals to make significant differences in support or in opposition to it. Assuming the superiority of some such modified theory, the historically based

157

antiretrievalist view is weaker than on either the capitalism-as-organism or a capitalism-as-plot viewpoint.

### THE 'FIT' WITH CAPITALISM.

Assuming a weaker historical thesis, then, the retrievalist might grant that there is a fit between capitalist needs and liberal-democratic values and institutions. This means that while it is not necessary for the survival of capitalism, liberal democracy facilitates meeting requirements for capitalism to be ongoing and secure. The requirements in question have been well treated by socialist theorists. They are: an antitraditionalist political culture; a relatively free labour market; and a facility for settling intra-capitalist disputes without weakening the entire class. Political authority on the liberal-democratic view is not based on tradition. Effective enforcement of legally formal equality and freedoms allows capitalists to rent labour power in a way that gives them (nearly) complete say over how it is used during the hours of the day when it is required and for the period of time it is profitable to keep someone employed, but with no responsibilities after work hours or when workers are unemployed. Favoured liberal-democratic political institutions, such as parliamentary-democratic ones, provide forums for representatives of different capitalist interests peacefully to negotiate, and the rule of law (for example, regarding contracts) also helps to limit hypercompetition.

What follows from these considerations is that liberal democracy facilitates capitalism. What does not follow is that only someone who values capitalism can value liberal democracy. A socialist can consistently hold that in general it is a good thing to free political authority from traditional rule, to prohibit legally sanctioned forced labour, and to facilitate peaceful resolution of conflict. To value these things is not also to value that capitalism has replaced traditional authority with moneyed authority and legally forced labour with economically forced labour, or that parliamentary forms and the rule of law work largely to capitalist advantage. Not all liberal democrats are procapitalists. Many are distressed that capitalism limits and subverts their favoured values, and they may regret what they view as an accident of history that this economic system has become associated with liberal democracy. Some retrievalists might share this lament, but there is a more realistic perspective.

This is to take stock of an existing situation where capitalism and its requirements are still in place and ask what possibilities exist in this environment to develop liberal democracy's positive potentials. From this point of view the very requirements of capitalism become things that those favouring the values of liberal democracy can make use of to weaken capitalism itself. The importance for democratic progress of the challenge to traditional authority has already been discussed, and if earlier arguments that democracy is like a spiral subject to laws of impetus and that capitalism severely limits it are sound, this should have anticapitalist consequences. Successful pressure by some unions to achieve legislation regulating working conditions and grounds for dismissal shows that the notion of a free labour market can also be construed in the interests of workers.

Procapitalist legislators are in a perpetual bind in trying to provide forums and extend rights to capitalists while denying them to others. That they often succeed is undeniable, but that they sometimes fail is evidence that these institutions are also double-edged swords. Capitalists are also in a bind in their efforts to contain popular pressure for democracy. The point is made by Maurice Goldring in his critique of the 'Trilateral Commission,' a think tank founded in 1973 by leading U.S. and European capitalists.[38] The report of this group purported to seek ways 'to make democracy more viable in the future,'[39] by limiting what the Commission's members saw as its immediate negative political and economic effects. The argument of Goldring's book, *Democracy: Zero Growth*, is that rather than seeking ways to strengthen democracy, these capitalists (none of whom had shown commitment to democracy in his own factory or bank, his own country, or in the third world) were responding to popular pressure for more of it: 'What exists of democracy today is the result of an enormous, permanent pressure. Just as a dam takes its form from the pressure of water on it, the back of existing [capitalist] power is bent by democratic pressure. When the pressure is strong, this power suffers curvature and calls the corrective exercises it is forced to employ "democracy." '[40]

Goldring's image expresses an approach to the relation between economic systems and democracy that inverts a standard socialist

159

one. For the retrievalist it is possible and desirable to make advances in democracy. Some political institutions and the norms appropriate to them represent at least potential advances. Thus possibilities offered by the cultural, demographic, geographic, technological, and economic conditions within which one finds oneself must be understood and developed or, in the case of constraints, removed or gotten around. The challenge to retrievalism based on historical associations of capitalism and liberal democracy gains what plausibility it has when an alternate viewpoint is adopted wherein political values and structures are seen as nothing but more or less adequate media for the promotion of economic class objectives.

## CLASS-RELATIVIZED VALUES

This is the point of view taken by Milton Fisk. He weds an historically and sociologically based theory pairing political values and class interests to a version of ethical relativism. Thus Fisk notes how liberal values such as toleration for others' views is appropriately valued both by capitalists who can restrict it and by members of oppressed groups when they need to propagate their views. However, he does not conclude that therefore unrestricted toleration is justified any more than is any other norm, because '[t]he liberal view of human nature reflects the tendency of a privileged minority to stabilize a social order in which its privileges are institutionalized. Similarly, the revolutionary view of human nature reflects the tendency of the lower classes to struggle to gain more control. These two conceptions belong to part of a historical antithesis. Neither can claim to be the basis of a system of right that is valid [across social classes].'[41] Unlike many antiretrievalists Fisk gives detailed arguments for his conclusions, full justice to which could not be done here. However, his approach is representative of class relativism, and examination of the following three problems common to all such approaches will help to defend the retrievalist position.

*Values of Group Members.* First, the position is in danger of being either self-refuting or without force. Central to it are the views that members of an oppressor class have different moral obligations than do members of an oppressed class and that it is in the interests of the oppressor class to promote a universalistic morality, while it is in the interests of the oppressed class to shun this.[42] Fisk gives reasons why an oppressed class should sometimes endorse and sometimes oppose such things as unlimited free speech, depending on when this serves its interests.[43] But it is hard to see why it would not also be in an oppressed class' interests that the precept, 'do whatever is in the interests of the oppressed class,' be universally believed both by its own members and by people from other groups. (It was, after all, largely because Frederick Engels, a capitalist, believed treatment of workers by fellow members of his class was immoral that he switched allegiance.[44])

If it is in an oppressed group's interests that the precept be universally believed, one wants to ask whether a member of that group should also believe in the precept's universality. If so, then a general morality is justified on relativistic grounds. If not, then the force of a deliberately relativized morality is called into question. What kind of motivation or sense of group unity could be provided by a belief of the form: 'I ought to do X in order to further the interests of my group; though persons not in my group have no such obligation'? This seems to mean no more than: 'I should do X because it is in my interests to do so insofar as these interests are linked to the fate of my group.' One might respond that at least being reminded that somebody is a member of an oppressed group is important due to the confusions some have about where their true interests lie. But this raises a second problem.

*Primary Groups.* To know how to act on a group-relativized ethics, one must identify his or her 'primary group' and its proper interests. The question of how group interests are identified is itself problematic, as the discussion of Chapter Ten will show, but so is the problem of identifying one's group. Fisk recognizes a difficulty here when simultaneous membership in a variety of conflicting groups makes it impossible to identify that group whose interests should serve as one's moral guide.[45] He holds that when somebody is a member of several *oppressed* groups (workers, women, racial minorities, and so on) there is no problem since 'in view of the coherence of interests between lower classes and oppressed groups, lower class obligations will become the obligations

161

of oppressed groups' and vice versa.[46] Left out is at least one group, the 'intellectuals of the ruling class,' who are such that their 'position does not allow them to have a valid and consistent ethics.'[47]

These views make a workable system of morality most precarious. On the face of it there are sometimes genuine conflicts of interest between oppressed groups, for instance, when women and nonwhite workers press for affirmative action and unions resist this to protect seniority. To say that in this circumstance people in one of the groups have misread their proper interests verges on begging the question. But even if this is avoided, there is still the difficulty that a person who is a member of two or more groups, who *believes* there is conflict, and who adheres to Fisk's view should also believe himself or herself to be unbound by any morality not only in respect of a specific conflict but generally. Regarding intellectuals, the force of the phrase 'of the ruling class' is not clear. Identifying with the ruling class and producing ideology for it (the traits Fisk mentions) cannot declass intellectuals any more than they could workers who identify with management. On this class-relativized ethics many or all of those in 'institutions of higher education, public relations offices, the bar, and the media,'[48] do not have a sufficiently well-defined group interest and are therefore literally beyond good and evil.

*Human Morality.*   The third problem with class relativism lies in denying one the ability to urge that interests of some groups *ought* to be furthered and those of others ought not to be. Anyone who knows Milton Fisk knows that it is by no means a matter of moral indifference to him whether there is a world with class oppression, sexism, racism, and war or a world without these things, and I'll wager this is true of any other socialist. Such socialists must also want members of oppressed groups to act in accord with what Fisk describes as their group interests and will welcome any class 'traitors,' like Engels, from the other side. Why deny oneself moral arguments to justify desired conduct of these sorts?

One possible response is to maintain that (nonrelativized) moral arguments are unnecessary, because how people will act is already determined by their class positions. Alternately, it could be urged that oppressive classes profit more from a general ethic favouring transgroup claims than does any oppressed group. The first response supposes the power-political or fatalistic views already criticized. The second response is the one Fisk gives. One problem with it is that capitalism can also profit from widespread belief in relativistic doctrines. For example, the popularly held view that morality is always just a rationalization of self-interest breeds a cynicism that inhibits political involvement, and it feeds a procapitalist possessive individualist culture.[49]

Another problem is that, while denying the socialist an argument that capitalism is out of accord with a general human morality, a class-relativized ethical theory is not needed to counter mystifying claims about universal morality. A better way is to grant transclass generality and charge the procapitalist with hypocrisy. Thus one can agree that freedom of speech should be allowed anyone, but point out the various ways this freedom is denied people when one needs money to be heard and when speaking out jeopardizes one's job. Nor is class relativization needed to justify denying people the ability to take unfair advantage of liberal-democratic rights. On most ethical theories one can favour general moral norms while granting that at least some of them admit of exception in the way that freedom of speech can be endorsed while prohibiting libel or giving false alarms. A class-relativized morality will thus be close in its concrete prescriptions to a nonrelativized one.

CAPITALISM AND HUMAN MORALITY

Why might a class relativist nonetheless reject (exception-admitting) general norms? It might be urged that addressing the question of whether procapitalists' uses of rights is justified on a case-by-case basis gives too much legitimacy to their position, glossing over irreconcilable hostility to the interests of the majority. Or it could be argued that depending on one's way of justifying exceptions to general norms, the procapitalist exploitation of rights will probably escape being prohibited. The point might be made that what is wrong with capitalism is its very continuing existence, that considered globally, capitalism itself is like shouting 'fire' in a movie house. However, since it will be very hard to establish the connection between this or that capitalist use of liberal-democratic rights and the system's continued existence, the blanket denial afforded by class relativism is needed. These are mainly practical considerations, which a retrievalist can grant while maintaining that a transition to socialism is possible in a political environment where procapitalists will be able to continue to exercise liberal-democratic rights provided their ability to monopolize this privilege can be curtailed.

To strengthen the projected antiretrievalist position, it would have to be linked with a power-political orientation where norms are rejected or adopted just as they further pregiven political ends. In addition to considerations already advanced against this orientation, it is questionable how, even on the power-political view, socialism is furthered by espousing relativized morality. Unless a large proportion of the population can be persuaded to agree, capitalists, armed with privileged access to media and educational institutions and advancing liberal-democratic values as universal, will be in a very good position to convey the opinion that socialists are power-hungry amoralists. If, conversely, socialists are capable of persuading people to be group-based ethical relativists, they are surely also capable of persuading them that procapitalists are hypocritical violators of generally applicable norms.

It is worth noting that Fisk, himself, admits general humanistic values. He says that when he encounters an anonymous victim of a car accident or plays baseball with a stranger, he has moral obligations to them no matter what their class, since he has entered a 'gap' in his 'class existence,' which 'provides a foretaste of life apart from the conflict resulting from the relations of domination within class society.'[50] This foretaste is of life in a projected classless society where there is 'a universal human nature' which can ground a morality relative to the one group of human beings.[51] If there can be a morality for any human, and if it can be operative while there is still class oppression, then (even if it is described in terms of 'gaps') there can be general humanistic values, and socialists need not be put off by liberal-democratic normativism.

### iv. Liberal-democratic Limitations

Defending liberal democracy against antiretrievalist charges does not commit the (nonpuritanical) retrievalist to full acceptance of it. Socialist critics of liberal democracy have found negative things to say about all aspects of its theory and practice. Just as liberal democrats approach consensus on only some positions, so there is only partial convergence among critics. Nonetheless, there is consensus on at least two major clusters of criticisms: those challenging the uncritical acceptance of the existing preferences of a population and those charging liberal democracy with failure to account for the systematic roots of oppression.

*Unquestioned Values.* The first sort of criticism attacks that version of individualism wherein society accommodates given individual preferences. Citing the passage earlier quoted from Dworkin, William Connolly argues that a political theory with this orientation will tend to accept people's existing values rather than challenge them.[52] Macpherson supplements a negative concept of liberty with a positive one whereby to be free people must be able to develop their human potentials.[53] And like many other socialists Fisk notes the way that people's preferences can be manipulated.[54]

Also in this category is Barber's charge that liberal-democratic society is nothing but a 'multilateral bargaining association,' where people with fixed interests compete.[55] Or there is Dorval Brunelle's criticism that 'one may characterize liberal democracy as being that [political system] where social relations are not called into question but where, on the contrary, the system is sufficiently flexible to integrate the permanent individual contestations of the woman, the black, the ecologist, the militant, without in normal times affecting the equilibrium of the social order. In such circumstances, democracy is no less or more than the legal "price" to pay to guarantee a minimum social peace.'[56] Brunelle's objection is not to liberal-democratic pluralism per se but to a social structure that assumes antagonism and does not encourage challenging antagonistic values with an eye to changing them.

*Structured Oppression.* Fisk also criticizes liberal-democratic pluralism, but for the different reason that in a capitalist society some 'groups,' the capitalists, have disproportionate power.[57] This is one species of the argument that liberal democrats attend to the surface of society and ignore the structural determinants of people's values and the social fields within which conflicts take place in ways biased for or against certain social agents. The criticism is often levelled against the mainstream liberal-democratic emphasis on equality of opportunity, as, for example, Zillah Eisenstein's charge that Harriet Taylor and J.S. Mill 'most often adopt the ideology of liberal individualism in that they work within an exclusionary framework which assumes an equality of opportunity where economic class inequalities in actuality exist. [They] view the individual as a finite being, separate and apart from society, a property unto itself, with the rights of control over itself. This notion of liberal individualism is structured tightly in relation to the values of the bourgeois market; the individual owning him/herself.'[58]

Eisenstein argues that opportunities can never be equal as long as capitalist markets and patriarchal social structures remain in place. This same point is made against a liberal-democratic trust in the rule of law. In a society where economic power imbalances are entrenched, some can get around the law, and to the large extent that the judiciary is integrated into structures perpetuating this imbalance, laws are interpreted to serve capitalist interests.[59] In this case, as in the case of equality of opportunity and pluralism, the entrenching structures are not just economic and political but also cultural, because people come to think of themselves in a narrowly 'juridic' way compatible with being interchangable wage workers, and to regard themselves as equal, forgetting that this is only equality before the law, and biased laws at that.

This point has been made by many Marxists, beginning with Marx, when he treated what he saw as a deceptive and pernicious demarcation of the public and the private realm. He argued that whereas public life could and should be a locus of self-fulfilment where a community of people cooperatively sets and pursues joint goals, this realm had instead become a main cause of alienation where people are abstractly regarded as little more than legally defined citizens, where affairs of state are determined by moneyed interests hidden from view and protected in the privacy of civil society, and where people are expected to develop their potentials in the mutual isolation of this very, capitalist-dominated, realm.[60] Applications of this critique to liberal democracy by present-day socialists are well-known, and typical liberal-democratic political practice, confined as it is to limited and piecemeal measures that leave oppressive social and political structures largely unchanged, should persuade the socialist that 'puritanical' retrieval of liberal democracy is inconsistent with socialist goals.

166

This poses the question of whether socialist theory and practice can still 'retrieve' liberal democracy or whether, as Levine concludes, 'a different kind of theory altogether' is needed.[61] If retrieval is to succeed, it must be by supersession.

# 8 Superseded Liberal Democracy

THOUGH HE DOES NOT employ the term, Macpherson's approach is of the supersessionist variety, where this is a matter of subtraction. He divides liberal democracy into its possessive individualist and its humanistic, developmental aspects, arguing in favour of shedding the former. The main problem confronting this or any other attempt at supersession by subtraction is to maintain continuity with liberal democracy.

## i. 'Supersession'

If political perspectives are viewed on an organic model, where parts mutually support one another, subtracting a component can so alter the integrity of the whole as to constitute radical departure. The same problem would confront supersession by adding new elements to a perspective, unless the addition can be justified from within the perspective itself. The retrievalist must conclude that a concept other than subtraction or simple addition is required.

### EXTENSION

A statement by Macpherson of his developmental powers thesis suggests one method, which might be called 'supersession by extension':

> The powers which liberal-democratic society actually and necessarily maximize are different from the powers it claims to maximize, and the maximization it achieves is inconsistent with the maximization that is claimed. The powers which it claims to maximize are every man's potential of using and developing his human capacities; the powers it does maximize are some men's

168

means of obtaining gratifications by acquiring some of the powers of other men as a continued net transfer.[1]

This is close to puritanical retrievalism, where a liberal-democratic concept is taken at face value. It is a supersession since Macpherson acknowledges obstacles in the way of the liberal democrat's acting on the concept (such as commitment to a capitalist market). He insists that the socialist, unencumbered by such obstacles, should be a *consistent* liberal democrat.

Another example is Macpherson's prescription for extending the liberal-democratic concept of 'property' when he argues that it should be redefined to include a 'right not to be excluded from the use or benefit of the accumulated productive resources of the whole society.' One ground for advancing this as an extension and not as a new concept is that by the mid-20th century, welfare rights such as old age pensions were already accepted within the liberal-democratic tradition.[2] Continuity in the case of the developmental powers argument is secured by demanding consistency of the liberal democrat. It is secured in the property example by taking note of prefiguring practices of liberal democrats. An example of a liberal-democratic value that can be superseded by extension either by demanding consistency or by noting practice that already starts to go beyond it is substantive equality of opportunity, which (according to Chapter Five's arguments) is superseded by extension to equality of benefits and burdens.

### REORIENTATION

To supersession by extension may be added supersession by 'reorientation.' To supersede something by reorientation is to retain its elements, but to place them in a context that changes one's way of acting on them. Though he did not conceive of it in terms of supersession, Felix Oppenheim's treatment of democracy and liberal rights is a good example. Oppenheim argues that rights such as freedom of speech can be justified as conditions required for democracy to be secure. This approach affords a way to avoid piecemealism in making social policies or, worse, the stymied inactivity that can result from having to make trade-offs among unweighted values.

*Value Conflicts.* Instead of taking freedom, equality, and democracy as norms always in irreconcilable conflict without criteria for adjudication, the supersessionist accords democracy prescriptive pride of place. When trade-offs must be made the retrievalist prescribes appeal to a criterion of progress in democracy. It is important to be clear about what can and cannot be accomplished by such a method. If appeal to this standard could eliminate any and all tensions between freedom and equality it would have squared the circle on a liberal-democratic perspective, and retrievalist continuity would likely be lost.[3] But this is not required for supersession by reorientation.

It should be recalled that the 'mixed mode' ideal democracy toward which progress is made includes room for negotiation when there is conflict. Many conflicts suppose different stands over the relative weight allotted in a specified circumstance to freedom and to equality, or over the location of the line between the public and the private, or about when representation is to be preferred to direct participation. Insisting that, ideally, negotiation should always be an option, is thus a retrievalist extension of the hypothesized liberal-democratic principle that whatever choice is made in adjudicating conflict, the direction of future trade-offs among conflicting values should not be biased.

But even if only the consensus dimension of perfect democracy were used as a standard, the retrievalist would still not be committed to believing that value conflicts will sometime cease to exist. One approaches perfect democracy only asymptotically. This means that as more democracy is attained, the severity and frequency of value conflicts can be expected to diminish, but not to be eliminated. Progress in democracy should not be seen as an overriding super value, but as a means for ameliorating value conflicts. The point will be further illustrated by reference to representative democracy and the public/private distinction.

*Representative Democracy.* Contrary to those who counterpose representative to participatory democracy, the retrievalist sees a place for representative democracy in the project of expanding democracy. The typical liberal democrat regards representative structures as simultaneously mechanisms for the expression of public will and as a hedge against the 'tyranny of the majority' and public inexpertise. On the retrievalist view, in which democracy is the pivot of reorientation, representative democracy is to be valued for serving the first of these functions, while the hedging functions will be regarded as usually inadequate responses to real problems. Though not denying that relatively undemocratic representation sometimes protects minority rights or facilitates the use of special expertise, the retrievalist will favour extension of democracy (the 'democratic fix') to address these problems.

*Public and Private.*   While some socialist theorists reject the notion that there should be any demarcation between the public and the private, others agree with Zillah Eisenstein that the problem is not the distinction itself but its location and the way people are constrained in both realms.[4] Her view accords with a retrievalist prescription that these matters be subject to democratic control. Public decisions about what should be areas of private decisions in one way gives the edge to the 'public,' but it also offers a nonarbitrary means for people to escape an oppressive private realm (for example, to be abused in their family without recourse). Democratization of this distinction also makes a 'private' realm more secure, since its privacy would have public support.

The puritanical liberal democrat might argue that this is not supersession of the public/private distinction, but obliteration of the private realm. In meeting this charge, retrievalists might appeal to the notion of a 'public realm' or 'sphere' as employed by Hannah Arendt and developed, among others, by Habermas and Lefort.[5] For instance, Habermas argues that essential to a liberal, postfeudal society was the creation of this sphere, which 'mediates between society and state,' access to which 'is guaranteed to all citizens,' and in which 'something approaching public opinion can be formed.' Habermas does not prescribe the creation of such a sphere as a modification of liberal democracy, but laments its loss through degeneration into a field occupied by violently competing individual interests.[6] Though one might question the extent to which a public sphere existed in early postfeudal periods, it is plausible that at least the idea and positive evaluation of such a realm is implicit in liberal-democratic theory.

This notion of a public sphere provides a way simultaneously to go beyond and to maintain contact with practices associated with the public/private distinction. The sphere in question is more public than private, since nobody may be excluded from it, but it is more private than the state in being a noncoercive locus for debate over what should be public or private. The effect of a

171

retrievalist insistence that public spheres be maintained is not that the private realm be obliterated, but that, as Iris Young puts it, 'no social institutions or practices should be excluded a priori as being the proper subject for public discussion and expression.'[7]

## ii. The Rule of Law

In the remainder of this chapter socialist retrieval – by both extension and reorientation – will be further illustrated by more detailed examination of some key elements of liberal democracy, taking up first the rule of law. In its core meaning 'the rule of law' refers to existence of laws (or less formal rules, as in voluntary organizations) applied and enforced in a nondiscriminatory way to everyone falling within their purview.[8] Some advocate strict obedience to any law that has been the product of due process, but this is a narrower, conservative conception of the rule of law than that typically endorsed by liberal democrats. For them the rule of law is justified to avoid discrimination. Thus the liberal democrat may not only object to violation of the 'letter' of the rule of law, when laws are differentially enforced (the slum dwelling thief is sent to prison, the white collar thief is given a stern lecture), but also to violation of its 'spirit,' when a law is uniformly enforced but discriminatory in its content (all blacks shall sit at the back of the bus).

The main defence of the rule of law in this core sense is that universal laws apply alike to ordinary citizens and to people in positions of power, thus inhibiting abuse of this power. That in capitalist societies important laws are skewed or limited to favour capitalists and that laws which should inhibit abuse of moneyed or political power are regularly ignored are not by themselves arguments against socialist retrieval of the rule of law. They may also be taken as grounds for supersession by extension. That is, socialists can argue that if there are to be laws guaranteeing, for example, access to educational facilities, there should also be laws guaranteeing access to uniformly high quality education and that laws not be selectively enforced. Some socialist critics of the rule of law are unimpressed with such arguments.

The strongest challenge is that of Lenin: 'The revolutionary dictatorship of the proletariat is rule won and maintained by the use of violence by the proletariat against the bourgeoisie, rule that is unrestricted by any laws.'[9] This passage appears in Lenin's polemic with Kautsky, where he simultaneously charges Kautsky with failing to see that democracy is class relative and opportunistically holding that the bourgeois state apparatus can be carried over into socialism intact. One does not need to endorse Kautsky's also problematic views[10] to take issue with Lenin's alternatives. His comments might be analysed into a variety of claims. One might ask a) whether socialists should press for certain sorts of laws in a capitalist society or b) what laws, if any, should be promulgated in a socialist society. One group of antiretrievalist arguments questions whether there can or should be any continuity between these two enterprises. A second objection challenges the value to socialists of championing the rule of law at all, whether in a socialist or in a capitalist environment. These approaches will be examined in turn.

### CONTINUITY

On the first approach the value of the rule of law is not questioned, but continuity between laws in a socialist and in a capitalist society is denied. This is the way some comments of Marx that bear superficial similarities to the passage from Lenin should be interpreted, for instance: 'After successfully carrying out a revolution one can hang one's opponents, but one cannot convict them. They can be put out of the way as defeated enemies, but they cannot be arraigned as criminals. After a revolution or counterrevolution has been consummated the annulled laws cannot be used against the *defenders* of these laws.'[11]

Marx was referring to capitalism and feudalism, not to socialism and capitalism, but his point could be generalized to insist on the essential dissimilarities of pre- and postrevolutionary laws. In one respect, this is undoubtedly the case; if socialism is structured to favour equality and capitalism is not, then the laws must differ. To go beyond asserting what the retrievalist can agree with, the antiretrievalist argument may be buttressed in one or more of three ways: by an appeal to theoretical relativism; by challenging continuity with respect to rights; or by appeal to the requirements of revolutionary practice.

*Legal Relativism.* Most of the arguments against the relativization of morality apply to any theory of legal relativism. Moreover, laws

173

do not determine norms but enforce behaviour in accord with them, and the retrievalist will claim that it is possible in a capitalist society at least sometimes to force through laws in accord with norms favoured by socialists. This puts antisocialists in the position of having to break or get around such laws – a situation more favourable to the socialist than if there are no such constraints. To assume on abstract left-wing principle that no such laws can be forced through or that they will make no difference is a species of what one socialist lawyer aptly calls 'infantile antilegalism.'[12]

*Rights.*   Since the most important sorts of laws presently under consideration are typically justified by appeal to rights, the anti-retrievalist might argue either (as Marx is alleged to have done regarding communism) that socialism is 'beyond rights,' or that the rights endorsed by capitalists and by socialists differ not just in content but in form, capitalists favouring individual rights, socialists collective ones. To take the first tack is to maintain that whatever functions law in socialist society serves, it is not to defend rights. William McBride argues that Marx and Engels were committed to the notion of a role in socialism for justice (defined by reference to rights).[13] This would make their views compatible with those of retrievalists, who must deny that protection of rights is unnecessary in a socialist society.

The summary of Allen Buchanan's convincing case in this regard is worth paraphrasing. He concludes that rights in socialism are required:

1. as constraints on democratic procedures to ensure minority rights and equal participation;
2. as constraints on paternalism;
3. as constraints on what may be done to maximize welfare or some similar good;
4. as constraints on the use of coercion in provision of public goods; and
5. to specify the extent and limits of sacrifices for future generations.[14]

One might avoid these conclusions by defining 'socialism' to refer to a society sufficiently harmonious that coercive sanctions to enforce rights are never necessary. However, we would then entertain a distant possibility which, if ever attained, would not suddenly appear full-blown from a society that was capitalist the day before. Rather, transitional institutions will be required where it is hard to envisage the absence of need for enforced rights for the reasons Buchanan gives.

Against this consideration Michael Sandel argues that systems of rights encourage people to regard conflict as inevitable, thereby impeding development of harmonious, consensual society.[15] No doubt there is some truth in such an objection, but retrievalists have available to them several lines of response. One, of course, is to question alternatives to rights in a world far short of harmony. Even if a group possessed of a consensual counterculture were able to effect a social transformation after which everyone else is educated to this culture, there would be the problem of whether to preserve rights prior to such an enormous project and prior to complete education of everyone else. Indeed, one might question whether a completely consensual society is either possible or even desirable.[16]

In Chapter Three 'mixed mode perfect democracy,' which allowed for both regulating conflict and promoting harmony, was regarded the goal of the democrat precisely to minimize the self-reinforcing dynamic that worries Sandel, just as it worries those on the other side who fear an imposed consensual ethic. In a perfect democracy coercive sanctions would not be required, since people would voluntarily accept compromise to maintain means of continuing negotiation and efforts to reach consensus; however, one could still talk of rights as things people recognize as justified constraints that ought to govern their behaviour to these ends. At least 1) and 4) in Buchanan's list would be required to protect the continuing ability to negotiate; whereas 2), 3), and perhaps 5) would be needed as constraints on what negotiated outcomes might be in the interests of keeping open future efforts to build consensus.

*Group Rights.*   Buchanan's list admits of rights being interpreted either as individual rights or group rights or both. For example, the notion of protection of a minority can be interpreted to mean either protection of individuals who happen to be in a minority on any one issue or protection of groups who are permanently in a minority of a population. Thus the antiretrievalist might grant there are rights in both capitalist and socialist societies, but claim that their natures are different – individual and group. It is no accident that socialists champion laws supporting group rights and note the relative absence of them in capitalist societies.

One socialist, Stuart Rush, defines 'group' or 'collective rights' disjunctively either as 'those rights which accrue to individuals because of their placement or membership in an identifiable group.... [or as] rights which accrue to groups as groups.'[17] Rush gives as an example of the first, working-class rights such as to employment and of the second, the rights of native people to jurisdiction over aboriginal lands. Referring to the Canadian Constitution's 'Charter of Rights,' he notes the conspicuous absence of either kind in procapitalist legal systems. However, Rush does not argue that the only value for socialists in raising the question of collective rights is to project an alternative for socialist society, and he lists several collective rights that could have found their way into the Canadian Constitution, albeit with great effort on the part of the left.[18] If such collective rights can find even minimum representation in the legal systems of capitalist societies (legislation guaranteeing old age pensions or affirmative action are examples), the retrievalist can gain a toehold and argue for supersession by extension.

Mainstream liberal democrats are concerned that laws defending group rights are themselves discriminatory when they lead to the disadvantage of some individuals just in virtue of their not being in a group protected by such a law. However, the justification of such legislation is that *extralegal* discrimination against individuals of protected groups already exists and is sufficiently entrenched that only the active promotion of group rights will help dismantle discriminatory social structures. The libertarian position, limited as it is to formal equality of opportunity, cannot be retrieved by socialists, but liberal democracy is here interpreted as going beyond this to defend some measure of substantive equality of opportunity. Thus conceived, the consistent liberal democrat ought to favour legal advancement of group rights insofar as this attacks systemic impediments to such equality.

The point is usually debated with reference to preferential hiring, which is said to constitute 'reverse discrimination' against members of nontargeted groups, but the same considerations apply in the case of any legally supported group right. Provision of child care is one way that goes beyond merely formal prohibition of discrimination in hiring practices to make it possible for women to get out of a gender ghetto. Therefore the consistent liberal democrat ought to entertain as legitimate the legal enforcement of a right to affordable, quality child care. However, this will put a tax on the public purse and increase the number of women on the job market – both measures which, like preferential hiring, will probably disadvantage some who would not be otherwise disadvantaged.[19] (Recently when debating some colleagues about preferential hiring I was struck by a discrepancy between their amenability to some far-reaching measures to make opportunities more than just formally equal and their strong hostility to preferential hiring. I wondered whether the fact that each of them was an able bodied, white, middle class male could have had something to do with this.)

The antiretrievalist might argue that such extensions result in something too far from a liberal-democratic individualist picture of the social world to be genuine retrieval if it involved belief in irreducible group entities. However, it is not clear that this is the case. Group rights in the first of Rush's characterizations obviously accrue to individuals; perhaps less obviously they also accrue to individuals in the second. What makes the right of native peoples to national self-determination a *group* right is not that it belongs to some mysterious superindividual entity, but that, like the right to strike, it can only be made use of by individuals acting in concert with other individuals of a specified group.[20]

It could be urged that one cannot identify groups at all without supposing a holistic social ontology, but it has already been argued that there is no convergence of liberal-democratic opinion on such ontological matters. If there were, perhaps the retrievalist would have to defend an individualist, 'reductionist' ontology. However, there are reasons to think that one can adopt such an ontology without foregoing the ability to promote social groups.[21] Indeed, many theorists agree with E.P. Thompson (a strong defender of the rule of law) in seeing an individualist social ontology as something it is vital for the democratic socialist to embrace.[22]

*Political Practice.*   A crude argument against continuity is that one cannot expect capitalism to be legislated out of existence. Though retrievalists are sometimes charged with holding the contrary view, few claim that pushing for the right laws alone will effect a socialist transformation of society. The more reasoned retrievalist view is that pressure for passage of laws should be *part of* a democratic-socialist's activities. Also required are: mobilization for the enforcement of laws hypocritically supported by procapitalists or passed against their wishes; organization of movements of people in work places, communities, and schools around issues not directly related to the law; civil disobedience; exposing lies and spreading truths; and so on.

Harry Glasbeek and Michael Mandel raise a legitimate concern for the retrievalist in arguing that socialist attempts to change laws may be counterproductive, since the legal and sociological apparatuses of the courts are loaded against the socialist. Instead of providing useful political forums, they can just drain energy and money.[23] No doubt battling in the bourgeois courts is costly and frustrating. So also is any activity that runs counter to powerful foes, and in any case it is something that cannot easily be avoided; nor should it be avoided. Defending this claim brings us to the second question raised by Lenin about why socialists should endorse the rule of law at all.

### THE LAW AND DEMOCRACY

Here the *purport* of socialist retrieval needs to be questioned, and we return to a basic point of difference between the democratic socialist and the instrumentalist socialist. For the latter, if there is any good reason for engaging in activities relating to the law it is to advance working-class power. Some instrumentalists grant that a few laws favourable to the working class have been forced on an unwilling bourgeoisie, but they will correctly see these as limited in scope and easily circumvented. In any case, the most important criterion in sorting laws is the extent to which they advance the interests of the working class.

The anti-instrumentalist socialist employs a broader criterion and sees any law favourable to the expansion of democracy as worth securing. This not only changes the field of laws to support, but it also gives the democratic socialist a stake in defending the concept in modern political culture of the rule of law itself. It is probably because this idea was a product of major democratic advances that Thompson describes it as an 'unqualified human good,'[24] marking a break with rule by tradition. From this perspective, the frailty of the law noted by many antiretrievalists is good reason not to ignore it, but rather to create a climate of opinion in which people are not cynical and passive when government officials, the rich, police agencies, or the military break the law. This is important not just for inhibiting undemocratic procapitalist measures, but for helping to ensure that government, police, and military officials in a projected socialist society will not be above the law either.

*The Law and Minority Rights.* The democratic socialist will also value the rule of law as a way of protecting minority rights. This was one of the things on Buchanan's list, and its importance for democracy was discussed in earlier chapters. John Ely's work on the rule of law usefully explicates the theory behind this point. In his book, *Democracy and Distrust*,[25] Ely, like Oppenheim, discusses the way that ongoing democracy requires the protection of minority rights, and explicates the liberal-democratic view that laws, being general in scope and interpreted by people who are not mandated to represent specific interests, are well suited to this task. What differentiates Ely's approach from most defences is that he regards the rule of law as a requirement for democracy, not as protection against supposed democratic 'excesses,' and he prescribes that rather than being extrademocratically responsive moulders of political policy, the courts may only intervene politically when this is required to preserve democracy.[26] In this way Ely's approach suggests a supersession of the rule of law by orientation around democracy.

*The Distance of the Law.* Between the instrumentalist and the democratic socialist there may be no room for rapprochement. But some socialists who are prodemocratic yet sceptical about the retrievalist project will surely still have doubts. In my experience, however, these doubts often pertain more to judicial activism than to the rule of law proper and have to do with the unresponsiveness of law to popular needs and issues. Thus Glasbeek and Mandel argue that to promote the rule of law as a way of protecting minority rights today is antimajoritarian and that the abstractness of laws makes them insufficiently sensitive to the context of real politics thus obscuring systematic oppressions and supporting a conservative judicial establishment.[27] These observations are surely on target.

179

Majority rule is hardly sufficiently advanced to pose a democratic threat. If every important aspect of the social environment of any large social unit were determined by the preferences of its majority, all democrats should be celebrating. In a world where this has not been attained, measures that further limit majority rule are suspect. Regarding the context insensitivity of the law, an example verging on the surreal may be found in a recent decision of Canada's Supreme Court against a woman who challenged on the grounds of sex discrimination an act requiring pregnant women to work longer than others to receive unemployment insurance. The presiding judge justified the court's denial arguing that if the act 'treats unemployed pregnant women differently from other unemployed persons, be they male or female, it is, it seems to me, because they are pregnant and not because they are women.'[28] Rich and poor alike are prohibited from sleeping under bridges, and neither pregnant women nor pregnant men are exempted from the act.

The problem for the retrievalist is not just that a conservative judiciary can use the law in undemocratic ways, but that the very abstractness and distance of the law required for it to do its proper job make this possible. This can be seen as a dilemma. If the law is to protect minority rights against a potentially tyrannical majority, then judges must not be directly responsive to the majority, but this gives the antidemocratic judge the freedom required to exercise illegitimate power. Similarly, abuse of the law's abstractness is made possible by the fact that laws must, as Dworkin and other legal theorists have argued, escape discriminatory application for utilitarian reasons.[29]

Socialist supersession of the rule of law by orientation around the project of protecting and expanding democracy suggests that these dilemmas may be approached in the way the 'paradoxes' of democracy were in Chapter Four, as problems amenable to ongoing practical solution. Though most of their arguments are directed against standard liberal-democratic conceptions of the role of the courts, Glasbeek and Mandel, themselves, adopt this point of view. Distinguishing between the 'rule of law' and the 'legalisation of politics,' they maintain: 'The rule of law is a democratic ideal under which the judicial function is impartially to apply the law to the facts of each case. The ideal of the rule of law is most closely approached when laws are specific and leave little room for personal discretion. It is most democratic when there is popular participation in law-making.'[30]

As in the case of many practical problems this prescription involves trade-offs. The more a law is spelled out in detail, the less abstract it is, but the more secured against undemocratic interpretation by the courts. However, it seems arbitrary to deduce from theoretical statements of the problem that there is no space for movement between two extreme and unacceptable positions. Similarly, one need not choose between a situation where judges are completely unresponsive to a population or where they are mandated legislators. A middle position might be one where judges are elected for specified periods of time and recallable between elections only in extraordinary circumstances. This is roughly the situation of *legislators* in parliamentary democracies today, who, the democrat argues, should be much more directly accountable.

### iii. Freedom

The retrievalist approach to freedom is in one respect straightforwardly a case of supersession by extension. The retrievalist can make use of Norman Daniels' criticism of Rawls for this purpose. Rawls, like Berlin, tried to distinguish between freedom and the worth of freedom.[31] Generalizing his formulation, the position is that people are free when they are not deliberately constrained from doing what they want to do at the time they want to do it by the actions of other people. People may be constrained by the existence of institutions, for instance, of private property, or states of affairs like poverty, and it is recognized that these institutions are maintained by human activities, though not usually constructed for the purpose of constraining specified others. When people are constrained in these nondeliberate ways they are said not to suffer unfreedom, but to be in a situation where their freedom is worth less than the freedom of those not thus constrained.

Daniels persuasively argues that someone who values freedom should abandon this distinction and extend the boundaries of what counts as constraints on freedom.[32] The point is also made by D.F.B. Tucker in defence of Macpherson on property: '[F]or reasons which I have never found convincing, liberal theorists are

181

reluctant to count property claims ("trespassers will be prose-cuted") as constituting a violation of the freedom of others. This is the case despite the obvious fact that one person's fence de-marcating his or her property manifestly bars others from entry.[33] Tucker also notes that even in the absence of nondeliberate im-pediments people might be able to act in accord with their wishes, but only at the leave of those who could prevent it. He accordingly wishes to extend the notion of freedom to mark someone's power of action.[34]

This is the position of most socialist theorists. It is summarized by Lawrence Crocker: 'Freedom is not the absence of constraint, but rather the presence of alternatives. Anything that enlarges the set of alternatives open to the individual enlarges freedom.'[35] Freedom is regarded a matter of potential choice. People would be completely free if they could do (or avoid or retain) anything at all should they choose to try. This extends the liberal-democratic perspective by considering nondeliberate conditions and potential choices. Unless it can be shown that these extensions radically change the concept of freedom, this effort at retrieval maintains contact with liberal democracy. For it to be a socialist retrieval, arguments must be given that capitalist structures limit and so-cialist structures expand freedom. Some socialists address this task by noting that one who values *equal* freedom must also value socialism insofar as socialism removes material impediments to equal enjoyment of freedom.[36] An alternative approach is that socialist equality is required to advance democracy (Chapter Six) and that maximizing freedom is best served by democratic prog-ress (Chapter Four). Success of these arguments would complete the retrieval.

### FREEDOM AND SELF-DEVELOPMENT

That is, it would succeed at socialist retrieval of freedom if free-dom of potential choice is strong enough for the socialist. Socialist theorists who emphasize self-development may not find it so. Mac-pherson's treatment of this subject is interestingly ambiguous. He agrees with Berlin's criticism that positive liberty doctrines are used to force people to be free, but he wants to retain a concept of freedom as 'self-development' defined as 'the ability to live in accordance with one's own conscious purposes, to act and decide

182

for oneself rather than to be acted upon and decided for by others.[37] Shortly thereafter he characterizes this kind of freedom as 'virtually the same as what I have called men's developmental powers.'[38] But in discussing this concept, Macpherson had drawn the following contrast: 'It may be allowed that some men (especially as shaped by modern market society) might, given the greatest freedom, wish to be no more than consumers of utilities. But it must be allowed that some do wish to be active exerters and developers and enjoyers of their human capacities.'[39]

On the face of it this generates a contradiction, since someone who chose to consume utilities would be designated unfree in the important sense for Macpherson even if this choice were in accord with his or her own purposes and not 'decided for by others.' These views are not likely results of slips of the pen, but derive from a worry of many other democratic socialists about the way life in a capitalist society can warp people's values and deaden their aspirations. Macpherson responds by marking off a favoured sense of 'freedom' which is incompatible with acting on these values. There are several reasons for avoiding this move, some of which were given in Chapter Four. Macpherson, himself, recognizes the main problem in acknowledging Berlin's point about the pernicious potential of positive freedom concepts. There may be good reasons to inhibit people's acting against development of certain of their capacities, but this should always be seen as a limitation of their freedom. Paternalism should be recognized as such and not allowed to function as an exercise of freedom.

### GOOD AND BAD FREEDOM

Another problem with distinguishing freedom and the worth of freedom is that this strains retrieval by specifying the content of wants in defining 'freedom.' One response to this situation, suggested by Macpherson and advanced by Carol Gould, is to retain two or more different concepts of freedom and argue for their compatibility. Thus Gould holds that 'abstract' freedom of choice, where the content is not specified, should be defended by democrats as a 'necessary condition' for the more important 'concrete' freedom of self-development.[40] It is questionable how compatible these two sorts of freedom are. Abstract freedom is a necessary condition for concrete freedom only in a requirement of the latter that people be able to make choices. However, some choices that people make surely work against their future ability to develop their capacities, hence limiting concrete freedom.

Closer to liberal democracy is Crocker's argument that in terms of life prospects people are free with respect to alternatives open to them should they choose to avail themselves of these alternatives and unfree with respect to blocked alternatives. People who are unable for any reason to do something they choose to do at the time they want to do it are unfree with respect to that choice. A person who willingly does something the effect of which is to close off future alternatives which he or she later wishes were not closed off no doubt makes a mistake, and there may be grounds for paternalism in some such situations. A serious problem with paternalism already discussed is that it sets in motion dynamics that themselves close off options by limiting democracy. But even when paternalistic measures are taken, they can at most be justified by appeal to the need to expand the future alternatives available to people and not as somehow a present exercise of their freedom.

### FREEDOM AND SOCIAL STRUCTURES

Socialists may still object to this characterization because it leaves unspecified the content of preferences and because it does not address the question of whether or how society should be structured in ways that would constrain or facilitate the choices people might realistically make. Both concerns can be taken into account in a retrievalist supersession. The objection of Barber and others that on the liberal-democratic view society is nothing but a 'bargaining association' can be formulated as the claim that society should be viewed as a potentially cooperative venture in which certain alternatives are deliberately and democratically created and others closed or at least severely constrained.[41] The retrievalist can agree with this prescription, thus differing from a mainstream liberal-democratic viewpoint in which deliberate structuring is discouraged.

However, this would still be a supersession (by reorientation around democracy) instead of a full departure. The point was made in Chapter Three that democrats must strive to provide means for negotiation; so what is envisaged is not exclusive homogeneity of viewpoint. The main difference between superseded

184

and nonsuperseded liberal democracy on this score, then, is that for the retrievalist, alternative creating/closing structuring should be *deliberate*. Macpherson echoes the point of all socialists who address the subject in arguing that an unplanned, capitalist market is nonetheless a structure with predictable and pervasive effects regarding the alternatives it opens to some and closes to many.[42] The difference between the socialist, who wants deliberate egalitarian structuring of a society, and the mainstream liberal democrat is not over whether the societies they favour are or are not structured, but over *how* they come to have the structures they do.

### JUDGING INTERESTS

Supersession of the liberal-democratic view that people are the best judges of their own interests is also possible. This view has been strongly objected to by socialist theorists, such as Evan Simpson and Charles Taylor, who think that people's values must be evaluated.[43] The retrievalist can agree and point out to liberal democrats that they, themselves, are committed to this when they criticize people for having intolerant or discriminatory values. In one respect, the retrievalist can also agree with the liberal democrat about not judging interests. While arguing in defence of deliberately structuring society to close off some alternatives, the retrievalist will still favour a proliferation of alternatives. Indeed, a major reason to disfavour the unplanned structuring of capitalist society is that this narrows people's life options. A socialist may regret that with many courses open to them, people sometimes take certain of them or pass over others. However, like the liberal democrat the retrievalist will be optimistic about people making decisions that are not destructive of themselves or others as their options for action become increasingly open.

Marković specifies as required for 'self-determination' that a person be aware of available alternatives and of the sorts of consequences that are likely to follow from taking a course of action,[44] implying that when free choices are made with such knowledge the results will be compatible with what a democratic socialist values – a progressively democratic society in which people develop their various humanistic capacities. Such optimism is not an unreasoned hope. It is based partly on empirical claims about nonaccidental connections between antihumanistic attitudes and counter democratic practices, on the one hand, and beliefs about human nature, including the effects of such practices on one's society and own personality, on the other. Rather than pursuing this important argument, a second justification will be addressed: that the pluralism made possible by a proliferation of options should also be retrieved by socialists.

### iv. Pluralism

For the pluralist, people ought as far as possible to pursue their own goods in their own ways including joining with others to promote shared ends. The mainly U.S. Pluralist movement of the 1950s and '60s came in for strong criticism from theorists of the left for obscuring structural imbalances of power among those designated 'interest groups,' and for helping to entrench these imbalances by prescribing no more than an umpire role for the state, when what was and is needed is a restructuring of society to remove the imbalances.[45] By contrast, Stanislav Erhlich and Branko Horvat prescribe that socialism itself be pluralistic.[46]

The question of pluralist socialism may be the most important one faced by a democratic-socialist theorist. It is one of those pivotal questions where a choice must be made, in this case between a vision of society as 'heterogeneous' or 'homogeneous.' Prescriptions for social institutions and activist practices will differ depending on whether the desired end is a society where people may as far as possible pursue their various goods or one where there is commonality of purpose around shared highest goals. Given that one cannot have it both ways, I do not see any other choice for the democratic socialist than pluralism. In addition to being subject to the charge of communitarian mind control often levelled by antisocialists, the alternative surely requires strong and persistent paternalism, the antidemocratic effects of which have already been touched on and will be treated again in Chapter Ten. Drawing on the work of theorists who share this conviction, this chapter concludes by treating some problems facing the socialist supersession of liberal-democratic pluralism.

The difficulty is to reconcile the egalitarian goal-directedness of socialism with the pluralist prescription that society accommodate people with a wide variety of goals. Thus Robert Dahl (whose evolution from mainstream liberal-democratic pluralism two decades ago to what seems a socialist pluralism today may be one indication of the feasibility of the retrievalist project) describes this as the central tension of contemporary democratic politics in his *Dilemmas of Pluralist Democracy*.[47] A similar point is made by Bob Jessop who describes as a major task of the democratic socialist to find ways to promote the creation of 'a unified people' while protecting 'individual autonomy.'[48]

Insofar as the problem here is that deliberate structuring of a society is thought incompatible with autonomy, the retrievalist can employ arguments used above in connection with freedom. At one point Dahl interprets the problem as specific to the structured promotion of equality, which he identifies with uniformity.[49] However, if, in accord with the definitions of Chapter Five, socialism aims to promote equality of benefits and burdens subjectively interpreted, this will not yield uniformity and in fact would allow people to pursue goals that they are now prohibited from pursuing due to lack of material means.

### SHARED VALUES

The retrievalist's problem is the most difficult insofar as socialist structures, if they are to be democratically supported, must be guided by goals broadly *shared* by members of a society. Elizabeth Rapaport states the difficulty in her examination of Rawls's attempt to give collective spirit to classic liberal individualism. The potential merit she sees in Rawls's theory is to achieve an *'Aufgehebung* of the contradiction between individualism and vicious collectivism,'[50] but she is sceptical about anyone's succeeding:

> There is reason to suspect an incompatibility between Rawls' ideal of pluralistic communitarianism and the value of autonomy in the formulation of a life plan. Once we conceive lives as centering around voluntarily undertaken communitarian activities, the idea of autonomous life planning – (in the traditional liberal manner where each selects his own personal goals) – altogether loses its applicability. Common ends and activities can only be the result of a common plan. The value of autonomy, if 'autonomy' is to retain any meaning, must be transformed into the value of participation in the formulation of a common plan for social unions. . . . Not to participate in common planning is to

187

lose an effective say altogether. But such participation means that no one can operate in terms of radical, individual autonomy.[51]

One attempt at the supersession of pluralism is to urge that whatever differing values people may have, they should also have overriding, communitarian values. This might mean that each takes an overriding interest in the interests of others being advanced[52] and/or that democratic participation in communal projects be a prime and uniting value.[53] Rapaport questions the feasibility of these projects and suspects we may only have the choice between unsuperseded liberal individualism or participatory communitarianism – crudely between Hobbes and Rousseau, or what she describes as 'classical individualism' and 'a holistic view of community.'

## MEANS AND INSTRUMENTS

The first step in approaching this problem is to regard expanding democracy as a means and not an end. If people can come to see the perfection of means for making shared decisions in ways that make progress toward complete freedom as important for the furthering of their own, unique goals rather than as an end in itself for which their goals ought to be sacrificed, then communitarianism will be reconciled with individual autonomy as means to end. This is the way that classic Pluralism defended representative government, a balance of powers, protection of minority rights, and the rule of law, but the project was not without limitations.

Its main obstacle is to avoid the 'instrumentalist' approach to democracy criticized by democratic socialists. The problem is analogous to one of contract theory regarded as pertaining to actual mechanisms of political practice (as opposed to an intellectual device to yield prescriptions), since there is nothing to prevent self-interested people from tearing up a contract whenever it is in their power and interests to do so. One who enters a democratic or any other arrangement to further interests other than to preserve that arrangement will be prepared to abandon or try to subvert democracy when it is thought expedient. Indeed, this is what happened in the case of the Philippines and South Korea whose constitutions were drawn up after World War II along

Pluralist lines and with advice from U.S. Pluralists only shortly thereafter to become totalitarian states (again with U.S. help). And it was a main charge of C. Wright Mills and William Domhoff that formal pluralism in the United States itself is systematically subverted by capitalist interests.[54]

How might the subversion of democracy by special interests be avoided? The retrievalist cannot insist that it somehow be brought to pass that all parties' values are changed to be in harmony without losing continuity with pluralism, but if no effort at all is made to alter people's values, then democratic progress will be difficult to achieve and levels of democracy once gained will be insecure. Democratic-socialist approaches to this problem seek ways to avoid a strict dichotomy between political structures and strategies that accommodate people's heterogeneous values, on the one hand, and attempts to shape their values to include a shared commitment to democracy, on the other. It will be instructive to look at two approaches to this endeavour, one of Bowles/Gintis and one of Laclau/Mouffe.

Perhaps one reason many democratic theorists insist that democracy be regarded as both a means and an end is to meet the problem before us. But, by itself, this does not so much resolve the problem as restate it. If democracy, valued as a means, facilitates satisfaction of existing interests, while, valued as an end, it requires people having shared interests, one still wants to know how these two aspects of democracy are related; a theory motivating integration of democracy as 'end' and as 'means' is required. Bowles and Gintis suggest one attempt. A recurring theme in their critique of liberalism and Marxism is that the 'models of individual behavior' employed in each perspective 'fail because they posit action as oriented toward the satisfaction of ends existing prior to social action, rather than resulting from it,' whereas in fact, 'individuals enter into practices with others not only to achieve common goals, but also to determine who they are and who they shall become as social beings.'[55]

This observation relates to an earlier judgment that once 'the pregiven nature of preferences is rejected, it is clearly inconsistent to consider a society to be democratic when the rights of popular determination and individual choice do not extend to the social relations through which preferences themselves are formed.'[56] Though resisting the claim that this ability is a condition for there being any democracy at all (indeed, gaining popular control over the 'production of wants' as they were called in Chapter Six would constitute a very high degree of democracy), the suggestion can be usefully followed by the retrievalist. However, some medium-large qualifications are required, one of which is to question a way of viewing democracy as an end as well as a means.

The key assertion is that people 'enter into practices with others' both to achieve common goals (that is, goals common to members of a group practicing together to advance their interests as they see them, but varying from group to group) *and* to determine 'who they are and who they shall become.' The approach to the problem at hand suggested here is that insofar as people try to advance their group-specific interests, democracy facilitates this as a means; while democracy serves as a common end insofar as people simultaneously determine their future characters. Obviously not everybody who enters into practices with others does so with this latter intent, so the claim must be that people *ought* to recognize the value of such self-determination. Bowles and Gintis come close to making this point explicitly in their rejection of 'liberal neutrality concerning the good life.'[57]

The task of the democratic socialist on this orientation is to promote people's coming to accept collective self-determination as a value. This is no mean feat, and requiring of superseded pluralism that those in a pluralist society must thus value democracy as an end may lose sufficient contact to constitute a retrieval (perhaps this is why Bowles and Gintis talk of *post*liberal democracy). However, independently of people's values, it remains the case that social interactions do affect their future interests and that democratic participation affords them the best chance of having control over how this process works and its results. Thus, it is not democracy as a normatively valued end that the retrievalist needs people to adopt, but the recognition that democratic institutions, habits of thought, and practices are of special importance to anyone whose interests are not completely fixed.

Someone who recognizes this will value democracy not just to the extent that it promotes furthering interests he or she already has but also because it affords more control over ways that interaction among people creates new interests. It might be said that such a person will see pluralistic, democratic institutions and modes of comportment as *means*, but not as *instruments*. A means

190

is to be valued insofar as it promotes or makes possible something else, and it has been argued that advancing democracy is to be valued insofar as it promotes freedom. Commitment to democracy, then, will be stronger for one who values the freedom not only to further some specific goal, but to keep open the widest possible range of possibilities for achieving other goals in recognition of the fact that in social interaction new, though as yet unknown, goals will be pursued. The instrumentalist, by contrast, values democracy or any other means only insofar as it promotes a known and specified goal and regards it as disposable whenever it stands in the way of furthering that goal.

What people might become is thus simultaneously shaped by the goals they presently seek to further (roughly their 'fixed' dimensions) and by their interactions with others similarly engaged to further their goals (the 'nonfixed' dimensions). When, as Bowles and Gintis prescribe, this process is subject to deliberate popular control, it might be called 'people's self-management.' On the (retrieved) pluralist view, those who are conscious of the need both to promote present goals and also to keep the future open will see that this requires pluralistic respect for the pursuits of others. However, to promote widespread acquisition of this consciousness it is not necessary to persuade people to value democracy as an end. Rather education about the advantages of democratic practices is needed, and this is accomplished in large measure by helping to engage people in these very practices. Theory to support the supersession of liberal-democratic pluralism thus requires less in the way of defending a moral norm in favour of democracy and more in the way of explicating the nature of nonfixity.

### NONFIXITY AND PEOPLE'S SELF-MANAGEMENT

The retrievalist may now urge that pluralism be superseded by orientation around the project of people's self-management. That is, the retrievalist can urge that measures be taken to make people aware of the nonfixity of their values and of the importance of democratic progress if changes are to be increasingly under one's own control. Crucial to this approach is that interests are in fact nonfixed and that there are ways of making people aware of this fact and its consequences. Some arguments regarding the second claim have been given in earlier chapters. The work of Laclau and Mouffe may be seen as a defence of the first claim produced explicitly in support of socialist retrieval.

In *Hegemony and Socialist Strategies* they argue that a society's basic components or 'subject positions' are never more than partially fixed and that in relating to one another each is changed ('articulated'). This applies both to 'antagonistic' relations when subjects regard both themselves and others as having fixed interests and to 'hegemonic' projects where subjects attempt to articulate 'floating elements' in ways consistent with their aims. The conclusion is that nonfixity is pervasive. In antagonistic relations, attempts are made by one pole to fix and hence to change the characteristics of the other (as when racists try to force people to live according to their stereotypes of them); while in hegemonic relations, the dominant subject is articulated, just as is the subordinate one.[58] In their support of these claims Laclau and Mouffe draw upon contemporary discourse theory. Support can also be found in Hegelian dialectics (Hegel's example of master and slave perfectly fits both antagonistic and hegemonic relations), Phenomenological social psychology, Symbolic Interactionism, and Pragmatism, to mention some sources.

Against their background theory, Laclau and Mouffe note that there is a sectarian tendency for those engaged in political struggles (women against sexism, workers against capitalism, visible minorities against racism, and so on) to regard their own interests as fixed and as antagonistically related not just to those of their immediate oppressors, but to everyone else who does not recognize the priority of their struggle. Counteracting this tendency is the practical necessity for those in each member movement of a coalition to recognize the equal claim to support of the other members. This in turn both requires and promotes interaction in such a way that participants' values change or at least that they view them as capable of 'articulation.' Writing from a holistic perspective and wishing to avoid Cartesian subjects to which are ascribed fixed essences, Laclau and Mouffe take subject 'positions,' rather than discrete individuals, as their basic units of analysis.[59] However, another circumstance favourable to recognizing nonfixity can be noted if the individual is focussed on.

Sheila Rowbothom makes the point that 'arguing in terms of a series of separate "oppressions" can have an ironic consequence.

We can forget that people are more than the category of oppression. . . . [W]e do not experience a single defining relationship of subordination in our lives any more than we possess trade union consciousness. We live within a complexity of relationships. This means we have certain sources of comparison and contrast. We can imagine how relationships might be different.'[60] For example, a person whose values are such that she is primarily concerned to resist and combat patriarchy is also of a certain race, nationality, economic class, sexual orientation, and so on, some of which are no doubt also subject to oppression. This provides a basis from which she can potentially recognize the legitimacy of other people's priorities and the possibility of her own priorities changing. The point can obviously be made starting with any priority.

Assuming that one may take individuals as central categories of social and political analysis without making them substrata for fixed essences, Laclau/Mouffe and Rowbothom thus suggest two ways that contemporary political struggle facilitates recognition of nonfixity. The same realities also suggest the value of pluralistic democracy. As Mouffe and Laclau put it: 'a left alternative [to the right's hegemonic project of legitimizing inequalities] can *only* consist of the construction of a different system of equivalents, which establishes social division on a new basis. In the face of the project for the reconstruction of a hierarchic society, the alternative of the left should consist of locating itself fully in the field of the democratic revolution and expanding the chains of equivalents between the different struggles against oppression. The task of the left therefore cannot be to renounce liberal-democratic ideology, but on the contrary, to deepen and expand it in the direction of a radical and plural democracy.'[61]

### TOLERANCE

These arguments in support of the feasibility of pluralism assume the existence of oppressive relations and people's organization against oppression, and some socialists might see this as problematic for the retrievalist. It might be held that consistency requires pluralistic toleration and respect for everyone's values including those of the capitalist, the sexist, the national chauvinist, and so on. But this is no more true for socialist pluralism than for classic Pluralism. Its heyday was in the post-World War II period, when

Pluralists located themselves as at odds with both socialists and the recently defeated fascists. In both cases their argument for nonrespect of right and left alike was that each held values incompatible with pluralism itself, and their justification for Cold War intolerance of the left was the claim that unless checked, left activities would undermine pluralistic institutions.

There is nothing self-contradictory about the *form* of this justification. To be intolerant of some values because they run counter to pluralism does not make pluralism an overriding value, since pluralism can only be valued insofar as it protects as much as possible the autonomy of people to pursue a variety of goals. Values motivating oppressors are worthy of disrespect by the pluralist not just because they lead to harmful behaviour but also because they promote relative fixity on the part of both oppressor and oppressed. Racists, for example, define themselves and others one-dimensionally, and in perpetuating systemic discrimination, they promote fixity in the self-images of those discriminated against as well.

Should such values become so destructive of pluralist institutions and practices as to threaten their continued existence, active intolerance by the pluralist, that is, treating them as crimes, might also be justified. The flaw in Cold War Pluralism was at best ignorance and at worst hypocrisy. It is now generally conceded that claims of the McCarthyites and their analogues in other countries represented gross fabrications against the left, as some liberal-democratic Pluralists found out when they, themselves, were caught in the net. Antipluralistic values and activities must not only be alleged; they must also be proven to be unworthy of respect or, in extreme cases, to merit intolerance.

### SOCIALIST MOVEMENTS

Another misgiving that some socialists express about pluralism pertains to socialist movements. Is a socialist movement organized to promote socialist values one movement among many others, whose values are to be pluralistically respected like the others, or is it more than this? There are two retrievalist responses to this question depending on what is meant by 'socialist movement.' Neither response will satisfy all socialists. If the goal of a socialist organization such as a Socialist or Communist political party is to combat capitalist oppression of workers and in general to promote specifically working-class interests, then on the retrievalist view it should be considered one movement among others. Claims that its goals should take precedence over the goals of other organizations (for women's liberation, for national self-determination, and so on) should be looked on with mistrust. If people in a working-class organization think that only a coalition of different organizations led by it can make significant gains, then it is incumbent on them to specify what is involved in 'leading' and to convince potential coalition members by word and deed that they are right in this claim. This applies to people in any alternate sort of organization.

Laclau and Mouffe doubt that a movement organized around working-class or any other specific goals has a universally privileged claim to leadership.[62] Traditional socialists, already put off by the style and mode of argumentation of Laclau and Mouffe, have been the most incensed about this conclusion and have charged them with forsaking the working class. Ellen Wood's attack on them (and on Bowles and Gintis, Poulanzas, Hall, Gorz, Jessop, Hunt, and several others) is representative. In her book, *The Retreat from Class: A New 'True' Socialism*, she associates the socialist-pluralist conclusions reached by Laclau and Mouffe with intellectualistic elitism, post-Structuralist idealism, and Eurocommunistic electoralism, all of which she sees as following from rejection of working-class revolutionary centrality.[63] On Wood's criticism, these views imply that no social fact is more important than any other 'in determining [people's] life-situations;' there are no 'clearly opposed social interests;' no agents can provide a 'social basis for *any* kind of politics' and instead intellectuals must lead, counting on 'a disembodied democratic impulse' and 'universal humanitarian goals;' and capitalism can be transformed to socialism through a 'non-antagonistic process of institutional reform' which all classes 'have an equal interest in attaining.'[64]

On my reading of Laclau, Mouffe, and the others Wood attacks, I do not see them advocating these things. Social movements are not disembodied discourses, but concrete things, often including intellectuals, but not a product of their persuasive leadership. Movements are partly constituted by modes of discourse in virtue of which their members identify themselves, but these people suffer from real oppressions, putting them into severe conflict around which they organize for specific (not just universal humanitarian) goals. In pursuit of these goals, hostile obstacles, including capitalism, are confronted, and overcoming these obstacles will constitute radical social change. This much is clear from an only barely charitable reading of the works Wood criticizes. Of course, it can be alleged that despite their intentions Laclau, Mouffe, and the rest are committed to the conclusions Wood describes, but this requires much more argumentation than she or other critics have so far produced.[65]

A socialist movement may also be conceived as a movement to promote socialism as the term is used in this work.[66] In this case it will be organized as a movement for a *means*. Socialism will be favoured as a way to advance democracy and, as part of this endeavour, to create a pluralist environment conducive to the pursuit of other goals, some of which movement participants themselves share. Though socialists whose main motivation is just to secure socialist equality are to be found, and while all socialists in the sense now under consideration are no doubt at least partly motivated by moral outrage at the degradation, pain, and suffering caused by capitalist inequality, most participants in such a movement likely see socialism, hence democracy and pluralism, as a means for furthering other values of theirs: rewarding work and decent wages, national self-determination, a full life for women, humanistic municipalities, life itself as in the case of the peace movement, and so on.

A problem many socialists see with this pluralistic approach to socialist activism is in locating the cement, so to speak, that might hold together a coalition of movements or the members of a socialist movement broadly conceived. This is no doubt a problem for continuing work by democratic socialists. However, there are many examples of the more or less successful coalescence of movements: workers and peasants in the Russian Revolution; the student, civil rights, and antiwar movements during the latter period of the war in Vietnam; or the women's, peace, and ecological movements in Europe and the United States. Assuming that what is actual (even if only sporadically) is possible, then there must be some basis for such unified activities.

Perhaps doubt depends on accepting as exclusive a traditional socialist alternative expressed in some Marxist polemics against

196

of movements is given its unity of action by the dominant role of revolutionary workers, or else it is held together by moral visions shared by the leaders of each member of the coalition. Somebody sceptical that this is a dependable source of unity, especially in the face of determined adversity, but who also rejects as both unlikely and undesirable the hegemony of any one group, might despair of finding a basis for effective cooperation. However, there is an alternative perspective in which motivations for multimovement unity define a scale from those approaching narrow self-interest near one limit, to motivations approaching moral vision near the other.

A.  That people are complex and 'nonfixed' means that there will be a motivation for each to wish well the efforts of those pursuing goals which may not be their first priority at some one time. The nonwhite woman who is mainly concerned to resist racism, also has a stake in there being a strong women's movement. Even the young, able-bodied, straight white male worker is well-advised to seek mutually strengthening unity between a working-class movement of which he is a part and other movements. Inhabiting a domicile, community, and planet, he has good reason to favour strong tenants' rights, municipal, ecological and peace movements. He will not always be young; he may become handicapped; his (acknowledged to himself) sexual preferences may change; and he may find himself in a situation where he is in a racial or ethnic minority. Hence he will have reasons to support movements appropriate to these things as well.

B.  To the large extent that oppressive practices and structures sustain one another – patriarchy and capitalism, racism and national chauvinism, and so on – there is a clear motive for those opposing them to form coalitions. Not always clear is that a precondition for effective unity of action is genuine mutual toleration and respect among the parties of such a coalition. 'A nation cannot become free and at the same time continue to oppress other nations,' argued Engels in urging unity among the workers of the European nationalities,[67] and the point can be generalized. Without mutual perception of respect, a coalition will be weakened by suspicion and factional intrigue. For the perception to

197

be sustained, respect must be thought sincere and, actions speaking louder than words, this will require concrete measures including ones to ensure that each participant maintain equal footing in the coalition.[68]

C. Being adaptable even to the most dismal circumstances, human beings do not undertake to improve their lot unless they can envisage a better possible future for themselves. If, however, they can envisage this for themselves, they can envisage it for others as well. At the very least, to view one's own liberation as possible is to view general human liberation as possible. The question to ask, then, is how great a step is it also to view human liberation as desirable? Considerations just advanced about individual complexity and mutual respect go some way toward bridging this gap, but they are largely negative, pertaining to what is necessary to overcome oppressions. A stronger motive for making the struggles of others one's own is provided by the positive vision of a world beyond oppression, where people may set out on creative projects with whatever other people they want without fear either that this will be met with hostility or purchased at the expense of projects yet others have set themselves. Thus are people united, as one civil rights activist put it to me, not by their chains but by their dreams.

Like the question of whether equality is to be morally preferred to inequality, I doubt it can be proven to a sceptic that such a dream can be a unifying force. Nevertheless, those of us who recall the day in April, 1975 when the people of Vietnam finally freed themselves of U.S. imperialism, remember an exhilaration centred, to be sure, on joy for the Vietnamese themselves, but extending beyond them to anticipation of the possibility of liberation of all sorts including ones more directly affecting us. It is safe to say that all democrats of that time felt the victory of the Vietnamese as a victory for themselves as well. (The exhilaration of that experience was strong enough to carry some of us even through the '80s.)

Of course, none of these considerations touch the question of how, concretely, pluralistically conceived movements might be organized. Joshua Cohen and Joel Rogers call for a 'democratic alliance' which is more than an ad hoc coalition and less than a vanguard movement.[69] Most democratic socialists agree with them that something in this range is needed, and there are many crucial, though as yet quite inconclusive, debates about what forms of organization are required. This topic of pluralist democratic-socialist organization is the main subject of Chapter Eleven.

# III Practical Solutions to Theoretical Problems

# 9 Class Reductionism

THE QUESTION OF class reductionism arose as a practical problem within movement politics, and it is in this context that it makes sense to address reductionism as other than a merely intellectual exercise in historiography. The work of Laclau and Mouffe has a movement orientation, as do Jean Cohen's *Class and Civil Society* and Michèle Barrett's *Women's Oppression Today*. All these authors seek a way to characterize class reductionism and to explain how it comes to inform left-wing theory in order to counteract its negative effects on movement politics. Barrett addresses the shortcomings of Marxist analyses in relation to the oppression of women, while Cohen, Laclau, and Mouffe address the full range of extraclass movements.

Cohen takes Marx to task, arguing that in his earlier writings he regarded all social actors normatively as 'representing' historical forces progressing toward the full development of 'productive capacities of mankind,'[1] while in later writings, on her view, Marx was reductionistic in an economically deterministic way, seeing individuals as 'personifications of functions of production, classes as personifications of [economic] value categories, and domination relations as purely economic.'[2] Barrett describes reductionism as the main failure in Marxist analyses of women's oppression. For her, the reductionist argues 'that such and such a phenomenon may appear in one set of terms, but is really only explicable in another,' or that 'gender relations are reduced to an effect of the operation of capital.'[3] The political orientations of Barrett and Cohen are shared by all socialists, who agree that social theory is worth pursuing to assist people in overcoming oppressions.

Conceptions vary of 'oppression' or of 'domination' or similar terms, none of which is ideal for our purposes, given that they

203

are often used in exagerated ways. Still, I think that in one standard sense, the word is appropriately descriptive. It refers to the unjustified thwarting of people's aspirations which is 'systematic' – that is, ongoing and pervasive across categories of people (workers, women, the handicapped, children, and so on) in such a way that this cannot be explained by reference to accident, such as the accident of powerful people happening to be possessed of ill will.[4] It is taken that there are many systematic oppressions throughout the world today. Those who doubt this may find the arguments of this chapter pointless. Such people are urged to look around them, read newspapers, leave sheltered homes or jobs for a while, and then return to the topic.

Similarly, rather than trying to persuade unconvinced socialists that class reductionism is something to be avoided, this chapter will first sharpen the meaning of 'reductionism' and then prescribe an approach to social inquiry that should help to avoid reductionism without prejudging very much in the way of substantive social-theoretical conclusions. (Since we are addressing a topic at the forefront of contemporary socialist theory, the first task calls for some relatively close analysis. Readers who wish may avoid this by picking up the broad outline of the argument at the subsection, 'Reductionism' on page 214.)

### i. Ways of Being Reductionistic

In addition to their movement orientation, Barrett and Cohen have in common with other critics of reductionism that it is *theories* which are said to be reductionistic by illegitimately positing relations ('personifying,' or 'being an effect of') among certain things. A full definition of 'reductionism' will require specifying the nature of reductionistic relations, the sorts of things to which they are attributed, and what makes the attributions illegitimate. Some classificatory groundwork will help to situate debates over these matters.

#### UNICENTRIC AND POLYCENTRIC THEORIES

On a 'unicentric' social theory one group, form of oppression, struggle, or putatively deeper lying source of these things is said to constitute a unifying force which orders other phenomena.

204

Most socialist theories of this sort view society in Lukács' term as a 'totality,' the principle of unity of which is found in relations among economic classes.[5] Also in this category are claims such as Althusser's that production relations constitute 'structures in dominance'[6] and one of Habermas's claims that each 'social formation' (for instance, 'liberal capitalist') has its proper 'fundamental principle of organization' ('the relation of wage labour and capital').[7] These views may be interpreted as weaker than a full-blown theory of society as a totality, but they still count as unicentric theories since, in the first case, one structure is designated 'dominant' and, in the second case, each period of history is organized around some one 'fundamental' principle.

Adherents of 'polycentric' approaches charge unicentrists with reductionism and insist that no pride of place be given any one group or source of struggle. Bowles and Gintis sketch a polycentric approach premised on the 'heterogeneity of power,' as does Juliet Mitchel when she analysed society into the 'structures,' production, reproduction, sexuality, and the socialization of children, no one of which is dominant over the others.[8] Another example is Alain Touraine's theory which 'dismisses the image of society as a system, with its own language, or as an instrument of repression, and instead ... chooses to set out from the event, i.e., the drama, the conflict, the clash of interests [of different social groups] and the sway of the dominator over the dominated. ... '[9] It bears mention that, like unicentric approaches, polycentric ones admit of differences, as for example, between Touraine's, which takes groups in struggle against domination as basic facts and Laclau and Mouffe's, which purports to explain such facts.

Some theories appear to mix elements of unicentric and polycentric approaches, but on examination they can be located, if not neatly, into one category. Thus, 'dual systems' theories, such as Heidi Hartmann's or Zillah Eisenstein's, postulate the two systems, class oppression and patriarchy, as jointly dominant over other social phenomena while neither is dominant over the other.[10] This should probably be considered a unicentric approach, since it still makes the one, complex system, 'class oppression in interaction with patriarchy,' a privileged centre of social analysis.[11] Jean Cohen's prescription to unite a structural with an action approach, on the other hand, should be considered a defence of polycentricism, since the function of structural analysis for her is to help 'develop a theoretical framework capable of defending and promoting the potential complimentarity [not prioritization] of emancipatory struggles.'[12]

## BASE AND SUPERSTRUCTURE

Another classification is useful for locating Marx's base/superstructure model. Following terminology in the philosophy of science which designates the object of an explanation an 'explanandum' and a putative explanation of it an 'explanans,' we might designate that which is or is alleged to be reduced a 'reducendum' (plural: reducenda) and that to which it is thought reduced a 'reducens' (plural: reducentia). A distinction can then be made between theories which are said to be reductionistic or which their adherents wish to protect against becoming reductionistic in terms of sorts of reducenda and reducentia involved.

Reducenda may be divided into specifically group-related states of affairs like group oppression, organized resistances, and certain group entities themselves (for instance, nations), on the one hand, and things that support or resist oppression (mainly, institutions of the state and ideas comprising an ideology), on the other. Charges that Marxist use of the base/superstructure model is reductionistic often mix together two distinct complaints. One charge is that some aspect of the base (for example, activities of conflicting economic classes) is a reducens in respect of a reducendum composed of a society's ideological and political superstructure. Or, it might be alleged that the reducenda are (apparently) extraclass oppressions, and the reducentia those elements of the entire base/superstructure complex of which these oppressions are putative effects or forms.[13]

These classificatory points are made to indicate the varieties of reductionism. For example, while polycentric approaches to social theory are protected against reducing one group phenomenon to another group phenomenon, this does not make them reduction proof altogether, since they may still be reductionistic of ideas and political institutions. Thus, it might be held that irreducible patriarchal and class 'bases' independently yield parallel ideological and political superstructures in a reductionistic way. Conversely, rejection of the base/superstructure model does not by itself mean that a position cannot be reductionistic, since it may still be a unicentric reduction.[14]

The classifications also help to specify the scope of putative reducenda and reducentia. An approach that allows something to be an effect or form of something else should not always be counted reductionistic. A theorist may be wrong about when something is such a form or effect, but to be a reducendum it must be a member of a class of things all of which are reduced. This stipulation is meant to capture the objectionably sweeping nature of claims typically called reductionistic. It also allows one to admit that sometimes things are related as cause and effect or form and essence. To allege that *any* putative cause or essence is a reducens unnecessarily transposes the debate between reductionist and antireductionist to problematic philosophical terrain.

Similarly, whether something is a reducens partly depends upon the relative depth of generality of an hypothesis asserting the (universal) relation of a possible reducendum to it. The point is best made with reference to the base/superstructure model. One reason that the two sorts of reductionist charges against this model are easily conflated is that it is used in both more and less general explanations. At one level (call it level-1) some extraclass oppression or political institution is purportedly explained by reference to economic class relations and an hypothesis asserting that these are the causes or essences of any such oppression or institution. At a deeper level of generality (level-2) a theoretical model is constructed that explains why and how extraclass oppressions are effects of economic relations.[15] At this level social theories ought to be sufficiently flexible to account for exceptions to connections postulated in level-1 assertions (if, of course, theorists constructing the models believe there can be any exceptions).

Marxist attempts to temper economic determinism with a concept of determination 'in the last instance,' conjoined with a dialectical view of the relation of base and superstructure, are examples. Analogous distinctions can be made about: structuralist Marxism regarded as a general social theory (level-2) and hypotheses that economic structures are 'dominant' (level-1); a general theory such as Habermas's uniting critical social theory with aspects of systems analysis (level-2) and level-1 views about the 'fundamental principles' of a social formation; or any other approach (neo-Hegelian, Psychoanalytic, and so on) that both produces unicentric or base/superstructural hypotheses and attempts to explicate a general social theory.

In this chapter it is prescribed that reductionism be regarded as generated by level-1 hypotheses and that agnosticism be maintained regarding level-2 theories. A charge directly linking level-2 theory with reductionism might be derived a priori from some philosophical principle which castes aspersion on the pursuit of general social theory per se, or it could be based inductively on a survey of actual such attempts. However, (despite their economy) the justification of philosophical metatheories is surely at least as problematic as justification of the social theories they question, and (despite the confidence with which they are usually advanced) extant, general social theories must be regarded as sufficiently tentative to admit of considerable future development and hence as providing an inadequate sample on which to base blanket charges. Moreover, not all reductionist views have any clear or explicit connection with theories at level-2 generality.

The intent of the above observations, then, is to limit the range of things that may count as either reducenda or reducentia and to loosen the link between conceptualizations of reductionism and attitudes toward social theories and philosophical principles of explanation. Further, it does not by itself stand as proof of reductionism that one embraces level-1 hypotheses, either of a unicentrist or a base/superstructuralist variety. This does not mean that these things may not prove to be reductionistic, but to see how they might be, the concept needs to be made more precise. This will be accomplished by relating it to 'sectarianism,' which must itself be defined.

## MOVEMENT SECTARIANISM

Movement sectarianism is the attitude that one's movement is the most important for anyone at all to support and that the oppressive features of life necessitating it are the most grave and far-reaching of all oppressions. Sectarianism is to be found in all movements: working class, civil rights, national liberation, ecological, women's, peace, gay liberation, even movements to expand democracy itself (for example, those insisting a favoured 'kind' of democracy be regarded an overriding goal). In each case the attendant sectarian practice insists that people in other movements not divert energy from the 'primary' movement or at least that they subordinate their aims to it whenever both cannot be simultaneously advanced. Anyone who resists this subordination is regarded as part of the enemy camp.

This is not the place to speculate on the origins of sectarianism, except to note that it likely shares common causes with the oppressions that movements plagued by sectarianism combat. Systematic oppression isolates people from one another, making it difficult to gain overviews and promoting a sense of desperate urgency regarding one's local situation. Whatever the causes of sectarianism, its antipluralist consequences impede progress in democracy and hence ultimately movements aim themselves. Also, there is a tendency for a movement sectarian to be an organizational sectarian as well. Once somebody is in the frame of mind to prioritize movements, he or she is also prone to prioritize forms of organization within a movement. The resulting factional infighting constitutes another well-known impediment to successful advance of movements.

This chapter addresses class reductionism, which is seen as an attitude growing out of and reinforcing the sectarianism of some who think of socialism as working-class power. At the same time it should be emphasized that to criticize class reductionism is not to deny that reductionist views support other kinds of movement sectarianisms,[16] and most of the hypotheses of this chapter apply equally to class and to extraclass reductionisms. The aim is the one Jean Cohen prescribes: 'to accept the diversity of identities and movements while attempting to develop a theoretical framework capable of defending and promoting the potential complementarity of emancipatory struggles.'[17] However, in one respect the approach adopted here contrasts with Cohen's.

### THEORY AND PRACTICE

Cohen's book concludes that an alternative to what she sees as irredeemable Marxist reductionism is needed which recognizes multiple social systems (Cohen cites the distinction made by Claus Offe and Habermas among political, economic, and normative systems), supplemented with an 'action' approach such as that of Cornelius Castoriadis and focussed in the manner of Alain Touraine's work on the plurality of social movements.[18] The analysis suggests that class reductionism is primarily a matter of an inadequate level-2 theory (that of Marx and Engels) to be rectified by devising a superior theory at the same level. This chapter prescribes measures to avoid sectarian reductionisms without committing one to a level-2 social theory, yet also without closing off (very many) options regarding the direction continuing theorizing might take.

In addition to justifications already cited, one can add that there is a danger in linking anticlass reductionism too closely with acceptance of a general theory, since this can generate its own forms of movement sectarianism. An example is Isaac Balbus's view:

> Since sexual, political, and technological domination do not owe their existence to the mode of production, the efforts to eliminate them cannot properly be subsumed under the (class) struggle to transform the mode of production. Nor should the three liberation struggles be aligned with this latter struggle: a struggle whose commitment to transform the particular mode of objectification is coupled with, and rooted in, an even more fundamental commitment to objectification as the essential, immutable relationship between humans and their natural surroundings is necessarily inconsistent with the participatory democratic, feminist, and alternative technological challenge to the domination of nature that objectification entails.... The proletariat... cannot be understood as the or even a revolutionary agent within contemporary industrial societies.[19]

Though Balbus states his 'neohegelian, feminist, psychoanalytic' theory in an authoritative tone, it is too speculative to justify those in women's, democratic, and ecological movements shunning alliances with working-class movements and regarding proletarian struggle as, in Balbus's term, 'reactionary.'[20]

Further, a full-blown and adequate nonreductionist social theory in my view is not yet at hand, and developing one (should this be possible) would itself require movement political activity more advanced than now exists as a base, reflection on which can formulate key questions, generate hypotheses and provide data.[21] Abstractly viewed we have a chicken-and-egg problem: theory is needed to guide movements, but movement politics is required to develop a theory. However, this is no more problematic (though no easier to succeed at either) than any enterprise requiring thoughtful practice. To claim that political practice is needed at the present time is not to claim that it should be uncritically carried out. On the contrary, for movement politics to provide the basis for improved theory, its conduct must always be interrogated.

Researchers who wish to support movements against oppression should try to give comparative answers to such questions as:

- When and how did a movement come into existence and what sorts of people support it?
- When do movement supporters take up sectarian stances toward other movements and when do they strive for unity?
- Under what circumstances do some people come to challenge oppressive ideology and practice?
- What forms of organization and ways of relating to other movements advance or impede a movement's aims?

This list can easily be extended with similar questions[22] all of them recalcitrant to solution either by armchair speculation or by appeal to uncritical activist instinct.

## THE LACLAU/MOUFFE ANALYSIS

The analysis of Laclau and Mouffe in *Hegemony and Socialist Strategies* continues Laclau's earlier critique of class reductionism. Having found attempts to understand the populist attraction of fascism in class terms wanting, Laclau concluded that populism had a responsive audience among those engaged in 'popular democratic struggles' (for example, for national renaissance), and that these struggles were not reducible to class struggles, although they needed self-interpretation as integrated with a major class' ideology to become historically effective. Thus, the battle for 'hegemony' was seen as the battle between the bourgeoisie and the proletariat to articulate extraclass aspirations.[23]

By the more recent work, the idea had been rejected that hegemonic articulation must be exercised by a major economic class in favour of the view that socialism is a matter of 'radical democracy,' the struggle for which may or may not be led by the working class. Explicating a social theory in support of these conclusions involved fuller treatment of class reductionism than this concept had earlier received, and a provocative hypothesis about what makes reduction possible was generated.[24] On one reading, Laclau and Mouffe attempt a level-2 general social theory of the sort called for by Jean Cohen (though not sharing her enthusiasm for the work of Offe and Habermas). On another reading it is a more transcendental effort to derive postulates for any antireductionistic perspective from the requirements (explicated in contemporary discourse theory) of human thought and action.

The reductionist mode of thought according to Laclau and Mouffe utilizes two sorts of 'argument':

> The argument from appearance: everything presenting itself as different can be reduced to identity. This may take two forms: either appearance is a mere artifice of concealment, or it is a necessary form of the manifestation of essence. (An example of the first form: 'nationalism is a screen which hides the interests of the bourgeoisie;' an example of the second: 'the Liberal State is a necessary political form of capitalism.') The argument from contingency: a social category or sector may not be reducible to the central identities of a certain form of society, but in that case its very marginality vis-à-vis the fundamental line of historical development allows us to discard it as irrelevant. (For example: 'because capitalism leads to the proletarianization of the middle classes and the peasantry, we can ignore these and concentrate our strategy on the conflict between the bourgeoisie and the proletariat.')[25]

Thus they describe three relations (contingency and two forms of appearance) alleged to hold between reducenda and reducentia and an implied view about what makes attributing them to social phenomena illegitimate. Comments are required about each of these components.

The two versions of the argument from appearance are often encountered in socialist literature. They are well described by Mouffe and Laclau, and versions of the situation where reducenda are 'manifestations' of something else are the main objects of attack in Cohen's discussion of 'representation' and 'personification.' The socialist historian Stanley Ryerson has noted that the term 'class expansionism' might be more apt,[26] but in keeping with present usage, this will be designated a kind of class reductionism, one in which nonclass phenomena are seen as *forms* of class phenomena. The argument from contingency allows that one who denies that everything is a form of class phenomena may still be a reductionist in thinking that whatever is not such a form is politically unimportant. But this still leaves out the *causal* reduc-

212

tionist, that is, the person who recognizes that extraclass oppression is important to combat, but believes it necessary and sufficient to engage in class struggle for this purpose. This opinion is consistent both with the view that class oppression is the origin of nonclass oppressions and with the weaker view that they have independent causes.[27]

It is problematic to make either the argument from appearances or that from contingency alone definitive of 'reductionism.' The key phrase in the passage above is 'the fundamental line of historical development.' Without it, a definition of 'class reductionism' by reference to the contingency argument would make anybody a reductionist regarding some state of affairs who holds that practical activity directed toward altering it is less important in existing circumstances than class struggle. Almost no socialist antireductionist holds that this is *never* the case; so if 'class reductionism' is pejoratively used, qualification is needed to indicate what it is that makes ascription of these relations among reducenda and reducentia illegitimate. The qualification employed by Laclau and Mouffe refers to historiographic theory, but they also refer to political practice.

According to them belief in a fundamental line of historical development involves thinking of history as a 'narrative' in which economic laws govern people's behaviour in accord with their objective class interests and where historical phenomena are considered 'equivalent' in virtue of hypothesized class positions.[28] A reductionist then deduces the centrality of waging class struggle and subordinating other struggles to it from such a theory, thus failing to take account of the varied political forces promoting or impeding 'radical democracy.'[29] These observations about the 'contingency' species of reductionism also apply to the 'appearance' species. It, too, yields political sectarianism, and thinking of history as a narrative involves seeing it as a process whereby things like class essences become less disguised.

On this reconstruction of the Laclau/Mouffe analysis, then, there are *two* possible sorts of criteria for reductionism: 1) being a theory of history with certain characteristics (necessary economic laws, objective interests, narration by enumeration of equivalences), and 2) having certain consequences for political practice (socialist sectarianism). The first criterion may be collapsed into the second when putative theories are nothing but rationalizations for sectarian behaviour. But to assume that any theory appealed to for justification of sectarian practices must be a rationalization is to beg questions about the connection between these theories and sectarianism. Alternate views are that some historical-developmental theory is a sound one from which sectarian prescriptions have been falsely drawn or that it is a mixed bag with sound and unsound elements, only some of which have yielded sectarianism. Moreover, there is an advantage to leaving theoretical options open, and hence to linking reductionism not to considerations of theory, but to those of practice. Here is an hypothesized way of doing this.

### 'REDUCTIONISM'

Charges of reductionism are appropriate to direct toward assertions at a relatively low level of theoretical generality which hold apparently nonclass phenomena (forms of oppressions, social movements, ideas, and political structures) to be: a) forms or expressions of class phenomena; b) effects of class phenomena; or c) such that even if they have extra-economic origins, it is necessary and sufficient to make changes in them that appropriate changes in class phenomena (like advancing or winning working-class struggle) are made. For such assertions to be class reductionistic, it must also be the case d) that sectarian practice would likely result from agreeing with them.

That many socialists advance theories as if they were abstractly motivated by a desire just to produce a true picture of society sometimes obscures their motivation by political goals. Rejecting this orientation for a more practical one does not mean that political acceptability be a criterion, Lysenko-like, of truth. Rather, it means that success or failure of theory-guided practice in attaining goals the theory was constructed to help attain is an important indicator of its adequacy. Suppose that the goal of overcoming some systematic oppression is thought realistic and a theory is advanced about the nature of this oppression which yields prescriptions for certain actions, but that the actions fail to make inroads in attaining the goal. This would be a good, objective reason to question the theory.

This chapter assumes that movement sectarianism does in fact work against the goal of overcoming the systematic oppression

214

that any movement is organized to combat. The assumption will not be defended here, because too much in the way of detailed historical evidence, argumentation about specific political circumstances, or for the benefit of some, vicarious experience in movement politics itself would be required to persuade the sceptic. He or she might think either that oppressions cannot be overcome at all or that they can only be overcome if one movement subordinates all the rest. No doubt there are many who believe one of these things. They may find not only this criterion of 'reductionism' but also the main arguments of this chapter unpersuasive. On the other hand, for a growing number of socialists, sectarian practice has for good reason become *evidence* against hypothesized connections among things which are supposed to help advance socialist and other movements and can accordingly be called into question when they support activities that are known from experience to retard such movements.

This characterization of class reductionism does not entail that all hypotheses of the forms designated a), b), or c) are reductionistic or that any prescription giving precedence to class phenomena is evidence of reductionism. The statement that an apparently free and equal exchange of work for wages is in fact a form of biased class relations is meaningful (and in fact true), and a prescription derived from it that workers recognize the limitations of what can be accomplished by legal action without organizing against institutions that support capitalism will give priority to group actions over individual, legalistic maneuvering. Sometimes imperialists make use of deep religious or national hostilities found among those they exploit, but sometimes the hostility has pretty clearly been *caused* by imperialists, and those recognizing this have appropriately prescribed that combatting imperialism is more important than pursuing activities based on artificial differences.[30] Cultural tensions between old and young workers with class independent, social-psychological origins are exacerbated by economic conditions (for example, in the way that youth unemployment keeps wages down and older workers cannot afford to retire early) such that changing those conditions is necessary and sufficient to eliminate the worst tensions.

To be sure, there is room for debate about the accuracy of such assertions, but a case can be made that believing them does

215

not lead to sectarianism. To do this, the assertions would have to be more sweeping in scope. A likely example regarding nations (from an article by Paul Belanger and Celine St. Pierre) is: '[N]ational oppression should be defined as an aspect of capitalist relations of exploitation and oppression in such a way that the national struggle, while completely retaining its specificity, should be considered a form of class struggle.'[31] Or, exemplifying c-type assertions, there is Milton Fisk's view that 'classes are "primary" among groups...in the limited sense that conflict among other groups are given their reason for present existence by conflicts among classes.'[32] From this Fisk derives the claims that 'the ideology of racism itself does not persist independently of the efforts by the owning class to promote profits.'[33] Or again, there is Althusser's comment that 'whatever their form (religious, ethical, legal, political) [ideologies] always express class positions.'[34]

Unqualified, these claims (at what were called level-1 generality earlier in the chapter) are sufficiently sweeping to promote socialist sectarianism. Were they accurate, it would make sense to insist that efforts to end national oppression or racism or to challenge and alter religious, ethical, legal, and political ideas be integrated with class struggle and that class struggle always be given pride of place in popular organization and in political programmes. To say that this 'makes sense' is not to say that prescribing these things is strictly entailed by such viewpoints, but rather that in a phenomenological way belief in them and sectarian prioritization of political activities make up a coherent orientation toward the political world. Insofar as such hypotheses are derived from more general (level-2) theories, this casts doubt on the adequacy of these theories while not fully disproving them.

One component of the position linking reductionism with sectarianism and low level theoretical hypotheses – that sectarianism is a reliable index of theoretical inadequacy – has been discussed. Two components remain: that belief in certain sorts of hypotheses leads to sectarian politics and that a level-2 theory yielding reductionist hypotheses may nonetheless be salvageable. These views will be defended before suggesting a nonreductionist way of relating antioppressive theory to political practice.

## REDUCTIONISM AND SECTARIAN PRACTICE

This characterization of reductionism can be challenged by questioning the intimacy claimed between sectarianism and a belief in a putatively reductionistic hypothesis. It might be argued that somebody can believe, for example, that all major social oppressions are effects of class oppression and still not behave in a sectarian way. The antireductionist can grant this but must then explain how somebody who believes that extraclass oppressions are effects of class oppression may refrain from sectarian insistence that movements against extraclass oppressions be subordinated to class struggle.

Four sorts of explanation come to mind:

1. The putative reductionist has doubts about whether the hypothesis in question (in our example that class oppression is the source of all other oppressions) is true;
2. It is believed that since the support of movements against other oppressions is required and that participants in them do not recognize the centrality of class oppression, nonsectarian behaviour is necessary to maintain this support;
3. It is thought that nonsectarian behaviour, though not required in the short run to advance some particular campaign, is important for longer-run goals such as recruiting others to one's movement;
4. The centrality of class oppression is believed to be compatible with giving struggles against other forms of oppression weight equal to or even sometimes greater than that given to advancing class struggle.

Situation 1) poses no problem; it means that however confidently the participant in class struggle espouses it, when push comes to shove in actual politics, belief in this centrality is not held after all. Situations 2) and 3) are less straightforward. Lacking knowledge of systematic research on such topics, I can only draw on my own experience and ask readers to appeal to germane experiences of their own.

Sectarian behaviour can be dampened by beliefs of sorts 2) or 3), but these checks are insufficient to prevent long- and short-term sectarian political practice. Sincere belief in the overriding importance of waging class struggle eventually yields sectarian behaviour – for example, as soon as one thinks the support of other movements is no longer needed or when it is thought that recruiting has proceeded as far as it can. Even in the short term, where coalition politics is pursued in a way that is not obviously sectarian, close examination reveals sectarianism. Thus sectarians who think it practically necessary to refrain from insisting on their movement's goals being placed first, are still less trustworthy in honouring commitments of support made to others or more energetic in the pursuit of others' goals in forums where their activities are visible than when they are not.

### SOCIALIST THEORY

Situations of sort 4) are more complex. Reductionist attitudes are general ones, but generality is a matter of degree. The analysis advanced here denies that holding certain general social theories or employing certain philosophical principles of explanation is conclusive evidence of reductionistic thinking. In addressing medium-general assertions about the relations between class and extraclass phenomena instead of addressing general social theories (for instance, neo-Hegelian dialectics or Marxist structuralism) or philosophical principles of explanation (such as causal determinism or functionalism), the analysis of class reductionism prescribed here leaves open the question of whether this or that theory or principle is bound to be reductionistic.

For example, should a neo-Hegelian socialist theorist advance hypotheses about class struggle being 'the truth of' patriarchy (or racism or national chauvinism), action on which would have sectarian consequences, then this would justify labelling these hypotheses 'class-reductionistic.' It would not immediately follow, however, that neo-Hegelianism is necessarily class reductionistic. To show this, one must demonstrate that reductionist hypotheses consistently and unavoidably follow from the theory. Similar points can be made about Structuralist and base/superstructure analysis and about competing explanatory principles. The fact that both reductionistic and antireductionistic claims are made by socialist theorists today writing in different theoretical camps suggests doubt regarding charges about essential connections.

What would make it possible to believe in the primacy of class struggle while also consistently denying that it always be made the top political priority is sufficiently sophisticated machinery of a general theory. Perhaps some attempts can be ruled out as rationalizations of *anti*sectarian practice. Thus someone might explain all oppressions as hidden forms of class oppression in a way that made no difference to political practice except that one might think to himself or herself that in nonsectarian activity what is 'really' being engaged in is class struggle. While people who find themselves in an environment with a workerist political culture may think of themselves in such a way, the sectarian practice necessary to call their views reductionist would be absent, and their class struggle centred self-image would be without practical content. It would parallel the way some pursue entirely secular aims in a secular way, but in the name of God.

For some antireductionists all theories that apparently allow one to have it both ways are either vacuous in this manner or disguised reductionistic theories; but there is a more charitable interpretation. A unicentrist may attempt to avoid reductionism by arguing that although one form of oppression and the struggles against it is 'dominant' or 'primary,' other forms have sufficient autonomy sometimes to be the most important to pursue. Or a 'base/superstructurist' can argue, as Marx and Engels did, that a political or ideological phenomenon possesses 'relative autonomy' from an economic base that is only determinant 'in the last instance.' Given that one is dealing with a high level of social theory in an underdeveloped domain, it is premature for the antireductionist to claim that these theories are rationalizations for antisectarianism, as is sometimes alleged in the case of Mao's descriptions of 'primary and secondary contradictions,'[35] or that they are conceptually incoherent.[36]

At the same time, if the test of leading to sectarianism is accepted as one that can falsify a theory designed to advance movement aims, there is a burden for the unicentrist and the base/superstructurist even if the charges about rationalization and internal incoherence are met. They still need a way to conceive of nonprimary movements and oppressions or of political and ideological phenomena as sufficiently 'relatively autonomous' from primary phenomena to avoid leading to sectarian behaviour, while not denuding concepts like 'structure in dominance' or 'ultimately determining' of practical significance. This is a heavy burden, but an antireductionist assertion that it cannot be borne is, it seems to me, as yet unwarranted. Nor *should* the antireductionist rest his or her case on this question. If a unicentrist or a base/superstructurist can produce a theory that consistently and usefully avoids sectarianism while advancing movements against oppressions, why complain? This result is the very aim of the antireductionist.

Moreover, unless the antireductionist defends foregoing social theory altogether, an alternative, antireductionist social theory will be required. Given the highly speculative nature of such theories, there is a danger in tying the justification of nonsectarianism to acceptance of any one of them. The theory of Mouffe and Laclau, drawn from contemporary poststructuralist discourse theory and neo-Gramscian hypotheses, contains many suggestive elements and has the merit of grounding antisectarianism, but it is surely premature to accept this theory as the last word on the nature of human interactions. Nor do Laclau and Mouffe advance it as such. Similar reflections pertain to Cohen's theory put together from views of Offe, Touraine, and Castoriadis, or Carol Gould's perception of an antireductionist individualistic action-theoretical core to Marx's social ontology. A fully developed antireductionist theory of history or society is not needed to pursue nonsectarian politics provided there is a perspective conducive to such politics that leaves open social-theoretical options, whether to try patching up a traditional theory, to construct a new or eclectic theory, or to defend permanently foregoing general social theory construction.

### ii. A Nearly Neutral Perspective

Required is a perspective allowing one to formulate nonreductionistic hypotheses (at level-1 of generality) without closing off options for more general (level-2) theoretical labour. The approach suggested here employs a pragmatized version of elements of Marxist materialism for this purpose, integrated in the project of expanding democracy. Its key theses are expressed in these famous quotations from Marx:

- Men make their own history, but they do not make it just as they please; they do not make it under circumstances chosen by themselves, but under circumstances directly encountered given and transmitted from the past.
- [M]ankind always sets itself only such tasks as it can solve; since ... it will always be found that the task itself arises

only when the material conditions for its solution already exist or are at least in the process of formation.[37]

I shall interpret these passages to describe a 'pretheoretical' perspective designating the task of the activist theorist to identify problematic circumstances, to generate hypotheses about them and about things like human capabilities, and to estimate the likelihood of success of alternate approaches to the pursuit of social tasks.

To say that this perspective is pretheoretical is not to say that it makes no assumptions about human nature and history, but that its theoretical assumptions are sufficiently unproblematic to gain the assent at least of those for whom avoiding reductionism in pursuing movement politics is a principal aim. In particular, it is assumed that tasks requiring the conjoined efforts of many do not get put on the agenda unless there are some live options available for carrying them out. Likewise, tasks would not need to be undertaken at all if there were no problems. These problems and the physical, social, and intellectual material available for confronting them are historically given. This is the realistic assumption of the first passage that tempers an optimistic assumption of the second. Those who consider these assumptions innocuous will not find it difficult to view the perspective as (relatively) pretheoretical, but not everyone will consider them innocuous.

## REDUCTIONISTIC POTENTIALITIES

The conditions with which Marx, himself, was concerned were 'economic' in having to do with the forces and relations of production. Such economic conditions are important, but there are other sorts as well, one of which − conditions of the reproduction of the species − Marx intended also to address.[38] What makes his comment part of a potentially reductionistic theory is not recognition of conditions that simultaneously pose problems and offer solutions, but the claim that one sort of condition, the economic, is most important.[39] It is true that in approaching social theory by isolating different major life conditions, one creates the possibility of reductionism in thus designating one sort of condition as in some sense primary,[40] but such prioritization need not result. If the antireductionist is to bar anything that *might* lead to reductionism, then use of language and thought itself should go. A

221

similar point can be made about objections to the sort of perspective Marx articulated which are voiced by Touraine and E.P. Thompson.

Referring to the first quoted passage from Marx, Touraine charges that '[s]ocialist thought recognizes that people make their history, but immediately adds that they do not know that they make it, which means that they are not actors but only instruments.'[41] And one of Thompson's criticisms is that structuralist Marxism considers structures as pregiven 'closed fields' of action.[42] Fatalistic use of the concept of limiting conditions is clearly possible, but the response must again be that one may recognize constraints without viewing them as entirely closed or thinking of people as pawns of historical conditions. Gramsci (for whom the second of Marx's passages quoted above was a point of theoretical focus)[43] puts it this way in describing his 'historicist' approach:

> The active politician is a creator, an initiator; but he neither creates from nothing nor does he move in the turbid void of his own desires and dreams. He bases himself on effective reality, but what is this effective reality? Is it something static and immobile, or is it not rather a relation of forces in continuous motion and shift of equilibrium? If one applies one's will to the creation of a new equilibrium among the forces which really exist and are operative – basing oneself on the particular force which one believes to be progressive and strengthening it to help it to victory – one still moves on the terrain of effective reality, but does so in order to dominate and transcend it (or to contribute to this). What 'ought to be' is therefore concrete; indeed it is the only realistic and historicist interpretation of reality, it alone is history in the making and philosophy in the making, it alone is politics.[44]

## DETERMINISM AND INDETERMINISM

This passage from Gramsci's *Prison Notebooks* is sometimes read as an effort to avoid commitment to causal determinism, and this raises a more substantive challenge to the innocuousness of a problem-solving perspective. Some interpretations of the way problems, solutions and limits are historically given would be considered too deterministic for those, like Carol Gould, for whom, 'it is . . . a basic feature of actions that choice is not limited to a given set of alternatives, but rather that agents can discover or create new alternatives. This feature of action is one of the bases for historical and social change as well as for individual self-transcendence.'[45] This view is part of a theory of human action which combines elements of indeterministic action theory and an Aristotelian model of causation, which Gould tries to attribute to Marx.[46] Whether the problem-solving perspective is compatible with indeterminism depends upon how both the perspective and indeterminism are interpreted.

They are incompatible if the second quotation from Marx is taken to mean that people are incapable of recognizing certain things as obstacles or of formulating alternative ideas about how to overcome them until historical forces bring them to recognition and formulation *and* if indeterminism is interpreted to mean that any such determination is unacceptably fatalistic. Relaxing either of these interpretations removes incompatibility. One might understand Marx's view to pertain not to what people can recognize as problems or entertain as solutions, but to what they can realistically be expected to succeed at and hence to attempt.[47] Or one may grant that there are historical causes of people's values and beliefs, but hold on philosophical compatibilist grounds that this does not detract from human freedom.[48] Or again, one might defend an intermediate position where one of the things that historically inherited conditions determine is the degree of receptiveness of a population to utopian proposals that may at any time be advanced by some people.[49]

These alternatives are not meant to be glosses of Marxist theory, but it is worth noting that democratic-socialist theorists otherwise as different as Marković and Levine see it in this light:

- What is essential for Marxist theory is the thesis of the objective possibility of self-government, and not of its necessary realization. The very idea of self-government presupposes that people themselves are the creators of history in given conditions, i.e., in the objectively determined framework of possibilities. In this way, the idea of self-government presupposes an open, activist interpretation of history in which the artificial gap between law and contingency, necessity and freedom has been overcome.— Marković

- The orthodox [Marxist] theory, reduced to its rational ker-

223

nel, will not by itself explain historical change; nor will it predict the outcomes of class struggles. But it does give an account of the conditions for the possibility of change and of the options available to classes in struggle.—Levine[50]

John McMurtry makes some useful suggestions in his interpretation of Marxist 'economic determinism' as the joint effect of 'limiting,' 'blocking,' and 'mapping.'[51] Or one might consider Eric Olin Wright's effort to define 'structural causality' in terms of a constellation of the relations: limitation, selection, reproduction/nonreproduction, limitation of functional capability, transformation, and mediation.[52] No doubt these terms can be further spelled out, and they can be employed both in reductionistic and nonreductionistic ways. McMurtry and Wright use them to trace relations among economic, political, and ideological phenomena in Marx's senses, but the explanatory machinery they suggest can also be employed to describe relations among phenomena associated with many different social tasks.

### SUBJECT/OBJECT EPISTEMOLOGY

Rapprochement may also be possible in the case of epistemological challenges to a problem-solving perspective. The most charitable interpretation of Marx's use of 'men' and 'mankind' is that he was following conventions which the largely unchallenged male chauvinism of his time inhibited him from questioning. The criticism can, however, be given philosophical content by accepting one feminist view that male-dominated theory is flawed in assuming a 'subject/object' epistemology.[53]

Insofar as this viewpoint is based on a criticism of a typically male 'instrumentalist' orientation to life, where nature and other people are seen as things to be dominated, it need not be in conflict with the problem-solving perspective. Viewing some conditions as posing problems to be overcome does not necessitate viewing them as hostile things to be dominated. Domination is one of a variety of means that might be taken to solve a problem, not a definitive feature of whatever makes something problematic. The contrary opinion may derive from the way that so much human problem-solving has been approached in oppressive ways. But this fact does not entail that the pretheoretical problem-solving orientation must incorporate a prodominating attitude, since sometimes people approach social problems in a nonoppressive spirit.

Whether anti-instrumentalism, conceived by some feminists (as by some nonfeminist Phenomenologists or Critical Theorists) as a specifically epistemological theory, is compatible with the problem-solving perspective again depends on how each is interpreted. If the critic of subject/object epistemologies is committed to a strong subjectivist or a voluntarist theory whereby there are no givens in the social world, no 'facticity' recalcitrant to alteration by an effort or will or change in perspective, the two orientations are no doubt incompatible. They would be compatible even on some antirealist epistemologies which allowed, Husserl-like, for a continuum from a 'subjective' (Husserl's noetic) pole of the integrated object 'the-world-as-experienced' to an 'objective' (noematic) pole, where the latter was marked precisely by its feature of placing obstacles to omnipotence in people's way.

That is, they are compatible if one employing the problem-solving perspective recognizes that interpretations of people's conditions are among those conditions. This raises the question of whether a problem-solving perspective can avoid commitment to a potentially reductionistic base/superstructure model, but surely it can. It is clear that among historically inherited problems and materials for solutions are ideas and political institutions themselves. Even those who think these things are always economically caused recognize them as conditions to be reckoned with, thus creating the onus to define terms like 'ultimately determining.' A proven theory that changing one kind of condition will always advance any social task better than changing another kind would be incalculably useful. The absence of such a theory, along with experience casting doubt on the hope of finding, one suggests a more empirical approach to problem solving which is prepared to 'weight' sorts of conditions differently when confronting different problems. This allows one to recognize that sometimes the most important conditions to change are ideas or political institutions.

For my part, I do not see why the problem-solving perspective, the 'indeterministic' viewpoint, and the antisubject/object epistemology cannot be made compatible by interpreting them in appropriate ways. But even if they cannot, reductionism is still avoidable. The approach prescribed here shares some characteristics of pragmatism and some of materialism: the first in viewing human activity, including the activity of theorizing, as a problem-solving enterprise, and the second in perceiving human activity as constrained by commonly encountered problems that are neither imagined nor capable of being imagined away. Some critics of reductionism may find this too materialistic. These critics would still be advised to wish this antireductionist well, since if he or she succeeds in explicating the perspective to avoid reductionism, antireductionism is all the more secure. Even the philosophically misguided materialists, the critic could say, reach antireductionist conclusions.

### MACROPROBLEMS

Central to the prescribed orientation is identifying social 'macroproblems,' that is, tasks which are addressed in all societies and persist through generations. Without suggesting that these are the only macroproblems or that they cannot be subdivided or combined, here are six examples:

1. The problem of maintaining the existence of the species in the face of natural and humanly constructed threats;
2. The problem of producing means of sustenance and other valued goods;
3. The problem of reproducing both the next generation of people and each day's ability to continue producing and reproducing;
4. The problem of caring for the infirm;
5. The problem of producing and reproducing culture;
6. The problem of coordinating ongoing society-wide tasks requiring a division of labour.

Identification of these macroproblems is not deduced from a general social theory, nor does it depend upon some list of supposed basic needs, and in fact not very much hinges on accepting just this list. Alternates are possible, and resulting modifications in the rest of the chapter should not affect its main argument. To say that the problems are universally faced is just to say that, for whatever reasons, enough people have placed a high enough priority on solving them that the species has continued to exist through enough generations for people to have lost track of them. If humanity is about two million years old, give or take a million, this is a short time as species survival goes, and one might be sceptical about whether the values that have kept people at it are rooted in something (like a universal species morality, biologically entrenched needs, or simply inertia) that will guarantee their persistence.

Similarly, accepting a sophisticated social or historical theory is not needed to recognize characteristics shared by these macro-problems. While there is room for controversy over claims about these characteristics, indication of social facts as opposed to conclusive proof of controverted theory is what is required to convince the sceptic. Two shared characteristics are of primary relevance to the antireductionist's project: the pervasiveness through all problem-solving domains of systematic oppressions and the fact that each macroproblem may be addressed more or less democratically.

*Oppressions.* Among the circumstances within which people find themselves when confronted with macroproblems are the many systematic oppressions sufficiently gravely felt to prompt organized movements to counter them: racism, classism, sexism, national chauvinism, ageism, heterosexism, oppressions of the handicapped, oppressions based on culture or religion, and perhaps others, such as state bureaucratic oppression of ordinary citizens (what Bob Jessop calls 'the officialdom/people contradiction').[54] Socialist theory, like that of other movement-oriented theories, is concerned to explain the origins of these oppressions and to trace their interconnections.

Relating the many hypotheses that have been produced about oppression to a list of macroproblems generates a complex classification of approaches. It might be held that efforts to solve each of the macroproblems themselves create oppressive divisions, each relative to some problem-solving domain: a division of labour for the purpose of production yields class divisions; reproductive divisions yield sex divisions; the development of state structures to administer social coordination generates bureaucratic oppression, and so on. As a variant, it might be speculated that one (or two or three) of these efforts creates oppressive forces in one domain, which in turn create oppression in other domains. Alternately, it can be urged that the division of people into oppressor and oppressed has biological or psychodynamic origins 'prior' to macro-tasks. Or there might be attempts to combine approaches.[55]

Movement theorists tend to produce theories that picture the oppressions each of their movements combat as the source of other oppressions or at least as the most important oppression to be overcome. It has been argued that the reductionist hypotheses generated by such theories creates a burden consistently to avoid sectarianism. But must one wait until an effort to meet this challenge has succeeded (or all have failed) to make progress in overcoming systematic oppressions while addressing macroproblems? A negative answer to this question is suggested in considering the shared characteristic of macroproblems that they may be more or less democratically confronted.

*Democracy.*   It should be evident that systematic oppressions place limits on the degree of democracy attainable in addressing macroproblems.[56] It is less evident, though true, that democratizing each sort of task by eliminating these oppressions would facilitate their solutions. It is true that one encounters defences of restricting the life options of women as being essential to avoid chaos in preparing food or raising children. Or it is claimed that effective workers' input to production decisions will result in inefficiency, that citizens are unable directly to govern themselves, that national security requires the domination of other nations, that society will suffer if children, the aged, or the handicapped are given important responsibilities, and so on. Arguments in Chapter Four about the efficiency of democracy and in Chapter Three about the 'democratic fix' apply to these allegations, which the democrat maintains are false.

It should also be noted that recognizing customs and beliefs as being among the given conditions of macroproblems does not commit one to uncritical acceptance of them. Critical thought is surely a prerequisite for good problem solving. Assumptions that people of certain races, nationalities, or ages can only do certain sorts of things, can and should be called into question no matter how widely believed. The fact that many socially important tasks are now carried out in ways that discriminate against the handicapped, calls for a critical examination of these ways, not an assumption that therefore the handicapped must be excluded from them. Other examples come readily to mind. Macroproblems are part of the human condition; they do not get solved once and for all, but must constantly be addressed. Since the ways they are addressed will have far-reaching effects, it makes sense to ask not just whether some mode of, for example, reproducing the species will succeed in raising a next generation, but what kind of a new generation will it succeed in raising and at what costs.

It must unfortunately be acknowledged that we now confront a situation regarding the survival of human life where the putative 'solution' of massive preparation for nuclear war could utterly fail, but this is an exceptional case where one can realistically imagine simple failure to solve a macroproblem. (Small comfort. As the bumper sticker says, 'One nuclear bomb can ruin your whole day.') Most often the question is not whether macroproblems can be solved, but how they can best be solved. Since we are concerned here with the most pervasive conditions of human life, technocratic value-neutral criteria of 'best' are not appropriate. Rather, one must ask what effects various solutions will have on the quality of people's lives, and it is hard to see how any criterion of this sort would not insist that macroproblems be solved without depending on continued systematic oppression.

It is against this background that the perspective advanced here prescribes that political theory and practice be pursued. Conditions that offer possibilities for solving macroproblems in ways that will advance democracy, and in particular that will contribute to the elimination of systematic oppression, are to be identified and actions taken to remove or circumvent limits and exploit possibilities. The perspective does not pretend to be itself a general social theory, but should be compatible with a variety of speculative theories including polycentric, unicentric, or base/superstructural theory, provided they avoid generating reductionist hypotheses.

### MOVEMENT RESEARCH

Thus political practice need not be viewed as antithetical to social theory construction. On the contrary, increasing success in democratic practice should increasingly provide experience on which such theory might build; though it is worth repeating that such experience needs to be interrogated to be useful for this purpose. Movements in industrialized countries include people possessed of research skills and facilities that can be used in the interests of coordinating and building upon movement politics in part by addressing questions like those on page 211. We may now add to this list the importance of: a) cataloguing means employed, society by society, to address macroproblems and noting the extent to which this is done critically; b) estimating the degrees of relative democracy and undemocracy with which macroproblems are addressed; and c) tracing the nature and effects of systematic oppressions confronting people in these endeavours.

Consideration of the history of research and theory construction designed to serve movement politics may illustrate how this process has already generated mutually beneficial theory and practice. Marxist theory did not originate organized struggle against class oppression, but found it already in existence and grew in reflecting on strengths and weaknesses, successes and failures in efforts to eliminate systematic oppression of workers, thus advancing the democratization of production. That Marxists have made theoretical advances with fruitful practical uses should be recognized by any champion of democratic movement politics. That the theory has also been rushed, so to speak, in a way that expanded it to cover more than is warranted with class reductionist consequences should also be realized. Though they have not had as long a history, similar comments can be made about other movement-oriented theories.

### AGAINST PRIORITIZATION

Critics might perceive a problem here. Macroproblems do not exist in isolation, but include one another's historically given conditions. For example, patriarchal institutions and values not only pose obstacles to the democratization of reproduction, but also constitute obstacles to the democratization of production. Both socialist and capitalist societies must care for the infirm, provide for administration of a complex division of labour, and transmit and provide for the creation of culture. One must recognize these problems as part of the limiting/solution-offering conditions of any mode of production, just as a specific mode of production is such a condition for addressing any other macroproblem.[57] The critic may therefore argue that it is necessary to rank macroproblems to identify those the democratic solution to which are most

230

favourable to general progress in democracy, and this requires a social theory.

An argument like this underlies Etienne Balibar's view:

> As soon as one admits that the state in some of its functions can escape class determination, as soon as one admits that it can be a simple 'public service' and represent the interests of the whole of society *before* representing those of the dominant class, *except* as historic interest of the dominant class, one is led inevitably to admit that class struggle between exploiters and exploited has limits, stops at a certain point. One is led to admit that exploiters and exploited 'also' have certain historical interests in common (those of the 'national collective,' for example), that their struggle does not determine the ensemble of social relations, that it is limited to a certain sphere of social life where it can be subordinated before certain more important exigencies.[58]

This argument depends on prior acceptance of a theory in which the struggle between exploiters and exploited is alleged to 'determine the ensemble of social relations.'

Generalized to contrast with the perspective under consideration, Balibar's argument asserts that: 1) capitalism is known to be the most important obstacle to the pursuit of any interests it is worthwhile pursuing, and 2) the practical consequence of failing to recognize this is that class struggle will sometimes be subordinated to other endeavours. The pretheoretical approach prescribed here maintains agnosticism regarding 1) and allows, regarding 2), that one can conceive of circumstances within which class struggle should in some sense take second place. Whether this is a mark against the approach depends on three factors.

*Capitalism as a Known Obstacle.*   Let us assume that macroproblems should be democratically confronted and also agree with Balibar that capitalism is the gravest obstacle for this task regarding every sort of problem. One must then ascertain whether this putative fact could be known in other ways than by derivation from a general social theory. If capitalism is such an all-pervasive obstacle and this can be known by experience, then it will be recognized in practice as the most serious limiting condition to be overcome in the democrat's approach to all macroproblems, and theoretical agnosticism will have made little practical difference.

Some socialist theorists think that anyone who agrees with them about the perniciously undemocratic effects of capitalism must do so in virtue of holding the same theory as themselves, such as some variety of Marxism, or else they must perceive the truth as through a glass darkly. An alternate view is that by our times the effects of capitalism have so intruded on various movements that (once questions about which oppressions are the 'worst' or how oppressions originate are put aside) what is required to gain assent about the antidemocratic nature of capitalism is to call people's attention to facts that can be recognized from within a variety of theoretical perspectives. Where there is disagreement that cannot be dispelled this empirical way, a case might be made that disagreement is not over whether capitalism is *an* impediment but over whether it is the *most grave* impediment. Against such a case, the defender of a pretheoretical problem-solving perspective might again argue that if capitalism really is the 'most grave' impediment to overcoming any oppression, then this, too, should impinge itself on the consciousness of anyone who does not have a vested interest in denying the fact.

*Ways of Struggling.*    Another consideration against prioritization concerns the ways class struggle might take second place. Balibar's view is common among socialists in suggesting that *either* one view class struggle as determining 'the ensemble of social relations' *or*, if this is denied in the case of any of these relations, it 'is limited to a certain sphere of social life where it can be subordinated before certain more important exigencies.' This is a false dichotomy. If it is agreed that capitalism is one obstacle to democracy and in particular to overcoming systematic oppressions, then whatever extraclass issues are taken up should be pursued in a way that is compatible with class struggle. There is no mystery about whether this can consistently be conceived of, though like any complex political project there are plenty of practical problems to overcome.

Balibar chastises those who think the state sometimes represents the interests of the whole of society. This is a challenge to the macroproblem perspective, since one employing it will no doubt hold that in some respects any state does represent such interests. Every state must address problems of society-wide coordination, and any that cannot will be attacked from all social sectors (when transportation to get the harvest to populations is unavailable, when education breaks down, when financial chaos makes national currency worthless, when the lights go out, when hospital space is altogether unavailable).[59] No doubt a state in a capitalist society will address this problem in ways that protect capitalists' economic freedom, but acknowledging this does not commit one to holding that therefore the *reason* it is addressed is to advance capitalism, any more than one should hold that the reason a socialist state addresses all problems of coordination is in order to promote equality.[60]

Similarly, forming common cause by socialists with a procapitalist state does not mean therefore that the anticapitalist struggle is shelved, but that pursuit of common causes is carried out so as *also* to combat capitalism. Taking an obvious example, in the case of a massive natural disaster few procapitalist state officials will take the attitude that nothing should be done unless capitalist profit is to be gained, and few socialists would wash their hands of cooperation with a procapitalist state that sought help to alleviate suffering caused by the disaster. However, in joining in this common cause one can expect that procapitalist state officials will try to keep down any expenses that intrude on profit, and where blame can partly be attributed to the inefficiency and corruption of capitalist agencies, they will downplay this. Forming common cause does not require endorsement of these things. More controversial instances of common cause can be viewed on this model.

In my own country, socialists have debated how to regard measures responding to a demand for national self-determination of Franco-Canadians against the dominant Anglo nation (when the Parti Québecois formed a Provincial government on this platform) and whether to support some limited actions on the part of a Liberal government to protect Canadian economic interests against U.S. domination. In both cases the majority of socialists perceived that state measures by these governments were carried out in ways that served the interests of local capitalists and concluded that therefore support was to be shunned. Nonreductionist socialists who saw the proposed state measures in the context of their potential to promote uniquely national ends supported these governments, but not uncritically. Support was seen as compatible with continuing organization against the procapitalist *ways* the Parti Quebecois and the Liberal Party pursued extraclass ends, not for the least reason that these ways worked against national self-determination itself.[61]

Making out a full case for the minority socialist views in these examples would, of course, require extensive argumentation. The point is that if situations of this sort may be considered on the model of the natural disaster, one need not accept either of the positions suggested by Balibar. In this respect, as in some others, socialists have something to learn from feminists. While a few feminists are across-the-board separatists, advocating no coordination with (nonfeminist) men in any organized effort, most neither see it as impossible to participate in patriarchally structured organizations (unions, organizations of the peace movement, socialist political parties) nor incumbent on one who does participate to acquiesce in the patriarchal ways of conducting these movements. With increasing success they have simultaneously advanced both the goals of these movements and feminist goals.

*Pluralism as Means and End.* This brings us to a third factor in evaluating the the macroproblem-solving perspective. It has been argued that the end of socialism is to advance democracy and that democracy is to be valued insofar as it promotes pluralistic freedom. Those who accept these conclusions might ask when efforts at promoting pluralistic tolerance and respect should begin – after capitalist impediments have been eliminated or before this? The response that pluralism should always be promoted is based on considerations similar to those advanced against the view that temporary democratic regress may be required for long-term advance.

Placing people whose primary concern is not to advance class struggle in a situation where they must choose either to subordinate other ends to the working-class struggle or to go it alone is likely to make cooperation among movements impossible.[62] Moreover, even if the forced choice is made and this leads to advance in class struggle, the result will be an unequal alliance which will work against construction of postcapitalist pluralistic political institutions and attitudes. The fact is that even should somebody demonstrate that one kind of oppression is in some useful sense 'primary,' people today differ on what they consider the most important problems and forms of oppression for them to con-

234

front. Not to respect this diversity in the conduct of political practice is to work against the end of pluralistic democracy.

A democratic unicentrist might attempt to avoid drawing a conclusion against prioritization, but with difficulty. One way to try would be to prescribe a two-stage approach to political practice whereby a movement for socialism in which specifically working-class concerns are dominant is preceded by a campaign to educate people to the fact that they should be dominant. Central to this problematic effort is a theory of false consciousness.

# 10 False Consciousness

IN *ONE DIMENSIONAL MAN* Herbert Marcuse expressed an opinion widely held among socialists:

> In the last analysis, the question of what are true and false needs must be answered by the individuals themselves, but only in the last analysis; that is, if and when they are free to give their own answer. As long as they are kept incapable of being autonomous, as long as they are indoctrinated and manipulated (down to their very instincts), their answer to this question cannot be taken as their own.[1]

This viewpoint is also voiced by feminists, antiracists, foes of national subjugation, and other activists frustrated by the fact that among the obstacles they confront are apathy or even resistance on the part of those whose interests they wish to promote.

## i. Oppression-sustaining Beliefs

A common antiactivist response is that such reactions indicate there are no such interests. However, putting aside for the moment the thorny question of how to identify interests, the legitimacy of the activist's concern can be supported by noting how oppression is often self-perpetuating. In the last chapter 'systematic oppressions' were described as situations where categories of people suffer unjustified thwarting of their aspirations in ongoing and nonaccidental ways. Socialist theorists were located among those wishing to overcome systematic oppression, in part by figuring out what it is that makes it nonaccidental. Like other antioppression theorists, socialists have almost always concluded that oppressive practices and institutions create beliefs and values which support them.

236

I take it as commonplace knowledge that when an educational system is biased against workers, women, or visible minorities receiving adequate training, this limits their ability to hold certain jobs, which reinforces their opinion that they are not capable of holding them. When a procapitalist press plays down evidence of support for movements against industrial pollution, trade with repressive regimes, or peace threatening 'defence' policies, this creates the opinion that such movements are only supported by a minority of malcontents thus dampening popular support. Beliefs of this kind are often also held by those who on the face of it gain by the perpetuation of oppression (middle and upper class white males, capitalists who pollute, produce arms, or trade with repressive regimes), which is why systematic oppression does not require the continuing ill will of specified 'oppressors,' but is properly called structural or institutional. Though it sometimes makes sense to ascribe false consciousness to people who profit from oppression, it is usually when those on the receiving end of sexism, racism, or class oppression hold such beliefs that the activist wants to employ this concept. How problematic such employment is depends in part on the nature of these beliefs.

*Fatalism and False Blame.* Two categories of belief straightforwardly sustain the oppression of those who hold them: fatalism and false identification of an oppression's source. It is not hard to demonstrate that the worker who is unable to pursue valued life goals due to inadequate wages and the threat of unemployment is a victim of systematic oppression. Nor is it hard to show both the falsity and the oppression-sustaining function of beliefs that this is one's inevitable lot in life or that the root cause of low wages and unemployment is, for example, immigrant labour.[2] These beliefs involve mistaken views regarding what Göran Therborn identifies as two of his three categories of 'ideology,' namely conceptions of 'what is' and of 'what is possible.' The situation is more problematic with respect to the third of Therborn's categories, 'what is good,'[3] interpreted to refer to one's aspirations.

*'Cheerfulness and Content.'* In the cases of fatalism and false blame, people's aspirations are continually thwarted partly because of false beliefs they hold. In the third category, aspirations are *not* thwarted. This is the situation that Marcuse has in mind when he

complains that a social system creates 'false needs.' Here some of a society's members are conditioned to have aspirations which can be satisfied within the system, even though the result is what someone with alternative aspirations will regard as a drone-like or unnecessarily arduous existence. It is as if the programme prescribed by the early defender of *laissez-faire* capitalism, Bernard de Mandeville, had been successfully implemented:

> [In] a free nation where slaves are not allowed of, the surest wealth consists in a multitude of laborious poor, [and to] make the society happy and people easy under the meanest circumstances, it is requisite that great numbers of them should be ignorant as well as poor. Knowledge both enlarges and multiplies our desires, and the fewer things a man wishes for, the more easily his necessities may be supplied. The welfare and felicity therefore of every state and kingdom require that the knowledge of the working poor should be confined within the verge of their occupations and never extended . . . beyond what relates to their calling. The more a shepherd, a plowman or any other peasant knows of the world and the things that are foreign to his labour or employment, the less fit he will be to go through the fatigues and hardships of it with cheerfulness and content.[4]

The situation de Mandeville hoped for is problematic, because there is good reason both to affirm and deny oppression in respect of it: on the one hand, there would technically be no oppression, but on the other hand, it does seem that de Mandeville's cheerful poor are wronged when their aspirations are thus constrained, and it is 'not in their interests' to deny them desire expanding knowledge. Moreover, when considering this category of belief, it makes the most sense to talk about the false consciousness of someone who profits from oppression. A capitalist who thinks that workers are fated to be factory fodder might be said to 'suffer' a conveniently self-serving false belief rather than false consciousness. However, it seems less inappropriate to attribute false consciousness to individuals who are capitalists insofar as they are conditioned to pursue limited goals, such as profit-making and conspicuous consumption.

### APPROACHES TO FALSE CONSCIOUSNESS

Political activists sometimes regard the harbouring of beliefs that perpetuate continuing oppression in elitist or moralistic ways. People who hold such views are thought either stupid or traitors to their groups. Perhaps some theorists share these attitudes, but their primary aim is to marshal social theory to understand the phenomenon. One may approach this topic from either a holistic or an individualistic direction. Most Marxists see false consciousness as a matter of ideology to be studied as an historical and political force, since they are mainly concerned with the false consciousness of entire groups of people.[5] Other theorists approach questions of political consciousness individualistically: either from the direction of rational decision theory (Allen Buchanan and Jon Elster are examples[6]) or psychologically (as does Joseph Gabel[7]). Traversing this distinction is another that sorts theorists of false consciousness into those who support socialist use of the concept and those who see it as confused or pernicious. Thus, Laclau and Mouffe subject the notion to criticism from a holistic orientation, while Cohen and Rogers express reservations from the direction of decision theory.[8]

Nearly all socialist theorists, both friends and foes of the notion of false consciousness, treat it on a par with that of objective interests. This chapter develops an approach that avoids appeal to objective interests while defending the usefulness of one concept of false consciousness. Also, though the approach is individualistic, it relates false consciousness to systematic group oppression. As before, agnosticism is maintained about philosophies of history or social-scientific supertheories. Instead, a stance toward false consciousness is derived from reflection on systematic oppression and on vanguardist paternalism. From this perspective, we shall address first the concept of objective interests and then the question of 'false consciousness' and what to do about it.

### ii. Objective Interests

The reason socialists are attracted to a theory of objective interests is clear. One defining feature of an objective interest (aspiration, want, or preference)[9] is that people can be said to possess one even though it is not among the current motivations for the sake of which they believe themselves to be acting, while conversely these conscious motivations or 'subjective interests' may not be objective. Thus de Mandeville's contented labourers are said not to be acting in their own interests in the cheerful pursuit of hard work. Beyond this, there is little agreement on what constitutes an objective interest. Here are possibilities to which reference is often made:

1. Interests belonging to an individual's group (such as a class or a nation) which are in some sense 'essential' to the group and hence to each of its members.
2. Needs of which one may be unaware.
3. Informed interests: consciously motivating interests a person would have with appropriate knowledge (for example, all there is to know about the causes and consequences of acting on alternative subjective interests).

Those who criticize socialist use of this concept often assume that 1) is taken as the primitive interpretation.[10] This is the most uncharitable view of a theory of objective interests, committing one to a social or historical metaphysics of transindividual group essences. Rather than joining debates over whether authors who have championed the notion of objective interests intended it in this way, the analysis presented here asks whether an unproblematic and useful theory of objective interests can be reconstructed.

### CLASS ESSENCES

References to objective interests expressed in the language of interpretation 1) – for example, in Marxist discussions of 'class interests' – can almost always be read to mean 'needs a person shares with all those in his or her class' (sense 2), or 'those interests which would motivate someone who understood the importance of uniting with others of their class' (sense 3). It is doubtful that any references in classic socialist texts can *only* be read to mean, 'interests that belong to a group entity called a class in virtue of that class' essence or role in a metaphysically grounded logic of history.' The charge of Laclau and Mouffe that the notion of objective interests 'only has sense' within 'the eschatological conception of history,'[11] overstates the case.

Or rather, if the charge is warranted it is because the concept of objective interest is used in sense 2) or 3) *conjoined* with a theory of the primacy of class struggle. Independent argument is needed to show that any such theory must be eschatological. One sometimes encounters fanatical sectarian socialists who use phrases like 'class interest' in eschatological ways appealing in fundamentalist fashion to texts of Marx and Engels for support; it is unlikely that the authors of *The German Ideology* and other works attacking historical metaphysics could intend their own views to be read in this manner.[12] Still, there are problems of interpretation because, like most socialist writers, Marx and Engels do not produce a theory interpreting group-property language. Moreover, even if 1), considered as an irreducible interpretation, is put aside, there are problems from the point of view of a theory of false consciousness with 2) and 3) as well.

We are looking for something that will count as an objective interest not just of a fatalist or someone who has falsely identified blame for oppression, but of someone content in his or her 'oppression.' Such an interest is not recognized as an interest by the person said to have it, while it may be identified by someone else. Additionally, the concept should be capable of integration with antioppressive, democratic political practice. A problem confronting any theory of objective interests is to satisfy all three of these requirements.

### NEEDS

Castoriadis describes needs as a myth of modern society, which (with the concept of rationality as calculation to achieve given ends) constitutes a core part of the 'social imaginary' of contemporary life.[13] Far from being a candidate to ground a theory of objective interests to combat false consciousness, belief in needs on Castoriadis' view contributes to false consciousness by encouraging uncritical acceptance of given goals in ignorance of their historical changeability.[14] This critique of the concept of needs is the strongest if 'need' is defined by references to group essences, metaphysically conceived, but it is also strong when needs are more naturalistically conceived as species of wants, namely, those called 'basic' that everyone has.

The fact that lists of basic wants change from time to time and from theorist to theorist warrants scepticism about whether there is any core to human motivations of this kind.[15] But even if there are core wants, the problem remains of meeting the requirement that people can be unaware of their having them. Using the notion of needs considered as core wants to explicate a theory of objective interests requires a supporting theory of potentially unconscious wants the nonsatisfaction of which is compatible with people

241

nevertheless feeling themselves content.[16] Perhaps such a theory can be found, but the requirement of justifying one creates a theoretical burden of no small dimensions.

On an alternate conception, needs may be regarded not as motivating wants but as states of affairs the securing of which is necessary to the satisfaction of certain (subjective) wants. Biological states such as being fed and kept warm are obvious candidates, but it is unlikely that people are ignorant of needs this close to survival or that they could be content in their absence. One might be ignorant and content lacking certain group-specific needs, but this raises other problems. A charitable interpretation of such claims as that all members of the working class need social revolution conceives needs as group-specific necessities. It means that some wants that all workers have will be frustrated unless there is a socialist revolution. In this case the ignorance requirement can be met without having to posit unconscious wants or improbable stupidity. Workers are surely aware of such aspirations as to have secure jobs; what they may be ignorant of is the necessity of revolution to attain this.

The problem, rather, is in making out the case for necessity while retaining room for (false) contentment. What would make it plausible to ascribe contentment to workers in the envisaged example is a belief that they can have enough security within a capitalist system. But what counts as 'enough'? If it means that within capitalism *some* progress can be made, then 'contentment' is justified, since, thanks largely to trade union activism, progress *has* been made. Or it might mean 'enough on balance,' where one would be content with modest reforms if anticipated dangers and costs of revolution outweighed a preference for full economic security. If the want in question is to have such full security that there is no danger of ever losing it (due, for instance, to an economic downturn), and this want is not offset by consideration of anticipated costs, then the case can be made that socialism is required, but it would be hard to find workers who falsely think they presently have enough security in this strong sense.

### POSTULATED CAUSES

An interpretation of objective interests as needs can be strengthened by thinking of them as theoretical entities postulated to explain the consequences of conjoined actions by some category of people.[17] Explicating Lukács, D.F.B. Tucker argues:

> [It] makes sense to identify 'interests' as part of a strategy analysis even where there is no direct evidence that people are actually aware of these interests. When a sociologist does this, he or she is usually referring to situations which are structured in such a way that some significant consequences of an agent's actions are clearly not intended.... Where liberals argue that each person acting rationally in his or her own interest contributes to the common good, Marx shows...that each rational calculator in fact (quite unintentionally) contributes to the ever increasing tensions between labour and capital, and he shows how this conflict of interests will eventually destroy market society itself.[18]

Since it stretches the concept of 'interest' too far to say that people can have an interest in the consequences of actions not intended and not even unconsciously wanted,[19] this approach must be regarded as the dubious but coherent imputation of unconscious motives to bring about certain historical consequences. Thus, just as it might be argued that the survival of the species is best explained on the hypothesis that most people have wanted to solve macroproblems (whether they thought of themselves as doing this or not), so one might maintain that a revolutionary confrontation between workers and capitalists is explained on a theory postulating conflicting objective interests.

One problem with this approach is that it requires inference to hypothesized causes from consequences, not many of which have as yet arrived on the scene. There have been few socialist revolutions and none in the circumstances envisaged by Marx: a confrontation between capitalists and a bloc led by industrial workers in an economically and politically advanced capitalist society. This does not mean the concept of objective interests thus hypothesized makes no sense, but it is hard to test its adequacy. A related difficulty is that sometimes consciously pursued class struggle has taken place in circumstances predicted by socialist theories, but other times it has not, as for example when a working class reacts conservatively to economic crises or even embraces fascist policies. These things have happened, and hence (let us deterministically suppose in accord with the interpretation under consideration) they were consequences of something. The problem is nonarbitrarily to rule out out the claim that it is as justified to postulate class collaborationist or fascist motives as it is to hypothesize socialist revolutionary ones in explaining working-class behaviour.

Marković grants that 'a disposition to dominate' has been conditioned into people by competitive and oppressive societies as a 'second nature' along with a nondominating, 'creative disposition.' He justifies regarding the latter, though not the former, as 'truly human,' because the creative disposition is 'much older, much more deeply rooted' and a 'necessary condition of human history' that allows for novelty in a way compatible with democracy and without oppressing others.[20] The key point is the one about history's preconditions, since without it an argument from duration could be countered by alleging that even if human nature was usually 'creative' in the past, it has since changed, and there is no reason to suppose it will not be 'dominating' for the indefinite future. Unfortunately, even a successful argument about a creative disposition being a precondition for human history will still not provide a criterion to isolate objective interests. Acceptance of this fact is compatible with holding that dominating dispositions are *also* objective and that what makes history possible is that the creative interests on balance outweigh the dominating ones but that there is no guarantee that the creative ones will always win out.

One response is to say that creative dispositions can serve to identify objective interests if the predominance of creative activities, and hence the continuation of human history, is *normatively* to be preferred to the dominance of activities following from contrary dispositions. This move would give one a straightforward criterion of objective interests, but it would do so by including normative evaluation of consequences said to result from acting on these interests. Some democratic-socialist theorists, like Seyla Benhabib and Ted Benton, charge that theories featuring a doctrine of objective interests are flawed precisely by such conflation of explanatory and prescriptive considerations.[21] This is a telling criticism. The problem with using normative criteria in sorting consequences as to postulated origins is that this vitiates attempted justifications of such postulations by reference to their explanatory power. Unless one employed a teleological theory whereby the normative worth of something explains why it comes to pass – the eschatology criticized by Laclau and Mouffe – an explanation would be vacuous. The fact that a morally valued state of affairs comes to pass would be explained on the postulate that people have acted on interests that lead to morally valued states of affairs.

Benton's alternative is to distinguish between 'powers,' which can figure as the objects of scientific explanation, and 'interests,' which are not explained but 'constructed' in practice.[22] Agnes Heller, by contrast, rejects the notion of objective interests (or 'needs') as in any way explanatory and takes a thoroughgoing prescriptive approach: '[W]e will not divide needs into "real" and "irreal," but we do make use of a moral norm. It can be formulated [that] all needs should be recognized and satisfied with the exception of those whose satisfaction would make people simple means. The categorical imperative [never treat others as means] then places a restrictive role in the evaluation of needs.'[23] Heller's interpretation is unproblematic in itself, but does not contribute (nor does she intend it to contribute) to a useful theory of false consciousness. We shall return to Benton's analysis.

### KNOWLEDGE

On this interpretation, people's objective interests are their presently motivating ones plus those they would have and minus those they would not if they possessed relevant knowledge. Connolly puts it that '[p]olicy $x$ is more in A's interest than policy $y$ if A, were he to experience the *results* of both $x$ and $y$, would *choose x* as the result he would rather have for himself.'[24] Mansbridge requires 'perfect knowledge,'[25] while in addition to the knowledge Connolly specifies, Nielsen includes understanding of the causes of one's preferences.[26] This interpretation of objective interests may be the strongest. It makes sense on it to say that people are both ignorant of an objective interest and content (blissfully ignorant). One can also be said to 'have' an objective interest of which he or she is unaware. This will happen when presently motivating (subjective) interests include a preference that objective interests be satisfied. Surely few people lack this subjective interest. Taking Connolly's definition, who, given a choice between being able to implement an informed or an uninformed policy, would opt for the latter? Still, this interpretation confronts conceptual and practical difficulties.[27]

The main conceptual problem is to specify what kind of knowledge and how much is needed for someone's objective and subjective interests to be in phase. Omniscience is the safest candidate, but then no mortal would be aware of his or her objective interests or those of anyone else. If the most advanced understanding of the time is considered enough, then one's objective interests would depend on how reliable this understanding happens to be. Or, to identify interests by reference to certain *objects* of knowledge, different objective interests will be yielded depending on whether one includes knowledge of the effects of acting in certain ways, knowledge of causes of preferences, moral knowledge, or combinations. Perhaps a satisfactory theory allowing for progress in knowledge of specified things to determine progress in objective interests can be devised, but a theory of false consciousness should not have to await such a problem-fraught epistemological project.

PATERNALISM

Moreover, there is a practical problem. This interpretation of objective interests lends itself to paternalism because of a familiar, often persuasive and sometimes sound justification of paternalistic measures. The paternalist undertakes actions that will have an effect on somebody who does not want them to be taken, justifying this by the claim that taking the actions is in that person's interests. On alternate conceptions of objective interests only such unconvincing justifications can be offered by the paternalist as: 'This is what you deeply want yourself;' or 'This is in the interests of that about you that has important historical consequences.' But if objective interests are regarded as informed preferences, the argument is the one we all grew up with: 'This is what you would want yourself if you knew better;' or 'When you see how things turn out, you'll agree this is the best thing for you.' Everyone has experienced paternalism thus justified, and it is therefore not difficult to fall into familiar parent or child roles in political contexts.

Additionally, paternalists can justify their activities to themselves in the belief that among the results will be that people acquire the needed knowledge both to see that the paternalist was right and also to eliminate the necessity for further paternalism. They will be vindicated, and paternalism will autodestruct. Herein lies the problem with paternalism. Viewed rationalistically, in abstraction from considerations of social-psychological dynamics and of social and political institutions, the approach makes political paternalism look compatible with efforts to increase democracy. But how, in actual practice, is the paternalist going to react when people fail to grant the wisdom of his or her decisions? One possible response is to call into question an earlier assessment of what is in people's interests, but another response is to conclude that *more paternalism* is required, since people have not yet learned about themselves. On this second response paternalism does not autodestruct but gets more deeply entrenched.

It is not accidental that paternalists – in small social units like families and work places and in larger ones like states – almost always respond in the second way. Paternalists have a stake in not admitting that they are wrong, as it is claim to special knowledge that justifies their paternalistic measures. (Also, not everyone who believes himself or herself to be in possession of special knowledge engages in paternalistic activity, and one might ask about the psychological profile of somebody who chooses to assume this altruistic burden.) In addition, there are structural inhibitions to reversing a paternalistic course once taken. The paternalist cannot consistently act for those ignorant of their interests in an environment with much democracy. The more easily more people can make decisions, the less effective paternalistic authority will be. Hence, protections against democratic advances are required.

In state institutions or political parties these range from formal and informal checks on the ease with which representative mechanisms can be employed (enormous cost and effort is required to reverse a 'representative's' decisions, or leaders can ignore public opinion with relative impunity) to outright police state measures. Once in place, such structures are hard to dismantle. Worse, they provide avenues for the abuse of power by nonpaternalistic authoritarians (Lenin is replaced by Stalin), and they create a self-reinforcing political culture as a frustrated populace either gives up hope of self-rule (thus strengthening the paternalist's opinion that they are not suited to it) or becomes bellicosely hostile to existing political leadership which responds by implementing further restrictions. Once again, less democracy leads spiral-like to still less.

If these practical dangers of paternalism are real, a further theoretical problem for a theory of objective interests is raised. It

247

was noted that people may have as a present subjective interest that their informed ('objective') interests be served, even though they do not yet know what these are. But if paternalism has antidemocratic consequences, knowledge of this fact should lead people to want to avoid paternalism. Thus, paternalism is out of accord with people's informed interests; it is in their objective interests (on the interpretation in terms of knowledge) to be allowed to make their own mistakes. Either a good argument against paternalism can be given from the point of view of objective interest theory, or doubt is cast about the usefulness of such a theory, since it yields contradictory policies. At this point the defender of a knowledge-grounded theory of objective interests might join a possible defence of one class-reductionistic position.

### PRACTICAL EDUCATION

It should be noted here that not all those who give prominent place to objective interests in a social theory are class reductionists. Indeed, they need not be unicentric reductionists of any variety, because in principle an individual could be visualized as comprising a plurality of objective interests. Thus an objective interest theory is not conclusive evidence of reductionism. Though the question does not directly concern the task at hand, it would be harder to argue the converse position that a reductionistic approach may dispense with any concept of objective interests. Perhaps a depersonalized class-reductionistic social theory could avoid a doctrine of objective, or indeed subjective, interests (as E.P. Thompson claims of Althusser's approach),[28] but most class reductionists hold that all workers have common objective interests. What differentiates them from nonreductionists, who may agree on this point, is that they also think furthering class interests is of overriding importance.

In the last chapter a prodemocratic class reductionist was envisaged who urged that multimovement political activity be prepared for by campaigns to educate people about the primacy of class struggle. Such a campaign might also be thought useful for bringing people's objective and subjective interests into phase without resorting to paternalism. A worry that any nonpaternalist will have about this approach is that it assumes, contrary to Marx's famous admonition, that the educator does not need to be educated.[29] How, the antipaternalist will ask, does somebody come to know what is in other people's objective interests so that he or she can teach this to them.? Pertinent to our present topic is a long-standing socialist view that important as research and abstract reflection are, engaging in actual political practice is also required.

Defence of this assertion might begin by noting that no attempt at blueprint politics – bringing to a political task a full plan of action derived from theoretical speculations – has ever succeeded. Rather, in the context-bound and rapidly changing world of active politics, hypotheses about what questions to ask and how to answer them are constantly revised and adjusted in the light of changing information close to the details of day-to-day practice and requiring reflection on successes and failures of actions actually taken. This fact, though typically overlooked by establishment academic theorists, is commonplace to socialist and other movement theorists. However, it follows that 'educators' must constantly keep informing themselves by theoretical-cum-practical engagement in actual politics.

Not only does the educator need to be educated in practice, but so do those to be in turn educated. On this point there is even more consensus among socialist theorists (the paternalistic wing of which now concerns us). John Dewey, addressing a problem of how to educate people to communitarian interests, remarked that 'the essential need' for this purpose is 'the improvement of the methods and conditions of debate, discussion and persuasion.'[30] Very few socialists will disagree that these are important skills and that an impediment to mobilization against capitalism is the difficulty with which people acquire critical abilities. However, still fewer would agree with Dewey that improvement in debate, discussion, and persuasion is '*the* problem of the [creation of a community-minded] public.'[31] They would rather endorse the spirit behind Brecht's remark on this point: 'People can only educate themselves; and they will establish popular government not when they grasp it with their minds but when they grasp it with their hands.'[32]

## VANGUARDISM

On the face of it, to agree that the educator needs to be educated in political activity is to abandon paternalism, since the would-be educator would have to give up claim to privileged knowledge that is brought to such activity. A paternalist response is that once the educators have come to have necessary knowledge (no matter how), they can then educate others by engaging with them in political practice. The difficulty with this response is seen in asking what practice is to be engaged in and how it is to be conducted.

Presumably the educators and those to be educated have different ideas about what the goals and forms of political activity should be (since otherwise the problem of paternalism would not exist). Whose ideas should be followed? To engage people in activity for which they see no need, in ways they do not favour guarantees that only a small group will be educated. To join people in projects with which the educator does not agree puts the latter in a pedagogically weak position. Either the differences are made known, in which case the would-be educator is perceived as an outsider, or the differences are kept secret, and when this is detected he or she is also regarded as a subversive.

Socialist vanguardism may be viewed as an attempt to solve this problem. Educators consolidate themselves in a political organization where they overtly proclaim their belief that they know better than others what is to be done. The problem of the pedagogic bind is supposedly avoided because the organization remains separate from what many vanguardists refer to as 'spontaneous' organizations of the people with which they cooperate, first by winning people's trust and respect (due to vanguardist dedication and organizational skills, made possible by 'correct understanding of the line of march'). The problem of educating the educator is solved by encouraging vanguard members to join 'spontaneous' organizations, or to remain in them, not just as educators but also to bring the organizations' experiences to party educational forums where the views of the vanguardists themselves are critically developed in their light.[33]

In my experience, this is a prime example of the failure in practice of a theory that may look attractive on paper. In practice, the vanguardist organization establishes at best distant relations with other organizations and at worst hostile ones, and vanguardist views get dogmatically entrenched rather than critically developed. Many antivanguardists attribute this to the psychological makeup of people attracted to vanguard organizations. An alternate (or if one wishes, supplementary) explanation is in terms of the political dynamics of paternalism. The fact that the formation of vanguard parties (or movements, or preparty formations, or caucuses) is partly paternalistically motivated is bound to be reflected in both their internal structures and their stances toward other organizations. The orientation of a vanguard organization is still paternalistic, confronting the apparent choice between self-isolating attempts to force policies on others or backfiring efforts to disguise one's differences. Vanguard party attempts to manipulate popular organizations and establish fronts are the unsatisfactory results of efforts to confront this dilemma.

Since knowledge admits of degree, the vanguard organization will itself tend to become hierarchically ordered, with those putatively best informed in positions of authority and suspicious of challenges to their views from below. This situation is not conducive to the ongoing self-education of the vanguardists. Moreover, when there are strong differences over what the correct line is, the vanguard organization is likely to divide into factions or split into separate parties such that the factions or parties become increasingly homogeneous in members' views, and each has a stake in holding firm so as not to give aid and comfort to the intra- or inter-vanguard opposing camps.

### ANALYSING 'INTERESTS'

The conclusion suggested by preceding sections is not that the notion of objective interests makes no sense, but rather that it makes too much sense. There are several ways to interpret the concept, each with problematic dimensions, and there is the danger of encouraging suspect paternalistic approaches to political activity. The response of this chapter is formally similar to that of Benton, which views objective interest theory as a confusion of normative and explanatory considerations. Without for the moment addressing the substance of Benton's view, his general strategy will be extended to urge that objective interest theory confuses at least four kinds of things which should be kept separate, namely:

1. A theory of false consciousness;
2. A theory of group interests;
3. Devices for explanation and prediction of political behaviour; and
4. Devices for moral evaluation and prescription.

251

Analytic philosophers of the 1950s enjoyed 'dissolving' philosophical problems by analysing them into components, the confusion of which they claimed generated pseudoproblems. The approach proved to be less useful than intended, since traditional problems of epistemology, political philosophy, and ethics remained, despite ingenious efforts to show that these entire disciplines rested on conceptual or linguistic 'mistakes.' However, more modest exercises of analysis sometimes do show that what appears to be a single problem that is both difficult to solve and hard to comprehend is in fact several problems, each relatively easy to comprehend if still difficult to solve. The problem of identifying objective interests is a good candidate. It is possible to show that different things said to be objective interests appropriately, but differently, figure in enterprises associated with the items in the above list. The prescription that follows is that one address problems specific to each enterprise, without relying on some general theory of objective interests appropriate to them all. (Perhaps this requires abandoning talk of objective interests altogether, but at the very least it should always be made clear which sense is being employed.)

Starting at the bottom of the list, objective interests thought of normatively (as interests that ought to be satisfied) appropriately figure in moral prescriptions. Considered as informed interests they also appropriately figure in one approach to ethical theory. This is the attempt of consequentialist ethicists, like Richard Brandt,[34] to solve a difficult problem for them. Classic utilitarians had seen a need to sort wants into what J.S. Mill called 'higher' and 'lower' to take account of the intuition that it is, in Mill's phrase, 'better to be Socrates dissatisfied than a fool satisfied.'[35] But it is difficult to produce a criterion for such a distinction without introducing extrautilitarian moral standards. Informed interests are appropriately employed in addressing this problem by identifying 'higher' wants as those people would likely have with knowledge.

However, as the arguments of the next section should illustrate, it is neither necessary nor plausible to insist that noncoincidence of subjective and objective interests in the senses we have been addressing constitutes political false consciousness. This applies also to interpretations of objective interests in terms of explanation or prediction. Interests thought of as postulated causes of behaviour or even as unintended consequences of joint activity are at home in the former undertakings. They might also be used to identify groups as those people who share certain postulated motives or whose unintended activities tend to converge in certain ways. But where groups are already identified on these or other criteria, group interests are probably best thought of as states of affairs necessary for the group to attain something it is thought (by members of the group or by someone else) they ought to attain.

### WORKING-CLASS INTERESTS

To illustrate these points, consider claims made about the working class, conceived broadly as those in an industrialized, commodity-producing society who exchange their ability to work for wages. This is a 'structural' criterion for identifying a social group that makes no essential reference to its members' 'interests' in any sense of the term.[36] Such reference becomes appropriate in the following circumstances:

A. It is noted that despite heterogeneity in their expressed aspirations, workers engage in behaviour like forming unions and supporting legislation that not only puts them in conflict with a boss, but limits society-wide capitalist ability and is resisted by procapitalist governments accordingly. These general effects can be noted as initially unintended consequences of behaviour caused by circumstances associated with being a worker, or such an explanation can include reference to postulated unconscious class-confrontational motives of the workers in question. These motives are 'objective interests' in one sense.

B. Aspirations most workers have – such as to gain secure employment with sufficient remuneration for lifetime postsubsistence survival – are shown to require socialism to be universally attained. Socialism is thus a necessity for them, another sense of 'objective interest.'

C. It is maintained that everyone ought equally to have such employment, and among the grounds for this prescription are that if workers understood their common situation, the quality of life in an egalitarian society, and the possibility of achieving it, they would agree with the prescription. These are moral and ethical uses of 'objective interests.'

253

### iii. False Consciousness and Interests

Let us extend this list of alternatives to a domain where false consciousness should be located. Figuring in social-scientific theory, morality, or ethics, the various senses of 'objective interests' so far discussed are highly abstract. The concept of false consciousness, by contrast, is required to respond to immediate political problems, such as:

D′. Some workers believe, to take an example of John Mc-Murtry's, that 'whatever rank is held by individuals in the social order represents their intrinsic worth;'[37] those who hold this belief resist efforts at organization to change oppressive conditions they falsely believe themselves lamentably unsuited to escape.

D″. Male workers think that women's incursion into traditionally male-dominated work is the root cause of job insecurity. This, too, is an instance of false consciousness insofar as the belief helps to keep the labour force divided.

The thesis of this chapter is that prescriptions for overcoming false consciousness that depend on a theory of objective interests will either be implausible or biased in a paternalistic direction and that, accordingly, 'false consciousness' should not be defined by reference to them. This section will sketch a theory of false consciousness designed to help discover the conditions under which certain beliefs and values, such as those of D′ and D″, may be changed. In doing this, only passing comments will be made about another practical political problem:

E. A nonfatalistic, nonsexist male worker who recognizes the need for collective action is nonetheless inactive, wishing to avoid the risks and effort required and reckoning that long-term benefits secured by those workers who do work to improve the collective lot will accrue to him whether he participates or not.

In his *Making Sense of Marx*, Jon Elster discusses 'class consciousness' by reference to attempts to overcome this problem of the 'free rider.'[38]

It is not clear whether Elster would want class consciousness tempered by 'rational' inactivity to count as an instance of false consciousness, but in this chapter it will not be taken in this way. For consciousness to be 'false,' it must include certain kinds of false beliefs, and the main political problem addressed will be to find conditions conducive to change in these beliefs rather than asking after conditions in which people without them are likely to take action. Critics of the view Elster expresses, such as Richard Miller,[39] charge that it incorporates a reified model of individuals. They might argue that once D-type problems are solved, E-type ones will atrophy. The chapter remains agnostic on this question.

## FALSE CONSCIOUSNESS AND OPPRESSION

False consciousness in this narrower sense is found in 'political culture' – roughly, beliefs widely held across some or all portions of a society's population as common-sense social and political descriptions with recognized normative implications. This field is sometimes referred to as 'ideology,' but since opinions regarding the scope of ideology and its relation to false consciousness are so varied, the less theoretically loaded term will be used here.[40] Within a political culture, false beliefs that sustain one's own oppression count as instances of false consciousness. Though there may be other types, clear cases are fatalistic beliefs and those assigning false blame. Not all such beliefs exemplify false consciousness, only those held by people whose own continuing oppression is partly maintained by their holding them and only if the beliefs are sufficiently widespread and motivating of social practice to be part of a society's political culture.

Some might be tempted to generate yet another sense of 'objective interests' from false consciousness thus construed. Workers who understand that social ranks have no correlation with intrinsic worth or who know that women workers are not the root cause of job insecurity do not suffer false consciousness in respect of beliefs about these matters. They might therefore be said to realize that their 'true interests' are to resist practices that reinforce their subordination and to form common cause with women workers. However, we are not here *defining* 'objective interests' as 'interests one would have with knowledge,' but noting that in order to overcome false consciousness, certain false beliefs must be shed. If one insisted on using the misleading term 'objective interests,' a phrase like 'it is not in male workers' objective interests to believe that females should be kept out of the work force' just means, 'holding this belief contributes to the systematic oppression of male workers.'

### TRUTH AND CHEERFULNESS

Essential to this approach to false consciousness is that certain beliefs do in fact sustain people's own oppression and that they are false. Each claim can be challenged in a variety of ways. One obvious challenge is to argue that true beliefs also sustain oppression. Sometimes it is the very truth of a belief that gives it force. For example, in a capitalist labour market, demands by women for equal job opportunities *are* a threat to male workers. Another challenge is to question how the 'cheerful and contented oppressed' are accounted for.

In response to the first objection, it can be observed that beliefs implicated in false consciousness are usually parts of common-sense explanatory theories, the kind that make everybody a 'philosopher,' as Gramsci puts it.[41] A male worker's belief that attempts by women to enter his segment of the labour force is a threat to his job may be true and thus would not constitute false consciousness. It becomes so when conjoined with the further belief that this is an inevitable feature of the labour market (a low-level theory conjoining elements of fatalism and false blame) or with a view that women are illegitimately making these attempts since their proper place is in the home (a theory attributing primary responsibility for job competition to unjustified women's demands). It is the mutual reinforcement of discriminatory practices, true beliefs about their effects, and false assignment of causes for these effects that sustains oppression. A challenge that the approach cannot take account of those 'content' in their oppression takes us back to Marcuse's point.

A first response is to grant that someone who is entirely cheerful and content in his or her life indeed cannot be counted as oppressed, but that this is justified and does not exclude very many things one might want to count as oppressive. It is lamentable that some people have aspirations that can be satisfied by leading lives many would consider intolerable, and it is morally reprehensible that some try to engineer such a state of affairs after the manner of de Mandeville's prescription. But one can harbour attitudes of lament and moral outrage without imputing false consciousness to the subjects in question. Consider people who have adapted to life in a harsh natural environment. One might lament that life is so hard for them, and one might condemn it if others who had a stake in their remaining in that environment deliberately kept knowledge of alternatives from them. But if the people in question had adapted in such a way as to be satisfied with their lives, it would be odd to attribute false consciousness to them.

From the point of view of democracy, the danger in counting contented people oppressed parallels that involved in questioning the democracy of a 'closed society.' In both cases, this can be used to rationalize paternalistic measures where people are forced to 'enjoy' a life that it is thought they ought to like or would like if they knew enough. However, as in the case of closed societies, persons are rarely completely contented through manipulation. Such a person would have to lack both the power to imagine alternative life prospects and contradictory wants. These circumstances are especially unlikely in present societies which raise false hopes and create desires that cannot be satisfied.[42] It is also important to note that there is a difference between satisfaction and resignation. These are confused when fatalistic attitudes lead to making the best of what is perceived as an inevitably bad situation and to expressing 'satisfaction' that at least one has succeeded in doing this.

It is also relevant to distinguish between abstract and practical expressions of aspirations. The point is illustrated in Gramsci's challenge to the view that workers who express procapitalist values are therefore entirely lacking in anticapitalist consciousness, since this is often also expressed in everyday life. The result is 'the coexistence of two conceptions of the world, one affirmed in words and the other displayed in effective action.' Gramsci described this not as self-deception, but as a product of the simultaneous influences of one's daily life and work conditions, on the one hand, and workers' 'intellectual subordination,' on the other, producing a 'contradictory consciousness.'[43] Socialist researchers sometimes describe practically expressed views as workers' 'real' views, but it is not necessary to the general point about aspirations to do this.

257

Rather, one can note that there are often tensions within individuals between contradictory values and beliefs, some of which are not explicitly articulated by them.

A more controversial way that apparently contented people may be regarded 'oppressed' is when the satisfaction of aspirations at one time in their lives contributes to nonsatisfaction at a later time. Being content in a sex-, race-, or class-ghettoized form of work, recreation, and education in one's youth is later regretted when it is seen what options were cut off. Perhaps this is as far as one can go in allowing for 'contented oppression,' but it should be seen as a limiting case of oppression. The analysis requires a view of personal identity which allows the contented 'bearer' of certain aspirations to be the same person as the later discontented bearer of other aspirations, and this already begins to raise more general theoretical challenges to the present analysis. Two of these will now be addressed, one concerning rationality and one concerning the relation of knowledge and practice.

### RATIONALITY AND MADNESS

Joshua Cohen and Joel Rogers avoid discussion of false consciousness – which they associate with theories of 'mass delusion' or an 'innate inability to understand' – and they explicate instead a view about working people's consent in capitalism being a rational response to life in a system that rewards seeking short-term, material benefits ('demand constraints') while making it very hard for anyone to change the system ('resource constraints').[44] Joseph Gabel argues a contrary view that the 'false consciousness of political groups is related both to child thought, through the prevalence of egocentric mechanisms, and to schizophrenia – and more particularly to morbid rationalism and geometrism – through the reification of interhuman relationships and the spatialization of historical duration.'[45] On one of these views, what some have called false consciousness is rationality within a constraining system, and on the other it approaches madness.

Each view has something to be said for it, while also being problematic. Cohen and Roger's approach makes it possible to view false consciousness as society-wide without attributing stupidity or insanity to whole populations. Such attribution requires accepting highly speculative and counterintuitive social-

258

psychological theories or drastically constraining the range of false consciousness. The weakness of their view is that while it makes sense in explaining people's economic behaviour, it is hard to see how it could be used to explain right-wing politics on the part of those who have nothing to gain even in the short range from capitalism or (without joining the Cohen/Rogers theory to a class-reductionistic perspective) views like sexism and racism, which support extraclass oppressions.[46] To explain these things a psychodynamic theory (whether Gabel's or an alternative)[47] is more attractive, especially when such views take extreme yet widespread form as in popularly based fascist movements.[48]

Though we presently lack general theories of rationality or of the personality sufficient to account for all aspects of false consciousness, perhaps it is not too rash to suggest that these contrasting approaches may be regarded as addressing two aspects of the phenomenon rather than as contradictory interpretations. Thus persisting fatalism might adequately be explained by reference to the effects on people's beliefs of structurally entrenched carrots and sticks; while a more specifically psychodynamic theory may be required to explain how people doggedly sustain such superficial and antihuman views as racism and sexism.

### PRACTICE AND KNOWLEDGE

Althusser's definition of 'ideology' places it in a realm of practice, distinct from one of knowledge: '[An] ideology is a system (with its own logic and rigour) or representations (images, myths, ideas or concepts...) endowed with a historical existence and role within a given society.... We can say that ideology, as a system of representations, is distinguished from science in that in it the practico-social function is more important than the theoretical function (function as knowledge).'[49] Insofar as this view sees ideology as the way people 'live their actions,'[50] it emphasizes its normative nature for everyday activity – part of political culture. The view has also been fruitfully employed in post-Althusserian theories that oppressed people's identity, and hence their consciousness as members of an oppressed group, come into being in the process of group struggle, thus offering an alternative to a perspective where group consciousness is thought of as a matter of people somehow discovering preexisting class or other group identities said to be their true selves. However, when Althusser's view suggests a rupture between practical norms and social beliefs either such that the latter are and the former are not truth valuable, or such that they are true or false in different senses of these terms,[51] his approach differs from the one adopted here.

An example is Benton's analysis. He criticizes Stephen Lukes, William Connolly and others for defining 'interests' by reference to informed wants on the grounds that these things belong to different 'discourses' – wants belonging to that involved in ascertaining somebody's 'power,' and interests belonging to the discourse appropriate to engaging in 'ideological struggle.' Ideological struggles primarily concern 'the constitution and incorporation of individuals into opposed patterns of social identity, loyalty and commitment, together with the interests that these carry.' This discourse differs from one in which wants and preferences figure because, whereas ascertaining one's power and hence one's wants requires no more than evidence of 'cognitive and political inquiry,' assessing interests requires the 'application of moral, prudential and/or political standards,' and this is an 'evaluative' as opposed to a 'cognitive' activity. Benton concludes that rational persuasion is insufficient to change people's identity or loyalties, since such change requires practical activities like trade union activism.[52]

Two claims are fused in this analysis: that changing people's ideological attitudes is not primarily a matter of rational persuasion and that these attitudes are commitments to forms of activity subject to political and moral evaluation instead of beliefs to be judged true or false. On the approach to false consciousness prescribed in this chapter, the first of these claims is endorsed, but the second is contested. Many who share Benton's orientation refrain from talking of false consciousness precisely because they think it inappropriate to describe viewpoints within the field of popular political culture as true or false. One might defend this by appeal to the ethical noncognitivist position that attitudes of moral approval or disapproval are not the sorts of things that can be either true or false. However, a broader argument than this is required to challenge the approach to false consciousness advanced in this chapter, which is concerned not specifically about the truth valuableness of moral beliefs, but about the effects of a wide variety of true or false beliefs on people's aspirations.

The critic must claim there are no beliefs, discovery of the truth or falsity of which crucially affect one's 'social identify, loyalty, or commitment.' On this chapter's view of false consciousness, such a claim must be resisted, since a main point of advancing the viewpoint is to identify beliefs that can and must be changed in efforts to overcome antidemocratic, systematic oppression. Perhaps it is assumed that the truth of oppression-sustaining beliefs which shape one's character could only be challenged by rational argumentation about fundamental matters of ethics and morality. However, this is debatable. One alternative is that critical questioning of oppression-sustaining values people harbour is prompted when these values interfere with an overriding desire for autonomy. Another alternative is that certain sorts of knowledge about the origins of one's beliefs leads him or her to challenge them.

*Critical Thought.* William Connolly's theory of political consciousness illustrates the first alternative. He takes it that whatever else people aspire to do or be, humans wish 'to see themselves as responsible agents freely choosing to play the roles available to them,' but that the extent to which this is possible is advanced or impeded by institutional structures. Political consciousness changes as people, discovering that socially approved ends are 'empty or defeated by the institutional means . . . necessary to their attainment' and thwarted in efforts to be responsible, begin to think critically 'about the roles they play, the purposes they serve, and the assumptions underlying those activities. . . .'[53]

Connolly's point is well taken. Perhaps we can imagine a person who is conditioned in such a way that he or she has no desire at all to make autonomous decisions. Such 'people' appear in fiction as robots or zombies (though even they usually break ranks by the end of the movie and strike out on their own). Discovery by people that their attempts to be responsible and autonomous agents are thwarted by constraining social institutions is bound to be unsettling and will lead people to question the extent to which they have unwittingly accommodated their goals to these constraints, thus beginning to affect their sense of identity as potential political actors. This challenges fatalism in particular, when people question prior beliefs of theirs that institutional constraints are 'naturelike in form or . . . rational means to universal ends.'[54]

*Origins of Beliefs.* A related way that beliefs about the origins of beliefs affect one's attitude toward their content is central to Allen Wood's interpretation of the Marxist theory of ideology: '[For Marx] as long as they are ignorant of the fact that their beliefs are socially prevalent on account of the social function the beliefs

fulfil, people are likely to think that these beliefs are so widespread because they are justified (that they are either self-evident or authenticated by the experience of humanity through the ages). Ignorance of the material basis for beliefs can lend credibility to a great many commonly held moral, religious and philosophical ideas which would otherwise be recognized for the plain rubbish they are.'[55] This view implies that knowledge about the origins of previously held false beliefs undermines them.

Wood does not specify whether he thinks Marx held that this knowledge involves acceptance of a detailed and proven historical theory, but such full knowledge need not be required. It is enough to argue, as do proponents of the epistemological 'causal theory of knowledge,'[56] that a person who learns that the origins of a belief he or she has been holding likely have nothing to do with what would make the beliefs true cannot continue (sincerely) to believe it. For example, some biological connection between sex and work abilities would make it true that women cannot hold a type of job in virtue of their sex. Consider a person who had believed women are thus incapacitated on the authority of tradition or the word of socially designated experts assuming that this authority derived from recognition of the actual inability of women. Should this person now come to doubt that there had ever been such recognition, it would require extraordinary self-deception to continue believing that women are limited in this way. Unless there were additional sources of the belief, it would be suspended and behaviour based on false blame inhibited.

### iv. Democratic Practice

The argument has so far been that false consciousness should be thought of as the harbouring of beliefs that sustain one's own oppression and that nothing but confusion is gained by trying to interpret it in terms of objective interests. The approach is 'rationalistic' in seeing false beliefs as central to false consciousness, recognizable as false, and capable of being changed by those who hold such beliefs partly due to this recognition. It departs from rationalism in rejecting the view that winning people to a general theory of human nature or an ethical theory is required to overcome false consciousness. Instead, beliefs supportive of oppression are most effectively challenged in the very process of taking action against this oppression.

This is a traditional Marxist view, and it is well argued, too, by advocates of participatory democracy for its educative effects. The arguments of these theorists will not be rehearsed here.[57] Rather, the chapter concludes by coming once again at the chicken-and-egg problem that, given the necessity for overcoming false consciousness of practical education, engaging in antioppressive struggle requires challenging oppression-sustaining beliefs and vice versa. This problem admits of solution if antioppressive activities are carried out in such a way as to expand democracy, since this is both practically educative and, like democracy itself, admits of degrees so that some such self-educating practice provides a basis for yet more. Let us take the example of 'oppressed group consciousness,' that is, awareness by members of an oppressed group that they share a common oppression with common sources that can be combatted by conjoined activity.

### GROUP CONSCIOUSNESS

It is a recurrent claim of Adam Przeworski that 'classes do not emanate from social relations,' but 'constitute the effects of practices, the object of which is precisely class organization, disorganization, or reorganization.'[58] Przeworski probably does not want to deny that there are oppressions common to members of what may become a class which antedate their forming themselves into one. Rather he argues that there is nothing inevitable about the emergence of classes as comprised of people conscious of their group identity and consciously behaving jointly as a political force, and that people simultaneously become both conscious in this way and potent in the process of struggle: 'Class struggle [is] any struggle that has the effect of class organization or disorganization.'[59]

The point is relevant here, since it describes a situation where people come to have group consciousness in the midst of struggle itself. This is possible because, like the class consciousness attending it, 'struggling' is a complex process involving actions ranging from defiant nonacquiesence through organized resistance to reconstruction of a previously oppressive institution on new lines. Thus, Gramsci distinguishes three levels of a 'collective political consciousness': a feeling of unity with those who do similar work; solidarity with all the members of one's economic class; and a recognition of the need to take the lead in a general political transformation of society.[60] He concludes that the most elementary resistance has the potential to initiate an escalating process of increased struggle-cum-consciousness.

When democracy is considered a matter of the degree to which people exercise effective collective self-determination, class struggle is also seen to expand democracy, involving the same process of overcoming false consciousness by and in practice. In particular, it is the effort to extend control by workers over important aspects of their social environment. Crucial for overcoming false consciousness are identification of capitalist economic institutions and practices as the source of oppression and nonfatalistic conviction that capitalism can be combatted. The same can be said of any group struggle against oppression. People's confidence in their abilities to take charge of their lives grows as they are increasingly successful at identifying and challenging sources of oppression. However, if overcoming false consciousness is seen, like group consciousness and like democracy, as a matter of degree, the question must be asked whether this suffices, either for securing group aims or in generally advancing democracy. That it does not suffice is indicated by the fact that short-term successes are compatible with movement sectarianism with its self-destructive and antidemocratic consequences.

### THE LENINIST PROJECT

To see what more is required, it will be helpful to examine a limitation of what is often called the 'Leninist' approach to revolutionary working-class politics.[61] Lenin's justification for calling the dictatorship of the proletariat 'a million times' more democratic than bourgeois parliamentary democracy was that it involved the political self-determination of the large majority of the population. Struggle against the oppression of the working class was thus regarded a democratic struggle. On the Leninist view this struggle is a process requiring and providing practical education which should proceed through three stages:

1. Workers confronting capitalist oppression organize themselves defensively thus identifying the source of problems they share and beginning antifatalistically to learn their own strength;

2. Intellectuals help the most politically advanced of these workers to form a vanguard party, which educates other workers (by both persuasion and political practice) to the need for social revolution;

3. After a successful revolution, the now politically dominant vanguard begins autodestructing by engaging the rest of the working class and members of other formerly oppressed classes in increasingly responsible and broad participation in self-government.[62]

Scepticism has already been expressed about the likelihood of vanguard autodestruction, and in Chapter Five the identification of democracy with working-class power was challenged. Most left critics of Lenin have focussed their attention on step 2), criticizing what is seen as an elitist view that workers cannot educate themselves without the aid of intellectuals outside the working class.[63] No doubt there is a problem here, though as the next chapter argues it has less to do with elitism than with limited identification of workers and their intellectual mentors/allies as the main political actors. More important considerations for a theory of false consciousness concern step 1).

### PLURALISM AND CRITICAL SELF-CREATION

False consciousness may be a matter of degree in several ways. For example: beliefs involved in false consciousness may be more or less strongly or tentatively held; one may harbour more of less of them; they may be more or less severely oppression-sustaining; or they may range from something near mere lip service to deeply held convictions. They may also have more or less 'content.' A fatalistic attitude may be no more than the negative belief that things will never be different, or it might be held as part of a detailed world view, for instance of religious or biological determinism. Similarly, false blame can involve a more or less detailed explanation to oneself about the genesis of one's imagined nemeses. Now if false consciousness-constituting beliefs can have more or less content, so can true beliefs that replace them, and it is here that a limitation with step 1) of the Leninist project can be seen.

Beliefs by workers that capitalism is to blame for the thwarting of working-class aspirations may have more or less content regarding one's understanding of how capitalism originates and sustains oppression, and they may have more or less content regarding one's stance toward previously falsely blamed people. Mere belief that other workers or people of another race or nationality are not to blame constitutes 'slight' content; while 'fuller' content requires some understanding of the nature of these other people's own oppressions. Similarly, an antifatalist belief will have slight content when it is limited to the view that one need not give up hope of fulfilling so far thwarted aspirations. It will have fuller content when it includes critical evaluation of how and why one has the aspirations one does combined with belief that it is possible to take control of their future production, that is, that deliberate 'consciousness raising'[64] is a real possibility.

To be sure, overcoming false consciousness in struggle even when the contents of beliefs rejecting fatalism or false blame are slight is a real achievement, but it will be precarious. Fuller beliefs that incorporate recognition of nonfixity and endorsement of pluralism offer more secure support for challenging false consciousness. Mere identification of specific sources of one sort of oppression without understanding the concerns of those confronting other sorts lends itself to the stance that others are 'either for us or against us,' with the resulting sectarian practices. Absence of a vision to become autonomously self-creative reinforces sectarianism by leading to identification with a limited range of aspirations, and it promotes an approach to political activism that does not strive to make the major advances in democracy required for security against recurrent oppression. By contrast, struggles pursued in a pluralistic, nonsectarian way and including the conscious aim of participants to become self-creative are more likely to succeed and are less reversible. Moreover, people who recognize their own nonfixity will be aware that the way collective action is pursued importantly affects their very personalities.

Those who endorse the 'Leninist project' could agree with all this but note that we are still confronted with a chicken-and-egg problem (pluralism and full antifatalistic attitudes are required for successful struggle, engagement in which is supposed to educate one about them). Agreeing that people can educate themselves in spiral-like practices, the Leninist might argue that the spiral requires the minimum initiative involving 'slight' true beliefs described as step 1) to get started. This is exactly the point at which democratic socialists should challenge the Leninist project. Of course, a self-building process must be started somewhere, and it stands to reason that trying to achieve too much in early stages is doomed to failure. But why identify nonpluralistic pursuit of fixed aspirations as the most realistic point of entry?

As noted when discussing the dictatorship of the proletariat, actual people are not workers of no sex, race, or nationality, any more than they are women of no class or members of some nation with no sex. Moreover, whatever priorities different people have, such that impediments to certain aspirations are felt as more oppressive to them than impediments to other aspirations, they each interact daily with people who have different priorities.[65] Thus, what is described as a first step in the Leninist progression supposes a reified, one-sided view of people, and the paternalistic dilemmas of its subsequent steps are not accidental. The conclusion is that false consciousness can be overcome by a process of practically educating struggle against systematic oppressions realistically pursued in a pluralistic and critical manner from the start. Explication of some practical dimensions of this point is the main task of the concluding chapter.

# Conclusion

# 11 The Politics of Democratic Socialism

WELL, THEN, WHAT is to be done? Like most works of democratic-socialist theory, the directly practical opinions expressed thus far answer instead the question, What is not to be done?: paternalistic vanguardism should be avoided, direct and representative-democratic measures should not be counterposed, sectarianism should be resisted, and so on. One reason for this is that more in the way of critically pursued movement politics is required first. Several research projects were suggested in Chapter Nine (pages 211, 230) as essential if useful lessons are to be learned from such experience. Also, though there is some merit in advancing programmatic hypotheses,[1] the fact remains that there is nothing approaching consensus about who is to act on a programme and how. Aside from making detailed political recommendations, projecting programmes, and interrogating movement political efforts, there remain some general questions relating to organization.

### i. Organizing for Democratic Socialism

In his biography of Bernstein, Peter Gay formulates a problem that has vexed more than one democratic socialist:

> Is democratic socialism, then, impossible? Or can it be achieved only if the party [having it as a goal] is willing to abandon the democratic method temporarily to attain power by violence in the hope that it may return to parliamentarianism as soon as control is secure. Surely this second alternative contains tragic possibilities: a democratic movement that resorts to authoritarian methods to gain its objective may not remain a democratic movement for long. Still, the first alternative – to cling to democratic

271

procedures under all circumstances – may doom the party to continual political impotence.[2]

Traditional responses to Gay's formulation distinguish alternative orientations to the practical political question about what is to be done to achieve democratic socialism.

Crudely put these are:

1. Parliamentary procedures suffice to achieve democratic socialism provided enough skilled and dedicated representatives are elected to parliaments.

2. Democratic institutions and procedures shelved under pressures of political exigency can be regained after the revolution as long as its leaders are committed to democracy.

3. Parliamentary methods are not effective for securing socialism, but they are not democratic (or democratic in the good sense) either; though other, directly participatory, methods are both democratic and effective.

4. Parliamentary methods used in combination with extra-parliamentary, movement-based politics can provide effective means to democratic socialism.

Historically, these responses are roughly associated, respectively, with social democracy, revolutionary vanguardism, anarchism, and Eurocommunism, but since many permutations and qualifications are exhibited in socialist practice, labels are not very helpful. Moreover, somebody employing a concept of democracy as a highly context-sensitive matter of degree will be wary of making detailed general prescriptions, to which the use of labels lends itself. This does not mean that nothing at all can be said about the practical politics of democratic socialism, and among this work's prescriptions is to favour some version of option 4) at least in relation to contemporary liberal-democratic, capitalist societies.

Such a prescription is consistent with the hypothesis that representative and direct democratic mechanisms are potentially compatible and mutually strengthening. At the same time, contesting false consciousness and building support for a democratic-socialist alternative require that people increasingly engage directly in the collective determination of schools, families, work places, neighbourhoods and other shared social units. If the retrieval of liberal democracy requires pluralism and recognition of nonfixity, then the dictatorship of the proletariat (or any other

272

one social group) should not be seen as essential to democratic-socialist struggle, quite the contrary. The aim of this chapter is to make more precise what a prescription for combined parliamentary and movement politics involves, first by considering the complex goals of the democratic socialist and then by challenging the perspective of 'reform and revolution' within which relevant debate is usually carried out.

## ii. Capitalism and Authoritarian Socialism

The democratic socialist is confronted with a dual task: to secure socialism against capitalist opposition and to do so in a way that will develop socialism's democratic potentials. Anyone who thinks that the first task is easy must be blind to contemporary history. Capitalist freedom from egalitarian constraints in the deployment of wealth, combined with competitive pressures that check significant philanthropic ventures, ensure that capitalism requires force or the threat of force to function. Such a system is bound to thwart too many people's aspirations to expect dutiful acquiescence from everybody. One does not need to endorse the now largely discredited view that procapitalist states function only by force[3] to recognize its permanent role in a capitalist society. It is employed on a daily basis, as, for example, when capitalists are confronted with strikes or organizing drives. A system to which force is integral is prone to turn to violent repression ranging from economic blackmail and blockade to use of the police and military when confronted with potentially effective socialist movements.

Difficulties confronting the second task – securing *democratic* socialism – need fuller explication. Defenders of the use and threatened use of force exercised against their own populations in existing socialist countries explain this as a response to capitalist force. In their crudest forms, the justifications allege direct capitalist-inspired internal subversion. The more sophisticated (and I think usually sincere) position acknowledges the relative undemocracy of existing socialisms, and alleges that force or its threat is necessary to prevent an unenlightened population from unwittingly playing into the hands of capitalists. It is required ultimately to save socialism from capitalist counterrevolution by means of paternalistic restriction of self-determination. Critics of

273

CONCLUSION

Stalinism – the most brutal employment of force in relatively authoritarian (or 'thin') socialism – who occupy official positions in socialist states may be seen as objecting to the immoral and counterproductive Stalinist use of force, but not to paternalistic justification of systematic antidemocratic measures of some form.[4]

One weakness in this justification is associated with class reductionism. If it is believed that 'protecting and building socialism' is the overriding task of a socialist society in such a way that having any other priority means one is antisocialist, then large numbers of people will be too hastily labelled as such. Thus, a defence of the military suppression of Poland's Solidarity movement was that those whom it attracted were motivated by religious or national concerns, as if this proved that they were also antisocialists. This is closely related to a second weakness, in which it suffices to be considered antisocialist to question the necessity of vanguardist institutions and practices (one thinks of justifications for the 1968 military suppression by the Soviet Union of the Dubchek government in Czechoslovakia). More serious is the attitude that a paternalistically imposed socialism can contribute to progress in democracy. Since this supports antidemocratic spirals which not only impede democratic progress, but threaten egalitarian advantages gained in thin socialism, as a population becomes cynical.

## HISTORICAL SPECIFICITY

It might be thought that avoiding authoritarian socialism is not a problem for those in the 'first' world which, thanks to relatively advanced economic and political structures and attitudes, lacks the conditions that prompt it.[5] No doubt such things as a postsubsistence economy and a political culture in which democratic progress is favoured are advantageous to the aims of first-world democratic socialists. However, it would be a mistake to see them as guarantees. Considerations of the historical specificity of conditions promoting and impeding democratic advance are better employed to explain existing socialist authoritarianism than to exonerate first-world socialists from taking appropriate precautions.

Thus Marković hypothesizes that the relative absence of democracy in Soviet and Eastern European socialisms was abetted by a political culture combining elements of European and

274

'Byzantine-Oriental' societies yielding 'possessive individualism without Western libertarian tradition,'[6] and Hannah Arendt discusses implications of the fact that the Russian Revolution occurred in a country with an already centralized bureaucracy and a large 'massified' population, structured neither by 'the remnants of the rural feudal order nor the weak, nascent urban capitalist classes.'[7] However, neither Marković nor Arendt believe it impossible for authoritarian socialism to result from socialist revolutions in presently liberal-democratic societies.

Also, while this work addresses the 'first world,' it should be reiterated that observations such as those of Marković and Arendt are not meant to justify fatalistic acceptance of authoritarian socialism resulting from third-world revolutions. Many third-world revolutionaries note the inappropriateness of first-world democratic practices and institutions to their environments. The democratic-socialist conclusion to draw from this is not that therefore undemocratic socialism is inevitable, but that third-world socialist struggles should be integrated with movements to expand democracy that are appropriate to local traditions and situations.

If a distinction can be maintained between the 'ground of possibility' of authoritarian socialism and the 'origins of its specific forms,' then observations about things like the relative lack of prior democratic traditions should be cause neither for first-world complacency nor for third-world resignation. The point concerns the nature of democratic progress. Understanding the context-bound nature of democracy alerts one to special problems in the third world, but understanding the pervasiveness of some measure of democracy should also prompt one to seek local conditions for its expansion. Thinking of democracy as a spiral helps one to recognize advantages provided by a liberal-democratic tradition for avoiding authoritarian socialism, but it does not follow that democratic progress is inevitable.[8]

It hardly seems necessary to argue that authoritarian practice is not foreign to those raised in a liberal-democratic political culture. Offices and factories, families, schools, trade unions, churches, public and private sector institutions of all kinds are typically organized on authoritarian lines. More ominously for the democratic socialist, so are political organizations of the left, including social-democratic parties and movements the official policy of which is to maximize internal democracy as well as vanguardist parties. There is no reason to suppose that such organizations would suddenly change should they gain state power. Indeed, even when authoritarian socialism has been largely sustained from without, as in the Czechoslovakian and Polish examples, a significant measure of internal willing complicity has not been lacking.

Compatibility of liberal democracy with authoritarianism is partly explained by negative features of (nonsuperseded) liberal democracy. Use of representative-democratic institutions primarily as bulwarks against direct and majority participation in government lays the basis for their transformation into paternalistic organs of minority rule.[9] Also, insofar as liberal democracy sanctions uncritical acceptance of values of the status quo, it leaves unchallenged authoritarian attitudes embodied in patriarchal, racist, and national chauvinist values. The concept of the 'empty space' of modern democracy is also pertinent.

One might argue that the democracy of countries that have undergone democratic revolutions is in one respect more precarious than that of others. In dispensing with traditionally dictated sources of authority, political power becomes, as Gorz puts it, 'functional' and 'without a subject.'[10] This theory, shared by Gorz with Lefort and Furet, suggests that once the idea of political rule is separated from that of specified agents of rule, possibilities for great democratic progress are opened up, but so are antidemocratic possibilities, among them rule by a faceless bureaucracy and socialist or populist 'partyism,' where a political party claims somehow to embody the popular will. A system that may thus replace the form of traditional rule, but not its content is conducive to a secular religious sort of political culture noted by many as central to Stalinism.

These considerations pertain to the immunization to authoritarianism putatively provided by the liberal-democratic traditions of advanced capitalism. They do not touch an alternate view that it is the especially violent counterrevolutionary measures now confronted by movements for socialism in the underdeveloped world that lay the basis for authoritarian socialism by necessitating undemocratic revolutionary measures. This observation could only be ignored by the first-world democratic socialist foolish enough to think that procapitalists are not prepared to employ any means they can get away with to resist socialism in developed countries

276

too. However, the conclusion that undemocratic socialist measures are therefore required is contested by many socialists, most notably, those in the 'Eurocommunst' tradition, who contended that the stronger the opposition, the more important is wide support, which is alienated by undemocratic socialist practices.

### A 'EUROCOMMUNIST' APPROACH

An argument sometimes advanced to defend Eurocommunist-type programmes against criticisms of traditional socialist revolutionaries was that in advanced capitalism, motivations other than hunger are required to impel people to the socialist cause, and only the massively widespread and active support of the large majority of a population could hope to neutralize and finally eliminate capitalist state opposition. This means that extra-economic, democratic political demands for self-government must be part of the motivation for socialism, and only a socialism supported by a large majority made up of different groups with mutual democratic respect can succeed in achieving socialism. If socialism can be attained at all in developed capitalism, it will of necessity be democratic.[11]

Like the view about historical specificity, this argument has much to be said for it. In the 1970s many socialists seeking an answer to the 'what is to be done?' question, were encouraged by the efforts of 'Eurocommunist' parties (including the Japanese Communist Party), and it still does seem that mobilizing people with various priorities around a shared anticapitalist, democracy-enhancing political project is the way to go. However, this is a case where the *orientation* with which such mobilization is undertaken is all-important. In retrospect, the argument seems often to have been more a legitimization of democracy to other socialists than a major shift in political perspective.[12]

### INSTRUMENTALISM

The Eurocommunist argument is compatible with an instrumentalist approach to socialist politics in which democracy is favoured just insofar as it is an indispensable means to replacing a capitalist with a socialist system. One problem with such a narrowly pragmatic defence of democracy is that it is in a way self-refuting. The aim is to build massive support for socialism by linking it with democracy. This support, however, is only as strong as its members' confidence in the genuinely democratic values of each other. Unless the instrumentalist is a supreme master of fooling all of the people all of the time, then he or she will have to be a sincere, noninstrumental democrat. But even if instrumentalist 'democrats' were able to pull off the deception, indeed especially in this case, the result could not further democratic socialism, since instrumentalist members of a postcapitalist society would be prone to act in antidemocratic ways when expedient.

There is also a problem with the political culture which an instrumentalist perspective promotes. In Chapter Eight a distinction was made between seeing democracy as a 'means' and as an 'instrument,' where the former requires strong commitment to a pluralism that promotes mutual toleration and 'people's self-management.' But despite its virtues, a political culture favouring these things will surely be difficult to sustain; instrumentalism is not enough. The problem with the old Pluralism resided in its assumption of fixed interests, and a similar criticism can be made of an instrumentalist approach to democratic socialism. It is no accident that instrumentalist perspectives are usually conjoined with sectarian reductionist ones. Advancement of specified interests are given as the goal, and building a democratic alliance is seen (when it is) as the means. Absent from this perspective is the view that members of such an alliance can and should have a variety of interests, the rankings of which are changeable as they interact with one another.

### PARTIES AND MOVEMENTS

Gay poses the problem of democratic-socialist politics in terms of the choice between traditional vanguardism and social democracy. Many consider this alternative restrictive and call for a 'third way.'[13] Claus Offe suggests replacing 'the political party as the dominant form of democratic mass participation' with increased activism on the part of social movements, the political efficacy of which is made possible due, in a contradictory way, to the increasing breakdown of bourgeois party politics in corporatist capitalism.[14] While not all agree with the details of Offe's analysis, many

278

other democratic socialists see increased activity of social movements as the alternative.[15]

Conceived as mutually exclusive alternatives for replacing capitalism with nonauthoritarian socialism, parties and movements present a trade-off situation. With the admittedly large assumption that intermovement sectarianism can be overcome, a socialism resulting from the activities of movements would have many democratic advantages. It would encompass pluralist principles from the start and contain already politically experienced people. However, it is doubtful that movement politics alone could suffice to achieve a transition to democratic socialism. Regardless of debates over whether perfect democracy should dispense with a system of government where political parties compete for votes, the fact is that these are the systems that exist in present-day liberal democracies. It is hopelessly unrealistic to expect that political change will come about by absenting oneself from involvement in this process. There is also the problem of achieving sufficient coordination to combat anticipated capitalist resistance. Socialist political parties contain the potential for coordination, but this is just their problem.

## DEMOCRATIC CENTRALISM

Though only the vanguardists use the term, democratic centralism is the operative principle of all socialist political parties (and maybe of all other types of party as well). Considered as a rule for decision-making and a matter of party mores, this principle exhibits a range from the Stalinist limit, where even secretly harbouring an opinion contrary to that of the leadership constitutes a breach, through strong Leninism (where opinions opposed by a majority of the party may not be expressed once a vote is taken) and weak Leninism (where such opinions may continue to be expressed provided they are not acted on and their expression is not organized by a faction) to non-Leninist forms that permit factions, but not activity by them counter to duly established policy. Those with experience in left-wing political parties have reason to suspect a tendency for practice in accord with democratic centralism to shift toward the Stalinistic end of the spectrum, as the 'democratic' dimension of this principle slips away in the heat of inner party struggle.

279

## CONCLUSION

This de facto lack of democracy is no accident. Based on my own experience and that of others from a range of left-wing political organizations, I conclude that it results from lack of adequate protection of minority rights in organizations that consider themselves different from the rest of society in having homogeneous interests. They are organized as if what was called in Chapter Four an 'anonymous majority' could only exist within them as an aberration. It is no business of the party to arbitrate among competing interests within it or to facilitate mutual toleration and respect, because either there should be no competing interests (the Stalinist and Leninist approaches), or, if there are, they should be subordinated to the common interests of the party as a whole (the approaches that admit impotent factions).

If this is the source of the breakdown of democratic centralism in its operation internal to political parties, then there is a connection between this dimension of democratic centralism and a party's relation to the social movements around it. In prescribing that democratic centralism be discarded, Radoslav Selucky refers to the 'split loyalty' that the principle imposes on party members who belong as well to institutions outside the party.[16] The ban on effective factions in left political parties has the primary effect of forcing members to put party loyalty above movement loyalties. There may exist within a party a trade unionists' caucus, a women's caucus, or a black caucus, and (with the exception of the lifetime party hack) members of these caucuses include activists in corresponding social movements. However, in the interests of achieving the coordinative ability of a unified party, caucus members are expected to carry out party policy no matter what opinions are held by movements themselves. To the extent that this deployment of democratic centralism is successful, it clearly militates against democracy in a society (pre- or postsocialist) where the political party is an influential force.[17]

### THE PCI AND THE GREENS

In their defence of democratic socialism, Cohen and Rogers call for an alternative to vanguardism and ad hoc coalition politics, involving an alliance the members of which share the common goal of advancing democracy.[18] Here the 'third way' sought is something that is neither a party nor a coalition of movements.

280

The difficulty is to specify what such a thing might be and how it could be constructed, especially in a political culture that so widely accepts party politics.[19] An alternate approach is *combining* movement-based and party politics in ways that can counter the problems associated with each. Unlike Cohen and Rogers' projected 'democratic alliance,' this approach has been pursued on a large scale, though in two rather different ways. One effort was proposed by Gramsci and has been more or less consistently pursued by the Italian Communist Party.[20] The other effort is best exemplified today by the Green Party in the Federal Republic of Germany.

One difference between the PCI, at least on Gramsci's prescription, and the Greens concerns their stances toward the working class. Where the Green Party aims to encompass a variety of movements without prioritizing them, the PCI both draws its main base of support from Italian workers while pursuing Gramsci's project whereby socialism is to be achieved by a broad alliance of people from all subordinated sectors of the population, in which alliance the working class has hegemonically won leadership through participation in democratic struggles.[21] This is an important difference, but more relevant to our purposes are their alternate approaches to integrating party and movement politics.

The Green Party sees itself as a vehicle with minimum structure of its own through which social movements (most prominently ecological, feminist, and peace movements) can gain political leverage within the existing parliamentary system while maintaining independence from representative-democratic institutions and without subordinating themselves to a political party. By contrast, the PCI aims to be a disciplined political presence as a party 'organically' related to movements. (In addition to major trade unions in Italy, this has grown to include linkage with municipally-based movements, too.)[22] The relation is organic to the extent that party members are active in movements and continuing negotiation is maintained with extraparty interests represented within the party. Gramsci thought this would inhibit a party 'bureaucracy' from dominating its mass membership and the 'social groups' of which the party is a political outgrowth.[23]

These are different approaches to the effort to combine parties and movements. The Green Party aims to be more than an umbrella of independent movements, but not to be much more than this; it faces as its major difficulty to coordinate these movements' efforts. The PCI strives to be an organized political party with built-in mechanisms to ensure responsiveness to movements outside of itself and to protect against party domination of them. A tendency toward 'partyism' is nonetheless hard to counteract. All too often, when experiments of these sorts are addressed by socialists it is to adduce them as models either to be emulated or to be rejected in total. (The North American socialist-theoretical establishments are especially good at finding fault with the efforts of people in other parts of the world. Obvious comments on this propensity come to mind.) More useful is close study of these and lesser-known attempts to see what can be learned from them.

To be useful, examination of others' attempts must surely be integrated with close analysis of the nature of one's own institutions, as Jean Cohen insists[24] or, more generally, with what Gramsci calls the study of 'situations.'[25] Perhaps such inquiry would reveal the feasibility of an alternative to combined movement and party politics. But even in the combined approach there are many alternatives regarding form (for example, parties that embody a variety of movements, coalitions of parties each representing different movements, coalitions of movements and of parties, movements of movements, or standing networks) and regarding process (involving mixtures of the transformation of existing parties or movements and the creation of new ones). Without addressing the potentialities of a local situation, little can be said in a theoretical study regarding the politics of democratic socialism. This chapter thus concludes by challenging a traditional perspective from which more concrete analyses are often pursued.

### iii. Reform and Revolution

Despite the left-wing charge of reformism sometimes levelled especially against the PCI,[26] neither this organization nor the Greens easily lends itself to analysis within a standard socialist reform/revolution perspective. Many democratic socialists recognize that there is something amiss about this perspective. For example, Marković replaces this distinction with one between 'revolutionary reformism' and 'pragmatic reformism.'[27] Gorz similarly analyses 'reform' into revolutionary and nonrevolutionary species,[28] and Poulantzas saw the identification of revolution with a 'sweeping transformation of the state apparatus' as a dangerously antidemocratic commitment to what this work calls a fragmentist, 'kinds-of-democracy' orientation.[29]

As democratic socialists who express such views quickly learn, to challenge the reform/revolution distinction is to invite criticism by self-described revolutionaries for being reformists and by reformists for being sugar-coated revolutionaries. This should give one additional cause to question the adequacy of the reform/revolution perspective. Its difficulties are at once semantic and political. Perhaps there is agreement that whatever else a revolution is, it constitutes a change from what existed before it, which is in some sense 'major,' 'radical,' or 'qualitative.' Those who think that no meaning can be attached to such terms when referring to social matters must deny that there can be social revolutions. The democratic socialist need not take this approach.

In Chapter Six it was urged that a 'major advance' has the potential of being global, that is, of achieving progress across a wide variety of social domains and of generating snowballing effects. This will apply to a transition from capitalism to socialism. Egalitarian structuring of a society's economy should affect all aspects of life, and once people begin to take advantage of new freedoms allowed in an environment where economic necessity does not facilitate subordination, it requires extraordinary events to cause them to give up this potentiality. Of course, antisocialists challenge this claim, but what is at issue here is an intrasocialist controversy over reform and revolution.

The democratic socialist need not question either the the notion of revolution itself or the claim that socialism constitutes a revolution. But certain attitudes toward revolution, considered both as a process and as its product, do need to be questioned. We shall discuss four related but separate claims often fused in the perspective of reform and revolution:

1. A socialist revolution is a radical transformation of a society; while the reformist thinks of socialism as continuous with capitalism (that is, similar to it in important social and political respects).
2. The revolutionary sees the need for an extra-electoral, probably violent transition to socialism, unlike reformists who think socialism can be voted in.
3. Socialism regarded in a revolutionary way centrally in-

283

volves the working class, both as the principal agent in a socialist transition and as the ruling group of a socialist society; the reformist denies both these things.

4. A socialist revolution will be a relatively quick and all-of-a-piece change, but reformists falsely believe a socialist transformation can be achieved by gradual incremental changes.

The motivation for rejecting the reform/revolution perspective as a way of organizing one's political thought and action is that, on the one hand, none of these characterizations of the reformist position accurately describes a democratic-socialist viewpoint (as conceived in this work), but on the other hand the democratic socialist will indeed want to reject certain aspects of 'revolution' as envisaged by its proponents. The point will be illustrated under three headings.

### WORKERS' POWER AND SOCIAL DEMOCRACY

Relevant to examining the concepts of revolution in 2) and 3) are some observations about social democracy. Though democratic socialists are often identified with social democrats (including by the latter themselves who sometimes describe their position as 'democratic socialist,' depending on the audience), there are differences between these two things both in respect of socialism and in respect of democracy. Social democracy as understood here aims to promote egalitarian measures, but not beyond what can be accommodated within a capitalist economy (albeit uncomfortably). Regarding democracy, the democratic socialist complains that social-democratic political parties typically do not promote self-determination beyond the electoral mechanisms of weak representative democracy, and they share with explicitly vanguard organizations a top-down internal structure and a paternalist stance toward the population.[30]

A more complex feature of social democracy concerns its relation to social movements, particularly workers' movements. On the one hand, social-democratic parties depend on trade union support and often serve as political arms of the organized work force, but on the other hand, they propose themselves as representatives of transclass interests. Przeworski sees this as a nonaccidental feature of the essentially reformist nature of social democracy. On his theory, social democracy is fully integrated into the system of 'capitalist democracy' in which workers may pursue limited economic gains in an electoral system. Insofar as they aim to serve workers, social-democratic parties compete with other sectors of a population for the crumbs, relatively speaking, that capitalists leave to be squabbled over, but insofar as they do this by making electoral gains, they must present themselves as more than workers' parties.[31]

Central to Przeworski's analysis is the claim that '[c]lass shapes the political behaviour of individuals only as long as people who are workers are organized politically as workers. If political parties do not mobilize people *qua* workers but as "the masses," "the people," "consumers," "taxpayers," or simply "citizens," then workers are less likely to vote as workers. By broadening their appeal to the "masses," social democrats weaken the general salience of class as a determinant of the political behaviour of individuals.'[32] Przeworski's conclusion is that any party with a working-class base that remains within the system of 'capitalist democracy' will always face this dilemma. Many socialist revolutionaries agree and call for a break with the 'capitalist-democratic' system whereby a revolutionary party mobilizes workers *qua* workers to play the leading role in gaining working-class political power. Anything short of this is reformist and hence a form of social democracy.

Reasons to reject the identification of socialism with working-class power have already been given. Regarding the leading role of the working class as a means to socialism, a democratic socialist might begin by distinguishing the question of whether or how the working class should be considered a primary agent in this endeavour from the organizational question about whether or how political parties should represent class interests. On the general question, the democratic socialist will ask what is to be gained by insisting that the working class is a primary agent. Why not simply assert that vigorous working-class participation in a transformation to socialism is a necessary component of this task? Two responses are often given: that workers have the most to gain from eliminating capitalism, and that due to working-class organization, discipline, and numbers, it is the strongest opponent of capitalist resistance to revolution.

The first of these claims probably requires rejection of the concept of socialism as an essentially egalitarian system. If socialism is conceived in egalitarian terms and if the arguments of Chapter Six carry any weight, then anyone suffering systematic oppression, working class or otherwise, has as good a reason as anyone else to eliminate capitalism in favour of it.[33] It is true that women, the handicapped, native peoples, those seeking an end to national oppression, and so on, can make *some* headway in a capitalist system, but so can workers. Socialism is required to make major advances in democracy, which in turn is required for the elimination of a variety of oppressions.

Insofar as the superior strength of the working class as a revolutionary agent goes, there is no doubt room for debating what counts as strength and who has how much of it. However, it is unnecessary to enter into these questions to see the flaw in this concept of 'primacy.' Unless it is thought that the working class can go it alone, coalition efforts are needed. But a coalition is only as strong as its weakest link, and there is nothing to be accomplished by ranking links according to relative strength except to threaten the coalition itself by inviting sectarian debates.

This brings us back to the question of organizational frameworks. Perhaps the perspective of reform and revolution has nowhere been more confining than in its effects on thinking about this subject. Social democracy is a problematic anomaly within a viewpoint that sees movements against capitalist oppression like trade unions as reformist, but with more or less revolutionary potential, and political parties as class-based institutions which are either revolutionary or counterrevolutionary. (Hence, a social-democratic party which is largely class-based and not revolutionary must appear either as an atypical party to be classified with reformist movements or a force of counterrevolution.) The focus of a democratic-socialist perspective will be on systematic oppressions and the many different movements that originate to combat them, some of which may find expression in political parties, both socialist and social-democratic.

The chief question of political organization, then, is how coordinated efforts that have a chance at securing democratic socialism might best be formed and win support from a variety of movements and parties. Since most such existing movements and parties contain democratic-socialist members, they might well start in their own back yards by finding ways to facilitate their movement or party coming to embody a nonsectarian, democratic political culture, 'radical and plural democracy,' as Mouffe and Laclau put it.[34] Without this, no coordinated anticapitalist effort will achieve the dual goals of democratic socialism.

## CONTINUITY AND RADICAL POLITICS

There is something amiss in asking whether a projected democratic socialism is continuous or discontinuous with capitalism. Even to grant that socialism might be continuous with part of capitalism and discontinuous with other parts would miss the depth of the democratic socialist's challenge to this reform/revolution orientation. In the first place, the transformation envisaged is continuous with preexisting political norms and institutions in a retrievalist sense, by extension and reorientation. There is also a fundamental difference between how people view their own history-making activities on the two perspectives. The democratic socialist sees an egalitarian transformation of a society's economy in which he or she is a participant as *part of* an ongoing process to democratize all aspects of that society by opening up possibilities for advances in democracy far beyond anything that exists today.

This makes the democratic-socialist perspective more radical than each of those embodied in conception 2) and 3). Regarding the process whereby a socialist transformation of society is attained, Richard Miller attributes to Marx the more traditional opinion (apparently shared by Miller himself) that a socialist transformation must take place outside normal channels of government and involve violence, ranging from 'disruptive demonstrations, wildcat strikes, ghetto rebellions and mutinies' to civil war.[35] Miller correctly assumes that capitalists are not prepared to allow activity through accepted governmental channels to unseat their positions of economic and political privilege. However, the conclusion that therefore true revolution must involve violence is too hastily drawn.

The democratic-socialist must agree that capitalists will not willingly relinquish power in the face of such things as the election of socialist candidates or the securing of legislation that challenges their interests. What follows from this, however, is not that violence is necessary (as it may sometimes be), but that anticapitalist, egalitarian gains require great effort and that to avoid violent

287

reversal, massive and active popular support must be won. If sound, the prescriptions and hypotheses of this book entail that more democracy leads to yet more, that at a certain point capitalist inegalitarianism is a block to progress in democracy, and that democratic participation creates ever-broadening ability and desire on the part of people to secure and protect democratic gains. The socialist who accepts these views will thus see all efforts to expand democracy – both through formal governmental channels and outside of them, both in ways that involve civil disobedience and in ways that do not – as revolutionary activities. Democratic struggles in their many forms thus constitute a 'permanent democratic revolution.'

The democratic-socialist perspective is also more radical than one which sees socialism in accord with 3) as reaching an historical plateau, where one group acquires dominant political power. In retrieving liberal democracy, the democratic socialist does look to maintain continuity with the past, but it would be mistaken to view this as preservation of capitalism. Democratic gains already made are celebrated and seen as important touchstones. They are viewed in the way that Marx viewed Prometheus rather than in the way he viewed Bismarck. If, however, one's goal is primarily negative – to get rid of capitalism – there will be little incentive to carry into a socialist society democratic advances already achieved. The result is likely to be a much more conservative socialism. Stalinism, for example, did a thorough job of attacking a capitalist economy. But at the same time it was hyperconservative in retaining the most backward political and cultural practices of capitalist and precapitalist eras.

These points about the radical nature of the democratic-socialist approach can be sharpened by considering the way democratic socialists estimate their success, which is by reference to advance in democracy both before, during, and after a socialist transformation. Not only are the domains of democratic-socialist efforts not limited to elections, as sense 2) of 'reform' would have it, but they encompass more areas of life and work than those focussed on by traditional socialists, which are typically limited to organized workers and the state. Moreover, though the democratic socialist wants socialism to help lay the basis for making major advances in democracy, it would be wrong to view this as a simple two-step operation: first secure socialism, then work to make the advances.

Instead, the democratic socialist goes as far as possible toward making these gains in a presocialist environment. The socialist supersession of liberal democracy begins, so to speak, before the revolution.

### THE LONG DEMOCRATIC-SOCIALIST MARCH

Gramsci's theories are especially appropriate to differentiating a democratic-socialist orientation from the reform/revolution perspective labelled 4). His concept of the 'war of position' is an alternative to the viewpoint that identifies revolution with a massive, relatively quick assault on capitalism (a 'war of movement') and reform with incrementalism (or gradualism or piecemealism). Gramsci's theory prescribes a kind of political guerrilla warfare in a modern capitalist society aimed at winning increasing numbers of people to the socialist cause while avoiding a frontal confrontation (political or military) which will either be lost to procapitalists or won at unacceptable costs.[36]

It is incrementalism understood in this sense that is most often attacked by socialist revolutionaries. For example, referring to the PCI, Milton Fisk allows that 'gradualism' might work 'if one could assume that the dominant class would gracefully step down,' which Fisk notes they have never shown any sign of doing.[37] Like many socialists, Fisk adduces the case of Allende's Chile as an example, as does Eric Olin Wright in an argument pertaining both to reform sense 2) and gradualism. Thus, quoting Perry Anderson, Wright argues:

> The logic of Marxist theory indicates that it is in the nature of the bourgeois state that, in any final contest, the armed apparatus of repression inexorably displaces the ideological apparatuses of parliamentary representation, to reoccupy the dominant position in the structure of capitalist class power. This coercive State machine is the ultimate barrier to a workers' revolution, and can only be broken by preemptive counter coercion.... The historic lesson of Chile underscores the theoretical rationale of this argument. It is ultimately the capacity of the bourgeoisie to destroy violently any peaceful attempt at constructing socialism that makes such attempts so precarious.[38]

The case of Chile is, indeed, germane and is adduced by other socialist theorists against the position advanced by Wright and

289

Fisk. Thus, Poulantzas and Therborn argue that the failure of Allende's Popular Unity government resulted in part from yielding to leftist pressures in ways that inhibited building necessary alliances.[39] This debate is often represented as one between antigradualist militants and cautious incrementalists. Instead it should be seen as marking a radical difference between an antigradualist's stance and one linking the war of position with political activity designed to further democracy.

Shortly after the 1973 right-wing coup, Enrico Berlinguer argued not that the Popular Unity had proceeded either too slowly or too quickly, but that it needed to be more consistently democracy-oriented. Berlinguer generalized his analysis to explicate a democratic-socialist approach to politics:

> The essential task lying before us . . . is to extend this fabric of unity [among Italy's major prodemocratic forces] to rally the vast majority of the people round a programme of struggle for the democratic renewal of our whole society and the state and to build a coalition of political forces that corresponds to this majority and this programme and is capable of realizing it. Only this line, and no other, can isolate and defeat the conservative and reactionary groups; only this line can give democracy solidarity and invincible strength; only this line can advance the transformation of society.[40]

The advantage this democratic project has from the point of view of avoiding counterrevolution is the one referred to earlier in connection with a Eurocommunist argument.

The best protection against capitalist-inspired violence is a broad and committed alliance of popular forces. The war of position is designed to forge such an alliance, but a precondition for success is that it be carried out from a relentlessly prodemocratic, anti-intrumentalist perspective. No members of the Popular Alliance were opposed to forging a united front. The problem, rather, was that class reductionist and other attitudes that inhibit democracy prevented this – a point detailed by Alejandro Rojas in his history of the Chilean left from the last century through the Coup.[41]

A democratic-socialist approach to the war of position is by no means an easy task. It requires fashioning alliances among people based on partly divergent and partly converging interests while at the same time challenging the fixity of those interests. It requires

290

protecting and extending the unstable spiral of democracy. It requires retaining while going beyond existing gains in democracy in projects of retrieval. The approach is not properly described as 'gradualist,' since it is recognized that at certain conjunctures the moment must be seized and rapid progress made. But on the other hand, no progress (rapid or otherwise) will be achieved by democratic socialists unless the ground has been laid through persistent involvement in the midst of local and movement politics, and this takes time. The democratic-socialist march will in all likelihood be a long one.[42]

### DEMOCRATIC SOCIALISM AND OPTIMISM: A QUASISERMON

Is the prospect of a long march a pessimistic conclusion? That it is not is best evinced by indulging in a bit of socialist sermonizing – an activity so far avoided in the belief that there are enough socialist sermons passing as theory. Considering the formidable obstacles the democratic-socialist project confronts, uncertainty of success may be cause for pessimism. Perhaps such a point of view is partly responsible for the attitudes of desperate optimism, of secular messianic zeal with which some socialists proclaim the inevitable triumph of the cause, but any sober view of major human enterprises should convince one that there are never guarantees of success.

Full-blown socialist sermonizing that tries to mask uncertain success by predicting certain victory not only fails to instill an enduring optimism (except in the minds of fanatics), but it does harm to the cause of democratic socialism by promoting false hope and fatalism. What is more, it is not required. Recognizing the possibility of the triumph of antidemocratic tendencies is good reason for persistence and for a sense of urgency, but it ought not to be a cause for despair. That one might fail does not entail that one cannot succeed.

Legitimate bases for despair in projects of long duration are those attendant on delayed gratification and on lost bearings. Only the long-suffering martyr can be satisfied with an indefinite period without rewards, and anyone will be disoriented when there are no benchmarks by which to gauge whether progress is in fact being made. However, these sources of dejection do not confront the democratic socialist, who is always engaged in projects to expand democracy and for whom there is at least one standard by which to tell whether progress is being made. This is the extent to which the democratic socialist has succeeded – by word and especially by deed—in retrieving a political culture wherein socialism is positively associated with democracy.

# Notes

**Chapter 1**

1. Thus Thomas Carlyle and Frederick Engels shared this association in their opposing evaluations of the Chartists, when Engels observed that 'democracy nowadays is communism,' while Carlyle declared: 'Democracy ... is found but as regulated method of rebellion and abrogation. . . . ' Engels, 'The Festival of Nations in London,' in *Karl Marx Frederick Engels Collected Works* (New York: Progress Publishers, 1974– ) 3–14, written in 1845, at p. 14; Carlyle, 'Chartism,' *Critical and Miscellaneous Essays Vol. 6* (London: Chapman and Hall, 1872), at p. 146.

The *Neue Rheinishe Zeitung*, founded and edited by Marx in the mid-1840s was subtitled 'An Organ of Democracy,' and an influential work of the time, said by Karl Kautsky and by Harold Laski to be the model for the *Communist Manifesto*, was Victor Considérant's *Principles of Socialism: Manifesto of Democracy in the 19th Century*, published in 1843. See Dirk Struik's discussion of this in his *Birth of the Communist Manifesto* (New York: International Publishers, 1971) 64–7.

Struik is right to note that Marx differed with socialists like Considérant who did not centrally place working-class revolution in their prescriptions. Still, Struik thought Marx always situated himself within the democratic tradition. (See Pt. One.) For a similar approach to Marx's efforts see Hal Draper's *Karl Marx's Theory of Revolution, Vol. 1: State and Bureaucracy* (New York: Monthly Review Press, 1977).

The association of socialism and democracy by antisocialists is most clear in the case of political figures such as Adolph Thiers (responsible for putting down the Paris Commune) or Bismarck, but it was also true of leading intellectuals who were convinced, as Karl Polanyi put it, 'that popular democracy was a danger to capitalism.' (Polanyi's *The Great Transformation: The Political and Economic Origins of Our Times* (Boston: Beacon, 1970), first published in 1944, 226.

Alexis de Tocqueville's work might be thought problematic since he is sometimes claimed by 20th-century democrats as one of theirs. However, whatever lessons democrats can learn from de Tocqueville, it should not be forgotten that he was primarily motivated by suspicion of democracy. See Richard Heffner's introduction to his edition of *Democracy in America* (New York: Mentor Books, 1956) 11. A similar point can be made about Edmund Burke, an antisocialist insofar as such a stance could be identified at the turn of the century, yet sometimes also claimed as a democrat. C.B. Macpherson addresses this topic in arguing that Burke's 'liberalism' was antithetical to what we know as liberal democracy in his *Burke* (New York: Hill and Wang, 1980).

2. Defence of the claim that existing socialism exemplifies a new kind of democracy

295

may be found in V.G. Afanasyev, et al., *Soviet Democracy in the Period of Developed Socialism*, ed. D.A. Kerimov (Moscow: Progress Publishers, 1979), where it is maintained that 'the socialist system has completely new criteria by which to judge democracy. . . .' 12. Socialist democracy is the 'form of the political organization of socialist society' which starts as the dictatorship of the proletariat and later turns into the 'power of the whole people.' In both periods it includes 'the power of the working people headed by the working class' and the 'organizational fusion of party and state.' (See chaps. 2 and 3, at 58–9, 74.)

Defences of apparently antidemocratic practices of existing socialist governments as unfortunate necessities are, in my experience, by far the ones most commonly advanced *in conversation*. However, it is difficult to find this defence put into print, where even the most blatant antidemocratic measures, such as the 1968 invasion of Czechoslovakia or the 1980 imposition of martial law in Poland, are described as democratic.

A more honest approach is in Herbert Aptheker's defence of the Warsaw Pact invasion of Czechoslovakia as a 'grievous and tragic' act necessary, among other things, he alleged, to prevent war in Europe. Aptheker expressed hope that Czechoslovakia could soon experience 'the advancing of democratic renewal.' 'Czechoslovakia and the Present Epoch,' Parts 1, 2, *Political Affairs* 47(11, 12): 34–45, 23–36 (November, December, 1968).

3. The best known example is Joseph Schumpeter's definition of 'democracy' as: 'that institutional arrangement for arriving at political decisions in which individuals acquire the power to decide by means of a competitive struggle for the people's vote,' *Capitalism, Socialism and Democracy* (London: Allen and Unwin, 1943) 269.

4. The classic expression of this treatment is by Lenin in *The Proletarian Revolution and the Renegade Kautsky*, in *V.I. Lenin Collected Works* (Moscow: Progress Publishers, 1963–80) 28:226–325, written in 1918, see especially 231–250. From an otherwise quite different perspective Benjamin Barber distinguishes five different kinds of democracy in his *Strong Democracy: Participatory Politics for a New Age* (Berkeley: University of California Press, 1984), see 141. Criticisms of these types of division are, respectively, by Barry Hindess, 'Marxism and Parliamentary Democracy,' in *Marxism and Democracy*, ed. Alan Hunt (London: Lawrence and Wishart, 1980) 21–54; and Alain Touraine, *l'Aprés socialisme* (Paris: Bernard Grasset, 1980), see p.195.

5. Lenin, *The Renegade Kautsky* 248.

6. Lest anyone doubt the extent and brutality of the Stalin regime, see Jean Ellenstein's documentation in *The Stalin Phenomenon*, trans. Peter Latham (London: Lawrence and Wishart, 1976).

7. Andrew Levine's, *Liberal Democracy* (New York: Columbia University Press, 1981) represents the first view, which I have criticized in a defence of the third in a 'Critical Notice' of this book, *Canadian Journal of Philosophy* 14 (2): 335–357(June 1984). Though Amy Gutmann is careful not to use the word 'socialist,' it is fairly clear that this position is a socialist one in a work supposing the second approach, *Liberal Equality* (Cambridge: Cambridge University Press, 1980). Other literature is referred to in the 'Critical Notice' and in Chapter 7 of this work.

8. The key work is Macpherson's *Democratic Theory: Essays in Retrieval* (Oxford: Oxford University Press, 1973).

9. See, for example, an exchange between Leo Panitch, 'Liberal Democracy and Socialist Democracy: The Antinomies of C.B. Macpherson,' and Ellen Wood, 'Liberal Democracy and Capitalist Hegemony: A Reply to Leo Panitch on the Task of Socialist Political Theory,' in *The Socialist Register* (1981) 144–189.

10. Examples are: Tomas Moulian, *Democracia y Socialismo* (Santiago: Flasco, 1983); and Sergio Bitar, *Democracia y Transicion al Socialismo* (Mexico City: Siglo 21, 1979). See

too the journals, *Opciones* from Chile (available from the Academia de Humanismo Cristiano, Catedral 1063, Santiago) and *Socialismo y Participacion* from Peru. Latin American literature in English translation written from a democratic-socialist perspective may be found in the publications of the Latin American Research Unit (Box 673, Adelaide St. P.O., Toronto, Ontario, Canada). Regarding possible socialist transformations in the Caribbean countries, see Clive Y. Thomas', *The Rise of the Authoritarian State in Peripheral Societies* (New York: Monthly Review Press, 1984), and Michael Kaufman, *Jamaica Under Manley: Dilemmas of Socialism and Democracy* (London: Zed Books, 1985), chap. 11.

11. Levine concludes his book on liberal democracy with this critique of Macpherson, 197–201.

12. There is a large body of literature in these two domains. Sample works with useful references are, in the case of nations, Arieh Yaari, *Le défi national: les theories marxistes sur la question nationale a l'épreuve* (Paris: éditions anthropos, 1978); and Jacques Mascotto and Pierre Yves Soucy, *Démocratie et nation* (Montreal: Albert Saint-Martin, 1980). Regarding women, see Michèle Barrett, *Women's Oppression Today* (London: New Left Books, 1980); and the essays in *Capitalist Patriarchy and the Case for Socialist Feminism*, ed. Zillah Eisenstein (New York: Monthly Review Press, 1979).

13. An example of the British work is the anthology *Marxism and Democracy*, ed. Alan Hunt. Representative works from France are: André Gorz, *Adieux au prolétariat: Au delà du socialisme* (Paris: Editions du Seuil, 1980); and Cornelius Castoriadis, *l'Institution imaginaire de la société* (Paris: Editions du Seuil, 1975). The American, Jean Cohen, draws on some of this work (and on that of Alain Touraine and Claus Offe) in a sustained critique of Marxist class reductionism, *Class and Civil Society: The Limits of Marxian Critical Theory* (Amherst: The University of Massachusetts Press, 1982). Japanese work is hard to come by in English translation, but some of the articles of Shingo Shibata (editor of the *Yearbook for Social-Scientific Studies* in Japan) bearing on reductionism are available, e.g., his 'Fundamental Human Rights and Problems of Freedom: Marxism and the Contemporary Significance of the U.S. Declaration of Independence,' *Social Praxis* 3(3,4): 157–185(1975). These are no more than typical samples of large bodies of literature.

14. I do not know who coined this term, but Ernesto Laclau popularized its use in left-wing debates about Marxism in his *Politics and Ideology in Marxist Theory* (London: New Left Books, 1979), see essays 2 and 3.

15. Ted Benton, 'Realism, power and objective interests,' in *Contemporary Political Philosophy*, ed. Keith Graham (Cambridge: Cambridge University Press, 1982) 7–33, at p.15.

16. Michael Levin, 'Marxism and Democratic Theory,' in *Democratic Theory and Practice*, ed. Graeme Duncan (Cambridge: Cambridge University Press, 1983) 79–95, at p.84.

17. Examples of theorists who are otherwise quite diverse include: Göran Therborn, *The Ideology of Power and the Power of Ideology* (London: Verso, 1980) 4–5, and Ferenc Feher and Agnes Heller, 'Les "vrais" et les "faux" besoins,' in *Marxisme and démocratie* (Paris: Librairie François Maspero, 1981).

### Chapter 2

1. V.I. Lenin, 'Our Revolution,' in *V.I. Lenin Collected Works* (Moscow: Progress Publishers, 1963–80) 33:476–480, written in 1923, at p.480. Rudolf Bahro discusses this passage in his *The Alternative in Eastern Europe*, trans. David Fernbach (London: New Left Books, 1978), first published in 1977, 91.

2. These are in a letter (now called 'Lenin's Testament') to the Party Congress, De-

cember 23, 1922. It is translated in a pamphlet appended to the 1969 edition of the *Collected Works* 33 or on pp. 594–6 of the 1964 edition.

3. Among the authors who have addressed these historical questions are Roy Medvedev, *On Socialist Democracy*, trans. Ellen de Kadt (New York: W.W. Norton, 1977), and *Leninism and Western Socialism*, trans. A.D.P. Briggs (London: New Left Books, 1981), and Fernando Claudin, *The Communist Movement: From Comintern to Cominform*, trans. Brian Pearce (London: Penguin, 1975). These works exhibit both the value and the (not always acknowledged) tentativeness such conclusions must have.

4. It might be asked whether from the point of view of such an 'interactionist' orientation there is any space for rationality, that is, whether in admitting changes in one's goals midstream in decision-making, the orientation does not collapse into irrationalism. In this book it will be assumed that there is space between irrationalism and 'hyperrationalism.' To defend this assumption, one can challenge an individualistic orientation of most theories of rationality by pursuing a suggestion of Mary Gibson in 'Rationality,' *Philosophy and Public Affairs* 6(3): 193–225(Spring 1972), that 'institutional' and 'individual' rationality interact. Another approach is to argue a) that moral commitments can be taken account of in assessing rationality and b) that it is compatible with rational activity that these commitments change. A defence of a) is Amartya Sen's 'Rational Fools: A Critique of the Behavioral Foundations of Economic Theory,' *Philosophy and Public Affairs* 6(4): 317–344(Summer 1977). Point b) could be defended by pursuing a suggestion raised and too hastily rejected by David Gauthier that rationality and morality are in reflective equilibrium, 'Justice and Natural Endowment: Toward a Critique of Rawls' Ideological Framework,' *Social Theory and Practice* 3(1): 3–26(1975), at pp. 24–5.

5. Jon Elster, *Making Sense of Marx* (Cambridge: Cambridge University Press, 1985); Richard Miller, *Analysing Marx: Morality, Power and History* (Princeton: Princeton University Press, 1984); Allen W. Wood, *Karl Marx* (London: Routledge and Kegan Paul, 1981).

6. G.A. Cohen, *Karl Marx's Theory of History: A Defence* (Oxford: Oxford University Press, 1978); John McMurtry, *The Structure of Marx's World-View* (Princeton: Princeton University Press, 1978).

7. Allen E. Buchanan, *Marx and Justice: The Radical Critique of Liberalism* (Totowa: N.J.: Rowman and Littlefield, 1982). Two collections of articles illustrate the debate over whether Marx's writings contain some theory of justice or morality: *Marx and Morality*, eds. Kai Nielsen and Steven C. Patten (Guelph: Canadian Association for Publishing in Philosophy, 1981); and *Marx, Justice, and History*, eds. Marshall Cohen, Thomas Nagel, and Thomas Scanlon (Princeton: Princeton University Press, 1980).

8. Jean Cohen, *Class and Civil Society: The Limits of Marxian Critical Theory* (Amherst: The University of Massachusetts Press, 1982); Leszek Kolakowski, *Main Currents of Marxism*, in 3 vols., trans. P.S. Falla (Oxford: Oxford University Press, 1981).

9. Those acquainted with my primer in Marxism, *Understanding Marxism: A Canadian Introduction* (Toronto: Progress Publishers, 1978), will note that I now take an agnostic approach to the thesis of the centrality of class struggle as a principle of macrohistorical explanation. Those who have read my earlier attack on Pluralism, 'Pluralism and Class Struggle,' *Science & Society* 39(4): 385–416(Winter 1975–76), will recognize in addition a willingness to incorporate some of this tradition's positive contributions.

The distance between the orientation of these works and the present one is not very great. The anti-instrumentalist approach to democracy and socialism in Chapter 9 of the primer is central to the present endeavour. Readers who were uneasy about *Understanding Marxism* from one traditional Marxist direction warned that this chapter in particular was dangerously opening the door to heterodoxy; perhaps they were right. As to Pluralism, I have not changed my earlier opinion that the neo-Hobbesian views of U.S. Pluralists in the 1950s were both inadequate explanatory theories and biased to favour capitalism. Moreover, as a normative approach, the pluralism I defend in subsequent chapters rejects power-political views implicated in the classic Pluralism. In general it seems to me that nothing is to be gained by insisting that socialist theorists declare themselves to be 'Marxists,' 'non-Marxists,' 'post-Marxists,' and so on. It can be argued (as was recently suggested to me by Alejandro Rojas) that any socialist theorist today should be both a Marxist and a non-Marxist in the same way that a contemporary physicist must be both a Newtonian and a non-Newtonian.

10. See Marx Wartofsky's critique of Kolakowski, 'The Unhappy Consciousness: Leszek Kolakowski's *Main Currents of Marxism*,' *Praxis International* 1(4): 288–306 (October, 1981). Also pertinent are Hal Draper's *Karl Marx's Theory of Revolution, Vol. 1: State and Bureaucracy* (New York: Monthly Review Press, 1977); David McLellan's *Karl Marx: His Life and Thought* (New York: Harper Colophon, 1973); and John P. Burke, Lawrence Crocker, and Lyman H. Legters, eds., *Marxism and the Good Society* (Cambridge: Cambridge University Press, 1981), especially the essays of Burke, Crocker, and Fischer.

11. Here are sample references: Mihailo Marković, *Democratic Socialism: Theory and Practice* (New York: St. Martin's Press, 1982); Samuel Bowles and Herbert Gintis, *Democracy and Capitalism: Property, Community, and the Contradictions of Modern Social Thought* (New York: Basic Books, 1986); Ferenc Feher and Agnes Heller, *Marxisme & démocratie* (Paris: Librairie François Maspero, 1981); David Schweickart, *Capitalism or Worker Control?: An Ethical and Economic Appraisal* (New York: Praeger Publishers, 1980); Carol C. Gould, 'Socialism and Democracy,' *Praxis International* 1(1): 49–63 (April 1981); Kai Nielsen, *Equality and Liberty: A Defence of Radical Egalitarianism* (Totowa, N.J.: Rowman and Allanheld, 1985); Philip Green, *Retrieving Democracy: In Search of Civic Equality* (Totowa: N.J.: Rowman and Allenheld, 1985); William E. Connolly, *Appearance and Reality in Politics* (Cambridge: Cambridge University Press, 1981); Zillah Eisenstein, 'Developing a Theory of Capitalist Patriarchy and Socialist Feminism,' in *Capitalist Patriarchy and the Case for Socialist Feminism*, ed. Zillah R. Eisenstein (New York: Monthly Review Press, 1979) 5–40; Heidi Hartmann, 'The Unhappy Marriage of Marxism and Feminism: Towards a More Progressive Union,' in *Women and Revolution*, ed. Lydia Sargent (Boston: South End Press, 1981) 1–41; Benjamin Barber, *Strong Democracy: Participatory Politics for a New Age* (Berkeley: University of California Press, 1984); Carole Pateman, *Participation and Democratic Theory* (Cambridge: Cambridge University Press, 1970).

12. Ernesto Laclau and Chantal Mouffe, *Hegemony and Socialist Strategy: Towards a Radical Democratic Politics*, trans. Winston Moore and Paul Cammack (London: Verso, 1984).

13. For example: André Gorz, *Adieux au prolétariat: Au delà du socialisme* (Paris: Editions du Seuil, 1980); Claude Lefort, *L'invention démocratique: les limites de la domination totalitaire* (Paris: Fayard, 1981); Alain Touraine, *The Voice and the Eye: An Analysis of Social Movements*, trans. Alan Duff (Cambridge: Cambridge University Press, 1981).

14. Sammuel Bowles and Herbert Gintis, *Democracy and Capitalism: Property, Community, and the Contradictions of Modern Social Thought* (New York: Basic Books, 1986) 3–4.

15. Joshua Cohen and Joel Rogers, *On Democracy: Toward a Transformation of American Society* (Harmondsworth, England: Penguin, 1983).

16. Jürgen Habermas, *Legitimation Crisis*, trans. Thomas McCarthy (Boston: Beacon Press, 1975).

17. Habermas, ibid., pt. 3, see pp. 123–4, 137. Also, Habermas's, 'Toward a Theory of

Communicative Competence,' in *Recent Sociology No. 2*, ed. Hans Peter Dreitzel (London: Macmillan, 1970), see 122–3; Laclau and Mouffe, *Hegemony*, chap. 4. See, too, Note 20 below.

18. Claus Offe, *Contradictions of the Welfare State*, ed. John Keane (Cambridge, Mass.: MIT Press, 1984).

19. Andrew Levine, *Liberal Democracy: A Critique of Its Theory* (New York: Columbia University Press, 1981), and *Arguing for Socialism: Theoretical Considerations* (Boston: Routledge and Kegan Paul, 1984).

20. Robert K. Merton, in *Social Theory and Social Structure* (Glencoe, Ill.: Free Press, 1949), used 'theories of the middle range,' 9, as part of a plea for social scientists to find room between narrow empiricism and grand system building. I use the phrase related to philosophy in a similar spirit and also to mark off a terrain called 'middle level' theorizing by Richard Miller in which social philosophers 'describe or clarify explanatory questions that are worth asking, explanatory strategies that are worth trying,' *Analysing Marx: Morality, Power and History* (Princeton: Princeton University Press, 1984) 101.

21. Thus Michèle Barrett, having surveyed the work of a large range of feminist theorists (Nancy Chodorow, Jane Flax, Juliette Mitchell, Anne Foreman, Eli Zaretsky, and others), concludes with explicit reference to Chodorow, but compatibly with all the others, that 'the possibility of women's liberation lies crucially in a reallocation of childcare...,' *Women's Oppression Today* (London: Verso, 1980) 20. Jane Flax reports a similar convergence, 'The Family in Contemporary Feminist Thought: A Critical Review,' in *The Family in Political Thought*, ed. Jean Bethke Elshtain (Boston: University of Massachusetts Press, 1982) 223–253, at p. 250.

22. Branko Horvat, *The Political Economy of Socialism* (Armonk, N.Y.: M.E. Sharpe, 1982), pt. 1, chap. 2 and pt. 2, chaps. 2, 3; Svetozar Stojanović, *In Search of Democracy in Socialism*, trans. Gerson S. Sher (Buffalo: Prometheus Books, 1981). pt. 2, 81; Mihaly Vajda, *The State And Socialism* (London: Allison and Busby, 1981), chap. 8, 128. These works were reviewed by me in *The Insurgent Sociologist* 12(1–2): 178–182(Winter/Spring 1984).

23. Described by Rawls in *A Theory of Justice* (Cambridge, Mass.: Harvard University Press, 1971) 20–1, 48–51.

24. Norman Daniels suggests an extended use of Rawls's principle, 'Reflective Equilibrium and Archimedean Points,' *Canadian Journal of Philosophy* 10(1): 83–103(March 1980). Kai Nielsen uses the principle thus extended against some of Rawls's own conclusions, *Equality and Liberty*, chap. 2.

25. One example is in the late Alvin Gouldner's *The Two Marxisms* (New York: Seabury Press, 1980): 'since it is here supposed [by scientific as opposed to critical Marxism] that the decisions and moralities which the people make are grounded only in their conditions, and that the former mirror the latter, then people who have been subjected to the corrupting influence of past institutions cannot be trusted to make the right decisions,' 57. Another is in Benjamin Barber's *Strong Democracy*: 'There are epistemological alternatives far more suitable to democracy and to politics in general [than a Cartesian "politics of applied truth"]. An epistemology of process, which could understand truth to be a product of certain modes of common living rather than the foundation of common life, would be free of the metaphysical problems posed by rationalism and empiricism,' 65. These are typical views of a large range of democratic theorists, and despite use of (also typical) hedging words like 'only' or a narrow interpretation of 'foundation,' they convey the view that those who favour some version of causal determinism are committed to paternalism and those favouring epistemological realism to social passivity.

26. On the question of whether determinism is 'compatible' with freedom, see my review

of Gouldner's book in *Science and Society* 45(3): 372–375(Fall 1981), and the *erratum*, recorded in 45(4): 436. I have defended the compatibility of social-scientific realism and activism in *Objectivity in Social Science* (Toronto: University of Toronto Press, 1973), chap. 6, and in 'Marxism and Epistemological Realism,' coauthored with Daniel Goldstick, *Social Praxis*, 6(3–4): 237–253(1979). I am disinclined to think that more recent changes in some of my views are somehow essentially connected to the philosophical theories expressed in these and other works, since I think pursuit of political theory and practice *as* a consistent critical realist and compatibilist has partly led me to these changes.

27. A well-known and, for those who respect his stature as a creative Marxist intellectual, tragic example is the forced recantation of his critique of realism by Georg Lukács in the 1967 Preface to *History and Class Consciousness*, revised ed., trans. Rodney Livingston (Cambridge, Mass.: MIT Press, 1971), first published in 1967.

28. Some of the core ideas of Chapter 9 were read at the 1983 World Congress of Philosophy meetings where I was gavelled down by the Soviet chair of the session to make time for a queue consisting of some of his compatriots and of GDR philosophers who read prepared criticisms of my paper and that of Shlomo Avineri. Later this paper was rejected by a journal specializing in democratic-socialist theory. One of its editors subsequently told me that the paper was considered too 'orthodox,' a judgment that could only have pertained to its philosophical orientation and not its political views.

29. In Laclau and Mouffe, *Hegemony*: 'Political conclusions similar to those set forth in this book could have been approximated from very different discursive formations – for example, from certain forms of Christianity, or from libertarian discourses alien to the socialist tradition . . .,' 3.

30. It might be thought that this approach is biased against someone who thinks that certain philosophical beliefs are involved in political action, not just in theory. Thus Barber: 'it is capitalist logic and epistemology that offends democracy rather than capitalist institutions or even capitalist values,' *Strong Democracy*, 253. If Barber means that having epistemological views somehow endemic to capitalism leads political actors to behave in certain, antidemocratic ways, this is still compatible with holding that this very conclusion should, or even can only, be reached in a dialectical way by use of this (putative) epistemology, itself. More argumentation than Barber provides is needed to establish a necessary link here.

### Chapter 3

1. Arne Naess, Jens A. Christophersen, and Kjell Kvalo, *Democracy, Ideology and Objectivity* (Oxford: Basil Blackwell, 1956); and see Raymond Williams, *Keywords: A Vocabulary of Culture and Society* (New York: Oxford University Press, 1976) 82–87.

2. A treatment of the value-laden nature of definitions of 'democracy' is in an article by Michael Davis, 'Liberalism and/or Democracy?,' *Social Theory and Practice* 9(1): 51–72(Spring 1983).

3. One might think of an 'action' as typically what J.L. Mackie calls an INUS condition, an insufficient but necessary member of a set of conditions unnecessary but sufficient to produce a result, *The Cement of the Universe: A Study of Causation* (Oxford: Oxford University Press, 1974) 62. This is what it means to say that the result occurs 'partly in virtue of' an action taken to bring it about. Such an action will never be sufficient, if for no other reason than that the state of the nonhuman world will have to be conducive to the result. Some results may be such that they could only come about

by the action of whoever has control, but most of the ends people aim at could be brought about otherwise.

When someone with a monopoly of power over a social unit benevolently acts to make things conform to the preferences of people in it, these people do not exercise control even though their preferences are satisfied. By contrast, the active members of a club or union might, as the only ones who attend meetings, make all its decisions with results in accord with the absent members' preferences, and if part of the motivation for their making these decisions is that the absent members have (in some way knowingly) given them reason to believe they might quit or start showing up to meetings and contesting the 'inner circle's' privileged role, then the absent members could be said to exercise some control. Indeed, it is largely thanks to this mode of control that representative government lacking formal accountability can still contain a measure of democracy.

If the absent members falsely believed that they had an effect on the decisions of the inner circle, they would lack control. It might be the case that the absent members' implied threats *would* lead the inner circle to act in the desired way, except for the fact that they are already doing so out of benevolence or that the inner circle acts to preclude being subject to the deliberate influence of absent members who have not yet formed an intent to exert influence. These are grey areas where debate over whether control is exercised is appropriate.

4. See David Harris's, 'Returning the Social to Democracy,' in *Democratic Theory and Practice*, ed. Graeme Duncan (Cambridge: Cambridge University Press, 1983) 218–234, at p.220.

5. As in Jane J. Mansbridge, *Beyond Adversary Democracy* (New York: Basic Books, 1980), see p. 25.

6. One problem not addressed is ascertaining just who has how much control in a situation where not only an environment is shared but so is control over it. Also set aside is examination of the differences between a) those means of shared control that more than one person *may* employ but that are effective if only one person takes advantage of them (like voting), and b) means that more than one person *must* employ (like mass demonstrations). As will be seen in the arguments of Chapter 4, the approach taken in this work is to try displacing theoretical problems of these sorts to ones of practice. Hence, to the extent that equal participation is achieved the problem of ascertaining who has control is less acute than otherwise, and prescriptions between types of means are made depending on circumstances.

7. Carl Cohen, *Democracy* (New York: The Free Press, 1973) 68–71.

8. Ibid. 7, italics omitted.

9. See the discussion of political compromise by Anthony Downs, *An Economic Theory of Democracy* (New York: Harper and Bros, 1957), chap. 4. A concise discussion of the Prisoner's Dilemma is in Andrew Levine, *Liberal Democracy: A Critique of Its Theory* (New York: Columbia University Press, 1981) 77–84.

10. By an alternate definition suggested to me by Derek Allen, things are judged more or less democratic depending on how many people participate in using means of potential control (rather than succeeding in the exercise of control). Or, an 'acceptable' outcome could be considered imperfectly democratic. I suspect that by making suitable alterations in what follows, either of these alternatives could be made to do well enough.

One reason for adopting a definition of 'more democratic' couched in terms of actual control is to capture an intuition I think I share with many that the telos of democracy is control, not the just having a chance for control. Also, as will be seen in Chapter 4, focus on control facilitates meeting Arrow-type concerns about the coherence of the notion 'democratic decision.' A reason to include reference to acceptability in a criterion of perfect democracy is that this fits well with the notion of 'mixed mode' ideal democracy described in section iii of the chapter. I was persuaded by David Schweickart that the democratic theorist must decide whether a perfectly democratic society is one where there is complete consensus or whether (as the notion of mixed mode democracy allows) it may contain conflict.

11. At this point it is worth averting confusion over how comparisons appealing to the criterion of progress toward perfect democracy might be made. Radical employment of this criterion would estimate how far any institution, action, habit of thought, and so on carries forward progress in democracy and call this limit of its potential, somehow characterized, its 'degree of democracy,' which could then be compared to the similarly assessed degree of democracy possessed by anything else.

In place of such a complex and probably philosophically muddled enterprise, this work prescribes instead that progress in democracy be appealed to in situations where different outcomes would result from applying one or the other of the three measures of democracy or where other complicating features make it unclear which of a number of live options constitutes more people having control over more and important aspects of their social environment than the alternatives. In these circumstances the idea of perfect democracy serves as a paradigmatic model to help one in thinking about the specific features of things compared rather than being regarded as a property of the most democratic of these things to be discovered 'in' it. Things taken by themselves may be thought of as approximating perfect democracy by comparing them to what they had been and to what they are likely (other things being equal) to become, thus estimating democratic progress or regress.

12. Robert Dahl, *Dilemmas of Pluralist Democracy: Autonomy vs. Control* (New Haven: Yale University Press, 1982) 96ff. My own view is that securing national self-determination in the circumstances of today's world is not in conflict either with democracy internal to a nation or external to it. Hence campaigning for national self-determination is a good place to start for those concerned to expand democracy when such large units are at stake. See my 'Quebec Self-Determination and Canadian Interests,' in *Philosophers Look at Canadian Confederation/La confederation canadienne: qu'en pensent les philosophes?*, ed. Stanley G. French (Montreal: The Canadian Philosophical Association, 1979) 97–102.

13. This problem should be distinguished from one I do not think this work need address. Political theorists who place social groups at the centre of their explanations, such as Pluralist use of 'interest group' or Consociationalist use of 'subcultural segment,' have difficulties nonarbitrarily identifying these groups. For a criticism of the Consociationalists on this point see Jörg Steiner and Robert H. Dorff, *A Theory of Political Decision Modes: Intraparty Decision-Making in Switzerland* (Chapel Hill: University of North Carolina Press, 1980) 6–8; and for the Pluralists see my, 'Pluralism and Class Struggle,' *Science & Society*, 39(4): 385–416(Winter 1975–76), at pp. 394–399.

The present endeavour does not confront this problem. Social units are nothing but collections of people whose actions affect one another to greater or lesser extents, and while any individual will be a member of a very large number of such groups, the complexity of their numbers and interrelations will not be problematic conceptually. Sought here are grounds for prescribing more democracy in units that have been identified rather, than defining 'basic social group,' or the like, as part of the construction of a general explanatory theory of society.

It does not qualify this comment too much to note that social units may be more or less 'cohesive,' i.e., they may persist through longer or shorter times and have more or less far-reaching and numerous effects on the lives of their members. In general one might say that the more cohesive a social unit the more important that it be democratic; thus it is more important for London to be made more democratic than the bus passenger unit. However, this itself should be qualified, because it will be in the interests of democracy sometimes to promote more cohesiveness, sometimes less. An example of the first case is people's alienation from one another in work places and communities, an example of the second is the cliquishness that isolates bureaucratic agencies from popular responsiveness.

14. John Dewey, *The Public and Its Problems* (Denver: Alan Swallow, 1957), first published in 1927, 148.

15. Karl Marx, *Contribution to the Critique of Hegel's Philosophy of Law*, in *Karl Marx Frederick Engels Collected Works* (New York: International Publishers, 1974– ) 3:3–129, written in 1843, at p. 29.

16. Antonio Gramsci, *Selections from the Prison Notebooks* (New York: International Publishers, 1971), ed. and trans. Quintin Hoare and Geoffrey Nowell Smith, written 1929–1935, 263 and sec. II.2, 'State and Civil Society.' Relevant to this point is Anne Showstack Sassoon's discussion, *Gramsci's Politics* (London: Croom Helm, 1980) 55–6, 109–119.

17. In their argument for a 'postliberal democracy,' *Democracy and Capitalism: Property, Community, and the Contradictions of Modern Social Thought* (New York: Basic Books, 1986), Samuel Bowles and Herbert Gintis define 'democracy' substantively, while wishing to draw conclusions that are in the main compatible with those of the socialist retrievalist. This results in fence-sitting formulations, for example: '[while] departing from the liberal tradition, we are not suggesting that liberal-democratic society step outside its historical trajectory to inaugurate a new order,' 179, or 'postliberal democracy departs so significantly from both capitalism and liberal democracy that one can hardly consider it a new form of accommodation. It is more accurately described as a process leading to a new social order,' 203.

Bowles and Gintis do not need to retain a substantive conception of democracy, and their analyses would be improved without one. Their view of democracy as a spiral, 187–8, requires a degrees approach, and we shall see that the key terms of their substantive definition of 'democracy' – as the combination of popular sovereignty and individual liberty, 4 – are quite complex ones designating phenomena amenable to degree.

18. Nicos Poulantzas, *State, Power, Socialism*, trans. Patrick Camiller (London: Verso, 1978) 252–3.

19. Alain Touraine, *l'Après socialisme* (Paris: Bernard Grasset, 1980) 195.

20. The eight are: liberal-progressive, authoritarian, distributive, ritualistic, democracy of well-being, stagnant, popular-liberal, and national, listed in Touraine's *Sociologie de l'action* (Paris: Editions de Seuil, 1965) 328–9.

21. Some theorists address this diversity itself, with results that are potentially useful for the project of the present work. One example is the approach to political theory of Robert R. Alford and Roger Friedland, *Powers of Theory: Capitalism, the State, and Democracy* (Cambridge: Cambridge University Press, 1985), who classify a large number of democracy-related concepts according to whether one is employing a 'pluralist,' a 'managerial' or a 'class' approach to political issues; see the summary chart at 449. Or, there is Russell L. Hanson's, *The Democratic Imagination in America: Conversations with Our Past* (Princeton: Princeton University Press, 1985). He argues that the concept of democracy is 'essentially contested,' and traces debates over how it should be interpreted from post-Revolution Republicanism through liberal democracy in the U.S.

The approach of this work is compatible with efforts like these. Hanson expresses the apparently contrary opinion that an 'objectivist' view, which appeals to 'a transhistorical ideal' denies 'the integrity of historical conceptions of democracy by sub-

ordinating them to the truth of a "timeless" conception, which . . . turns out to be a
projection of contemporary prejudices about democracy,' (3–4, and see 392). This
objection would have force against someone who tried to *combine* a substantive with
a degrees approach to democracy where some form of government was designated
'perfectly democratic,' and progress measured by seeing how close to it other forms
are. This is not the approach of the present work, which is even further from the
one Hanson castigates than is his own. Using one interpretation of Habermas's
theory of an ideal speech situation, he argues that progress in *rhetoric* about 'democracy' (that is, in debates over its meaning) can be ascertained by seeing how far
from undistorted, ideal speech such rhetoric is (chap. 1). In allowing that relations
of power can facilitate or impede progress in debates about democracy (49), he thus
introduces a specific (and certainly time-bound) standard of democratic progress,
namely to favour those relations that promote ideal discourse.

22. Alan Ryan, 'Two Concepts of Politics and Democracy: James and John Stuart Mill,'
in *Machiavelli and the Nature of Political Thought*, ed. Martin Fleisher (New York:
Atheneum, 1972) 76–113, at p. 112.

23. The thesis is explicated in C.B. Macpherson's *Democratic Theory: Essays in Retrieval*
(Oxford: Oxford University Press, 1973), see essay III.

24. Benjamin Barber, *Strong Democracy: Participatory Politics for a New Age* (Berkeley: University of California Press, 1984) 231. Macpherson specifies that those
entering the negotiating market are egoistically motivated (they could, like
Locke's negotiators, be partially morally motivated), and Barber specifies that
those who seek to be self-developing agents value community itself as well as
sharing community projects (they could strive to develop their potentials minus a potential to be community minded). The association of the three distinctions is thus an historical one.

25. This is the organizing principle of Brian Barry's book, *Sociologists, Economists and
Democracy* (London: Collier-Macmillan, 1970).

26. William Connolly calls these the 'arena' and the 'umpire' theories of the state in his
'The Challenge to Pluralist Theory,' in *The Bias of Pluralism*, ed. William Connolly
(New York: Altherston Press, 1969) 3–34. For discussions by Pluralists see: V.O.
Key, *Politics, Parties, and Pressure Groups* (New York: Thomas Crowell, 1958) e.g.,
24; and Robert Dahl, *Pluralist Democracy in the United States* (Chicago: Rand McNally,
1967), see 7.

27. For example, Dorval Brunelle: 'one may characterize liberal democracy as being
that [bad form of democracy] where social relations are not called into question but
where, on the contrary, the system is sufficiently flexible to integrate permanent
conflicts on an individual level of women, blacks, ecologists, militants . . . without in
normal times affecting the equilibrium of the social order. In such circumstances,
democracy is no less or more than the legal "price" to pay to guarantee a minimum
social peace,' in *Socialisme, étatisme et démocratie* (Montreal: Editions Saint-Martin,
1983) 48.

28. It is a curious fact that democratic theorists who fragment the concept of democracy
and who appeal to classic sources for illustration are not in accord over which source
illustrates which conception of democracy. Alan Ryan identifies negotiationism with
James Mill and self-developmentalism with John Stuart Mill, 'Mill and Rousseau:
Utility and Rights,' in Duncan ed., *Democratic Theory*, 39–57. While in their contributions to this collection, David Miller identifies something very like the first position
with John Stuart Mill and the second with Rousseau, 'The Competitive Model of
Democracy,' 133–155, and Richard Krouse identifies them respectively with Madison and de Tocqueville, ' "Classical" Images of Democracy in America: Madison
and Tocqueville,' 58–78.

29. See Jürgen Habermas's essay, 'Wahrheitstheorien,' in *Wirklichkeit und Reflexion: Festschrift für Walter Schulz*, Helmut Fahrenbach, ed. (Pfullingen: Neske, 1973) 211–265. The view is summarized by Thomas McCarthy, in his introduction to Habermas's *Legitimation Crisis*, trans. Thomas McCarthy (Boston: Beacon, 1973): 'The very act of participating in a discourse, of attempting discursively to come to an agreement about the truth of a problematic statement or the correctness of a problematic norm carries with it the supposition that a genuine agreement is possible. If we did not suppose that a justified consensus were possible and could in some way be distinguished from a false consensus, then the very meaning of discourse, indeed of speech, would be called into question,' xvi. Habermas' views are further explicated by McCarthy in his *The Critical Theory of Jürgen Habermas* (Cambridge, Mass.: MIT Press, 1978), sec. 4.3.

30. Decision theorists treating the problem include Stefan Valavanis, 'The Resolution of Conflict When Utilities Interact,' *The Journal of Conflict Resolution* 2(2): 156–169(1958), see 164–6; and Norman Frohlich, 'Self-Interest or Altruism, What Difference?,' *The Journal of Conflict Resolution* 18(1): 55–73(March 1974).

31. A classic attempt, associated with the decision theorist Vilfredo Pareto, is to specify that whatever preferences people have in the ideal society, nobody in it would prefer an alternative society to it. However, as critics of this 'Pareto optimality' condition have shown, it fails to distinguish between social arrangements among which people are indifferent, even though these may be very different societies. See Philip Pettit's accessible treatment in, *Judging Justice: An Introduction to Contemporary Political Philosophy* (London: Routledge and Kegan Paul, 1980) 143–4.

32. Amartya Sen has argued that rational normative decision-making does not require completeness in his *Collective Choice and Social Welfare* (San Francisco: Holden Day, 1970), chap. 7, and in his 1984 Dewey Lectures, 'Well-being, Agency and Freedom,' *The Journal of Philosophy* 84(4): 169–221(April 1985), at pp.178–181; Sen provides several additional references in this publication.

33. Joshua Cohen and Joel Rogers, *On Democracy: Toward a Transformation of American Society* (Harmondsworth, England: Penguin, 1983) 49.

34. Ibid. 149.

35. Ibid. 169.

36. Ibid. 60–71.

37. Ibid. 51–60.

38. Karl Marx and Frederick Engels, *Manifesto of the Communist Party*, in *Collected Works* 6:477–517, written in 1847–8.

39. See *From Max Weber: Essays in Sociology*, eds. Hans H. Gerth and C. Wright Mills (New York: Oxford University Press, 1946), especially the section, 'Bureaucracy,' from Weber's *Wirtschaft und Gesellschaft*, first published in 1922, 196–244; and Weber's, 'Socialism,' a 'Speech for the General Information of Austrian Officers,' in *Max Weber: The Interpretation of Social Reality*, ed. J.E.T. Eldridge (London: Nelson, 1972), delivered in 1922, 191–219.

40. John Keane, *Public Life and Late Capitalism: Toward a Socialist Theory of Democracy* (London: Cambridge, 1984) 26–7, chap. 3.

41. Jane J. Mansbridge, *Beyond Adversary Democracy* (New York: Basic Books, 1980) 25.

42. Macpherson, *Democratic Theory* 4. For Macpherson one can be mistaken about what 'essentially human' capacities are; see 51ff.

43. Mihailo Marković, *Democratic Socialism: Theory and Practice* (New York: St. Martin's Press, 1982) 104. Marković allows that sometimes people can voluntarily give someone power to dominate for the purpose of creation. His example – members of the Berlin Philharmonic giving power to von Karajan – casts doubt on whether there are circumstances where this happens. Recently, the Berlin

Philharmonic went on strike against von Karajan precisely in protest against his dictatorial ways.

**44.** Benjamin Barber, *Strong Democracy* 132 (italics omitted).

**45.** V.I. Lenin, *The Proletarian Revolution and the Renegade Kautsky*, in *V.I. Lenin Collected Works* (Moscow: Progress Publishers, 1963–80) 28:226–325, written in 1918, at pp. 227–325, especially 248–9.

**46.** For example: 'the exploiters inevitably transform the state (and we are speaking of democracy, i.e., one of the forms of the state) into an instrument of the rule of their class, the exploiters, over the exploited.... A state of the exploited must fundamentally differ from such a state; it must be a democracy for the exploited....' Ibid. 250.

**47.** In defending the claim that socialism is 'a million times more democratic than the most democratic bourgeois republic,' Lenin writes: 'Is there a single country in the world, even among the most democratic bourgeois countries, in which the average rank-and-file worker ... enjoys anything approaching such liberty of holding meetings in the best buildings, such liberty of using the largest printing-plants and biggest stocks of paper to express his ideas and to defend his interests, such liberty of promoting men and women of his own class to administer and to "knock into shape" the state, as in Soviet Russia?' ibid. 248.

**48.** In his analysis of the French Second Republic, Marx argued that a parliamentary form of government was a condition for the joint rule of competing capitalist factions. Karl Marx, *The 18th Brumaire of Louis Boneparte* in *Collected Works* 11:99–197, written in 1851–2.

Several contemporary authors have developed arguments that capitalism and representative, parliamentary democracy 'fit' one another. A sample discussion is in Adam Przeworski's, *Capitalism and Social Democracy* (London: Cambridge University Press, 1985) chaps. 4, 5, see 140. This book collects several of Przeworski's earlier published articles. The two pertinent to this discussion are 'Material Bases of Consent: Economics and Politics in a Hegemonic System,' *Political Power and Social Theory* 1: 21–66(1980) and 'Proletariat into a Class: The Process of Class Formation from Karl Kautsky's *The Class Struggle* to Recent Controversies,' *Politics and Society* 7(4): 343–401(1977); Jürgen Habermas, *Legitimation Crisis* 36–7; Claus Offe and Helmut Wiesenthal, 'Two Logics of Collective Action: Theoretical Notes on Social and Class Organizational Forms,' *Political Power and Social Theory* 1: 67–115(1980), see 94.

**49.** Rosa Luxemburg, *The Russian Revolution*, ed. Paul Levi and trans. Bertram D. Wolfe (Ann Arbor: University of Michigan Press, 1961), posthumously published in 1922, 71. Samuel Bowles and Herbert Gintis describe the hostility to representative government as a 'romantic notion,' which 'precludes the possibility of a reasoned defense of representative institutions.' *Democracy and Capitalism: Property, Community, and the Contradictions of Modern Social Thought* (New York: Basic Books, 1986) 148.

**50.** Carole Pateman, *Participation and Democratic Theory* (Cambridge: Cambridge University Press, 1970), but see her stronger statement that participationism 'is a return to the tradition of Rousseau ... and a rejection of the political theory and practice that developed as an integral part of the development of the capitalist economy and its liberal, constitutional state.' In Stanley Benn, et al., *Political Participation* (Canberra: Australian National University Press, 1978) 59–60.

**51.** Isaac Balbus, for example, maintains that representatives cannot interpret the will of the people, but 'inevitably develop interests of their own ...,' in his *Marxism and Domination* (Princeton: Princeton University Press, 1982) 358. Balbus never explains how this is inevitable, but this is not atypical of his book. Words like 'necessarily' and 'inevitably' are liberally employed.

52. Ibid. 359ff.
53. A useful source of illustrations is in *Public Participation in Planning*, eds. Bruce O. Watkins and Roy Meador (London: John Wiley, 1977).
54. Philip Green, *Retrieving Democracy: In Search of Civic Equality* (Totowa, N.J.: Rowman and Allenheld, 1985), discusses measures to strengthen representative democracy, chap. 9.
55. Cohen and Rogers, *On Democracy* 49–167. The first four items on their list are background conditions which in turn have 'more specific institutional requirements of the democratic order,' listed as 5 through 11.
56. Michael Margolis, *Viable Democracy* (Harmondsworth, England: Penguin, 1979) 158–179.
57. Radoslav Selucky, in his *Marxism, Socialism, Freedom* (London: Macmillan, 1979) 183.
58. J. Roland Pennock, *Democratic Political Theory* (Princeton: Princeton University Press, 1979) chap. 6
59. Ibid. 206–7.
60. Ibid. 247.
61. Ibid. 247–54.
62. Cohen and Rogers, *Democracy* 169.
63. See for example Pennock, 7, and Margolis, 22. Examples of exceptions are: Carl Cohen, *Democracy* 5–6; Lawrence Crocker, 'Marx, liberty, and democracy,' in *Marxism and the Good Society*, eds. John P. Burke, Lawrence Crocker, and Lyman H. Legters (Cambridge: Cambridge University Press, 1981) 32–58, at p. 51; and Roy A. Medvedev, *On Socialist Democracy*, ed. and trans. Ellen de Kadt (New York: W.W. Norton, 1977) 34.
64. V.I. Lenin, *What is to be Done?* in *Collected Works* 5:347–529, written in 1901–2, at p. 472.
65. For example John Hoffman, *Marxism, Revolution, and Democracy* (Amsterdam: Gruner, 1983) 77, 89.
66. An example is Bob Jessop on 'the officialdom-people contradiction' as the arena of democratic politics. See his 'The Political Indeterminacy of Democracy,' in *Marxism and Democracy*, ed. Alan Hunt (London: Lawrence and Wishart, 1980) 55–80, at pp. 57ff; see, too, Dorval Brunelle, *Socialisme* 35.
67. Barber, *Strong Democracy* 120 (italics omitted).
68. Later Barber summarizes this absence of independent grounds condition (which he calls his main innovation) with the phrase, 'where consensus stops, politics starts,' ibid. 129. Were this conjoined with a consensus theory of truth, the point would be less subject to this criticism, but, depending on what 'independent grounds' means, it makes the condition redundant, since 'conflict' is already listed as another condition.
69. In Michael Walzer's *Spheres of Justice: A Defence of Pluralism and Equality* (New York: Basic Books, 1983) 31.
70. Cohen, *Democracy* 44, makes this point in arguing that 'consent' is one of the 'presuppositions' of democracy.
71. See John Locke's *The Second Treatise of Government*, in *Two Treatises of Government*, ed. Peter Laslett (Cambridge: Cambridge University Press, 1963), first published in 1690, paragraph 115.
72. Cohen, *Democracy* 41.
73. Ibid. pt. 2; also see Michael Davis, 'Avoiding the Voter's Paradox Democratically,' *Theory and Decision* 5(3): 295–311(October 1974), at p. 301.
74. Davis is primarily concerned to set down conditions to obviate Arrow's paradoxes, 'Voter's Paradox.'

75. John Harris, 'The political status of children,' in *Contemporary Political Philosophy*, ed. Keith Graham (Cambridge: Cambridge University Press, 1982) 35–55, at p. 49.
76. Moses Finley argues that democracy and politics were born with Athenian society, *Democracy: Ancient and Modern* (New Brunswick, N.J.: Rutgers University Press, 1973) 14. Mansbridge, *Beyond Adversarial Democracy* 10–14, takes a contrary view and in fact sees tribal society as a paradigmatic representative of one kind of democracy.
77. Marković, *Democratic Socialism* 25.
78. Macpherson, *Democratic Theory* 51.

### Chapter 4

1. See David Gauthier's attempt, *Morals by Agreement* (Oxford: Oxford University Press, 1985). In addition to the question of whether Gauthier's approach can ground morality as he envisages it, there is an additional question of whether it can ground the egalitarian moral prescriptions of the present work's Chapter 6. Gauthier, himself, is not concerned to endorse such prescriptions.
2. William Nelson, *On Justifying Democracy* (London: Routledge and Kegan Paul, 1980), pp. 90–1.
3. An adequate morality for Nelson is a set of principles that 'produce benefits and prevent harm,' that can be the fundamental charter of a well-ordered human association,' and that can function 'in a society of free and independent persons,' ibid. 109–10.
4. Seymour Martin Lipset, *Political Man: The Social Bases of Politics* (Garden City: Doubleday, 1960) 403. Quoted and discussed by Felix Oppenheim, 'Democracy – Characteristics Included and Excluded,' *The Monist* 55(1): 29–59(Jan. 1971), at p. 30. (This issue of *The Monist* has several contributions on democratic theory.) See, too, Robert Paul Wolff, *The Poverty of Liberalism* (Boston: Beacon, 1968) 181, 193–4.

   It is interesting to note that in his expanded edition of *Political Man*, 2nd ed. (London: Heinemann, 1983), Lipset, a defender of the 'end of ideology' thesis as a welcomed development of modern times, criticizes the New Left of the '60s and '70s for attempting to revive antipluralistic ideological viewpoints, 524–544. My clear recollection is that the main 'ideological' orientation shared by streams of the New Left was that democracy is to be valued as an end in itself.
5. Philip Green, *Retrieving Democracy: In Search of Civic Equality* (Totowa, N.J: Rowman and Allenheld, 1985), see pts. 1 and 4 for an overview of the argument. 'Political democracy' is given this short definition at 5, and is elaborated on in chap. 8. Green has many good criticisms of antidemocrats. In my view his work would be helped by abandoning his fragmentist distinction between pseudodemocracy and real democracy. Note 40 below suggests one way this approach hinders his analysis. Another problem is that it is hard to imagine what 'democracy' is supposed to be 'retrieved.'
6. Ibid. 242. Green cannot mean that this is a main motivating desire of people consistently with his lament that thanks to living in a pseudodemocracy they think of their social being more in terms of 'competition and withdrawal into the life of privatized consumption' rather than of 'cooperation and participation,' 5.
7. Brian Barry, in Stanley Benn, et al., *Political Participation* (Canberra: Australian National University Press, 1978) 47. The target of Barry's criticism is the contribution of Benn in this collection. Barry contests Benn's contention that it is impossible due to the free-rider problem for any rational person to engage in democratic politics for any reason other than for its own sake.

8. Roy A. Medvedev, *On Socialist Democracy*, ed. and trans. Ellen de Kadt (New York: W.W. Norton, 1977) 39. The instrumentalist view is expressed by John Hoffman, *Marxism, Revolution, and Democracy* (Amsterdam: Gruner, 1983) 87. Hoffman and I corresponded about a draft of this book, and I am cited for support in it; I am also acknowledged, in a later book by Hoffman on Gramsci, with thanks for urging him to read the Eurocommunist writers. Though John Hoffman is kind to refer to me in his books, I should note that my evaluations of Gramsci and 'Eurocommunism' differ from his, and the main point I made to him was that Stalinism should be explicitly addressed.

9. For example, Medvedev also argues that democracy is necessary to cultivate genuinely capable political leaders and to allow them to be recognized, while the 'uncompromising sectarianism' typically associated with class instrumentalism inhibits this, *Socialist Democracy* 311.

10. See the argument that respect for rights is consistent with a consequentialist ethics in Wayne Sumner, *The Moral Foundation of Rights* (Oxford: Oxford University Press, 1987).

    Here is a representative account: 'Instrumental justifications value democracy for the way in which it translates people's wishes into government policy.... Intrinsic justifications value democracy for the benefits that the act of policy-making confers directly on the participants: democracy is desirable either because political participation is an intrinsically worthwhile activity or because it develops qualities of character ... that are valuable in other areas of life,' David Miller, 'The Competitive Model of Democracy,' in *Democratic Theory and Practice*, ed. Graeme Duncan (Cambridge: Cambridge University Press, 1983) 133–155, at p. 151. Miller does not explain how an activity could be 'intrinsically worthwhile,' but supposing democratic participation to be such a thing, the prescription for more society-wide democracy could be seen as a prescription to make it possible for everyone to enjoy the direct benefits of participation. Democratic activities would then be both a means and an end.

11. Kenneth J. Arrow, *Social Choice and Individual Values* (New York: John Wiley, 1951), chap. 3. Arrow summarizes his argument in 'Public and Private Values,' in *Human Values and Economic Policy*, ed. Sidney Hook (New York: John Wiley, 1951) 3–21. The four conditions are: 1) that a collective choice rule will always determine a unique ordering of preferences for the collectivity in question ('collective rationality'); 2) that if everyone ranks some possible outcome higher than an alternative the rule will rank it higher as well (the 'weak Pareto principle'); 3) that a collective choice depends only on the individual preference rankings of those in the collective ('independence of irrelevant alternatives'); and 4) that no individual's choice is automatically the collective choice ('nondictatorship').

12. See, Amartya Sen, *Collective Choice and Social Welfare* (San Francisco: Holden Day, 1970) 44ff., and Duncan Black, *The Theory of Committees and Elections* (Cambridge: Cambridge University Press, 1971) 19.

13. An example is Michael Davis, 'Avoiding the Voter's Paradox Democratically,' *Theory and Decision* 5(3): 295–311(October 1974). Davis points out that *Robert's Rules of Order* contains straightforward provisions for dealing with cyclical majorities.

14. This point is ably argued by N.M.L. Nathan, 'On the Justification of Democracy,' *Monist* 55(1): 89–120(Jan. 1971).

15. Andrew Levine, *Liberal Democracy: A Critique of Its Theory* (New York: Columbia University Press, 1981) 61. Levine does not suggest how the nonliberal-democratic choice mechanisms he calls for might escape this criticism.

16. Arrow, in Hook ed. *Human Values* 13. Arrow defines a 'constitution' as a rule for making social decisions which have this capability.

17. In his survey of 'processes for revealing social preferences,' Dennis Mueller discusses the following: a unanimity rule, the optimal majority, simple majority rule, cycling, logrolling, plurality rule voting, Condorcet voting, use of the Borda count, exhaustive voting, and approval voting. *Public Choice* (Cambridge: Cambridge University Press, 1979), chap. 3. Mueller's discussions include methods to encourage individuals to reveal their actual preferences, a problem not discussed in the present work. See his Chapter 4.

18. A selection of positions on this dilemma may be found in Stanley Benn, et al., *Political Participation*, cited above.

19. Anthony Downs discusses what is here called autocompromizing among other places in *An Economic Theory of Democracy* (New York: Harper and Bros., 1957), chap. 4.

20. In the 'prisoner's dilemma,' two prisoners are separated from one another and offered the following conditional options (each knowing the other is offered them): if neither confesses to a crime they are charged with having committed together, each will receive the same light sentence; if one confesses and the other does not, the one who confesses will get off and the one who does not will receive a heavy sentence; if both confess, each will receive the same medium heavy sentence. Since neither can trust the other to refrain from confessing, they both confess with the result that they are rationally led to a situation known by each to be worse than the available alternative where each would receive a light sentence.

21. There is a division among socialist theorists over the extent that the free-rider problem ought to be of such concern. Some, like Allen Buchanan and Jon Elster, not only take it seriously, but place the problem at the centre of their analyses of political consciousness. See Buchanan, *Marx and Justice: The Radical Critique of Liberalism* (Totowa, N.J.: Rowman and Littlefield, 1982) 88–102, and Elster's, *Making Sense of Marx* (Cambridge: Cambridge University Press, 1985) 345–371. Richard Miller challenges this approach, charging that it supposes an atomistic view of people as having preferences that are independent of their role-determined characters, in his *Analysing Marx: Morality, Power and History* (Princeton: Princeton University Press, 1984) 63–76. Similarly, Samuel Bowles and Herbert Gintis, *Democracy and Capitalism: Property, Community, and the Contradictions of Modern Social Thought* (New York: Basic Books, 1986), argue that it is a mistake to hold (as is supposed in statements of the free rider-problem) that people participate only 'to meet preexisting ends,' because 'preferences are as much formed as revealed in the exercise of choice,' 138–9. There are germs of a solution to the free-rider problem here, albeit a less decisive solution than one might want.

If peoples' characters are importantly formed by the nature and degree of their participation in joint actions with others, and if they want to have some control over this process, then they are ill advised to absent themselves from participation. That people are in fact thus formed is a claim almost all democratic socialists are prepared to defend. That people want to participate to this end is more problematic. Miller seems to accept a doctrine of motivating objective interests (107, 143, 149), but we shall see that this is itself problematic. Bowles and Gintis (who do not employ an objective interest doctrine, 149–50) imply either that people have or that they ought to have social formation of their characters through participation as a goal. Elster or Buchanan could reply that not everyone has this aim, and that the free-rider problem is not dissolved, but highlighted, by prescribing that people participate. Still, the number of those tempted to be free riders can be reduced by encouraging recognition of the way social processes affect one's personality and of the possiblity of affecting these processes through participation. Chapter 8, section iv pursues this topic.

311

22. I believe the term was coined by Alvin Weinberg, who used it to describe the superiority of technology over 'social engineering' (including both attempts to eliminate the causes of social problems and to change people's values) due to the relative economy of making technological innovations, 'Can Technology Replace Social Engineering,' *University of Chicago Magazine* 59: October(1966), 6–10; reprinted in *Technology and Man's Future*, 2nd ed., ed. Albert Teich (New York: St. Martin's Press, 1977) 22–30.

23. Studies of public apathy bear this out. For example, in explaining decreasing public participation in environmental policy formation, Steven Schatzow concludes that there is 'a general suspicion and dislike for greater public participation' on the part the government, and he lists a variety of realistic measures that could rectify inhibitions to participation by creating more possibilities for it. 'The Influence of the Public on Federal Environmental Decision-making in Canada,' in *Public Participation in Planning*, eds. W. Derrick Sewell and J. Coppock (London: John Wiley, 1977) 141–158. See, too, the essay, 'Citizen Participation in Practice: Some Dilemmas and Possible Solutions,' by Timothy O'Riordan in the same collection, 159–171.

24. Mueller, *Public Choice*, makes use of the work of Kurt Wicksell to distinguish between 'allocative' and 'redistributional' decisions, showing that they require different voting procedures.

25. Ibid. 268. Mueller's distinction between majority rule and unanimity is summarized in a chart on 216–17. Chaps. 11 and 12 treat the book's larger themes. And see Robert Dahl, *Dilemmas of Pluralist Democracy: Autonomy vs. Control* (New Haven: Yale University Press, 1982) 81–95.

26. Michael Davis makes a similar point in criticizing Arrow. He compares a 'deliberative' body to a scientific community, each of which makes decisions both about means and ends in an already partially shaped environment, 'Voter's Paradox,' 303. Examination of what political theorists and philosophers have had to say about real-life constitutional questions can be found in the case of Canada/Quebec in *Philosophers Look at Canadian Confederation/La confederation canadienne: qu'en pensent les philosophes?*, ed. Stanley G. French (Montreal: The Canadian Philosophical Association, 1979).

27. Allusion to a 'world history of democracy' is not only made for heuristic purposes. Given the complex ways that the world's societies overlap, a synoptic history sufficiently detailed to be of interest would be an undertaking of mind-boggling proportions. This does not mean, however, that historians cannot address fair-sized portions of our pasts to exhibit the things that impede or facilitate progress in democracy. Something like this has already been a principal focus of some historians.

Thus, historians in the tradition of Charles Beard looked critically at political institutions of the United States to ask, as Richard Hofstadter observes, not what laws or policies exist, but 'who has control and what do they want?' in Hofstadter's, *The Progressive Historians* (New York: Alfred Knopf, 1968). Barrington Moore's, *Social Origins of Dictatorship and Democracy: Lord and Peasant in the Making of the Modern World* (Boston: Beacon, 1966), is another example, where he tries to show how different 'routes to the modern world' led to either (parliamentary) democracy or to (left or right) dictatorship. Raymond Williams studies cultural history to chart the changing conceptions and evaluations of 'democracy' and related ideas, *Culture and Society: 1780–1950* (London: Chatto and Windus, 1958). Then again, there are the labour historians, such as Herbert Gutman whose focus is on the everyday experience of working people (not just of labour organizations and leaders) both in and outside of the workplace to produce what James R. Green calls 'labor history from the bottom up,' *The World of the Worker: Labor in Twentieth-Century America* (New York: Hill and Wang, 1980). And, of course, there is E.P. Thompson's *The Making of the English Working Class* (London: Penguin, 1980), first published in 1963, which integrates a bottom-up orientation with institutional and cultural ones.

Perhaps it is not presumptuous to suggest that historians could profit from the work of democratic theorists in pursuit of detailed histories of democracy and that much more such historical study should be undertaken. Without question, the fruit of this work would benefit democratic theory and practice.

28. Bowles and Gintis, *Democracy and Capitalism*: 'Two possibilities present themselves. In one, a democratic dynamic, a democratic set of rules induces a more democratic culture, and this in turn leads actors to render the rules more democratic, further enhancing democratic culture and eventually leading, perhaps, to a highly democratic institutional equilibrium. Equally possible, however, is an antidemocratic dynamic, in which the rules promote a less democratic culture, [fostering] the progressive erosion of democratic rules,' 187.

29. It is true that this possibility is hypocritically appealed to by authoritarians, and a political unit of any size in which elections were indefinitely postponed would no doubt be grossly deficient in democracy. However, it should be remembered that elections are culminating events of complex processes, requiring mechanisms for identifying issues, formulating platforms, nominating candidates, carrying on debate, determining what counts as a decisive result, and providing structures for assumption of political authority after the election, not to mention holding the election itself. All this takes time.

Shortly after the Cuban Revolution many antisocialist politicians in the United States (in the main those who had been conspicuously silent during the Batista years) loudly demanded that the new regime hold immediate elections. Making reference to the social and economic difficulties that had to be overcome to allow for elections, Castro is reported to have reminded his critics that the Cuban people were still armed and thus had the means to effect a change of government directly if they had wanted this.

30. Benjamin Barber, *Strong Democracy: Participatory Politics for a New Age* (Berkeley: University of California Press, 1984) 224.

31. Jürgen Habermas, *Legitimation Crisis*, trans. Thomas McCarthy (Boston: Beacon Press, 1975) 123, and pt. 3. See also William Connolly's *Appearance and Reality in Politics* (Cambridge: Cambridge University Press, 1981), especially chap. 3.

32. Barber, *Strong Democracy* 198.

33. Felix Oppenheim, 'Democracy,' see 32–40.

34. Oppenheim is right to conclude his article by observing that democracy 'cannot provide a solution to all social problems,' but he is too pessimistic, and indeed inconsistent, when he says that 'not more, but less democracy,' is required to better the lot of outvoted and deprived minorities in the contemporary United States, ibid. 50.

35. Carl Cohen, *Democracy* (New York: The Free Press, 1973) 71–4.

36. Kenneth O. May, 'A Set of Independent, Necessary and Sufficient Conditions for Simple Majority Decision,' *Econometrica* 20(4): 680–4(October 1952). (Those of us who worked with Ken May before his sudden death in 1977 recall that he was an active democratic socialist as well as a gifted theorist.)

37. Elaine Spitz, *Majority Rule* (Chatham, N.J.: Chatham House Publishers, 1984), chaps. 9 and 10. Spitz's response is compatible with that of Oppenheim and, while she does not explicitly express it, also with the theory of the anonymous majority.

38. In addition to Oppenheim and Spitz, the point is made by Dahl, *Dilemmas* 6; Joshua

Cohen and Joel Rogers, *On Democracy: Toward a Transformation of American Society* (Harmondsworth, England: Penguin, 1983) 149–50, and Medvedev, *Socialist Democracy* 42, 45.

**39.** Green, *Retrieving Democracy* 171–2.

**40.** Green argues later in his book that an adequate defence of minority rights cannot be derived from empirical or logical considerations about the requirements for democracy, but must rather appeal directly to considerations of morality, ibid. 214. The worry Green expresses is less severe for somebody who thinks of democracy as a matter of degree. Such a one can agree that the necessity of protecting minority rights is neither a logical nor an empirical requirement for there being any degree of democracy whatsoever, while still maintaining that protection of minority rights is an empirically necessary condition for making advances in democracy.

**41.** Ibid. 171.

**42.** Claude Lefort, *L'invention démocratique: les limites de la domination totalitaire* (Paris: Fayard, 1981) 92, see especially chaps. 2 and 3. And see François Furet's *Interpreting the French Revolution*, trans. Elborg Forster (Cambridge: Cambridge University Press, 1981). Claus Offe, citing Max Weber, makes a similar point, *Contradictions of the Welfare State*, ed. John Keane (Cambridge, Mass.: MIT Press, 1984) 134.

**43.** Daniel Goldstick makes this point in an exchange with Richard Wollheim over whether it is a 'paradox in the theory of democracy' that a majoritarian in the minority on some issue is committed to having contradictory values regarding that issue. Goldstick's article is 'An Alleged Paradox in the Theory of Democracy,' *Philosophy and Public Affairs* 2(2): 181–189(Winter 1973).

**44.** See in this connection Y. Michael Bodemann, 'The Fulfilment of Fieldwork in Marxist Praxis,' *Dialectical Anthropology* 4: 155–161(1979).

**45.** Moses Finley, *Democracy: Ancient and Modern* (New Brunswick, N.J.: Rutgers University Press, 1973) 103.

**46.** Benjamin Barber does a good job of discussing these various aspects of the requirements for participation in his *Strong Democracy*, pt. 2. In my view, his suggestions can be accepted without also accepting his problematic classification of 'politics as epistemology,' 166–7.

**47.** Michael Walzer, 'Philosophy and Democracy,' in *What Should Political Theory Be Now?*, ed. John S. Nelson (Albany: State University of New York Press, 1983) 75–99, at p. 93.

**48.** Examples are Roger Scruton, *The Meaning of Conservatism* (London: Macmillan, 1980) and Russell Kirk, *The Conservative Mind* (Chicago: Henry Regnery, 1953): '...the essence of social conservativism is preservation of the ancient traditions of humanity,' Kirk, 7.

**49.** 'Efficient' is here used as a quality of means, not ends. Given that a social goal has been set, alternative sorts of activities, institutions, or modes of organization will be ranked as more or less efficient by estimating their relative likelihood of success at attaining the goal in question and taking account of costs incurred (which costs are in turn determined by reference to other goals). In much contemporary economic theory 'efficiency' is used in a different sense, not to be confused with this one, to describe a certain sort of social outcome, namely one which is 'Pareto optimal.'

**50.** Seymour Martin Lipset, *The First New Nation: The United States in Historical and Comparative Perspective* (New York: Basic Books, 1963), chap. 6.

**51.** Habermas, *Legitimation Crisis* 133–8.

**52.** John Stuart Mill was good at describing the first of these advantages but in an elitist way singularly blind to the second. See the critique by Zillah Eisenstein, *The Radical Future of Liberal Feminism* (New York: Longman 1981), chap.6.

**53.** In Canada a 'War Measures Act' suspending civil liberties was used sporadically during World War I and systematically on only two occasions – against Japanese Canadians during World War II and against Quebec nationalists in 1973 – both times inflicting unjust material and psychological harm on innocent people. The pretext in the first case was that Canadians of Japanese descent were Fifth Column threats; in the second it was declared that an 'insurrection' was underway. In both cases the justifying claims have been shown not only false, but known false by leading government officials at the time. See Ann Gomer Sunahara, *The Politics of Racism: The Uprooting of Japanese Canadians During the Second World War* (Toronto: Lorimer, 1981), and Aubrey Golden and Ron Haggart, *Rumors of War* (Toronto: New Press, 1971). I dare say that readers from any other country in the world can produce their own examples.

### Chapter 5

1. Adam Przeworski, *Capitalism and Social Democracy* (Cambridge: Cambridge University Press, 1985) 138. Przeworski's critique of the 'objectivity of classes' (Essay 2) need not be interpreted as incompatible with a 'structural' definition. See Note 36, Chapter 10. The notion of a surplus is seen by some as problematic if it is interpreted by reference to 'subsistence' considered as a primitive term. See the discussion by Dušan Pokorný, 'Marx's Philosophy of Surplus Value,' *The Philosophical Forum* 16(4): 274–292(Summer 1985). Sense can, however, be made of a surplus without supposing an ahistorical or naively value-neutral concept of subsistence. One might appeal to the difference that must surely exist in any society between some level of wealth that could be portioned so that everybody (or at least nearly everybody) would consider his or her share barely sufficient to deter opting out of any directly or indirectly productive activity (on an assumption that welfare or charity is not available) and a level of wealth that in addition would afford at least some people a standard of living they would prefer to the one considered barely sufficient.

2. G.A. Cohen, *Karl Marx's Theory of History: A Defence* (Oxford: Oxford University Press, 1978), chap. 8.

3. One seeking a fuller definition might want to specify whether it suffices for somebody to be a capitalist that he or she owns means of production and hires workers or whether it is also required that profit actually be realized. Also, some might think that a noncapitalist society must be devoid of any capitalist ownership of means of production. It seems to me that a noncapitalist society, and in particular a socialist one, is compatible with there being a measure of capitalist ownership; though in an egalitarian society the attraction of traditional private ownership to some that it affords disproportionate allocative powers would be absent. Those who wish may make absence of any private ownership a definitionally necessary condition for socialism and the main line of argument in this part of the book should not be adversely affected.

4. This is a 'functional' definition. The equivalent 'structural' definition of 'capitalism' is 'the society whose immediate producers own their labour power and no other productive force,' Cohen, *Karl Marx*, 181.

5. See Samuel Bowles and Herbert Gintis, *Democracy and Capitalism : Property, Community, and the Contradictions of Modern Social Thought* (New York: Basic Books, 1986) 67, 99.

6. See the treatment by John Roemer, *A General Theory of Exploitation and Class* (Cambridge, Mass.: Harvard University Press, 1982), especially chap. 7, summarized at 233–237; and Roemer's article, 'Should Marxists be Interested in Exploitation?,' in *Philosophy and Public Affairs* 14: 30–65(1985), reproduced in *Analytic Marxism*, ed.

John Roemer (Cambridge: Cambridge University Press, 1986) 260–282. See, too, Jon Elster, *Making Sense of Marx* (Cambridge: Cambridge University Press, 1985), chaps. 3 and 6.

7. One point of tension is in the chapter's focus on distribution. In the *Critique of the Gotha Programme* Marx maintains that: 'Any distribution whatever of the means of consumption is only a consequence of the distribution of the conditions of production themselves.... If the elements of production are [distributed so that the material conditions of production are in the hands of nonworkers] then the present-day distribution of the means of consumption results automatically. If the material conditions of production are the co-operative property of the workers themselves, then there likewise results a distribution of the means of consumption different from the present one,' *Karl Marx and Frederick Engels, Selected Works in One Volume* (New York: International Publishers, 1968) 319–325, at p. 325. The concepts of socialism and capitalism in the present work overlap with Marx's more than this may suggest.

It should be noted in the first instance that Marx's assertion about distribution following production relations 'automatically' is hyperbolic, as Marx elsewhere recognized the many mediations between production and distribution. This caveat aside, the concept of capitalism employed in this work is compatible with Marx's claim. On the concept, in a capitalist society ownership of means of production is unequally distributed and those who own such means have largely unconstrained control over the distribution of wealth for consumption. Marx's claim is that whenever ownership of productive means is unequally distributed, then there will be unequal distribution of wealth for consumption (hence, no constraints to prevent this). Rather than building this causal hypothesis into a definition, the approach here highlights what is taken as the most important effect of capitalism in contrast with an egalitarian conception of socialism in respect of the life options of society's various members. The often quite strongly expressed opposition to such an approach derives, it seems to me, either from fear that it constitutes rejection of a Marxist theory of history or adoption of a utopian, moralistic orientation toward social change.

However, while the approach in terms of effects is incompatible with Historical Materialism embraced as matter of unquestioned faith and with amoral instrumentalism, it is not incompatible either with Marx's causal hypothesis or with approaches to social activism that go beyond moral exhortation. (Chapter 9 further addresses the first of these points, Chapter 7 the second; see, too, Note 26.)

8. Claus Offe, *Contradictions of the Welfare State*, ed. John Keane (Cambridge, Mass.: The MIT Press, 1984), see especially the interview with John Keane (chap. 12) in which he gives an overview of his work.

9. A good explication of the various things that jointly constitute a 'fit' of this sort is in John McMurtry's, *The Structure of Marx's World-View* (Princeton: Princeton University Press, 1978) 160–171.

10. Christine Buci-Glucksmann and Göran Therborn advance typical socialist criticisms of the right-wing dimension of social democracy, while remaining alert to its complexity, *Le défi social-démocrate* (Paris: François Maspero, 1981) 257–265.

11. Mihailo Marković, *Democratic Socialism: Theory and Practice* (New York: St. Martin's Press, 1982) 88; Andrew Levine, *Arguing for Socialism: Theoretical Considerations* (Boston: Routledge and Kegan Paul, 1984) 6–7.

12. It is evidently necessary to include the clause about how decision makers *understand* benefits so as not to rule out those societies in which they have bad judgment. It is only now with the growth of socialist economies that the question of the grounds of such judgments has come to the forefront. Heretofore, it has not been too difficult

to agree that food, shelter, education, employment, and medical care have been the main priorities. The condition about relative equality of distribution is also not too difficult to live up to when need satisfaction at a relatively basic level is the main task.

13. Robert Nozick, *Anarchy, State, and Utopia* (New York: Basic Books, 1974) 28–32. Of course, Nozick denounces such systems, which indicates one advantage to making this part of a definition of 'socialism.' One wants to be defending something that a radical procapitalist, like Nozick, is actually against.

14. Major events in this decade which strain it are those in Afghanistan and Poland. For analyses from the left see Alexandre Adler and Jean Roney, *L'Internationale et le genre humain* (Paris: Mazarine, 1980); 'Afghanistan, Issue at its Origin,' *Akahata*: Bulletin of Information for Abroad, Japanese Communist Party (451): 1–17(January 10, 1981); and Enrico Berlinguer, et al., *After Poland: Towards a New Internationalism*, eds. Antonio Bronda and Stephen Bodington (Nottingham: Spokesman, 1982).

15. This point is difficult to prove. It is partly based on my own impressions in limited but first-hand experience in Cuba and four countries of Eastern Europe and partly on consideration that a state populated by determined anti-egalitarians would have been able by now at least to dampen what seem to be essentially egalitarian practices and institutions. That there is at least a strong presumption that these exist in countries of existing socialism is exhibited in comparative statistics about such matters as income spreads, accessibility to education and health facilities, or housing prices. One must compare comparables (e.g., Cuba and Jamaica or Honduras, China and India, Bulgaria and Turkey) and consider trends, but a few days in a library looking through U.N. statistics can be instructive in this respect.

   Useful documents are the *Statistical Yearbooks* of UNESCO, publications for the U.N. Economic Commissions for Latin America and for Asia and the Pacific, and surveys of the International Labour Organization. There are many other sources, among them: David Lane, *Soviet Economy and Society* (Oxford: Basil Blackwell, 1982), chap. 2; Charles Allan McCoy, *Contemporary Isms* (New York: Franklin Walts, 1982), chap. 2; Peter Wiles, *Distribution of Income, East and West* (New York: Elsevier, 1974); Harold Lydall, *Property and Industrial Organization in Communist and Capitalist Nations* (Bloomington, Ind.: Indiana University Press, 1973); and Paul S. Shoup, *The East European and Soviet Data Handbook: Political, Social, and Developmental Indicators, 1945–1975* (New York: Columbia University Press, 1981).

   Those who think that anybody harbouring anything but the most uncharitable view of the motivations of socialist state personnel is an idiot or a knave are requested to blot this note and the parenthetical remark to which it is attached from their minds and evaluate the main arguments of the book on their merits.

16. Louise Marcil-Lacoste, 'Cent quarante manières d'être égaux,' *Philosophiques* 11(1): 125–136(April, 1984). Along with other papers in this and the next number of *Philosophiques*, this draws on research compiled in an impressive annotated bibliography of recent philosophical work on equality coordinated by Marcil-Lacoste: *La thématique contemporaine de l'égalité: Répertoire, résumés, typologie* (Montreal: Presses de l'Université de Montréal, 1984). I suspect that most, if not all of her 140 ways can be classified under one of the three concepts of equality treated here, but this hypothesis need not be defended for present purposes. A less comprehensive but useful treatment of equality is the concise text by Bryan S. Turner, *Equality: A Sociological Inquiry* (Chichester, Essex: Ellis Harwood, 1986).

17. Yvon Gauthier characterizes this distinction as one between 'homotopic' and 'heterotopic' properties. The former are 'not linked to a concrete condition, to a given place, to an epoch, but answer to an ideal of rational equivalence,' whereas the latter are subject to variation depending on circumstance and are better thought of as

317

'tasks' than as 'states of affairs.' Possession of a right is a homotopic property; freedom from discrimination is a heterotopic one. 'Note sur la syntaxe et la semantic du concept d'égalité,' *Philosophiques* 11(2): 349–353(October 1984), at p. 351.

18. For an extended treatment see Ronald Dworkin's article, 'What Is Equality?' Parts 1, 2, *Philosophy and Public Affairs* 10(3,4): 185–246, 283–345(Summer, Fall 1981).

19. Nondiscrimination for Barry requires that people are not disrespected in virtue of irrelevant characteristics such as their race, and integration is incompatible with a 'separate but equal' policy, *Political Argument* (London: Routledge and Kegan Paul, 1965), chap. 7, 119–24. An egalitarian as conceived here would be justified in prescribing against discrimination and nonintegration because they almost certainly work against substantive equality of opportunity or equality of benefits and burdens. In the unlikely event that some discriminatory or separate but equal practice had no effects on people's opportunities and/or benefits and burdens in life, there may still be good reasons to object to them, but it is not clear that in such a circumstance the grounds would be properly called 'egalitarian.'

In Philip Green's *Retrieving Democracy: In Search of Civic Equality* (Totowa, N.J.: Rowman and Allenheld, 1985), he defines 'constrained inequality,' as the principle 'that whatever work people do should receive roughly the same socially standard reward at similar phases of their life-cycles,' 57. A few lines later, 'the [egalitarian] democratic principle' is described as 'the principle of a standard, decent reward for a standard, decent effort,' and Green adds that in this way 'not only would everyone be provided with roughly the same resources for active citizenship, but the inevitable differentials in reward or earning power would appear as a series of deviations from an expected social norm....'

These would be unique concepts only if the references to life cycle differentials or to effort are part of the meaning of 'equality' rather than specifications of constraints on full equality. However, Green makes it explicit that reward for effort is a deviation from equality, and gives no reasons not to regard life cycle differentials similarly. His use of the phrase 'for active citizenship' suggests that baseline equality is equality of opportunity; though when discussing 'absolute equality' as a desirable but unrealistic goal, Green seems to have in mind full equality of benefits and burdens. In his earlier book, *The Pursuit of Inequality* (New York: Pantheon Books, 1981), Green is less equivocal, describing equality as equality of opportunity plus reward for merit and with protection against inequalities becoming systemic, constituting class privilege, or being passed on to the next generation, 81.

Michael Walzer, *Spheres of Justice: A Defence of Pluralism and Equality* (New York: Basic Books, 1983), divides social life into the 'spheres' community membership, security and welfare, money and commodities, office, hard work, free time, education, kinship and love, grace, recognition, and political power. 'Complex equality' is a situation where, 'no citizen's standing in one sphere or with regard to one social good can be undercut by his standing in some other sphere, with regard to some other good.' 19. This makes Walzer's basic prescription one for equality of substantive opportunity, which he narrows by spelling out kinds of opportunities and ways they might be made unequal.

20. Levine, *Arguing for Socialism* 61–2. This is also an argument of Onora O'Neill in her paper, 'How Do We Know When Opportunities Are Equal?,' in *Feminism and Philosophy*, eds. Mary Vetterling-Braggin et al. (Totowa, N.J.: Rowman and Littlefield, 1977) 177–89.

21. In different ways this conclusion is argued for by Kai Nielsen, *Equality and Liberty: A Defence of Radical Egalitarianism* (Totowa, N.J.: Rowman and Allanheld, 1985), pt. 3, and by Christopher Ake, 'Justice as Equality,' *Philosophy and Public Affairs* 5(1):

68–89(Fall 1975). This conclusion is the one at which Levine himself arrives. He notes that 'a desire to distribute social benefits and burdens more equally is, historically, an important motive of socialists of all sorts' (*Arguing for Socialism* 64), and he concludes from his discussion of equality of opportunity that: 'If I am right about how equality of opportunity is best understood, and if socialism can reasonably be expected to promote material equality better than capitalism, then there is a case for socialism (including state bureaucratic socialism) over capitalism with respect to equality of opportunity,' 62.

22. Jeffrey Reiman, 'The Possibility of a Marxian Theory of Justice,' in *Marx and Morality*, eds. Kai Nielsen and Steven C. Patten (Guelph: Canadian Association for Publishing in Philosophy, 1981) 307–322, at p. 321. A discussion of equity and equality may be found in Stuart Nagel, 'Equity as a Policy Goal,' Original Papers, No. 2, (Bowling Green, Ohio: Social Philosophy and Policy Center, 1983): 'Equality in a policy analysis context means that two or more places, groups, or people receive equal treatment. Equity generally means they receive proportionate equality, not absolute equality,' 1.

23. While expressed in complex ways, these are the considerations that lead Ronald Dworkin to reject the notion of equality of 'welfare' in favour of equality of 'resources,' 'What is Equality?,' Part 1. See Nielsen's criticism of Dworkin, *Equality and Liberty*, 293–302. Some interesting approaches to this topic may be found in work of Thomas Scanlon, 'Preference and Urgency,' *Journal of Philosophy* 72(19): 655–670(November 6, 1978), and Evan Simpson, 'The Priority of Needs over Wants,' *Social Theory and Practice* 8(1): 95–112(Spring 1982). On their views individual preferences are to be evaluated by reference to social standards (though Scanlon admits the possibility of an unanalysed 'naturalistic' one as well), thus moving relativity from the individual level to that of predominant social norms. This approach is biased against a prescription that social norms favour equality of benefits and burdens subjectively regarded.

24. Kai Nielsen, *Equality and Liberty* 283.

25. Nielsen, himself, tries to distinguish between wants and needs, leaving the latter concept 'unanalysed,' ibid. 301. But there is nothing in his defence of equality that prevents him from treating needs as sorts of wants, and he usually does treat them in the same way; see, for example, 283–285. A critique of approaches to political philosophy employing the category 'need' is that of C.B. Macpherson, 'Needs and Wants: An Ontological or Historical Problem?,' in *Human Needs and Politics*, ed. Robert Fitzgerald (Sidney: Pergamon, 1977) 26–35.

26. A forceful statement of this interpretation of Marx is that of Allen Wood, 'Marx and Equality,' in *Issues in Marxist Philosophy*, eds. John Mepham and David Hillel-Ruben (Sussex: The Harvester Press, 1981), 195–221; and see Wood's book, *Karl Marx* (London: Routledge and Kegan Paul, 1981), chap. 9. Wood claims that Marx was 'highly critical' of socialist views favouring equal rights and 'indifferent' to equality of what are called benefits and burdens in this chapter as a goal, Mephan, ed., 198. In this Wood differs with Lucio Colletti, who argues that the value Marx places on material equality is the crucial difference between Marx and Rousseau, *From Rousseau to Lenin: Studies in Ideology and Society*, trans. John Merrington and Judith White (New York: Monthly Review Press, 1972), first published in 1969, 192. For other interpretations of Marx as an egalitarian and as a nonegalitarian see, respectively, Jon Elster, *Making Sense of Marx* (Cambridge: Cambridge University Press, 1985), chap. 4, and Richard Miller, *Analysing Marx: Morality, Power and History* (Princeton: Princeton University Press, 1984) 19–40.

In my view, Marx's scepticism about equal rights was motivated by belief that this deludes people into thinking socialism can be legislated or somehow brought into existence just by recognizing and proclaiming its moral superiority to capitalism. Marx's worry about unrealistic, moralistic approaches to socialism can be taken account of, however, without denying the moral superiority it is here claimed socialism has over capitalism, and socialist activists can try to pursuade people of this fact as a way of gaining popular support for socialism without confining themselves only to such activity.

27. To my knowledge, the only references to this slogan in Marx's writings pertain to its second part, emphasizing need-adjusted equality under communism, *The German Ideology*, co-authored with Frederick Engels, in *Karl Marx and Frederick Engels Collected Works* (New York: International Publishers, 1974– ) 5:19–539, written in 1845–6, at p. 537, and *Critique of the Gotha Programme*, 321–5. For an egalitarian analysis of the *Gotha Programme* see Kai Nielsen, 'Marx, Engels and Lenin on Justice: The Critique of the Gotha Programme,' *Studies in Soviet Thought* 32(1): 23–63 (July 1986).

28. Relevant debates on this topic may be found in *Marx, Justice, and History*, eds. Marshall Cohen, Thomas Nagel, and Thomas Scanlon (Princeton: Princeton University Press, 1980), see the exchange between Allen Wood and Ziyad Husami; and Nielsen and Patten, eds., *Marxism and Morality*, see especially the papers of Derek Allen, Gary Young, Allen Buchanan, and Jeffrey Reiman. A good survey of Marx's opinions on the subject is provided by George Brenkert, 'Marx and Human Rights,' *Journal of the History of Philosophy* 24(l): 55–77(January 1986).

29. This approach is available to Levine when he argues that socialism is more egalitarian than capitalism in lacking private ownership, 'the distinctively capitalist mechanism for generating material inequalities,' rather than arguing that socialism possesses equality-promoting mechanisms, *Arguing for Socialism* 63.

30. C.B. Macpherson, *Democratic Theory: Essays in Retrieval* (Oxford: Oxford University Press, 1973), chap. 6; G.A. Cohen, 'Capitalism, Freedom and the Proletariat,' in *The Idea of Freedom: Essays in Honour of Isaiah Berlin*, ed. Alan Ryan (Oxford: Oxford University Press, l979) 9–25.

31. John Rawls, *A Theory of Justice* (Cambridge, Mass.: Harvard University Press, 1971) 74. Lest the fact that it is Rawls, a nonsocialist, who is quoted here suggest this cannot be a socialist view, see Nielsen's defence of Rawls on this very point, *Equality and Liberty*, 140–1, and Jeffrey Reiman's similar defence, 'The Possibility of a Marxian Theory of Justice,' in Nielsen and Patten, eds., *Marx and Morality*, 307–322.

32. Etienne Balibar, *Sur la dictature du prolétariat* (Paris: Librairie François Maspero, 1976) 44 (italics omitted), and see 108–122.

33. Publishers of the *Oxford Advanced Learner's Dictionary of Current English*, 3rd ed. (Oxford: Oxford University Press, 1981) complained that in the edition of this work used in the Soviet Union, the definition of 'socialism' had been altered: *British edition*: 'Socialism... philosophical, political and economic theory that land, transport, the chief industries, natural resources, e.g., coal, water-power, etc. should be owned and managed by the State or by public bodies, and wealth equally distributed.' *Soviet edition*: 'Socialism... first phase of Communist social economic formation; social system which is replacing capitalism, based on the public ownership of the means of production and the abolishing of the exploitation of man by man.'

34. Isaac Balbus argues for a postcapitalist society uniting feminism, participatory democracy, ecological and 'post-instrumental' movements. 'Proletarian class struggle,' he says, is 'a reactionary struggle' incompatible with these. *Marxism and Domination* (Princeton: Princeton University Press, 1982) 353–4.

35. Some socialists doubt that communism can be without legal structures, for example, Allen Buchanan, *Marx and Justice: The Radical Critique of Liberalism* (Totowa, N.J.: Rowman and Littlefield, 1982), chap.7. Also, even as a stateless society, communism is envisaged to be informally structured to promote equality. Its culture and social

structure are to be ones where 'the freedom of each is the condition for the free development of all,' as Marx and Engels put it in the *Communist Manifesto, Karl Marx and Frederick Engels Collected Works* (New York: International Publishers, 1974–   ) 6:477–517, written in 1847–8, at p. 506.

**36.** Karl Marx and Frederick Engels, *Manifesto*, 495.

**37.** Selucky wants to replace 'workers' self-managment' with 'labour self-managment' for this reason, 180.

**38.** Kai Nielsen, *Equality and Liberty*, pt. 4, and several articles by G.A. Cohen, chief among them: 'Robert Nozick and Wilt Chamberlain: How Patterns Preserve Liberty,' in *Justice and Economic Distribution*, eds. John Arthur and William H. Shaw (Englewood Cliffs, N.J.: Prentice-Hall, 1978) 246–262; 'Capitalism, Freedom and the Proletariat,' 9–25; 'Illusions about Private Property and Freedom,' John Mepham and David-Hillel Ruben, eds., *Issues in Marxist Philosophy* (Sussex: Harvester, 1981), pp. 223–239.

### Chapter 6

**1.** Lawrence Crocker, 'Marx, liberty, and democracy,' in *Marxism and the Good Society*, eds. John P. Burke, Lawrence Crocker, and Lyman H. Legters (Cambridge: Cambridge University Press, 1981) 32–58, at p. 51.

**2.** Carol Gould, 'Socialism and Democracy,' *Praxis International* 1(1): 49–63(April 1981), at p. 53.

**3.** Carl Cohen, *Democracy* (New York: The Free Press, 1973) 111–118.

**4.** Ibid. 117.

**5.** Arthur M. Okun, *Equality and Efficiency: The Big Tradeoff* (Washington, D.C.: The Brookings Institution, 1975) 61.

**6.** Ibid. 61.

**7.** Okun loads the case by setting aside the vital questions about capitalist ability to manipulate consumer wants and the potential of workers' self-management arrangements to provide socialist flexibility and innovation. (Okun simply asserts that the latter is something U.S. labour does not want.) More seriously, Okun does not address the question of how efficient massive waste spending by capitalists is, ibid. 2–3.

For empirical criticisms of the putative efficiency of capitalism see Samuel Bowles, Daniel M. Gordon, and Thomas E. Weisskopf, *Beyond the Wasteland* (New York: Anchor, 1984); and Seymour Melman, *Profits Without Production* (New York: Alfred Knopf, 1983), chaps.10–12. See, too, Samuel Bowles and Herbert Gintis, *Democracy and Capitalism: Property, Community, and the Contradictions of Modern Social Thought* (New York: Basic Books, 1986) 79–87. A useful discussion of incentives is in Philip Green, *Retrieving Democracy: In Search of Civic Equality* (Totowa, N.J.: Rowman and Allenheld, 1985) 155–164.

**8.** David Schweickart *Capitalism or Worker Control?: An Ethical and Economic Appraisal* (New York: Praeger Publishers, 1980) 58–60.

**9.** Seymour Melman's, *Pentagon Capitalism: The Political Economy of War* (New York: McGraw Hill, 1970), describes the economic and social costs of military production in the United States, Chap. 8.

**10.** An exception is Pennock, but his arguments are weak. He defends the relative egalitarianism of capitalism by contrasting it to *feudalism*, excusing himself from comparing capitalism and socialism by erroneously claiming that statistics are not available. J. Roland Pennock, *Democratic Political Theory* (Princeton: Princeton University Press, 1979) 230–1. At another point he says that contrary to the predictions of anticapitalist and anti-imperialist theorists, developing nations which have gained independence 'appear to be sinking farther and farther into a morass of poverty, corruption, and undemocratic regimes,' 515, 516 note 12. No comparisons are made of countries like Cuba with the Dominican Republic or Haiti, of Bulgaria with Turkey, of China with India, and so on.

Pennock's assertions call attention to the fact that relative economic comfort of some noncapitalists in the wealthier capitalist societies is partly purchased at the expense of the most appalling poverty in the developing world. The reason that liberally inclined procapitalists almost never address this question is that they cannot. It is hard to imagine how one could morally justify imperialism, and to deny its effects would require explaining facts such as those documented by Noam Chomsky in his books. See, for example, *Turning the Tide: The U.S. and Latin America* (Montreal: Black Rose Books, 1986) or *The Washington Connection and Third World Fascism*), co-authored with Edward S. Herman (Montreal: Black Rose Books, 1979).

11. Philip Green, *The Pursuit of Inequality* (New York: Pantheon Books, 1981) 1.
12. John Rawls, *A Theory of Justice* (Cambridge, Mass.: Harvard University Press, 1971) 83.
13. Representative critics are Milton Fisk, 'History and Reason in Rawls' Moral Theory,' in *Reading Rawls*, ed. Norman Daniels (Oxford: Basil Blackwell, 1975) 53–80; and Robert Paul Wolff, *Understanding Rawls* (Princeton: Princeton University Press, 1977). Allen Buchanan surveys ten different sorts of Marxist critics of Rawls in *Marx and Justice: The Radical Critique of Liberalism* (Totowa, N.J.: Rowman and Allanheld, 1982), chap. 6.
14. Kai Nielsen, *Equality and Liberty: A Defence of Radical Egalitarianism* (Totowa, N.J.: Rowman and Allanheld, 1985) 309. Though he is defending 'abstract egalitarianism' (roughly, substantive equality of oportunity), his argument better applies to equality of benefits and burdens. Nielsen is developing a point made by Richard Norman that pro-egalitarianism is essential for having 'a moral point of view.' He cites Norman's 'Critical Notice of Rodger Beehler's *Moral Life*,' *Canadian Journal of Philosophy* (11)1: 157–183(March 1981).
15. Andrew Levine, *Arguing for Socialism: Theoretical Considerations* (Boston: Routledge and Kegan Paul, 1984) 133.
16. Main sources are: Robert Nozick, *Anarchy, State, and Utopia* (New York: Basic Books, 1974); Milton Friedman, *Capitalism and Freedom* (Chicago: University of Chicago Press, 1962); and Friedrich A. Hayek, *The Constitution of Liberty* (South Bend, Ind.: Gateway, 1972).
17. To my mind G.A. Cohen and Kai Nielsen, in works cited in the last chapter (Note 38), have put to rest the main theses of Nozick's defence of libertarianism. See too, Schweickart, *Worker Control*, chap. 5; Stephen Newman, *Liberalism at Wits' End: The Libertarian Revolt Against the Modern State* (Ithaca: Cornell University Press, 1984); C.B. Macpherson's criticism of Friedman, *Democratic Theory: Essays in Retrieval* (Oxford: Oxford University Press, 1973), chap. 7; and Christian Bay, 'Hayek's Liberalism: The Constitution of Perpetual Privilege,' *The Political Science Reviewer* 1: 93–124(Fall 1971). Libertarians seldom take account of the fact their plans would have to work on a worldwide basis, thus confronting the difficulties Bowles and Gintis discuss about the 'global market,' *Democracy and Capitalism* 188–93.
18. See Nozick, *Anarchy* 268–271.
19. See Peter Dworkin's detailed account, 'Chile's Brave New World of Reaganomics,' *Fortune* (Nov. 2, 1981) 136–144.
20. Michael Parenti, *Democracy for the Few* (New York: St. Martin's Press, 1974) 165. Parenti's conclusion is not only to reject capitalism but to reject representational democracy as well.

21. Bowles and Gintis, *Democracy and Capitalism* 88–9.
22. Alfred Lord Tennyson, *In Memorium: An Authoritative Text*, no. 127 (New York: W.W. Norton, 1973) 84. (There is some question about whether Tennyson wrote this before 1848, in which case the third democratic excess must have been something other than the events associated with the origin of the Second Republic.)
23. Mihailo Marković, *Democratic Socialism: Theory and Practice* (New York: St. Martin's Press, 1982) 38.
24. Ibid. 70ff and pt. 2.
25. Ernesto Laclau and Chantal Mouffe, *Hegemony and Socialist Strategy: Towards a Radical Democratic Politics*, trans. Winston Moore and Paul Cammack (London: Verso, 1984) 155.
26. Shingo Shibata, 'Fundamental Human Rights and Problems of Freedom: Marxism and the Contemporary Significance of the U.S. Declaration of Independence,' *Social Praxis* 3(3–4): 157–185(1975). Shibata's article sparked a debate including Silviu Brucan (Romania), Agnes Heller (Australia), Hermann Klenner (GDR), Howard Parsons and John Somerville (USA), and Anatol Rapaport (Canada), published in *Social Praxis* 6(1,2) (1977).
27. Laclau/Mouffe, *Hegemony* 156.
28. François Furet, *Interpreting the French Revolution*, trans. Elborg Forster (Cambridge: Cambridge University Press, 1981) 198.
29. One democratic theorist, Elaine Spitz, makes it definitive of 'sovereignty' that a sovereign political actor (she has in mind a majority) accept no authority outside of itself in coming to a decision, *Majority Rule* (Chatham, N.J.: Chatham House, 1984) 200.
30. Thomas Carlyle, *Critical and Miscellaneous Essays*, Vol. 6 (London: Chapman and Hall, 1872).
31. Catholic Church controversies over socialist-leaning orientations of Latin American worker priests and Canadian and U.S. Bishops further illustrate the point, as conservatives argue that this rejects Church tradition, while defenders argue that it represents critical extension of Christian charity. See the defence of the Canadian Bishops by Gregory Baum and Duncan Cameron, *Ethics and Economics* (Toronto: Lorimer, 1984). Regarding the U.S. Bishops see the papers in *Catholic Social Teaching and the U.S. Economy: Working Papers for a Bishop's Pastoral*, eds. John W. Houck and Oliver F. William (Washington: University Press of America, 1984).
32. In *The Socialist Decision*, trans. Franklin Sherman (New York: Harper and Row, 1977), first German edition in 1933, the theologian Paul Tillich integrated a prescription for socialism with an exploration of ways that a revolutionary proletarian movement could simultaneously turn Enlightenment antitraditionalist values against bourgeois society, while regaining prebourgeois links with originating communities. See pts. 1 and 2. See, too, the defence of liberal theology by Enrique Dussel where he discusses going 'beyond scholasticism and modernity,' *Ethics and the Theology of Liberation*, trans. Bernard F. McWilliams (Maryknoll, N.Y.: Orbis Books, 1978), first published in 1974, chap. 5, esp. 132–141; and see Gregory Baum's discussion of 'Critical Theology,' *Religion and Alienation: A Theological Reading of Sociology* (New York: Paulist Press, 1975), chap. 9.
33. Jürgen Habermas, *Legitimation Crisis*, trans. Thomas McCarthy (Boston: Beacon Press, 1975) 70.
34. In addition to Parenti's book, see Joshua Cohen and Joel Rogers, *On Democracy: Toward a Transformation of American Society* (Harmondsworth, England: Penguin,

1983), chaps. 4 and 5; and Michael Harrington, *The New American Poverty* (Harmondsworth, England: Penguin, 1985).

35. Norman Daniels, 'Equal Liberty and Unequal Worth of Liberty,' in *Reading Rawls*, ed. Norman Daniels (Oxford: Basil Blackwell, 1975) 253–282.

36. G.A. Cohen, 'Capitalism, Freedom and the Proletariat,' in *The Idea of Freedom: Essays in Honour of Isaiah Berlin*, ed. Alan Ryan (Oxford: Oxford University Press, 1979) 9–25.

37. Some sample sources on systemic discrimination are: Michael Reich, *Racial Inequality: A Political-Economic Analysis* (Princeton: Princeton University Press, 1981); and Paul and Erin Phillips, *Women and Work: Inequality in the Labour Market* (Toronto: Lorimer, 1983); the contributions to *Structured Inequality in Canada*, eds. John Harp and Jack Hafley (Scarborough, Ontario: Prentice-Hall, 1980); Laura Katz Olson, *The Political Economy of Aging* (New York: Columbia University Press, 1982); Angela Wei Djao, *Inequality and Social Policy* (Toronto: Wiley, 1983). Empirical work of this sort is very easy to come by and those who deny the existence of systematic oppression have a seldom confronted obligation to come to grips with it.

38. There is a large body of literature detailing this situation. A representative collection is *Hidden in the Household: Women's Domestic Labour Under Capitalism*, ed. Bonnie Fox (Toronto: The Women's Press, 1980). See, too, Pat Armstrong and Hugh Armstrong, *The Double Ghetto: Canadian Women and Their Segregated Work* (Toronto: McClelland and Stewart, 1984).

39. The strongest critics of affirmative action would not be satisfied with such measures, since they consider affirmative action as unfair to individuals in nontargetted groups. Green discusses these and other objections, *Pursuit of Inequality*, chap. 6, see 176–187.

40. As Levine puts it regarding freedom: 'It is ... pertinent to ask how free we are in the determination of what we want. Should it be that we are not very free in that determination, it is plainly a reproach against our institutions, no matter how well they deliver what we actually desire,' *Arguing for Socialism* 40.

41. Some democratic theorists think that admitting this entails denying that people have a power of free choice. Whether this charge can be maintained partly depends on what one means by 'choice,' and partly on one's stand on causal determinism.

A strong antideterminist position is espoused by Carol Gould who thinks determinism 'ideological' and expressing 'in theory the form of domination which characterizes economic and political life in capitalist societies.' Carol C. Gould, 'Beyond Causality in the Social Sciences: Reciprocity as a Model of Non-Exploitative Social Relations,' in *Epistemology, Methodology, and the Social Sciences: Boston Studies in the Philosophy of Science*, Vol. 71, eds. Robert S. Cohen and Mark W. Wartofsky (Boston: Reidel, 1983) 53–88, at p. 62. Other examples may be found in William E. Connolly, *Appearance and Reality in Politics* (Cambridge: Cambridge University Press, 1981), e.g. 20; and Cornelius Castoriadis, *l'Institution imaginaire de la société* (Paris: Editions du Seuil, 1975) 60ff, chap. 5.

In her *Marx's Social Ontology: Individuality and Community in Marx's Theory of Social Reality* (Cambridge, Mass.: The MIT Press, 1981), Gould cites many passages from Marx's works where he writes of human 'purposeful activity' or 'freedom' to support her claim that Marx saw human activities as 'fundamentally purposive' and not effects of causes, 73. Marx could be viewed a consistent determinist on the 'compatibilist' view, most famously argued for in recent Anglo-American philosophy by Donald Davidson, that reasons for actions are causes, 'Actions, Reasons and Causes,' *Journal of Philosophy*, 60(23): 685–700(November 1963), reprinted among several other places in *Free Will and Determinism*, ed. Bernard Berofsky (New York: Harper and Row, 1966) 221–240. Gould refers to Davidson in a note (n. 3 p. 186), but does not argue for her apparent rejection of compatibilism.

42. Habermas, *Legitimation Crisis* 123

43. Bowles and Gintis, *Democracy and Capitalism* 121–127.

44. Benjamin Barber, *Strong Democracy: Participatory Politics for a New Age* (Berkeley: University of California Press, 1984) 169.

45. Laclau/Mouffe, *Hegemony*, esp. chap. 3.

46. Ibid. 167.

47. Gilles Deleuze and Félix Guattari, *Anti-Oedipus: Capitalism and Schizophrenia*, trans. Robert Huxley, Mark Green, and Hellen R. Lane (Minneapolis: University of Minnesota Press, 1983), see chap. 4. Robert D'Amico's monograph, *Marx and Philosophy of Culture* (Gainesville: University Presses of Florida, 1981), summarizes the political relevance of their views.

48. If democratic politics were easy, then given the advantages of democracy and charitable views of human nature, the world would be far more democratic than it is. We have seen, however, that the deliberate pursuit of progress in democracy requires many difficult trade-offs involving fine and fallible judgment, sometimes militating against the civil libertarian position that certain rights may never under any circumstances whatsoever be infringed upon. A pertinent article on this point is by Marvin Glass, 'Anti-Racism and Unlimited Freedom of Speech: An Untenable Dualism,' *Canadian Journal of Philosophy* 8(3): 559–575(September 1978). However, the democrat should side with the civil libertarian in placing the burden of proof on the shoulders of those who favour abnegating generally supported rights to show not that this *may* be justified in some situation, but that it as a matter of fact is justified.

49. Jonathan Kozol puts adult illiteracy in the United States at 33%. *Literate America* (Garden City: N.Y.: Doubleday, 1985).

50. Macpherson, *Democratic Theory*, essays III, and IX–XI and *The Political Theory of Possessive Individualism* (Oxford: The Oxford University Press, 1962). The point is made by G.A. Cohen: 'We criticize capitalism not because it causes desires which might otherwise not have arisen, but because it causes desires the fulfilment of which does not afford an appropriate degree of satisfaction. The system requires the pursuit of consumption goods: it is indifferent to the quality of satisfaction which lies at the end of it....' *Karl Marx's Theory of History: A Defence* (Oxford: Oxford University Press, 1978) 320.

See, too, Claus Offe's argument that capitalism 'commodifies' things that ought not to be considered commodities, such as health and education, *Contradictions of the Welfare State*, ed. John Keane (Cambridge, Mass.: MIT Press, 1984) 144, and Bowles' and Gintis' discussion of capitalist production of an antidemocratic culture, *Democracy and Capitalism* 132–5.

51. Joshua Cohen and Joel Rogers, *On Democracy*: Toward *a Transformation of American Society* (Harmondsworth, England: Penguin, 1983) 51–60.

52. The principal texts are *Contribution to the Critique of Hegel's Philosophy of Law*, in *Karl Marx and Frederick Engels Collected Works* (New York: International Publishers, 1974– ) 3:175–187, written in 1844; and *On the Jewish Question*, ibid. 146–174, written in 1843. For an interpretation of these texts from the point of democratic theory see Norman Fischer, 'Marx's Early Concept of Democracy and the Ethical Bases of Socialism,' in Burke, et al., eds., *Marxism and the Good Society* 59–83.

53. Zillah Eisenstein, *The Radical Future of Liberal Feminism* (New York: Longman, 1981), passim and 220–24, 192–7.

54. Nicos Poulantzas discusses the pervasiveness of the influence of the state throughout

what is often thought of as civil society in his *State, Power, Socialism* (London: New Left Books, 1978), pt. 1, sec. 2, see 65–6.

55. Göran Therborn, *What Does the Ruling Class Do When It Rules?* (London: Verso, 1980) 66.

56. Speculating on one form a democratic-socialist society might take, John Keane asks: 'Can we therefore speak of the need for a post-liberal reconstruction of civil society – of . . . non-patriarchal public spheres that relate to state institutions only at the levels of criticism, negotiation, and compromise? Could the relations between autonomous public spheres within a socialist civil society come to resemble relations between federated and highly differentiated local communities, which temporarily surrender and entrust only such part of their powers as is necessary for the realization of their aims? So conceived, might not autonomous publics legitimately exercise rights to secede from this federation? Might autonomous publics with good reason redefine areas of life as private, as beyond the scope of legitimate state activity?' *Public Life and Late Capitalism: Toward a Socialist Theory of Democracy* (London: Cambridge University Press, 1984) 257. See the further discussion of this point in Chapter 8, pp. 171–2, of the present work.

57. Marx and Frederick Engels, *The German Ideology*, in *Collected Works* 5:19–539, written in 1845–6, at p. 47. See Green's similar discussion of the division of labour, *Retrieving Democracy*, chap. 5.

58. Iris Marion Young, 'Beyond the Unhappy Marriage: A Critique of the Dual Systems Theory,' in *Women and Revolution*, ed. Lydia Sargent (Boston: South End Press, 1981) 45–69.

59. Tony Honeré, 'Property, Title and Redistribution,' in *Equality and Freedom: Past, Present and Future*, ed. Carl Wellman (Wiesbaden: Franz Steiner, 1977) 107–115, at p. 114.

60. Thus Bowles and Gintis charge that liberal principles fail to justify placing the economy in a 'private' sphere, protected from democratic control, *Democracy and Capitalism* 64–71. And see their article, 'The Power of Capital: on the Inadequacy of the Conception of the Capitalist Economy as "Private",' *The Philosophical Forum* 9(3–4): 225–245(Spring-Summer 1983).

61. Cornelius Castoriadis, 'From Marx to Aristotle, from Aristotle to Us,' *Social Research* 45(4): 667–738(Winter 1978), at pp. 701ff, 723.

62. Karl Marx, *Grundrisse: Foundations of the Critique of Political Economy*, trans. Martin Nicolaus (New York: Vintage Books, 1974) 221–228.

63. J.R. Lucas, 'Against Equality,' in *Justice and Equality* , ed. Hugo Bedau (Englewood Cliffs, N.J.: Prentice-Hall, 1971) 138–151.

64. J.R. Lucas, 'Because You are a Woman,' in *Sex Equality*, ed. Jane English (Englewood Cliffs: Prentice-Hall, 1977) 111–120, at p. 117.

65. Gayle Rubin, 'The Traffic in Women: Notes on the 'Political Economy' of Sex,' in *Toward an Anthropology of Women*, ed. Rayna Reiter (New York: Monthly Review Press, 1975) 157–210, at p. 159.

66. On this point, Philip Green makes an unnecessary and unjustified concession to inflexibility: 'Of course any egalitarian must acknowledge, or even emphasize, that the biological difference between men and women is real. So too is their inevitably differential involvement in early child rearing, no matter what structures of social support for shared or communal parenting exist. . . . [Thus] a single standard of rights is not possible across gender lines,' *Retrieving Democracy* 103.

Radical theorists addressing the family and heterosexism have produced ample critiques of such naturalistic views. See, for example, the essays in *The Family in Political Thought*, ed. Jean Bethke Elshtain (Amherst: University of Massachusetts

Press, 1982), especially those of Elshtain, herself, "'Thank Heaven for Little Girls'": The Dialectics of Development,' 288–302; and Jane Flax, 'The Family in Contemporary Feminist Thought: A Critical Review,' 223–253; and Adrienne Rich, 'Compulsory Heterosexuality and Lesbian Existence,' *Signs: Journal of Women in Culture and Society* 5(4): 631–660(Summer 1980), reprinted in *Feminist Frameworks*, eds. Alison M. Jaggar and Paula S. Rothenberg (New York: McGraw-Hill Book Co., 1984) 416–420; and Monique Wittig, 'One Is Not Born a Woman,' also in Jaggar and Rothenberg, 148–152.

67. Eva Anscel, *The Dilemmas of Freedom* (Budapest: Akademiai Kiado, 1978) 74–5.

68. Georg Lukács, *History and Class Consciousness*, revised ed., trans. Rodney Livingston (Cambridge, Mass.: MIT Press, 1971), first published in 1967, quote at 186, and see 185–209. Many democratic-socialist theorists, reacting negatively to Lukacs's emphasis on social and historical 'totality,' overlook this importantly democratic dimension of his work.

69. Marx/Engels, *German Ideology*, sec. 1, passim, see 44–48.

70. See the papers in the collections: Fox, ed., *Hidden in the Household; Capitalist Patriarchy and the Case for Socialist Feminism*, ed. Zillah Eisenstein (New York: Monthly Review Press, 1979); *Feminism and Materialism*, eds. Annette Kuhn and Anne Marie Wolpe (London: Routledge and Kegan Paul, 1978), and the material referred to in these works.

71. For instance, Amy Gutmann argues that equality requires 'taking away from capitalists the collective power to determine wage rates,' 'ample training and employment for all,' a 'highly progressive rate of taxation upon owners of capital,' and 'industrial democracy or...legislation of more attractive job possibilities.' *Liberal Equality* (Cambridge: Cambridge University Press, 1980) 147–8. She expresses agnosticism about whether capitalism can accommodate these things. The socialist, by contrast, argues that no capitalist society in the world could tolerate more than token or temporary measures of these kinds.

Similarly, Michael Walzer argues that 'complex equality' requires that success in one domain not give one an edge in another and grants that 'the most common form of powerlessness in the United States today derives from the dominance of money in the sphere of politics,' which gives those who exercise this dominance an undue edge in other spheres as well. *Spheres of Justice: A Defence of Pluralism and Equality* (New York: Basic Books, 1983, 310, and see, 121–2. The spheres of life within which wealth ought not to give one an edge are: community membership, security and welfare, office, conditions of work, free time, education, kinship and love, grace, recognition, and political power.

Walzer does not explain how wealth in a capitalist system can be prevented from giving those who deploy it an edge in all these spheres. Instead he suggests that regulations for redistribution within a market system might be required. He gives as examples: 'blocking of desperate exchanges,' 'fostering of trade unions,' regulation of money 'directly through the tax system,' 'establishment of grievance procedures,'and 'co-operative control of the means of production,' ibid. 122. Socialists will argue that only the last-mentioned example in this unbalanced list has a ghost of a chance of promoting full complex equality.

Or one might consider pertinent views in Benjamin Barber's *Strong Democracy*. Defending thoroughgoing participatory democracy, Barber argues that 'neither capitalism nor socialism has much to do with the economic realities of the modern world' and that 'it is capitalist logic and epistemology that offends democracy rather than capitalist institutions or even capitalist values' 252–3. This is in contradiction with the major arguments of his chapter, which treat capitalism as a politically supported economic institution. Socialists holding different epistemological views will also maintain that dismantling capitalist institutions is required for anything as threatening to capitalist freedom as Barber's strongly participatory democracy. In fact, a few pages after the quoted passage Barber writes: 'The relationship of capitalism to democracy may remain problematic and controversial, but the relationship of the multinational, monopolistic corporation to democracy involves no such mysteries. The corporation is incompatible with freedom and equality, whether these are construed individually or socially,' ibid. 256. For socialists it is no accident that capitalism has largely turned to monopoly.

72. André Gorz, *Adieux au prolétariat: Au delà du socialisme* (Paris: Editions du Seuil, 1980) 87 and see 35, 60–1.

73. Ibid. 110.

74. Ibid. 108.

75. Laclau/Mouffe, *Hegemony and Socialist Strategy* 186.

76. Robert Michels's actual phrase in describing the antidemocratic structures of political parties was 'the iron law of oligarchy' *Political Parties: A Sociological Study of the Oligarchical Tendencies of Modern Democracy*, trans. Eden and Cedar Paul (New York: Dover, 1959), first published in 1915, pt. 6, chap. 2, but, as Eva Etzioni-Halevy notes in her survey of theories of bureaucracy, what Michels calls 'oligarchy' is closely akin to what Max Weber and Michels himself mean by 'bureaucracy,' *Bureaucracy and Democracy: A Political Dilemma* (London: Routledge and Kegan Paul, 1983) 20.

77. Connolly, *Appearance and Reality* 190–1.

78. In addition to works by Benjamin Barber and John Keane, anarchist theory has produced many examples of ways to increase participation. See Murray Bookchin's *Post-Scarcity Anarchism* (Berkeley: Ramparts Press, 1971).

Lenin comes in for rough treatment by democratic socialists, no doubt sometimes with justice. However, Lenin was also a participationist, who projected and started to implement much direct participation in the governing of the new Soviet society before he was succeeded by those less sympathetic to this or any other democratic measures. See the collection of relevant writings by him in V.I. Lenin, *On Participation of the People in Government* (Moscow: Progress Publishers, 1979).

79. Writing from first-hand experience, this phenomenon is described by Branko Horvat, *The Political Economy of Socialism* (Armonk, N.Y.: M.E. Sharpe, 1982) 182–90, and Roy Medvedev, *Leninism and Western Socialism*, trans. A.D.P. Briggs (London: Verso, 1981), chap. 2, see 60; and see Medvedev's *On Socialist Democracy*, trans. Ellen de Kadt (New York: W.W. Norton, 1977), chap. 7, where he calls for a rejuvenation of the soviets which were to have functioned as organs for direct participation independent of the state and the party, but had early on lost that independence.

80. In his *Contradictions of the Welfare State*, Claus Offe describes ways the competitive political party system supports capitalism by 'deradicalization of the ideology of the party,' bureaucratic 'centralization,' and 'deactivization' of rank and file members, 185ff. The list could be extended to include reference to the ways channelling socialist opposition to capitalism through political parties creates or exacerbates destructive sectarianism on the left. Offe sees hope for effective democratic and socialist politics in the demise of party politics even if this often takes the initial form of corporatism, 185ff.

81. Horvat devotes a chapter (11) of *Political Economy of Socialism* to this topic.

82. Buchanan, *Marx and Justice* 174–5.

83. References to various positions on this topic are in Notes 28 and 35 of Chapter Five. See, too, Levine's *Arguing for Socialism* 149–152.

84. Gorz, *Adieux* 166.

85. C.B. Macpherson, *The Real World of Democracy* (Toronto: Canadian Broadcasting Corporation, 1965), Lecture 1. This is the way to make Macpherson's point con-

sistent with a degrees-of-democracy approach. Sometimes Macpherson himself uses language that suggests a kinds-of-democracy orientation, for instance in his distinction between liberal-democratic, Marxian, and Rousseauean 'concepts of democracy,' each appropriate in some conditions; see 59. For reasons given in Chapter One, I think such descriptions should be rephrased in terms of degrees. While Macpherson would not condone it, I have heard some socialists from developing countries appeal to his distinction to claim that whereas authoritarian socialism is avoidable and unjustifiable in the first world, it may be appropriate to the third world.

86. Schweickart, *Worker Control*, and his article, 'Should Rawls be a Socialist? A Comparison of his Ideal Capitalism with Worker-Controlled Socialism,' *Social Theory and Practice* 5(1): 1–27(Fall 1978). Ferenc Feher and Agnes Heller, 'Forms of Equality,' in *Justice*, eds. Eugene Kamenka and Alice Erh-Soon Tay (London: Edward Arnold, 1979) 149–171.

87. Agnes Heller poses the question this way: '[W]ho makes the decisions about how productive capacity should be allocated?.... Marx's reply, of course, is *everyone* (this is precisely why he speaks of "associated individuals"). But how can every individual make such decisions? Marx did not answer this question, because for him it did not arise. For us, however, in our times, it has become perhaps the most decisive question of all. The focal point of contemporary marxism is to work out models for this (or at least it ought to be),' *The Theory of Need in Marx* (London: Allison and Busby, 1974) 124. And see her 'Forms of Equality,' 163.

88. Barry Clark and Herbert Gintis, 'Rawlsian Justice and Economic Systems,' *Philosophy and Public Affairs* 7(4): 302–325(Summer 1978), at p. 324 (italics omitted). Gintis's views as expressed in the more recent work coauthored with Bowles, *Democracy and Capitalism*, seem restricted to criticism of the capitalist market, 127–30.

89. Mihailo Marković, *Democratic Socialism* 39–41. See, too, Schweickart *Capitalism or Worker Control?* 51–55, 216–217.

90. Feher/Heller, 'Forms of Equality,' 163.

91. See Green's constructive discussions of this problem, *Retrieving Democracy*, chap.7 and 68–9, 132–137.

92. Crocker, 'Marx, liberty, and democracy,' 52.

93. William Nelson expresses this worry, *On Justifying Democracy* (London: Routledge and Kegan Paul, 1980) 49, but his conclusion is (as noted in Chapter Four) that democracy ought to be favoured because it creates morally desirable character types.

94. Jane J. Mansbridge, *Beyond Adversary Democracy* (New York: Basic Books, 1980) 4–5.

95. Medvedev, *Socialist Democracy*, chaps. 2 and 3.

96. Mihaly Vajda, *The State And Socialism* (London: Allison and Busby, 1981) 141.

97. Horvat, *Political Economy of Socialism*, see 468–9; Svetozar Stojanović, *In Search of Democracy in Socialism*, trans. Gerson S. Sher (Buffalo: Prometheus Books, 1981) 71ff. Medvedev describes the constitutionalists in *Socialist Democracy* 77–8.

98. Nozick, *Anarchy* 163.

99. G.A. Cohen, 'Robert Nozick and Wilt Chamberlain: How Patterns Preserve Liberty,' in *Justice and Economic Distribution*, eds. John Arthur and William H. Shaw (Englewood Cliffs, N.J.: Prentice-Hall, 1978) 246–262.

### Chapter 7

1. Alan Hunt, 'Introduction: Taking Democracy Seriously,' in *Marxism and Democracy*, ed. Alan Hunt (London: Lawrence and Wishart, 1980) 17.

2. Andrew Levine, *Liberal Democracy: A Critique of Its Theory* (New York: Columbia University Press, 1981) 206.
3. Levine's main arguments have been met in Chapter 4. See, too, my review article of his book, *Canadian Journal of Philosophy* 14(2): 335–357(June 1984).
4. '[A]n account must be given of liberal democracy which makes clearly visible not only its limitations but also the *discontinuity*, the radical break, between liberalism and socialism. If the defeat of capitalist hegemony rests on the reclamation of democracy by socialism . . . it cannot be achieved simply by "disarticulating" democracy from bourgeois class ideology. New, *socialist*, forms of democracy must be defined. . . .' Ellen Meiksins Wood, *The Retreat from Class: A New 'True' Socialism* (London: Verso, 1986) 153.

   And Milton Fisk argues that rather than viewing rights as applicable across different social systems, they 'must be based on the possibilities for change [which] can be of two sorts, either change that reforms an existing social order or change that creates a new social order. The possibilities of reforming and hence strengthening an existing order determine the rights of defenders of that order; the possibilities of creating a new order determine the rights of those opposed to the old,' *Ethics and Society* (Brighton: Harvester Press, 1980) 245. Fisk is here concerned with both liberal democratic and other kinds of rights. His chapter 7 deals with specifically liberal-democratic rights.
5. Levine, *Liberal Democracy*, passim. Levine defines 'social democracy' at 2. At 199 he describes Macpherson as also expressing a social-democratic view, 'in the accepted historical sense of a political movement rooted in the working class, that began as an attempt to replace capitalism and has become in country after country, an effort to reform and manage it.'

   This is a misleading description of Macpherson's views in two respects. Macpherson does not think that transformation to a more democratic society must or will be rooted in the working class, and he is a consistent anticapitalist (as Levine, himself, acknowledges at 200). See the interview with Macpherson (conducted, as it happens, by myself) in *Socialist Studies: 1983*, a publication of the Society for Socialist Studies (Winnipeg: University of Manitoba, 1984) 7–12. See, too, Macpherson's replies to earlier criticism by Levine and by Alasdair MacIntyre in *Canadian Journal of Philosophy* 6(2): 195–200(June 1976).
6. Amy Gutmann, *Liberal Equality* (Cambridge: Cambridge University Press, 1980), see chap. 5.
7. Zillah Eisenstein, *The Radical Future of Liberal Feminism* (New York: Longman 1981), chap. 4.
8. Renato Cristi, 'Hegel on Possession and Property,' *Canadian Journal of Political and Social Theory* 2(3): 111–124(Fall/Winter 1978).
9. Leo Strauss, *Natural Right and History* (Chicago: University of Chicago Press, 1953) 180–82.
10. Frank Coleman, *Hobbes in America* (Toronto: University of Toronto Press, 1977), see chap. 4. For a critique, see Terry Heinrichs, 'Hobbes and the Coleman Thesis,' *Polity* 16(4): 647–666(Summer 1984).
11. Carol C. Gould, *Marx's Social Ontology: Individuality and Community in Marx's Theory of Social Reality* (Cambridge, Mass: MIT Press, 1981). The phrase was likely coined by Lukacs.
12. C.B. Macpherson, *Democratic Theory: Essays in Retrieval* (Oxford: Oxford University Press, 1973), pt. 1.
13. As Levine does, *Liberal Democracy* 197–200.
14. Chantal Mouffe, 'Democracy and the New Right,' *Politics and Power* (4): 221–235(1981). And see her *Hegemony and Socialist Strategy: Towards a Radical Democratic*

*Politics*, trans. Winston Moore and Paul Cammack, coauthored with Ernest Laclau (London: Verso, 1984) 171–5. The point is also made by Philip Green, when he argues that some liberal critics of Rawls to the contrary, Rawlsian egalitarianism is central to the liberal tradition, *The Pursuit of Inequality* (New York: Pantheon Books, 1981) 4.

15. Isaiah Berlin, *Four Essays on Liberty* (Oxford: Oxford University Press, 1969) 121–2.

16. Ronald Dworkin, 'Liberalism,' in *Public and Private Morality*, ed. Stuart Hampshire (Cambridge: Cambridge University Press, 1978) 113–143, at p.127.

17. Levine, *Liberal Democracy* 145.

18. As for example, J. Roland Pennock, addressing the problem of conflict between such things as freedom of association and equality-promoting integration programmes: 'No "solution," practical or theoretical, is to be found, for they reflect tensions that are inherent in society, and indeed in man,' *Democratic Political Theory* (Princeton: Princeton University Press, 1979) 17.

19. Steven Lukes, *Individualism* (New York: Harper and Row, 1973). The species are: respect for the dignity of the individual; valuing autonomy; valuing privacy; valuing self-development; seeing individual aims as formed independently of society; espousing political individualist values; favouring economic individualism (laissez-faire); religious individualism (as in classic Protestantism); ethical egoism; epistemological egoism; and some versions of methodological individualism.

20. See John Rawls, *A Theory of Justice* (Cambridge, Mass.: Harvard University Press, 1971), sec. 74. Also pertinent to this point is Allen Buchanan's treatment of Rawls's changing use of the contract, *Marx and Justice: The Radical Critique of Liberalism* (Totowa, N.J.: Rowman and Littlefield, 1982), see 139.

21. A main charge of each is that the other cannot account for the phenomenon of human choice; see the well-known articles by R.E. Hobart, 'Free Will as Involving Determination and Inconceivable Without It,' *Mind* 43(169): 1–27(January 1934); and C.A. Campbell, 'Is "Freewill" a Pseudo-Problem?,' *Mind* 60(240): 446–464(October 1951). These are reprinted in *Free Will and Determinism*, ed. Bernard Berofsky (New York: Harper and Row, 1966).

22. Lukes, *Individualism* 73. Lukes pejoratively calls this individualist thesis 'abstract,' because he thinks it includes conceiving the individual 'as merely the bearer' of whatever given interests society may serve. The individualist, however, can agree with the prescribed characterization of the relation between society and the individual and deny the characterization of individuals Lukes attributes to this position by considering individuals not as 'bearers' of traits but autonomous agents with these traits.

23. David Schweickart, 'Should Rawls be a Socialist? A Comparison of his Ideal Capitalism with Worker-Controlled Socialism,' *Social Theory and Practice* 5(1): 1–27(Fall 1978); Jeffrey H. Reiman, 'The Possibility of a Marxian Theory of Justice,' in *Marx and Morality*, eds. Kai Nielsen and Steven C. Patten (Guelph: Canadian Association for Publishing in Philosophy, 1981) 307–322.

24. Derek P.H. Allen, 'The Utilitarianism of Marx and Engels.' *American Philsophical Quarterly* 10(3): 189–199(July 1973); and see Allen's further defence of this position in 'Marx and Engels on the Distributive Justice of Capitalism,' in *Marx and Morality*, eds. Kai Nielsen and Steven C. Patten, 221–250.

25. Carol C. Gould, 'Self-development and Self-management: A Response to Doppelt,' *Inquiry* 27(1): 87–103(March 1984), see 88–9. Gould holds that this 'follows from' the fact that each human has a power of choice, but since this does not entail that people have a moral right of access to means of self-development, a theory of primitive natural rights must be assumed.

26. Ellen Meiksins Wood, 'Liberal Democracy and Capitalist Hegemony: A Reply to Leo Panitch on the Task of Socialist Political Theory,' *The Socialist Register 1981*: 169–189, at p. 172. This continues an earlier criticism of Macpherson by Wood, 'C.B. Macpherson: Liberalism and the Task of Socialist Political Theory,' *The Socialist Register 1978*: 215–240. (Curiously, though three chapters of her recent book, *The Retreat from Class*, are devoted to strong criticism of cornerstone claims of the retrievalist project, no reference at all is made to Macpherson in this book.)

27. John Hoffman, *Marxism, Revolution, and Democracy* (Amsterdam: Gruner, 1983) 62–3.

28. Fisk, *Ethics and Society* 255.

29. An example is Richard Miller, *Analysing Marx: Morality, Power and History* (Princeton: Princeton University Press, 1984), chap. 10, whose negative argument (against the consistency of radical politics and morality) will be taken up shortly.

30. Leszek Kolakowski described Stalinism as 'the absolute institutionalization of Marxism as an instrument of power,' in which theory is consciously employed in the interests of specific political aims without concern for its integrity or truth. *Main Currents of Marxism*, Vol. 3, trans. P.S. Falla (Oxford: Oxford University Press, 1981) 2–4. Whereas Kolakowski's further claim that the seeds of this power-political approach are to be found in Marx and Lenin is a subject of ongoing debate among democratic socialists, there is general consensus on the point in relation to Stalin and other Stalinists.

31. Michael Teitelman, 'On the Theory of the Practice of the Theory of Justice,' *Journal of Chinese Philosophy* 5(3): 217–247(September 1978), at p. 239. See Reiman's criticism of Teitelman on this point, in 'The Possibility of A Marxian Theory of Justice,' 309–10.

32. Miller, *Analysing Marx* 17ff.

33. Ibid. 41–43.

34. Ibid. 43–45.

35. Ibid. 30.

36. Miller devotes most of his space in this argument to an explication of the view discussed in chapter five that Marx was an antiegalitarian and in general did not have a theory of rights, ibid. 19–30. These views, however, are beside the point at issue.

37. Ibid. 31–34.

38. In Goldrings's critique of this commission's analyses and recommendations, *Démocratie, croissance zero* (Paris: Editions sociales, 1978), he notes that when first published as a report, an appendix included a full list of founding 'private citizens,' but the main English language publication of this work, *The Crisis of Democracy*, eds. Michael Crozier, Samuel Huntington, and Joji Watanuki (New York: New York University Press, 1975), excised this list, leaving only the names of mainly academically-based intellectuals who had participated in the Commission's formal meetings. The excised list contained 31 names, all but two of big league capitalists, such as J.K. Jameson (Exxon), David Rockefeller (Chase Manhattan), and Edmond de Rothschild (Compagnie financière Holding). The two not in this league were Jimmy Carter and Raymond Barre. The Commission was chaired by Zbigniew Brzezinski. See Goldring's treatment including the full list at 10–11, 18–20. For additional socialist criticisms of the Trilateral Commission's report see the contributions to *Trilateralism: Elite Planning for World Management*, ed. Holly Sklar (Montreal: Black Rose Books, 1980).

39. Crozier, et al., eds., 3.

40. Goldring, *Croissance* 169.

41. Milton Fisk, 'History and Reason in Rawls' Moral Theory,' in *Reading Rawls*, ed. Norman Daniels (Oxford: Basil Blackwell, 1975) 53–80, at p.78; and see the relativized definitions of 'right' and 'obligation' in *Ethics and Society* 239.

42. '[P]eople in a group that conflicts with some other group do not have obligations to do things that would advance the internal historical needs of that other group. An owner has no obligation to make work safer, nor does a worker have an obligation to work faster....' *Ethics and Society* 128.
43. Ibid., 208.
44. It is not possible to read *The Condition of the Working Class in England*, in *Karl Marx and Frederick Engels Collected Works* (New York: International Publishers, 1974– ) 4:295–596, written in 1844–5, without being struck by Engels' strong moral outrage at the treatment of working people by his fellow capitalists.
45. '[A] person is subject to ethical principles only if, through the groups to which he or she independently belongs, a coherent human nature is developed. If, however, these groups conflict and thus generate conflicting forces within human nature, no comprehensive ethics compatible with ethical naturalism [his term for group-relativized ethics] can be applied to such a person.' Fisk, *Ethics and Society* 38.
46. Ibid. 128.
47. Ibid. 144–5.
48. Ibid. 144.
49. Barrows Dunham makes pertinent points in his *Man Against Myth* (New York: Hill and Wang, 1962), see chaps. 2 and 8.
50. Fisk, *Ethics and Society* 130.
51. Ibid. 259–61.
52. William E. Connolly, *Appearance and Reality in Politics* (Cambridge: Cambridge University Press, 1981) 96–102. Connolly may have some difficulty squaring this critique of Dworkin with a defence later in the same work of what is usually called negative liberty, chap. 7. Samuel Bowles and Herbert Gintis make this critique of liberalism an important part of their alternative political theory, *Democracy and Capitalism: Property, Community, and the Contradictions of Modern Social Thought* (New York: Basic Books, 1986) 22, chap. 5.
53. Macpherson, *Democratic Theory* 105.
54. Fisk, 'History and Reason,' 59.
55. Benjamin Barber, *Strong Democracy: Participatory Politics for a New Age* (Berkeley: University of California Press, 1984) 231.
56. Dorval Brunelle, *Socialisme, étatisme et démocratie* (Montreal: Editions Saint-Martin, 1983) 48.
57. Fisk, *Ethics and Society* 86–7.
58. Eisenstein, *Liberal Feminism* 126.
59. Ibid. 138.
60. Thus Marx's comments in 'On the Jewish Question,' in *Collected Works* 3:146–174: 'None of the so-called rights of man ... go beyond egoistic man, beyond man as a member of civil society, that is, an individual withdrawn into himself, into the confines of his private interests and private caprice, and separated from the community. In the rights of man, he is far from being conceived as a species-being; on the contrary, species-life itself, society, appears as a framework external to the individuals.... The sole bond holding them together is natural necessity, need and private interest, the preservation of their property and egoistic selves,' 164.

   See, too, the theory of law based on this perspective by Evgeny B. Pashukanis, *Pashukanis: Selected Writings on Marxism and Law*, eds. Piers Beirne and Robert Sharlet and trans. P.B. Maggs (London: Academic Press, 1980); from works written between 1924–36, see selections from *The General Theory of Law and Marxism* 37–131; Etienne Balibar, *Sur la dictature du prolétariat* (Paris: Librairie François Maspero, 1976) 555; Claus Offe, *Contradictions of the Welfare State*, ed. John Keane (Cambridge, Mass.: MIT Press, 1984), chap. 7; and Eisenstein, 238–40.

61. Levine, *Liberal Democracy* 200. In this work he thinks that 'the most likely direction for research in political theory...is that pioneered by Marx and later elaborated by Lenin (in *The State and Revolution*) and others,' 201. Like many socialists, Levine looks to Rousseau's work for help in this project. See his forthcoming, *The End of the State* (London: Verso, 1987) and his earlier work, *The Politics of Autonomy* (Boston: University of Massachusetts Press, 1976). Due, no doubt, to the richness of their respective theories, Marx and Rousseau are not straightforwardly brought into phase – a point that is made by both Lucio Colleti and Galvano della Volpe. From their differing perspectives, each sees a Rousseauean orientation as an important component of Marxist social/political theory: Colleti, *From Rousseau to Lenin: Studies in Ideology and Society*, trans. John Merrington and Judith White (New York: Monthly Review Press, 1972), first published in 1969, see pt. 3, essay 1; della Volpe, *Rousseau and Marx: And Other Writings*, trans. John Fraser (London: Lawrence and Wishart, 1978), first published in 1964, see secs. 2 and 4.

## Chapter 8

1. C.B. Macpherson, *Democratic Theory: Essays in Retrieval* (Oxford: Oxford University Press, 1973) 12–13.
2. Ibid., essay 6. The quoted passage is at 133. In his essay, 'Liberal Democracy and Property,' Macpherson confronts the question of whether this contradicts liberal democracy, arguing that it is 'consistent with the liberal-democratic ethic' and that a concept of property as the right to exclude others from use 'is unnecessarily narrow,' *Property: Mainstream and Critical Positions*, ed. C.B. Macpherson (Toronto: University of Toronto Press, 1978) 199–207, at pp. 206–7. Michael Walzer illustrates the same implied method of supersession by extension in his claim that a 'consistent liberalism' is 'one that passes over into democratic socialism,' *Spheres of Justice: A Defence of Pluralism and Equality* (New York: Basic Books, 1983) 323.
3. More fruitful for the theorist of democracy than either trying to square the liberty/equality circle or bemoaning unavoidable tensions is to reflect on the nature of these tensions in order to advance democratic theory and practice. It is in this spirit that Philip Green discusses the question of whether an egalitarian society should protect the right to strike, *Retrieving Democracy* 76–7.
4. Zillah Eisenstein, *The Radical Future of Liberal Feminism* (New York: Longman, 1981) 238–40; Mihailo Marković, *Democratic Socialism: Theory and Practice* (New York: St. Martin's Press, 1982) 151; André Gorz, *Adieux au prolétariat: Au delà du socialisme* (Paris: Editions du Seuil, 1980) 131.
5. Hanna Arendt, *The Human Condition* (Chicago: The University of Chicago Press, 1958), chap 7l; Jürgen Habermas, 'The Public Sphere,' *New German Critique*, trans. Sara Lennox and Frank Lennox, 1(3): 49–55(Fall 1974); Claude Lefort, *Essais sur le politique: XIX^e-XX^e siècles* (Paris: Editions Du Seuil, 1986), see 63–4.
6. Habermas, 'Public Sphere,' 49–54.
7. Iris Marion Young, 'Impartiality and the Civil Public: Some Implications of Feminist Critiques of Moral and Political Theory,' *Praxis International* 5(4): 381–401(January 1986), at p. 396. This is one of the two defining features of the slogan 'the personal is political' for her. (The other is that 'no persons, actions or aspects of a person's life should be forced into privacy.') Whether Young herself would perceive this view of the public sphere as a supersession of liberal democracy depends on how to interpret her call 'to break with modernism rather than recover suppressed possibilities of modern political ideas,' 38l. Her explicit interpretations of the prescription link it with a rejection of formal equality and universal rationality and

with a pluralist perspective that promotes 'heterogeneity in public life,' 382–3. The approach of this work is compatible with both these views (unless the first were to be employed along the lines of Richard Miller's critique of equal respect discussed in Chapter 7).

8. A standard 19th-century treatment of the rule of law, that of A.V. Dicey, *The Law and the Constitution* (London: MacMillan, 1886), describes this notion of equality before the law, 179, but also specifies that laws are to be created by judicial decision in the courts, 174, 210. This specification is unnecessarily restrictive of a liberal-democratic concept of the rule of law, pertaining as it does, not to its nature but to one possible origin.

   Pertinent discussions of the rule of law and socialism may be found in *Legality, Ideology and the State*, ed. David Sugarman (London: Academic Press, 1983); and Bob Fine, *Democracy and The Rule of Law: Liberal Ideals and Marxist Critiques* (London: Pluto Press, 1984).

9. V.I. Lenin, *The Proletarian Revolution and the Renegade Kautsky*, in *V.I. Lenin Collected Works* (Moscow: Progress Publishers, 1963–80) 28:227–325, written in 1918, at p. 326.

10. See the treatments by Barry Hindess, 'Marxism and Parliamentary Democracy,' in *Marxism and Democracy*, ed. Alan Hunt (London: Lawrence and Wishart, 1980) 21–54; and Ernesto Laclau and Chantal Mouffe, *Hegemony and Socialist Strategy: Towards a Radical Democratic Politics*, trans. Winston Moore and Paul Cammack (London: Verso, 1984), especially 59–60. These authors see a continuity between the views of Lenin and Kautsky. At a conference I attended, Laclau described Leninism as 'the surreal moment of Kautskyism.'

11. Karl Marx, 'The Trial of the Rhenish District Committee of Democrats,' *Karl Marx and Frederick Engels Collected Works* (New York: International Publishers, 1974–   ) 8:323–339, speech, Feb. 8,1849, at p. 324.

12. Charles Campbell, 'The Canadian Left and the Charter of Rights,' in *Left Perspectives on the Charter of Rights*, ed. Robert Martin, a special issue of *Socialist Studies/Etudes Socialistes: 1984* 2:30–44(1984), at pp. 31–2. Campbell's article is in a collection of contributions to a conference analysing an unfortunate experience in Canada's recent political history when the Liberal Party patriated the Canadian Constitution from Britain and added to it an entrenched Charter of Rights with many omissions. See, too, the collection *And No One Cheered: Federalism, Democracy and the Constitution Act*, eds. Keith Banting and Richard Simeon (Toronto: Methuen, 1983); and chap. 6 ('Constitutional Bonapartism') of Philip Resnick's book, *Parliament vs. People: An Essay on Democracy and Canadian Political Culture* (Vancouver: New Star Books, 1984).

   An effort by a minority of Canadian socialists (including Resnick and some of the contributors to the Martin collection) to promote active socialist input to debates that preceded entrenchment failed in the face of the response that it was a foregone conclusion that nothing of value could be gotten into the constitution. Meanwhile, although organized labour also sat on its hands, women, native peoples, and organizations of the handicapped vigorously campaigned for inclusion of some rights favourable to them. The gains they made were, to be sure, small, but they were no doubt better than what would have existed without their intervention.

13. William McBride, 'The Concept of Justice in Marx, Engels, and Others,' *Ethics* 85(3): 204–218: 'I do not see how Marx and Engels could, if pressed on the matter, logically avoid recognizing that justice . . . can meaningfully be referred to from a standpoint at least partially external to any particular past or present socioeconomic system. It, too, must . . . be said to be dualistic or pluralistic in meaning; so that . . . it cannot be understood strictly in terms of the standards of capitalism. . . . [Engels] spoke of the proletariat's "drawing more or less correct and more far-reaching demands"

out of the bourgeois demand for equality. I see no reason for not extending this pattern to the area of justice,' 213–14. For references to other views on Marx's stance toward rights see Note 28, Chapter 5.

14. Allen E. Buchanan, *Marx and Justice: The Radical Critique of Liberalism* (Totowa, N.J.: Rowman and Allanheld, 1982) 165ff.

15. Michael Sandel, *Liberalism and the Limits of Justice* (Cambridge: Cambridge University Press, 1983) 34–5.

16. Steven Lukes argues that even in 'a community of angels or saints,' conflict over goals that are not narrowly individualistic will require some means of resolution, 'Taking Morality Seriously,' in Ted Honderich, *Morality and Objectivity: A Tribute to J.L. Mackie* (Boston: Routledge & Kegan Paul, 1985) 98–109, see 104–9. And the desirability of a fully consensual community will be challenged on the grounds that this creates a closed society.

17. Stuart Rush, 'Collective Rights and the Collective Process: Missing Ingredients in the Canadian Constitution,' in Martin, ed., *Left Perspectives* 18–29, at p.18.

18. Ibid. 20–21.

19. See the articles and the bibliography in pt. 4 of *Feminism and Philosophy*, eds. Mary Vetterling-Braggin, Frederick Elliston, and Jane English (Totowa, N.J.: Littlefield Adams, 1977).

20. This way of characterizing a group right is explicated by Michael McDonald, 'The Rights of People and the Rights of A People,' in *Philosophers Look at Canadian Confederation/La confederation canadienne: qu'en pensent les philosophes?*, ed. Stanley French (Montreal: The Canadian Philosophical Association, 1979) 333–339, see p.334. The conference which spawned this collection was addressing philosophical dimensions of a major political tension within Canada between its Franco and Anglo nationalities when it had become especially acute (due to the election of a separatist government in Quebec). Other essays in the collection that bear on group rights are by David Copp, Daniel Goldstick, Charles Taylor, and Robert Ware.

Rush's own examples do not quite fit the characterization. For instance, affirmative action legislation, classified by him with national self-determination, can be enjoyed by individual women without acting in consort with other women. A right of women to form caucuses in a union, by contrast, would be an example of a collective right in this second sense. Rush's arguments can be reformulated to accommodate this modification.

21. See David Copp, 'What Collectives Are: Agency, Individualism and Legal Theory,' *Dialogue* 23(2): 249–269(June 1984).

22. See, especially, E.P. Thompson's, *The Poverty of Theory and Other Essays* (London: Monthly Review Press, 1978) 150ff.

23. See Harry Glasbeek and Michael Mandel, 'The Legalisation of Politics in Advanced Capitalism: The Canadian Charter of Rights and Freedoms,' in Martin, ed., *Left Perspectives* 84–124, see p.101.

24. E.P. Thompson, *Whigs and Hunters: The Origin of the Black Act* (London: Penguin, 1975) 258–269, quoted passage at 266.

25. John Hart Ely, *Democracy and Distrust: A Theory of Judicial Review* (Cambridge, Mass: Harvard University Press, 1980).

26. Thus Robert Martin cites Ely's work in support of his attack on 'juridical activism,' whereby decisions that ought to be made by legislators interacting with an electorate are made instead by judges interacting with lawyers. In Martin's 'The Judges and the Charter,' in Martin, ed., *Left Perspectives* 66–83, at pp. 69–73. Though he does not refer to Ely, Philip Green takes a similar approach, *Retrieving Democracy: In Search of Civic Equality* (Totowa, N.J.: Rowman and Allenheld, 1985) 214–218.

27. Glasbeek and Mandel, 'Legalisation of Politics,' 104, 108–110.

28. Bliss versus the Attorney General of Canada, 1979, l, S.C.R. 183 note 27 at 258. This and similar cases are discussed by Lynn McDonald, 'The Supreme Court of Canada and the Equality Guarantee in the Charter,' in Martin, ed., *Left Perspectives* 45–65.
29. Ronald Dworkin, *Taking Rights Seriously* (Cambridge, Mass.: Harvard University Press, 1977) 90–92. Dworkin's point is related by him to his thesis that the proper juridical method for making constitutional decisions is to construct a nonutilitarian justifying theory (see 107). Glasbeek and Mandel argue that this furthers conservatism, 'Legalisation of Politics,' 105ff., prescribing instead that judges' discretionary powers be greatly reduced. Still, their discretion is not likely capable of being narrowed to nothing. Ely's view that the guiding principle of judicial judgments should be protection of democracy is probably too consequentialist for Dworkin's taste, but it should be noted that this provides consequentialist defence of the importance for democracy of there being legally enforced 'trumps,' as Dworkin designates individual rights, against adverse effects a majority decision may have on a minority.
30. Glasbeek and Mandel, 'Legalisation of Politics,' 99. See, too, Mandel's 'The Rule of Law and the Legalisation of Politics in Canada,' *The International Journal of the Sociology of Law* 13(3): 273–287(August 1985). There he distinguishes between 'two opposing senses of the law: the *democratic* and the *juridical*,' and criticizes Thompson for overlooking the latter, see 277.
31. John Rawls, *A Theory of Justice* (Cambridge, Mass.: Harvard University Press, 1971) 204.
32. Norman Daniels, 'Equal Liberty and Unequal Worth of Liberty,' in *Reading Rawls*, ed. Norman Daniels (Oxford: Basil Blackwell, 1975) 253–282.
33. D.F.B. Tucker, *Marxism and Individualism* (Oxford: Basil Blackwell, 1980) 115.
34. Ibid. 116–117.
35. Lawrence Crocker, 'Marx, liberty, and democracy,' in *Marxism and the Good Society*, eds. John P. Burke, Lawrence Crocker, and Lyman H. Legters (Cambridge: Cambridge University Press, 1981) 32–58, at p. 38. Crocker more fully develops this case in his *Positive Liberty* (The Hague: Martinus Nijhoff, 1980).
36. Carol C. Gould, 'Self-development and Self-management: A Response to Doppelt,' *Inquiry* 27(1): 87–103(March 1984), at p. 89; Macpherson, *Democratic Theory*, 51; Richard Norman, 'Does equality destroy liberty?,' in *Contemporary Political Philosophy*, ed. Keith Graham (Cambridge: Cambridge University Press, 1982) 83–109, at p. 97.
37. Macpherson, *Democratic Theory* 109.
38. Ibid. see 117–119, quoted passage at 109.
39. Ibid. 51.
40. Gould, 'Self-development,' 89–90.
41. Macpherson thus criticizes liberal democrats for seeing society merely negatively, *Democratic Theory* 57.
42. Ibid. essay 3; and see G.A. Cohen, 'Capitalism, Freedom and the Proletariat,' in *The Idea of Freedom: Essays in Honour of Isaiah Berlin*, ed., Alan Ryan (Oxford: Oxford University Press, l979) 9–25.
43. Evan Simpson, 'Socialist Justice,' *Ethics* 87(1): 1–17(October 1976); Charles Taylor, 'What's Wrong with Negative Liberty?,' in *The Idea of Freedom: Essays in Honour of Isaiah Berlin*, ed. Alan Ryan, 175–193. Taylor argues that freedom involves 'my being able to recognize adequately my more important purposes, and my being able to overcome or at least neutralize my motivational fetters, as well as my way of being free of external obstacles. But clearly the first condition . . . requires me to have become something. . . . I must actually be exercising self-understanding in order to be truly or fully free,' 193.
    The plausibility of Taylor's analysis depends on the ambiguity of 'involves' and

'requires' in this passage. On the (retrieved) liberal-democratic concept of freedom, self-understanding is best regarded as an empirically necessary condition for keeping open a wide range of future options. But one can consistently recognize this while still defining 'freedom' by reference to people's abilities to do what they want to do when they want to do it. Freedom in respect of future options 'requires' self-understanding as a matter of fact, but 'freedom' need not 'involve' self-understanding as a matter of definition.

44. Marković, *Democratic Socialism* 106.
45. See the contributions to *The Bias of Pluralism*, ed. William Connolly (New York: Atherton Press, 1969); Peter Bachrach, *The Theory of Democratic Elitism* (Boston: Little, Brown, 1967); my 'Pluralism and Class Struggle,' *Science & Society* 39(4): 385–416(Winter 1975–76); and Richard Miller, *Analysing Marx: Morality, Power and History* (Princeton: Princeton University Press, 1984), chap. 4.
46. Stanislav Erhlich, *Pluralism On and Off Course* (Oxford: Permagon Press, 1982), pt. 2; Branko Horvat, *The Political Economy of Socialism* (Armonk, N.Y.: M.E. Sharpe, 1982), sec. 13.
47. Robert A. Dahl, *Dilemmas of Pluralist Democracy: Autonomy vs. Control* (New Haven: Yale University Press, 1982) 31ff.
48. Bob Jessop, 'The Political Indeterminacy of Democracy,' in Hunt, ed., *Marxism and Democracy* 55–80, at p. 70.
49. 'Equality means, precisely, identity. If A and B are to be treated as equal with respect to a thing of value, a right, opportunity, duty, or share in some social allocation, then the thing must be identical for A and B.... What might from an earlier perspective be justified as a proper difference, a desirable or ineradicable diversity, becomes an unjustified inequality, discrimination, unfairness, inequity. If equality is often desirable, then so is uniformity.' Dahl, *Dilemmas* 101–2.
50. Elizabeth Rapaport, 'Classical Liberalism and Rawlsian Revisionism,' *Canadian Journal of Philosophy*, Supplementary Volume III: 95–119(1977), at p. 119.
51. Ibid. 118.
52. This seems to be Isaac Balbus's solution: 'Although each liberation movement embraces elements of the others, each has nevertheless been reluctant fully and explicitly to endorse the goals of its counterparts,' *Marxism and Domination* (Princeton: Princeton University Press, 1982) 370–1. Balbus excludes working-class organizations from an alliance because he thinks their goals are objectionably technocratic, 353–4.
53. This is likely what Benjamin Barber means in his espousal of 'strong democracy,' which 'places the democratic process itself at the center of its definition of citizenship' so that a 'community of citizens' is one where '[c]itizens are neighbors bound together neither by blood nor by contract but by their common concerns and common participation in the search for common solutions to common conflicts,' *Strong Democracy: Participatory Politics for a New Age* (Berkeley: University of California Press, 1984) 219, and chap. 9. Some such view is likely also that counterposed to 'liberal individualism' by Alasdair MacIntyre in his *After Virtue* (Notre Dame: University of Notre Dame Press, 1981), see 233.
54. C. Wright Mills, *The Power Elite* (New York: Oxford University Press, 1956); William Domhoff, *Who Rules America?* (Engelwood Cliffs, N.J.: Princeton University Press, 1967). See also Domhoff's later *The Higher Circles* (New York: Random House, 1970); and Tod Gitlin, 'Local Pluralism as Theory and Ideology,' in *Recent Sociology*, No. 1, ed. Hans Peter Dreitzel (London: MacMillan, 1969) 61–87.
55. Samuel Bowles and Herbert Gintis, *Democracy and Capitalism: Property, Community,*

*and the Contradictions of Modern Social Thought* (New York: Basic Books, 1986) 150. Chapter 5 develops a theory of 'learning and choosing' as an alternative to a liberal view about preferences being pregiven.

56. Ibid. 131.
57. Ibid. 208.
58. Laclau/Mouffe, *Hegemony* 114–116.
59. See ibid. chap. 3, and Laclau's essay, 'Transformations of Advanced Industrial Societies and the Theory of the Subject,' in *Rethinking Ideology: A Marxist Debate*, eds. Sakari Hänninen and Leena Paldan (Berlin: Argument-Sonderband, 1983) 39–44, at pp. 43–4.
60. Sheila Rowbotham, 'The Women's Movement and Organizing for Socialism,' in *Beyond the Fragments*, eds. Sheila Rowbotham, Lynne Segal, and Hilary Wainwright (Boston: Alyson Publications, Inc., 1981) 21–155, at pp. 26–7.
61. Laclau/Mouffe, *Hegemony* 176, italics omitted.
62. This is a main point of difference that Laclau and Mouffe have with Gramsci, ibid. 137–8, 180–2.
63. Ellen Meiksins Wood, *The Retreat from Class: A New 'True' Socialism* (London: Verso, 1986), passim. The generic charge of Eurocommunism is levelled at 19–21.
64. Ibid., see (in order of allegations cited in the text) 63, 98, 75–6, 132–3, 175–6, 176–7, 136–7.
65. Two sorts of argument can be pieced together from Wood's criticisms. A philosophical argument cites Perry Anderson's critique of 'post-Structuralists' like Michel Foucault and Jacques Derrida from whom many authors Wood attacks draw. In his lectures, *In the Tracks of Historical Materialism* (London: Verso, 1983), Anderson criticized the post-Structuralists for adopting language as a model for all human activity, thus leading them to a subjectivist concept of truth and an anticausal viewpoint on history, chap. 2, cited in *Retreat* at 5 and 77–8. A second, social-scientific, argument is attributed by Wood to Marx. Its main claims are: 1) that the 'fundamental' interests of the working class are such that acting on them 'advance[s] the cause of socialism' even when not thus intended by workers; 2) that the working class has the 'capacity to destroy capitalism'; and 3) that neither 1) nor 2) is true of any other social group, summarized at 188–9.

To make out a 'guilt by association with post-Structuralists' case, much more justification of key premises is needed, in particular that Derrida and the rest are committed to the conclusions Anderson attributes to them and that anybody who adopts a pluralist, retrievalist position is thereby committed to these conclusions as well. The argument attributed to Marx could only be persuasive to somebody who had already adopted as unproblematic and proven the framework Wood defends. Her concept of 'socialism,' 165–6, probably makes 1) true by definition; though the question of how struggles against capitalism are related to other struggles (for example, against patriarchy or racism) remains to be addressed. A main question concerning claim 2) is whether the working class has this capacity acting alone or whether it requires joint activity with people organized to further other than working-class goals. In the latter case, a way of conceiving and justifying working-class priority in a coalition effort is still needed. This topic is further addressed in Chapter 9, pp. 230ff. and Chapter 11, Note 33.
66. Adam Przeworski refers to the ambiguity in the term 'socialist movement' in a way that bears on the point at issue here, *Capitalism and Social Democracy* (London: Cambridge University Press, 1985) 76–7.
67. Engels, 'Speech on the 17th Anniversary of the Polish Uprising of 1830,' *Collected Works* 6:389–90, made Nov. 29, 1847, at p. 389.

**68.** I have made this point more with specific reference to the need for Anglo-Canadians to support national self-determination in Quebec, 'Quebec Self-determination and Canadian Interests,' French, ed., *Canadian Confederation* 97–102.

**69.** Joshua Cohen and Joel Rogers, *On Democracy: Toward a Transformation of American Society* (Harmondsworth, England: Penguin, 1983) 172ff.

**Chapter 9**

**1.** Jean L. Cohen, *Class and Civil Society: The Limits of Marxian Critical Theory* (Amherst: The University of Massachusetts Press, 1982), see 39, 77, 89.

**2.** Ibid. 169.

**3.** Michèle Barrett, *Women's Oppression Today* (London: Verso, 1980) 24. Barrett distinguishes between reductionism and 'functionalism,' criticizing both. Functionalist Marxists on her account note that things like sexist oppression serve capitalist interests and conclude that this explains such oppression, 23–4. A functional explanation may be treated as a causal hypothesis connecting two phenomena ('X behaves in way W to serve the purpose Y' is extensionally equivalent to '[t]he fact that purpose Y requires X's W-like behaviour causes X to behave in a W-like way'). These sorts of hypotheses will be held to be reductionistic provided believing them has certain political consequences. Interpreted as a general approach (one in which society is pictured as an organic whole, the parts of which mutually support one another), functionalism may or may not yield reductionistic hypotheses.

**4.** The notion of 'oppression' thus contains two key elements: systematic thwarting of people's will and moral indefensibility of such thwarting. Most borderline candidates will clearly meet one but not the other of these conditions. By 'unjustified' is meant, 'morally unjustified' to capture the normative connotation of 'oppression.' The Ku Klux Klan ought not to be classified as oppressed when police agencies regularly impede its activities. (By contrast, chronically underemployed, frustrated whites some of whom join the Klan might be properly described as oppressed in their aspirations to secure a comfortable and meaningful life.) Prima facie evidence that the thwarting of some people's will is not accidental and hence 'structured' is when it is widespread. Proof that it is structured requires discovery of the mechanisms whereby it is sustained.

Samuel Bowles and Herbert Gintis outline a useful framework within which to express such mechanisms in their treatment of 'forms of domination.' They define a 'site' as a 'region of social life' where 'the manner in which whatever is done there is regulated by a set of social rules.' There is domination when these rules confer special power or privilege. For example, there is economic domination when 'rules of the game confer socially consequential power [etc.] on the basis of property rights,' and the patriarchal family is viewed 'as a system of rules in which social positions are organized according to gender, age, and kinship in such a way to confer special privileges on adult males,' *Democracy and Capitalism: Property, Community, and the Contradictions of Modern Social Thought* (New York: Basic Books, 1986) 98–9. It is not clear whether Bowles and Gintis would classify this perspective as a framework compatible with alternate theories of oppression or as a substantive social theory. A reason to place it in the first category is to reserve the term 'social theory' for something with hypotheses specifying the nature and functioning of the 'rules' in question and the relations among rules defining different sites.

**5.** One of Georg Lukács's discussions of totality is in *History and Class Consciousness*, revised ed., trans. Rodney Livingston (Cambridge, Mass.: MIT Press, 1971), first published in 1967, 183–186. Michael Mann employs this concept in a way most likely integrated with a forms-type of reductionism when he stipulates as necessary for working-class consciousness, '[T]he acceptance of [class identity and the opposition of classes] as the defining characteristics of (a) one's total social situation and (b) the whole society in which one lives,' *Consciousness and Action Among the Western Working Class* (London: Macmillan, 1973) 13.

6. Louis Althusser, *For Marx*, trans. Ben Brewster (London: Penguin, 1969), first published in 1965, 200ff.

7. Jürgen Habermas, *Legitimation Crisis*, trans. Thomas McCarthy (Boston: Beacon Press, 1975), pt. 1.

8. Juliet Mitchell, *Women's Estate* (Baltimore: Penguin, 1971).

9. Alain Touraine, *The Voice & the Eye: An Analysis of Social Movements*, trans. Alan Duff (Cambridge: Cambridge University Press, 1981) 21.

10. Heidi Hartmann, 'The Unhappy Marriage of Marxism and Feminism: Towards a More Progressive Union,' in *Women and Revolution*, ed. Lydia Sargent (Boston: South End Press, 1981) 1–41; and Zillah Eisenstein, 'Some Notes on the Relations of Capitalist Patriarchy,' in *Capitalist Patriarchy and the Case for Socialist Feminism*, ed. Zillah Eisenstein (New York: Monthly Review Press, 1979) 41–55.

11. A critique of the dual systems theory is offered by Iris Young, who thinks that a 'unified theory' can be produced by 'elevating the category of the division of labor to a position as fundamental as, if not more fundamental than, that of class,' 'Beyond the Unhappy Marriage: A Critique of the Dual Systems Theory,' in Sargent, ed., 45–69, at p. 53. To illustrate the classifications suggested here it is instructive to note the two directions in which this observation could be developed. One is to construct a general theory of society based on the division of labour which would provide putative grounding of a polycentric view of society analogous to the way that Mouffe and Laclau try to do this with a discourse-analytic theory of social equivalence and difference. Or a unicentric direction could be taken by following Young's own suggestion that the 'gender division of labor' is fundamental.

12. Jean Cohen, *Class and Civil Society* xiii, and see 220–225.

13. Representative examples of criticisms of the base/superstructure model from antireductionist directions may be found in Barry Hindess, 'Marxism and Parliamentary Democracy,' in *Marxism and Democracy*, ed. Alan Hunt (London: Lawrence and Wishart, 1980) 21–54; and Stuart Hall, 'Re-Thinking the "Base-and-Superstructure" Metaphor,' in *Class, Hegemony, and Party*, ed. John Bloomfield (London: Lawrence and Wishart, 1977) 43–72.

14. One criticism of the base/superstructure model is that it does not permit of a *sufficiently* totalized picture of society: '[The base-superstructure formulation] transposes from the arena of physical and spatial relations to the phenomenon of society. ...[T]he spatial content of the metaphor induces us to think of the elements of society as structures – "things" – existing as discrete objects in spatial relations.... This makes it difficult to "think" society, as Marx is at great pains to insist we should, as an "ensemble of social relations," as a totality which is not simply the sum of independently existing elements,' Maureen Cain and Alan Hunt, eds., *Marx and Engels on Law* (London: Academic Press, 1979) 49.

15. Though he did not intend it to serve this purpose, G.A. Cohen's analysis of Marxist modes of explanation in his *Karl Marx's Theory of History: A Defence* (Oxford: Oxford University Press, 1978) serves as an example. He maintains that superstructural phenomena are 'functionally explained' by production relations, while the latter are in turn explained by the development of productive forces. Accounts of the ways Cohen's Marx is supposed to have explained legal phenomena, 225–230, might be viewed as level-1 hypotheses, and the explanations of why production relations

should be thus explanatory by reference to development of the forces of production (chap. 6) might be regarded as level-2 explanations.

16. An example is in the following statement of Sandra Harding: 'From [the perspective of Chodorow and Flax] the underlying social dynamic of racism takes on a clear form. As a social institution, designed and controlled by men, as all social institutions have been, the vast panorama of the history of race relations becomes one more male drama in which the more powerful group of men works out its infantile project of dominating the other. Race relations are fundamentally social relations between men, where women find themselves supporting characters or, occasionally, thrust forward to leading roles in a script they have not written and cannot direct,' 'What is the Real Material Base of Patriarchy and Capital?,' in Sargent, ed., *Women and Revolution* 135–163, at p. 153.

17. Jean Cohen, *Class and Civil Society* xiii.

18. Ibid.; see the concluding chapter, 'Toward a Critical Stratification Theory.'

19. Isaac D. Balbus, *Marxism and Domination* (Princeton: Princeton University Press, 1982) 353.

20. Ibid. 354. For a critique of Balbus' work from a feminist direction, see Patricia J. Mills's review, 'Man-Made Motherhood and Other Sleights of Hand,' *Phenomenology and Pedagogy* 3(3): 207–217(1985).

21. Referring to Habermas, Dieter Misgeld challenges the opposing assumption that 'society is not known unless it is known in its entirety,' 'Critical Hermeneutics versus Neoparsonianism?,' *New German Critique*, No. 35, Special Issue on Jürgen Habermas: 55–82(Spring/Summer 1985), at p. 82.

22. Bowles and Gintis also call for such research, including of the 'discourses – over the way words are used, which flags are borne, and so on [as] a key to understanding the formation and solidarity of collective social actors,' *Democracy and Capitalism* 153, chap. 6.

23. Ernesto Laclau, *Politics and Ideology in Marxist Theory* (London: Verso, 1979), chaps. 3 and 4.

24. In their *Hegemony and Socialist Strategy: Towards a Radical Democratic Politics*, trans. Winston Moore and Paul Cammack (London: Verso, 1984), Laclau and Mouffe see both sectarianism and reductionism rooted in the open-ended or nonfixed nature of society. Engaging in movement politics supposes that there come to be 'subject positions' uniting those in the movement, which require that people see themselves as 'equivalent' to one another in being 'different' from others. Thus, just as the racist, the national chauvinist, or the sexist view certain features of people as exhausting their natures, so do the antiracist, the antichauvinist, and the antisexist tend to bifurcate the social world into abstractly characterized we's and they's. Mouffe and Laclau prescribe 'radical' (pluralistic) democracy largely to counteract this tendency on the left. See especially chaps. 3 and 4.

25. Ibid. 21.

26. See Ryerson's critique of reductionism regarding the national movements of Quebec in 'Quebec: Concepts of Class and Nation,' in *Capitalism and the National Question in Canada*, ed. Gary Teeple (Toronto: University of Toronto Press, 1972) 211–227. Also on this topic is Nicole Laurin-Frenette's criticism of Gilles Bourque's views in her *Production de l'Etat et Formes de la Nation* (Montreal: Nouvelle Optique, 1978). The point about the terms 'reductionism' and 'expansionism' was made by Ryerson in conversation.

27. Someone defining 'reductionism' could, of course, argue in the manner of Hegel that causation is such that an effect is a form of its cause. (Hegel argues this in his *Science of Logic*, the Doctrine of Essence: Three, III, B.) However, at issue is not what causation is, but what those criticized for being reductionists *think* it is, and it

would seem too restrictive to rule out as potential reductionists those with Humean concepts of causation.

28. Laclau and Mouffe, *Hegemony*, see 50–1 for a discussion of the historical narrative approach.
29. Ibid., see 177.
30. Examples treated by Marx concern English imperialism in Ireland and in the Indian Subcontinent. Several examples pertaining to contemporary Africa are discussed in John Saul's, *The State and Revolution in Eastern Africa* (New York: Monthly Review Press, 1979). He does a good job of illustrating the exacerbating effects of imperialism on preexisting tribal and internal class tensions. Essay 14, 'The Dialectics of Class and Tribe,' treats some theoretical dimensions of this task.
31. Paul Belanger and Celine St. Pierre, 'Dépendance économique, subordination politique et oppression nationale: le Québec 1960–1977,' *Sociologie et Sociétés* 10(2):123–147(October 1978), at p. 125.
32. Milton Fisk, *Ethics and Society* (Brighton: Harvester Press, 1980) xv.
33. Ibid. 49.
34. Louis Althusser, *Lenin and Philosophy and Other Essays*, trans. Ben Brewster (London: New Left Books, 1977) 150, from the essay, 'Ideology and Ideological State Apparatuses,' written in 1969, italics omitted.
35. Mao Tse Tung's abstract account of contradiction is in his 'On Contradiction,' in *Four Essays on Philosophy* (Peking: Foreign Languages Press, 1968), written in 1937, 23–78.
36. This is the charge of Hindess: 'the slogans of "relative autonomy," "determination in the last instance," and all the rest, are gestural evasions of a problem that cannot be resolved. There is no coherent way in which political life can be conceived as different from and irreducible to the economy and the distribution of the population into classes on the one hand and in which the economy is conceived as playing the ultimately determining role on the other,' 'Marxism and Parliamentary Democracy,' 40.

Two charges may be distinguished: that the concepts in question cannot be given any sense at all, and that they cannot be given sense in a way that will avoid reductionism. It is only the second charge that is pertinent to the topic of this chapter. Concepts like 'X is primary in relation to Y, though Y has relative autonomy' might be given sense in one of several ways. For example, if some notion of 'radical' or 'qualitative' change in respect of X- and Y-type phenomena is accepted, one might say that X is primary in that a radical change in X is necessary and sufficient for a radical change in Y, but not vice versa, while nonradical changes may work in either direction.

Or, one could develop an hypothesis of Milton Fisk's which distinguishes between 'frameworks' and 'stimulus causes' whereby the former allow the latter to have the effects they do in the way that the cellular structure of a plant allows the sun to produce carbohydrates in it. Economic structures for him are primary, since they alone are social frameworks, whereas such things as sexist or racist oppressions are admitted as extra-economic stimulus causes. This is explicated in his 'Feminism, Socialism, and Historical Materialism,' *Praxis International* 2(2): 117–140(July 1982).

These and other conceivable ways of making sense of the notions Hindess refers to become problematic when an antireductionist trying to make use of them comes to doubt, for example, that radical changes in the balance of class forces is sufficient to end racism or national oppression or that patriarchal structures have at least as much claim to be considered 'frameworks' as economic ones. In these circumstances one must decide whether to modify the theory or to discard it.

37. The first passage is from Marx's *The Eighteenth Brumaire of Louis Bonaparte*, in *Karl*

*Marx and Frederick Engels Collected Works* (New York: International Publishers, 1974–  ) 11:99–197, written in 1851–52, at p. 102. The second is from his 'Preface' to *A Contribution to the Critique of Political Economy*, in *Marx Engels Selected Works in One Volume* (New York: International Publishers, 1968)181–5, at p. 183.

38. Karl Marx and Frederick Engels, *The German Ideology*, in *Collected Works* 5:19–539, written in 1845–46, list as one of the material circumstances that humans face 'from the very outset of history,' that 'men, who daily remake their own life, begin to make other men, to propagate their kind: the relation between man and women, parents and children, the *family*,' 42–3. As is well-known it was Engels who followed up on this side of their materialistic theory of history, *The Origin of the Family, Private Property and the State*, in *Selected Works* 468–593, written in 1884.

39. For reasons given in Chapter 2, this work does not address the question of whether Marx's own views were reductionistic. Where Marxist theory is in danger of being reductionistic, it is likely not in seeing extraclass phenomena as either effects or forms of class phenomena, but in the weaker way labelled c) that recognizes a variety of important social phenomena, each with its proper nature or origins, but related to class struggle in such a way that it is both necessary and sufficient to make gains in class struggle to make other sorts of gains.

40. This is what Milton Fisk does in an approach in some ways closer to the one prescribed here than that centred on his framework/stimulus cause model. The core social-theoretical argument of his *Ethics and Society* is that there are basic needs (for food, sex, companionship, and so on) which are not 'made up' of one another and which in being met are subject to 'social patterning' in ways that produce new, nonbasic needs. Social groups are defined by reference to their basic and nonbasic needs and sorted into those which dominate and those which are dominated. Fisk claims that, '[t]he reason for having [nonclass] forms of domination is their reinforcement of class domination,' 50. See 110ff. for a discussion of needs.

41. Alain Touraine, *l'Après socialisme* (Paris: Bernard Grasset, 1980) 40.

42. E.P. Thompson, *The Poverty of Theory and Other Essays* (London: Monthly Review Press, 1978) 83.

43. James Joll calls attention to the importance for Gramsci of the 'Preface' passage, *Gramsci* (Glasgow: Fontana, 1977) 84. I am indebted to Esteve Morera-Dulsat for finding some references to uses of this passage in Gramsci's *Quaderni del Carcere*, 4 vols., ed. Valentino Gerratana (Turin: Einaudi Editori, 1975), at 1:455, 2:855, 3:1579, 1774. See, too, Stuart's Hall's interpretation of Gramsci's attack on economism, 'Base and Superstructure,' 46.

44. Antonio Gramsci, *Selections from the Prison Notebooks*, ed. and trans. Quintin Hoare and Geoffrey Nowell Smith (New York: International Publishers, 1971), written from 1929 to 1935, 172.

45. Carol C. Gould, 'Beyond Causality in the Social Sciences: Reciprocity as a Model of Non-Exploitative Social Relations,' in *Epistemology, Methodology, and the Social Sciences: Boston Studies in the Philosophy of Science*, Vol. 71, eds. Robert S. Cohen and Marx W. Wartofsky (Boston: Reidel, 1983) 53–88, at p. 58.

46. In addition to the deterministic language that permeates *The German Ideology, Capital*, and other works, Marx seems straightforward when he explicitly addresses this question, as for example: 'What is society, irrespective of its form? The product of man's interaction upon man. Is man free to choose this or that form of society? By no means. If you assume a given state of development of man's productive faculties, you will have a corresponding form of commerce and consumption. If you assume given stages of development in production, commerce or consumption, you will have a corresponding form of social constitution, a corresponding organization, whether of the family, of the estates or of the classes – in a word, a corresponding

civil society. If you assume this or that civil society, you will have this or that political system, which is but the official expression of civil society,' Letter to P.V. Annenkov, December 28, 1846, *Collected Works* 38:95–106, at p. 96.

47. This seems to be the view of Thompson: 'The critical concept ... is that of "determination" itself; hence the importance – as [Raymond] Williams and I and others have been insisting for years (and to the deaf) of defining "determine" in its senses of "setting limits" and "exerting pressures" ... ,' *Poverty of Theory* 159.

48. See the references to Hobart (Chapter 7, Note 21) and Davidson (Chapter 6, Note 41).

49. This is suggested by Touraine who notes that 'each sort of society forms an image of its creative potential,' and he plausibly hypothesizes that when members of a society fail, they conceive of their erstwhile creativity as having had an external source, *l'Après socialisme* 129–30.

50. Mihailo Marković, *Democratic Socialism: Theory and Practice* (New York: St. Martin's Press, 1982) 35, and see the summary of his interpretation of dialectics to justify this view, pp. 10–11; Andrew Levine, *Arguing for Socialism: Theoretical Considerations* (Boston: Routledge and Kegan Paul, 1984) 195.

51. John McMurtry, *The Structure of Marx's World-View* (Princeton: Princeton University Press, 1978) 160–170. McMurtry uses these concepts in a defence of 'technological determinism,' 189–198, but one need not take sides in debates over this thesis to recognize the usefulness of his definition of 'determinism' for explicating relations with which the indeterminist may be able to live.

52. Eric Olin Wright, *Class Crisis and the State* (London: Verso, 1979) 15–29. Like McMurtry, Wright is mainly concerned to explicate relations between productive forces, class struggle, and the state; also, one might challenge his grounds for allowing or disallowing the specific sorts of relations among these things he does (as summarized in a chart at 27).

    In his more recent book, *Classes* (London: Verso, 1985), Wright expresses a viewpoint closer to reductionism than that of the earlier one. Wright wishes to limit the concept of class to property relations in production. In itself, of course, there is nothing reductionistic about this. (Though Wright's further assertion that forms of exploitation other than of workers 'are essentially redistributive of a social product already produced within a set of property relations,' 98, detracts from the way that things like sexual or national oppressions are implicated in production.) A reductionist potential enters his analysis when he adds to his characterization of class an 'epochal theory of social change' where production is assigned first 'a pivotal role,' 97, and then one where 'the overall trajectory of social change ... is fundamentally limited by the dynamics of the dominant mode of production,' 111, and where no other field of oppression is assigned such a role.

53. A representative statement is by Elizabeth Fee: 'Women, who have already been defined as natural objects in relation to man, and who have traditionally been viewed as passive, have special reason to question the political power relation expressed in this [subject/object] epistemological distancing. The subject/object split legitimized the logic of domination of nature; it can also legitimate the logic of domination of man by man, and woman by man,' 'Is Feminism a Threat to Scientific Objectivity?' *International Journal of Women's Studies* 4(4): 378–392(September/October 1981) at p. 386.

    In the background of this view is the opinion of Nancy Chodorow that boys 'come to define themselves as more distinct, with a greater sense of rigid ego boundaries and differentiation. The basic feminine sense of self is connected to the world, the basic masculine sense of self is separate,' *The Reproduction of Mothering: Psychoanalysis and the Sociology of Gender* (Berkeley: University of California Press, 1978) 169. Unlike

Fee, Chodorow does not put this as a specifically epistemological thesis, but it is likely that Balbus does mean it this way when he draws on Chodorow and Dinnersteins' theses for a critique of what he calls 'the instrumental mode of symbolization,' *Marxism and Domination*, chaps. 8, 9. That scepticism about this theory is justified is indicated by the fact that some male philosophers share the criticism of a subject/ object distinction without themselves seeming to hold any feminist values.

Criticism of objectivist epistemologies is often merged with critiques of biased social research masking as disinterested or with advocacy of an approach to social science that starts with the local, lived experience of women (or of others whose pretheoretical orientations to the world are typically ignored or devalued by traditional social inquiry). Valuable insights into these things have been developed by feminists like (among many others) Margaret Eichler in her *The Double Standard: A Feminist Critique of Feminist Social Science* (London: Croom Helm, 1980) and Dorothy Smith, as in her 'A Sociology for Women,' in *The Prism of Sex: Essays in the Sociology of Knowledge*, ed. Julia Sherman and Evelyn Beck (Madison: University of Wisconsin Press, 1979) 135–187.

For a survey of the broad range of different feminist epistemological theories see Alison M. Jaggar, *Feminist Politics and Human Nature* (Sussex: Rowman and Allenheld, 1983), chap. 11. Jaggar describes the 'socialist feminist' position she favours as insisting that, whether recognized or not, all claims to knowledge are made from within social locations often involving oppressions and that 'the special social or class position of women gives them a special epistemological standpoint which makes possible a view of the world that is more reliable and less distorted than that available either to capitalist or to working-class men,' 370. Far from challenging the possibility and desirability of attaining some measure of objective knowledge, this view presupposes it.

54. Bob Jessop, 'The Political Indeterminacy of Democracy,' in *Marxism and Democracy*, ed. Alan Hunt (London: Lawrence and Wishart, 1980) 55–80, passim. See, too, Jessop's treatment in his book, *The Capitalist State: Marxist Theories and Methods* (New York: New York University Press, 1982) 247–252. An interesting empirical approach to aspects of this topic may be found in Eric A. Nordlinger, *On the Autonomy of the Democratic State* (Cambridge, Mass.: Harvard University Press, 1981).

55. An example of a mixed approach is that of Claus Offe. He combines systems theory with a viewpoint in which social movements such as the women's and ecological movements are viewed as 'decommodified organizations,' motivated by 'post material interests.' Offe speculates that though the oppressions that brought them into existence were originally caused by needs of capitalism, their members are 'no longer guided by the form of rationality appropriate to market behaviour' but by 'moral, political, and cultural values,' *Contradictions of the Welfare State*, ed. John Keane (Cambridge, Mass.: MIT Press, 1984), see 176, 248, 264.

One can envisage ways to make Offe's view about the common origin of movements that later take unique forms compatible with a nonreductionist theory. More difficult to accommodate is his additional reference to the three 'fundamental organizational principles of society as a whole,' the economic, political, and ideological, of which the latter two are today 'subordinate to the dominant organizational principle of exchange in capitalist societies,' 39. The nearly neutral perspective to be outlined in this chapter ought to be compatible with anything that does not have reductionist consequences in this and alternate movement-oriented theories, while at the same time providing a framework for sorting the various components of such theories for the purpose of advancing movement political theory.

56. In the essay, 'Technical Progress and the Social Life-World,' Jürgen Habermas

defines 'democracy' in a relevant way: 'We shall understand "democracy" to mean the institutionally secured forms of general and public communication that deal with the practical question of how men can and want to live under the objective conditions of their ever expanding power of control,' *Toward A Rational Society: Student Protest, Science, and Politics*, trans. Jeremy J. Shapiro (Boston: Beacon Press, 1970), first published in 1968.

57. Main attempts to trace such interconnections among macroproblem conditions have tried to explicate the relation between production and reproduction. A collection of illustrative works (among a very large and rapidly growing body of literature) is *Hidden in the Household*, ed. Bonnie Fox (Toronto: The Women's Press, 1980).

58. Etienne Balibar, *Sur la dictature du prolétariat* (Paris: Librairie François Maspero, 1976) 64.

59. A germane point of Radoslav Selucky's is that: 'the state is always a kind of social co-operation. People living on the same territory and performing different social functions are mutually interdependent. Whether divided into antagonistic (or co-operative) social classes, or not, in so far as they live in a given state, they are interested in its smooth functioning,' *Marxism, Socialism, Freedom* (London: Macmillan, 1979) 59.

60. In his *The Real World of Ideology* (Brighton: Harvester, 1980), Joe McCarney makes the point that one should 'distinguish the thesis that ideology serves class interests from the thesis that it is determined by class interests,' 32.

61. On the national question in Quebec see Note 26 in this chapter. A typical exchange between socialists over Canadian nationalism took place between Julian Sher and Mel Watkins in *Socialist Studies*, 1 (1983) and 2 (1984), regarding whether or how Canadian socialists should support a Liberal Party National Energy Policy. And see Daniel Drache's overview, 'The Enigma of Canadian Nationalism,' *The Australian and New Zealand Journal of Sociology*, Part 2, 14(3): 310–321(October 1978). More general critiques of reductionism in relation to the national question are: Arieh Yaari, *Le défi national: les théories marxistes sur la question nationale a l'épreuve* (Paris: Editions Anthropos, 1978); Jacques Mascotto and Pierre Yves Soucy, *Démocratie et nation* (Montreal: Albert Saint-Martin, 1980); and Rafael Ribo, *Débat ideologic y democracia interna*, (Barcellona: Edicions 62, 1979).

62. Gramsci addresses this question in the following way: 'If the union of two forces is necessary in order to defeat a third, a recourse to arms and coercion (even supposing these are available) can be nothing more than a methodological hypothesis; the only concrete possibility is compromise. Force can be employed against enemies, but not against a part of one's own side which one wishes rapidly to assimilate, and whose "good will" and enthusiasm one needs,' *Prison Notebooks* 168.

A debate over whether Gramsci had broken with a reductionist perspective may hinge on what the term 'assimilate' means here. Interpreted one way, Gramsci is arguing for short-term nonsectarianism in order finally to subsume all forces against oppression under class struggle, and his call for revolutionary working-class hegemony as an alternative to force is a call to persuade extraworking-class segments of a population willingly thus to subsume themselves.

An alternate (and admittedly less likely) reading is that assimilation simply requires nonantagonistic coordination among equals. In this case the call for working-class hegemony is a call for the revolutionary working class to take the lead in bringing such a coordination into effect. The disadvantage of the first, reductionistic, approach is that it requires members of extraclass movements to give up more than they should or may be prepared to give up as a precondition for overcoming class and other forms of oppression. This topic will be pursued in Chapter 11.

### Chapter 10

1. Herbert Marcuse, *One Dimensional Man* (Boston: Beacon Press, 1964) 20. An insightful survey of Marcuse's views bearing on the topic of this chapter is that of André Vachet, *Marcuse: La révolution radicale et le nouveau socialism* (Ottawa: Editions de l'Université d'Ottawa, 1986), chaps. 4, 5 and pp. 83–5.

2. It is not the aim of this chapter to defend the claim that the worker in question is systematically oppressed and that the beliefs are false. Rather, these things are assumed for the purpose of examining 'false consciousness' in democratic-socialist theory. The full argument invokes the following claims, which the antisocialist must contest and the socialist defend: a) low wages and the threat of unemployment are widespread across a capitalist society's working population; b) these thwart workers' aspirations to engage in the fuller and more rewarding life activities that are technologically and culturally possible today; c) this thwarting is unjustified – that is, neither somehow deserved by workers nor necessitated because of some higher goal like addressing a macroproblem or fulfilling the will of God; and d) that the continuation of this state of affairs is neither fated nor the fault of immigrants, women who don't 'know their place,' or any other oppressed group.

3. Göran Therborn, *The Ideology of Power and the Power of Ideology* (London: Verso, 1980) 94–7.

4. Bernard de Mandeville, *The Fable of the Bees* (London: Pelican, 1970), in an essay appended by de Mandeville to the 1723 edition (spelling updated), 294.

5. It should be noted that 'holism' as used here does not refer to the view that descriptions and explanations of social group phenomena are in principle unanalysable into language referring only to individuals and their relations. Rather the holist considered here need only prescribe that false consciousness be studied as a social/historical phenomenon, even if it could coherently be studied as a psychological one as well.

6. Jon Elster, *Making Sense of Marx* (Cambridge: Cambridge University Press, 1985) 345–371; Allen Buchanan, *Marx and Justice: The Radical Critique of Liberalism* (Totowa, N.J.: Rowman and Allanheld, 1982) 88–102.

7. Joseph Gabel, *False Consciousness: an Essay on Reification*, trans. from French by Margaret Thompson and Kenneth Thompson (Oxford: Blackwell, 1975), first published in 1962.

8. Joshua Cohen and Joel Rogers, *On Democracy: Toward a Transformation of American Society* (Harmondsworth, England: Penguin, 1983), chap. 3.

9. The term 'aspiration' will sometimes be used to refer to any desired goal of someone and sometimes to the most highly ranked goal; the context of usage should make it clear which is meant. There are, to be sure, important and difficult problems in defining terms like 'desire,' 'want,' 'preference,' and 'aspiration,' but it ought not to be necessary to enter this terrain for the purpose at hand. Rather these and similar terms will be used in an intuitive, preanalytic way, and those who think that differences among them are important for the problem at hand may make suitable substitutions in the terminology of arguments that follow.

10. This seems to be the view of Therborn, *Ideology and Power*, 4–5, and see Seyla Benhabib, 'The Marxian Method of Critique: Normative Presuppositions,' *Praxis International* 4 (3): 284–298(October 1984).

11. Ernesto Laclau and Chantal Mouffe, *Hegemony and Socialist Strategy: Towards a Radical Democratic Politics*, trans. Winston Moore and Paul Cannock (London: Verso, 1984) 83–4.

12. Edward Andrew argues that 'Marx never referred to classes in themselves or distinguished a class in itself from a class for itself,' in 'Class in Itself and Class Against

Capital: Karl Marx and His Classifiers,' *Canadian Journal of Political Science*, 16(3): 577–584(September 1983).

13. Cornelius Castoriadis, *l'Institution imaginaire de la société* (Paris: Editions du Seuil, 1975) 219.

14. This point is drawn out by Castoriadis in 'From Marx to Aristotle, from Aristotle to Us,' *Social Research*, 45(4): 667–738(Winter 1978).

15. Pertinent critiques of political-theoretical use of the concept of needs are by C.B. Macpherson, 'Needs and Wants: An Ontological or Historical Problem?,' in *Human Needs and Politics*, ed. Ross Fitzgerald (New York: Pergamon Press, 1977) 26–35; and Alkis Kontos' development of Macpherson's point in 'Through a Glass Darkly: Ontology and False Needs,' *Canadian Journal of Political and Social Theory*, 3(1): 25–45(Winter 1979), followed by a commentary by Macpherson.

16. Erik Olin Wright distinguishes two senses in which interests might be called 'objective,' one of which – those interests people would have in circumstances of 'maximum possible autonomy' – Wright rejects as problematic because it requires too much speculation. The other refers to interests 'buried deep in the unconscious waiting to be uncovered when psychological blocks are removed.' Wright's example is 'an interest in expanding [one's own] capacity to make choices and to act on them.' In *Classes* (London: Verso, 1985) 248–9. But this sense of 'objective interests' is also problematic.

   To be unconscious of this 'deep' want somebody would have to be able (consciously) to want to do something believing that an effect would be to prevent setting and achieving *any* future goals. It would not be enough to act on a want that will block specified future choices, since any action will have some such effects. (Indeed, sometimes this is surely desirable, as when somebody sets out to block a future choice to smoke.) It is doubtful that anybody lacks a conscious want to avoid turning him or herself into a complete automaton. It can plausibly be claimed that people ought to strive to keep open as many future choices as possible and that they (prudentially) ought to eliminate economic structures like capitalism that, perhaps unknown to them, are major impediments to the expansion of their freedom, but these claims require no reference to an unconscious desire for autonomy.

17. Possible explanations of the ongoing solution of macroproblems might serve as models. States of affairs required to solve macroproblems might be counted as *social* needs when these are interpreted as necessities. That macroproblems are solved (when they are) might generically be explained in two ways, one in which a desire to solve them is imputed to members of a population and one in which such desire is not imputed. In the former case, the claim is made that only if there were such a desire held (conciously or otherwise) by all but the few asocial ascetics or misanthropists in a society could they be solved.

   In the latter case, various things are seen to motivate people, few or none of whom may have as preferences to contribute to the solution of macroproblems, but the joint activity of these people is nonetheless recognized as having among its consequences their ongoing solutions. In the first situation imputation of certain motivations is an explicitly theoretical enterprise; while in the second, different theories (functionalist, teleological, instinctivist, behaviouristic, and perhaps others) may be invoked to explain why joint activities have such unintended consequences.

18. D.F.B. Tucker, *Marxism and Individualism* (Oxford: Blackwell, 1980) 37. An argument reaching similar conclusions is by Sheila Rowbotham, 'The Women's Movement and Organizing for Socialism,' in *Beyond the Fragments*, eds. Sheila Rowbotham, Lynne Segal, and Hilary Wainwright (Boston: Alyson, 1981) 21–155, at pp. 104–5.

   See also, Frederick Engels' formulation: 'Men make their own history, whatever its outcome may be, in that each person follows his own consciously desired ends, and it is precisely the resultant of these many wills operating in different directions and of their manifold effects upon the outer world that constitutes history. . . . But, on the one hand, we have seen that the many individual wills active in history for the most part produce results quite other than those they intended. . . . On the other hand, the further question arises: What driving forces in turn stand behind these motives? What are the historical causes which transform themselves into these motives in the brains of the actors?' *Ludwig Feuerbach and the End of Classical German Philosophy* in *Selected Works in One Volume* (New York; International Publishers, 1968) 596–632, at p. 623.

19. It is for this reason that Alan Wood describes as misleading Engels' view summarized in Note 18. *Karl Marx* (London: Routledge and Kegan Paul, 1981) 88–9.

20. Mihailo Marković, *Democratic Socialism: Theory and Practice* (New York: St. Martin's Press, 1982) 105.

21. See Seyla Benhabib, 'Marxian Method of Critique,' 294–7; and Ted Benton, 'Realism, Power and Objective Interests,' in *Contemporary Political Philosophy*, ed. Keith Graham (Cambridge: Cambridge University Press, 1982) 7–33.

22. Benton, 'Realism,' see 23.

23. Agnes Heller, 'Les "vrais" et les "faux" besoins,' in Ferenc Feher and Agnes Heller, *Marxisme & démocratie* (Paris: Librairie François Maspero, 1981) 243–263, at pp. 250–1.

24. William E. Connolly, 'On "Interests" in Politics,' *Politics and Society*, 2(4): 459–477(Summer 1972), at p. 472.

25. Jane J. Mansbridge, *Beyond Adversary Democracy* (New York: Basic Books, 1980) 25.

26. Kai Nielsen, 'On Justifying Revolution,' *Philosophy and Phenomenological Research*, 37(4): 516–532(June 1977), at p. 518.

27. In a critique of political-scientific Pluralism considered as an explanatory theory, I prescribed using a concept of objective interests thus defined on the grounds that this better lends itself than a subjective definition to useful theory construction, 'Pluralism and Class Struggle,' *Science & Society*, 39(4): 385–416(Winter 1975–76), at pp. 389–394. While I retain this criticism of the Pluralist power-political model of society, I would now either drop the term 'objective interest' to describe likely future (subjective) interests or at least be careful to specify exactly what and how much knowledge is to be definitive of one's objective interests.

28. E.P. Thompson, *The Poverty of Theory and Other Essays* (London: Monthly Review Press, 1978) 173ff.

29. This is the political dimension of Marx's 'Third Thesis on Feuerbach,' Karl Marx and Frederick Engels, *Collected Works* (New York: Progress Publishers, 1974–   ) 5:3–9, written in 1845, at p. 7, in which he criticizes Robert Owen for 'dividing society into two parts, of which one is superior to society' and forgetting 'that the educator himself needs educating.'

30. John Dewey, *The Public and Its Problems* (Denver: Alan Swallow, 1957), first published in 1927, 208.

31. Ibid. Dewey's italics.

32. This is from Brecht's 'Notes on Politics and Society,' quoted in Kai Nielsen, 'A Defence of Radicalism,' in Hector Hawton, ed., *Question Seven* (London: Pemberton, 1974) 53–66, at p. 53.

33. This description is an ideal type, constructed from classic and organizational pamphlet-style literature and from experience. The vanguardism thus described is more sophisticated than many nonsocialists and armchair socialists imagine. The straightforwardly elitist practices pictured by antisocialists and advocated only in ultraleft rhetoric would be too easy a target of criticism. Rather, the more sophisticated vanguardist project, even when in practice it degenerates into elitist sectar-

ianism, is designed to meet the problem of simultaneously leading and learning from mass movements of people.

Typical expositions of this project advocate weaving a path between the twin deviations of 'right opportunism' (subordinating the party in popular movements) and 'left sectarianism' (distancing the party from the movements). A representative example is M.I. Basmanov and B.M. Leibzon, *The Revolutionary Vanguard* (Moscow: Progress Publishers, 1977), see especially chaps. 5, 6, and 7. (Canadian readers of this general Soviet textbook will be interested to learn how the Communist Party of Canada initiated and organized 'massive campaigns... in 1974 to fight the energy crisis and the inflation,' described as an example of the effectiveness of correctly pursued vanguard activity, 241–2.)

34. Richard B. Brandt, *A Theory of the Good and the Right* (Oxford: Oxford University Press, 1979), chap. 13.

35. John Stuart Mill, *Utilitarianism* (London: J.M. Dent, 1910) 9.

36. Adam Przeworski resists describing class relations as 'objective' due to his view that, 'Classes are not prior to political and ideological practice [but] are organized and disorganized as outcomes of continuous struggle,' *Capitalism and Social Democracy* (London: Cambridge University Press, 1985) 70. His concern is to avoid an objectionably fatalistic approach which sees people acting out roles predetermined by their class positions. However, that classes exist and have certain properties independently of whether or not their members believe them to exist or have the properties (that is, that classes are 'objective') does not entail that class members are fated to act only in certain, predetermined ways. To draw this conclusion, the objectivist would have to hold that the objective social relations in which one stands completely determine all his or her actions and that people are thus determined only by their class relations.

Przeworski's own description of social relations as 'structures of choice given at a particular moment of history' (ibid. 73) is clearly compatible with considering these relations objective. The advantages of recognizing, contrary to Przeworski's advice, that classes are in respect of their objectivity 'prior' to political and ideological practice are that this facilitates delineating those structures of choice unique to people's class relations and that it leaves open the possibility of seeking circumstances within which class membership makes it probable that certain sorts of choices will be made. Surely the possibility of discovering such circumstances should not be ruled out a priori.

37. John McMurtry, *The Structure of Marx's World-View* (Princeton: Princeton University Press, 1978) 149. McMurtry distinguishes between 'ideology' and 'forms of social consciousness,' where the latter (from which the above example is taken) are the presupposed principles of the former. Full development of a theory of political culture, false consciousness and ideology would likely require sharpening and adding to this kind of distinction.

38. Jon Elster, *Making Sense of Marx* 345–371. As discussed in Chapter 4, Note 21, Elster goes so far as to write: 'I define (positive) class consciousness as the ability to overcome the free-rider problem in realizing class interests,' 347 (italics omitted). See the similar approach to 'revolutionary motivation' of Allen Buchanan, *Marx and Justice* 88–102.

39. Richard Miller, *Analysing Marx: Morality, Power and History* (Princeton: Princeton University Press, 1984) 65–75. (It is Allen Buchanan's version of this argument that Miller addresses.) If Miller's attack on the position of Buchanan and Elster succeeds, then this might work against the position he attributes to Marx (discussed in Chapter 7) that socialism is to be justified on extramoral grounds.

40. Gramsci's conception of ideology is probably close to that of political culture, since

he did not see it as necessarily oppression-sustaining. See Yvon Cloutier's treatment: 'The originality of Gramsci resides in his formulation of a broad and neutral definition of ideology – the ideological field encompasses implicit and explicit representations [which] are not deformed, occult, or reactionary by definition,' in 'Gramsci et la question de l'ideologie,' *Philosophiques*, 10(2): 243–253(October 1983), at p. 244 (italics omitted). See too: Antonio Gramsci, *Selections from the Prison Notebooks*, ed. and trans. Quintin Hoare and Geoffrey Nowell Smith (New York: International Publishers, 1971), written between 1929 and 1935, 344; Louis Althusser, *For Marx*, trans. Ben Brewster (London: Penguin, 1969), first published 1963, 232–4; Therborn, *Ideology and Power* 22ff.

**41.** Gramsci, *Prison Notebooks* 344.

**42.** Desires might be unsatisfiable either because conditions for their satisfaction cannot be met or, as G.A. Cohen notes in criticizing capitalism, because people are led falsely to believe they will be satisfied if the conditions are met, *Karl Marx's Theory of History: A Defence* (Oxford: Oxford University Press, 1978) 320.

**43.** Gramsci, *Prison Notebooks* 326–7. Joseph Femia summarizes the result of empirical work supporting Gramsci's thesis in showing significant disparities between responses by workers to questions depending on how they are put: '[I]t would seem that the average man tends to have two levels of normative reference – the abstract and the situational. On the former plane, he expresses a great deal of agreement with the dominant [procapitalist] ideology; on the latter, he reveals not outright dissensus but nevertheless a diminished level of commitment to the bourgeois ethos, because it is often inapposite to the exigencies of his class position,' in 'Hegemony and Consciousness in the Thought of Antonio Gramsci,' *Political Studies*, 23(1): 29–48(March 1975), at pp. 44–6.

See, too, Michael Mann, *Consciousness and Action Among the Western Working Class* (London: Macmillan, 1973), and Nicholas Abercrombie, Stephen Hill, and Bryan S. Turner, *The Dominant Ideology Thesis* (London: Allen and Unwin, 1980). These and other studies are well-used by Charles Mills in his 'The Concept of Ideology in the Thought of Marx and Engels,' Ph.D Diss. (University of Toronto, 1985), chap. 5.

**44.** Joshua Cohen and Joel Rogers, *On Democracy: Toward a Transformation of American Society* (Harmondsworth, England: Penguin, 1983) 51–87.

**45.** Jospeh Gabel, *False Consciousness* 139.

**46.** At a session of the 1985 Canadian Philosophical Association meetings devoted to a discussion of their book, Cohen and Rogers maintained that their theory was meant to complement, not replace, theories of false consciousness.

**47.** Gabel wishes to unite a psychoanalytic theory of schizophrenia with a Lukácsian theory about the effects of 'spatial' thought wherein phenomena are viewed in a reified way out of historical context.

**48.** Gabel's description of Nazi consciousness may not be far off: '[N]ational-socialist ideology as a whole depends on morbid rationalism in its worst form. By placing the essential value of man in the biological domain, racism denies History; one extra-historical axiogeneous source is supposed to enlighten the "outside" world without itself being exposed to the fates and fortunes of historicity. The result is that any unfavourable event for this racial pseudo value is itself extra-historicized and "understood" in terms of treason or conspiracy,' *False Consciousness* 118.

**49.** Althusser, *For Marx* 231.

**50.** Ibid. 233. The point is developed in Althusser's use of the concept of interpellation in arguing that ideology 'has the function . . . of constituting [interpellating] concrete individuals as subjects,' 'Ideology and Ideological State Apparatuses,' *Lenin and*

*Philosophy and Other Essays,* trans. Ben Brewster (London: New Left Books, 1977) 160ff.

51. Whether or how Althusser does this depends on how one interprets his view that ideology does not fail to represent real social relations, but adequately represents the imagined realities through which people live, *Lenin and Philosophy* 155.

52. Benton, 'Realism,' especially 29–33.

53. William E. Connolly, *Appearance and Reality in Politics* (Cambridge: Cambridge University Press, 1981), see 74–84.

54. Ibid. 75.

55. Wood, *Karl Marx* 119.

56. On this theory one is justified in holding a true belief if what (directly or indirectly) causes the holding of the belief is also what (directly or indirectly) causes the belief to be true. Acceptance of the conception of false consciousness advanced here does not commit one to this epistemological theory, but draws on one of its corollaries: that continuing sincere belief in the truth of a proposition is incompatible with full realization that the only factors that had led one to hold or to continue holding it have nothing to do with the belief's being true. On the causal theory of knowledge generally, see David M. Armstrong, *A Materialist Theory of Mind* (London: Routledge and Kegan Paul, 1968), chap. 9. For an application, see Daniel Goldstick, 'A Contribution Towards the Development of the Causal Theory of Knowledge,' *Australian Journal of Philosophy,* 50(3): 238–248(December 1972).

57. A large number of democratic theorists will agree with Harald Laski's argument (in both his pre- and post-Marxist periods), summarized in his example: 'When a man is trained to service in a trade union, he cannot avoid seeing how that activity is related to the world outside. When he gets on a school committee, the general problems of education begin to unfold themselves before him,' in *The Foundations of Sovereignty and Other Essays* (New York: Harcourt Brace, 1921) 247. Lenin argued the case in respect of the trade unions, which he called 'schools of communism,' in *Left-Wing Communism, an Infantile Disorder, V.I. Lenin Collected Works* (Moscow: Progress Publishers, 1963–1980) 31:17–117, written in 1920, at p. 51.

    People learn by doing, and this is especially important in areas of politically charged viewpoints where ideological bias and self-serving sophistry are the norm among those designated as authorities (professional political scientists, newspaper analysts, T.V. commentators, and the like). It does not take much realistic cynicism for people to come to the view that they can learn better from their own experience than from what the experts tell them. Then again, there does seem to be a difference of the sort Gramsci focussed on between abstractly agreeing to something and internalizing it as a principle of daily activity. For instance, one may refrain from disagreeing with assertions of teachers or in the press that racism is unfounded, but it often takes working closely together with those of another race on a project of common and pressing concern to come to a full understanding of how false and pernicious racist attitudes really are.

58. Przeworski, *Capitalism* 73. As to whether Przeworski ought to accept this 'objectivist' gloss of his view, see Note 36 in this chapter.

59. Ibid. 80 (punctuation altered).

60. Gramsci, *Prison Notebooks* 181–2; and see Anthony Gidden's distinctions among 'class awareness,' and 'class consciousness,' and his further analysis of the latter into perception of class unity and revolutionary consciousness, 'Class Structuration and Class Consciousness,' in *Classes, Power, and Conflict,* eds. Anthony Giddens and David Held (Berkeley: University of California Press, 1982) 157–174, at p. 164.

61. The view called 'Leninist' is here discussed in full recognition that there are continuing debates about what Lenin himself actually intended. This debate will not

be entered into for the same reasons that the work is not concerned to engage in textual analysis of Marx's writings. Considered as a representation of Lenin's intended meanings, this analysis is more charitable than, say, Kolakowski's but less charitable than that of, for example, Althusser and much less than the view of orthodox 'Marxist-Leninists.' That there are widespread practices matching these descriptions and carried on in the name of Lenin there can be no doubt.

**62.** Those wishing to analyse Lenin's own views on this subject could consider as a first step explicating this passage from a polemic of his with Trotsky: 'We now have a state under which it is the business of the massively organized proletariat to protect itself, while we, for our part, must use these workers' organizations [the unions] to protect the workers from their state, and to get them to protect our state,' in 'The Trade Unions, The Present Situation and Trotsky's Mistakes,' *Collected Works* 32:19–42, written in 1921, at p.25.

The problematic terms here are 'their' and 'our.' Interpreted one way, 'their state' means 'the socialist state insofar as it conforms to the not yet fully educated consciousness of the working class,' and 'our state' means 'the socialist state as envisaged by the vanguard party, whose members do not suffer false consciousness about what the state should be.' Vanguardists are to encourage workers to engage in the practical activity that will protect them from the shortcomings of 'their state' partly through education by direct participation in the governing of their affairs. As this activity closes the gap between 'their' actual state and 'our' anticipated state, one can expect the simultaneous merging of the state with voluntary organizations of the people (that is, the withering away of the former) and the autodestruction of an increasingly unneeded vanguard party. This projected process cannot but break down when the existing state becomes not 'their state,' but the dictatorship of the vanguard party itself.

For an interesting discussion of Leninism bearing on this point see Jerome Karabel, 'Revolutionary Contradictions: Antonio Gramsci and the Problem of Intellectuals,' *Politics and Society*, 6(2): 123–172(1976), see p. 163.

**63.** Femia, 'Hegemony,' 41; Karabel, 'Contradictions,' 127.

**64.** Claus Offe and Helmut Wiesenthal describe it as a 'paradox' that 'interests [of the working class] can only be met to the extent that they are partially redefined,' in 'Two Logics of Collective Action: Theoretical Notes on Social and Class Organizational Forms,' *Political Power and Social Theory*, 1: 67–115(1980), at p. 79. Their thesis is that since this is true of workers but not of capitalists, social, economic and especially political structures of liberal democracy are major impediments to working-class struggle since they favour people's acting on perceived interests rather than challenging them. This approach is only superficially compatible with the point made here, according to which: a) nonfalse consciousness admits of degree, and true beliefs of 'slight' content (where one does not challenge his or her present aspirations) count as one level, and b) insofar as liberal-democratic values and structures encourage pluralism and nonfixity, they do not inhibit confrontation of the 'paradox' Offe and Wiesenthal mention.

On consciousness raising, see Rowbotham's prescriptions for a socialist practice incorporating deliberate consciousness raising programmes of the kind central to the early feminist movement, *Beyond the Fragments* 132–149.

**65.** An 'exception that proves the rule' defence of this claim may be found in an argument of Alejandro Rojas that class-reductionistic attitudes and sectarian practices in the Chilean left had their origins in the life and work experiences of the politically powerful nitrate miners, who, Rojas argues, were atypically isolated from other than working-class struggles and hence approximated the abstract existence as 'pure workers' on which the Leninist project is predicated, 'The Problem of

Democracy and Socialism in the Chilean Political Process from the 1880's to the 1980's,' Ph.D. Diss. (York University, 1984), chap. 3.

### Chapter 11

1. Philip Green, *Retrieving Democracy: In Search of Civic Equality* (Totowa: N.J.: Rowman and Allenheld, 1985), chap. 11.
2. Peter Gay, *The Dilemma of Democratic Socialism: Edward Bernstein's Challenge to Marx* (New York: Octagon, 1979) 7.
3. There are, to be sure, major debates among socialist theorists regarding the state, a good example of which is that between Ralph Miliband and Nicos Poulantzas. Central books of theirs on this subject are Miliband's *The State in Capitalist Society* (London: Weidenfeld & Nicolson, 1969) and Poulantzas's *State, Power, Socialism*, trans. Patrick Camiller (London: Verso, 1978). They debated the issue in the *New Left Review* (Nos. 58 and 59), reproduced in *Ideology in Social Sciences*, ed. Robin Blackburn (Glasgow: Fontana, 1972).

   This debate is over questions of general methodology (Poulantzas charging Miliband with empiricism, Miliband criticizing Poulantzas for advancing an overly abstract structuralist analysis), over the boundaries of the state, and over the interpetation of such terms as 'state power' or 'relative autonomy of the state.' It is typical of contemporary socialist views of the state which, whatever their differences, agree that no state rules by force or the threat of force alone. Almost all would agree with the comment of James O'Connor that 'a capitalist state that openly uses its coercive forces to help one class accumulate capital at the expense of other classes loses its legitimacy and hence undermines the basis of its loyalty and support,' *The Fiscal Crisis of the State* (New York: St. Martins, Press 1973) 6.

   Bob Jessop provides a useful survey of this and other recent left theories of the state in *The Capitalist State: Marxist Theories and Methods* (New York: New York University Press, 1982); for analyses of the Miliband/Poulantzas debate that, from different directions, suggest ways to go beyond it see Laclau's, *Politics and Ideology in Marxist Theory* (London: Verso Editions, 1979), chap. 2; and Richard Miller's treatment in *Analysing Marx: Morality, Power and History* (Princeton: Princeton University Press, 1984) 129–136.
4. The characterization of Stalinism employed here sees it as the implementation of an extreme position regarding the *means* required paternalistically to check democracy rather than as a position regarding the putative necessity of antidemocratic mechanisms. This latter position is shared by all defenders of existing bureaucratic socialisms, though this is sometimes clouded by espousal of a kinds-of-democracy theory in which 'socialist democracy' is regarded as compatible with paternalism.

   In a book that bristles with examples of these defences, 'socialist democracy' is described as 'the form of the political organization' of socialist society – either 'democracy for the working majority' or 'for the whole people' depending on the society's 'stage of development,' D.A. Kerimov, et al., *Soviet Democracy in the Period Of Developed Socialism* (Moscow: Progress Publishers, 1977) 59.

   'Right revisionists' are chided for propagating 'petty-bourgeois theories about people's power, in denying the leading role of the working-class and its party in the building of a new society. But it is precisely this leading role that predetermines the socialist character of people's power and its purpose in social development. Furthermore, as it leads the struggle of the working people for the building of socialism and communism, the working class is expressing its own interests as well as the vital interests of all sections of the working people. That is why its leading role not only does not contradict popular sovereignty, understood as the real absolute power of the working people exercised in the interests of building a new society, but is also its necessary precondition,' 74.

Elsewhere in the book the relation of the working class to its party is clarified to note that 'the Communist Party expresses the general interests of the working class, and since under socialism . . . these objectively correspond with the interests of social progress, the party becomes the vanguard of the whole of society,' 212.

5. The view of Andrew Levine is typical in arguing that blame 'for the shortcomings of existing socialist societies cannot be ascribed in the main to their socialist economic organization. Fault lies with the absence of sustained democratic traditions; and, above all, with the extraordinary historical circumstances – the economic backwardness and overt hostility – with which socialist polities . . . have had to contend,' *Arguing for Socialism: Theoretical Considerations* (Boston: Routledge & Kegan Paul, 1984) 217.

6. Mihailo Marković, *Democratic Socialism: Theory and Practice* (New York: St. Martin's Press, 1982) 171–173.

7. Hannah Arendt, *The Origins of Totalitarianism*, 2nd ed. (New York: Meridian Books, 1958), first published in 1951, 318–323.

8. Mouffe and Laclau criticize Bernstein for replacing a class-reductionistic perspective with a democratic 'essentialist' one in holding that democracy will always advance as if in accord with evolutionary laws, *Hegemony and Socialist Strategy: Towards a Radical Democratic Politics*, trans. Winston Moore and Paul Cammack (London: Verso, 1984) 34–36. For references to pertinent arguments about the third world see Chapter 1, Note 10.

9. Though Poulantzas' point that Stalinism has its origins in the rejection of representative democracy, *State Power, Socialism* 255, is well-taken insofar as it challenges a left kinds-of-democracy approach to politics, this should not encourage one to forget that there is also a similarity between representative democracy where there is minimum accountability of the representatives and paternalistic vanguardism.

10. André Gorz, *Adieux au prolétariat: Au delà du socialisme* (Paris: Editions du Seuil, 1980) 68.

11. Perhaps a representative example of this sort of view is in the following defence of the espousal in its 22nd Congress of a democratic road to socialism by the French Communist Party: 'One of the fundamental tasks of [the envisaged democratically elected socialist] power will be precisely to respect and to make respected the freely-expressed will of the majority of the people. . . . But let it be well understood that it will be able to do this just insofar as, far from substituting its intervention [against reaction] for that of the people thus relegating them to passivity and disorganization, it always bases itself on them.' The authors, Jean Fabre, François Hincker, and Lucien Sève, *Les communistes et l'état* (Paris: Editions Sociales, 1977), describe this approach as the 'peaceful, democratic, pluralist . . . strategy of the 22nd Congress,' 223–4.

Joint statements made at meetings of European and Japanese Communist Party leaders between 1975 and 1977 are often taken as authoritative definitions of 'Eurocommunism.' A collection of such statements along with relevant reviews and articles may be found in *Recherches Internationales*, Nos. 88–89 (1976).

12. Alexandre Adler and Jean Roney discuss reversion of the Communist Party of France to a pre-Eurocommunist position in a way that bears on this point. '*Internationale et le genre humain* (Paris: Mazarine, 1980), pt. 2 and 151–155.

13. See, for example, Colin Mercer, 'Revolutions, Reforms or Reformulations? Marxist Discourse on Democracy,' *Marxism and Democracy*, ed. Alan Hunt (London: Lawrence

and Wishart, 1980) 101–137, who attributes the origin of the phrase to Pietro Ingrao, a leading theorist of the Italian Communist Party, 101.

14. Claus Offe, *Contradictions of the Welfare State*, ed. John Keane (Cambridge, Mass.: MIT Press, 1984), see essay 8, quote at 188.

15. For example, Alain Touraine comes to very similar conclusions from a social-theoretical orientation in many respects quite different from that of Offe. See Alain Touraine, *l'Aprés socialisme* (Paris: Bernard Grasset, 1980) 205–6, and *The Voice & the Eye: An analysis of Social Movements*, trans. Alan Duff (Cambridge: Cambridge University Press, 1981), first published in 1978, chap. 11.

16. Radoslav Selucky, *Marxism, Socialism, Freedom* (London: Macmillan, 1979) 113. Selucky is explicitly concerned with workers' self-managed enterprises, but the split loyalty problem equally confronts party members in any social movement.

17. This democracy-subverting feature of democratic centralism is overlooked by those, such as the authors defending the French Communist Party's version of Eurocommunism cited above, who wish to oppose to the Soviet practice one where democratic centralism remains operative in the party, but not in the state, Fabre, et al., 229–231.

18. Joshua Cohen and Joel Rogers, *On Democracy: Toward a Transformation of American Society* (Harmondsworth, England: Penguin, 1983) 172ff.

19. In the session on their book referred to in Chapter 10 (Note 46), Cohen and Rogers responded to a request for such specification by suggesting that all it could realistically mean in present-day North American politics is that those involved in a variety of movements be encouraged to approach their political work in ways that generally further democracy.

20. Arguments over the accuracy of this claim concern theoretical questions of the interpretation of Gramsci's views, especially over whether or to what extent he was a Leninist and debates over the continuity of the orientation of the Italian Communist Party. Representative positions regarding the first issue may be found in the contributions of Norberto Bobbio, Leonardo Paggi, Massimo Salvadori, and Biagio de Giovanni in *Gramsci and Marxist Theory*, ed. Chantal Mouffe (London: Routledge and Kegan Paul, 1979). Important for evaluation of the continuity thesis is interpreting the views of Togliotti; see Palmiro Togliatti, *On Gramsci and Other Writings*, ed. Donald Sassoon (London: Lawrence and Wishart, 1979), from essays written between 1925 and 1964, and Laclau's review of this collection in *Politics and Power* 2: 251–258(1980). See, too, the article by Enrico Berlinguer referred to in Note 40 of this chapter and the study by Giuseppe Vacca, *Saggio Su Togliatti: e la tradizione communista* (Bari: De Donato, 1974).

21. This is the main point of difference that Laclau and Mouffe have with the Gramscian approach. On their view, the hegemonic project around which alliances of movements should be forged is that of advancing radical and plural democracy, *Hegemony* 134–145.

22. Some pertinent accounts are in Elim Papadakis, *The Green Movement of West Germany* (London: Croom Helm, 1984); Werner Hulsberg, 'The Greens at the Crossroads,' *New Left Review* 152: 5–29(July/August 1985); and *Eurocommunism: Myth or Reality*, eds. Paulo Filo della Torre, Edward Mortimer, and Jonathan Storey (London: Penguin, 1979).

23. Antonio Gramsci, *Selections from the Prison Notebooks*, ed. and trans. Quintin Hoare and Geoffrey Nowell-Smith (New York: International Publishers, 1971), written between 1929 and 1935, 211.

Gramsci addresses the question of democratic centralism by distinguishing 'bureaucratic centralism' where a party leadership deduces how the party should relate to social movements from general principles and 'organic centralism': ' "Organicity" can only be found in democratic centralism, which is so to speak a "centralism" in movement – i.e., a continual adaptation of the organisation to the real movement, a matching of thrusts from below with orders from above, a continuous insertion of elements thrown up from the depths of the rank and file into the solid framework of the leadership apparatus which ensures continuity and the regular accumulation of experience. Democratic centralism is "organic" because on the one hand it takes account of movement, which is the organic mode in which historical reality reveals itself, and does not solidify mechanically into bureaucracy; and because at the same time it takes account of that which is relatively stable and permanent, or which at least moves in an easily predictable direction, etc. This element of stability within the State is embodied in the organic development of the leading group's central nucleus, just as happens on a more limited scale within parties,' ibid. 188–9.

24. '[O]ne cannot simply call for the "great alliance" among party, union, and movement, between reformist struggles against authoritarian tendencies in the state or economy and social movements for self-determination, without articulating the institutional domain (and alternatives) in which these forces might meet while retaining their difference.... The analytic dimension of institutionalization allows for the theorization of a plurality of democratic forms which, if partially institutionalized in every domain of social and political life, could serve as countervailing powers vis-à-vis one another,' Jean L. Cohen, *Class and Civil Society: The Limits of Marxian Critical Theory* (Amherst: University of Massachusetts Press, 1982) 227.

25. Gramsci, *Prison Notebooks* 175ff. It is to further such situational analysis that Gramsci introduces some of his most useful and innovative political ideas such as the distinction between 'conjunctural' and 'organic' movements and the various and complex 'moments' of the 'relations of forces,' and the importance of ascertaining the appropriate 'fixed proportions' among components of a movement such that it can become a political force (or party), ibid., pp. 177–8, 180–185, 190–192. A review of these and other key concepts of Gramsci is Anne Showstack Sassoon's *Gramsci's Politics* (London: Croom Helm, 1980).

26. North American Marxists often argue the case by pointing to the Communist Party of Italy's attempted 'historical compromise' with the Christian Democrats in the late 1970s as an example of revisionism. For a relevant treatment see Mimmo Carrieri and Lucio Lombardo Radice, 'Italy Today: A Crisis of a New Type of Democracy,' *Praxis International* 1(3): 258–271(October 1981).

27. For Marković revolutionary reformism is distinguished from pragmatic reformism in that: '[T]he former is a conscious, radical, critical, thought-inspired process of change, with a view of realizing the optimal historical possibility of society as a whole ...and as quickly as possible. The latter is a process of change determined by immediate practical necessity, with a view to solving specific tasks one by one, and to preserving all those institutions which are still able to function successfully,' *Democratic Socialism* 58. While an improvement on the traditional distinction, this one may still retain some of its elements insofar as it pejoratively regards what in this chapter will shortly be characterized as 'the long democratic march' (in Marković's use of 'quickly') and 'retrieval' (in his reference to the preservation of functions).

28. André Gorz, *Socialism and Revolution*, trans. Norman Denny (New York: Anchor, 1973) 136–167.

29. Poulantzas, *State, Power, Socialism* 261.

30. John Keane aptly criticizes social-democratic political parties for being 'dirigistes,' *Public Life and Late Capitalism: Toward a Socialist Theory of Democracy* (London: Cambridge University Press, 1984) 1–2, 17–20. See, too, the sustained analysis of social

democracy by Christine Buci-Glucksmann and Göran Therborn, *Le défi social-démocrate* (Paris: François Maspero, 1981), and contributions of the issue devoted to social democracy of the *Socialist Register: 1985–86*, eds. Ralph Miliband, John Saville, Marcel Liebman, and Leo Panitch (London: Merlin Press, 1986).

31. Adam Przeworski, *Capitalism and Social Democracy* (London: Cambridge University Press, 1985), see the essays, 'Social Democracy as an Historical Phenomenon,' 'Material Bases of Consent: Economics and Politics in a Hegemonic System,' and 'Proletariat into a Class: The Process of Class Formation from Karl Kautsky's *The Class Struggle* to Recent Controversies.' References to journals where these essays originally appeared are in Note 48 of Chapter 3.

32. Ibid. 42.

33. To accept this claim, according to Ellen Meiksins Wood, is either 'to make a gross strategic error or to challenge [a Marxist] analysis of social relations and power, and at least implicitly to redefine the nature of the liberation which socialism offers,' *The Retreat from Class: A New 'True' Socialism* (London: Verso, 1986) 15. On her interpretation of Marxism (one this work is not concerned either to challenge or to endorse), this is no doubt true. After discounting such hyperbolic and false claims that a socialist-pluralist view opposed to hers rejects seeing class as a 'principle of unity' or a 'motivation of action' at all, 98, or that it holds 'all classes have an equal interest in attaining [socialism],' 136, the perspective from which she argues probably does entail that the working class has a unique interest in socialism. On it, the working class is differentiated from other possible forces for social change, since socialism is in its 'fundamental' or 'material' interests.

    This conclusion, Wood claims, derives not from 'metaphysical abstraction' but from 'materialist principles' about 'the centrality of production and exploitation in human society,' from which follow several conclusions including that 'the working class is the social group with the most direct objective interest in bringing about the transition to socialism' and whose class interests require and make possible 'the abolition of class itself,' 12–15. Unfortunately, but not atypically of those defending this perspective, Wood seldom defines key terms, like 'fundamental,' 'centrality,' 'most direct,' 'objective interests,' or 'class.' The fullest definition of 'socialism' (presented in referring to 'the essential objective of socialism') as 'the abolition of class, and more specifically the classless administration of production by the direct producers themselves,' 189, illustrates how easy it is to make such claims true by definition.

34. Laclau and Mouffe, *Hegemony*, chap. 4.

35. Richard Miller, *Analysing Marx: Morality, Power and History* (Princeton: Princeton University Press, 1984) 113–114.

36. See Sassoon's summary, *Gramsci's Politics*, pt. 3, secs. 12, 13 and pp. 221–2.

37. Milton Fisk, *Ethics and Society* (Brighton: Harvester Press, 1980) 251.

38. Eric Olin Wright, *Class Crisis and the State* (London: Verso, 1979) 251. Richard Miller also alludes to the coup in Chile as evidence that revolution necessarily requires civil war, *Analysing Marx* 125.

39. Göran Therborn, *What Does the Ruling Class Do When It Rules?* (London: Verso, 1980) 268–9; Poulantzas, *State, Power, Socialism* 263–4.

40. Enrico Berlinguer, 'Reflections On the Events in Chile,' *Marxism Today* 18(2): 39–50(February 1974), first appeared in *Rinascita*, Oct. 12, 1973, at p. 43.

41. Alejandro Rojas, 'The Problem of Democracy and Socialism in the Chilean Political Process from the 1880s to the 1980s,' Ph.D. Diss. (York University, 1984). Unlike most treatments of the experience of the Popular Unity government of Allende (UP) by socialist theorists, which make sweeping statements about failure to arm the people and the like, Rojas traces its history in detail. On the assumption that

the coup initially required passive support of large sectors of the middle classes (a politically and numerically important sector of Chilean society), it is not implausible to argue that the coup might possibly have been headed off, but only if the UP succeeded in not alienating people in these classes. In turn this would have required maintaining rapprochement with the Christian Democratic Party (CD). On Rojas's account such an attempt was a realistic one to have tried, and opportunities presented themselves. The CD contained left- and right-wings, the latter of which wished to pull out of the coalition with the UP, and by the Fall of 1973 had succeeded in doing this. Rojas cites several incidents in the year before where the UP facilitated this victory of the CD's right-wing by refusing on what he convincingly argues were class-reductionistic grounds to pursue democracy-promoting policies in accord with initiatives of the CD's left-wing.

42. The phrase is used by Therborn, *Ruling Class* 271.

# Index

## SUBJECTS

361

# INDEX

362

# Index

# NAMES

# INDEX

# Index